John Almon

Anecdotes of the Life of the Right Hon. William Pitt, Earl of Chatham

John Almon

Anecdotes of the Life of the Right Hon. William Pitt, Earl of Chatham

ISBN/EAN: 9783337155148

Printed in Europe, USA, Canada, Australia, Japan

Cover: Foto ©ninafisch / pixelio.de

More available books at **www.hansebooks.com**

ANECDOTES

OF THE LIFE OF

THE RIGHT HON. WILLIAM PITT,
EARL OF CHATHAM,

AND OF

THE PRINCIPAL EVENTS OF HIS TIME.

WITH

HIS SPEECHES IN PARLIAMENT,

FROM THE YEAR 1736 TO THE YEAR 1778.

SIT MIHI FAS AUDITA LOQUI.——VIRGIL.

IN TWO VOLUMES.

VOLUME I.

London:

PRINTED FOR J. S. JORDAN, No. 166, FLEET-STREET.

1792.

PREFACE.

THE moſt proper apology for this publication, is a candid and unadorned ſtatement of Truth. Had a ſimilar work been executed by any of thoſe perſons, who are more capable, and more converſant with the period, and with the conduct of the noble Lord, than the Editor, the public would not have been troubled with this attempt. It is now almoſt fourteen years ſince Lord CHATHAM's death, and the writer has not heard, that any intention to offer a ſimilar work has been in the contemplation of any ſuch perſon. Every period in Hiſtory is intereſting. Undoubtedly ſome periods more than others; and, perhaps, none more than that of theſe volumes. But truth is ſo ſeldom the object of the hiſtorian of his own times, that it has, for ſome years paſt, been a trite obſervation, amongſt perſons of information, that nothing is ſo *falſe* as Modern Hiſtory. The writers in general, may, perhaps, have other views than the relation of facts. But it ſhould be further obſerved, that thoſe perſons, who are in poſſeſſion of the beſt and moſt authentic materials for hiſtory, are uſually perſons of faſhion and rank; and one of theſe very rarely ſits down to the laborious work of writing a volume. Hence ariſes the *falſhood* and ſterility of Modern Hiſtory. The important facts dying with the perſons who were beſt acquainted with them, the future writer frequently aſcribes motives and conſequences to events, with which they have not the moſt diſtant relation.

The writer has not the vanity to offer this work as a hiſtory. He preſumes no more, than having collected, and preſerved a fund of materials, which may afford light and information to the future enquirer; who could not have found them in any of the books hitherto printed [*]. He is conſcious, that his ſtyle, and ſome circumſtances, are not in his favour. But he is not conſcious of having advanced one falſhood. The anecdotes

[*] Except in a few inſtances; and theſe are ſo immediately connected with the ſubject of the work, they could not, with propriety, have been omitted. But the names of the books, or pamphlets, from which they are taken, are ſet down in the margin.

which

which he has here committed to paper, were, all of them, in their day, very well known. They were the subjects of public conversation. But they have not been published. His situation gave him a knowledge of them, and a personal acquaintance with several of the events. It was his custom to keep a diary; in which he minuted all such circumstances as seemed to him most worthy of remembrance. He has endeavoured to state the facts, as nearly as possible, in the original language; and with the original colouring in which they were spontaneously given at the moment——presuming he should thereby exhibit the most faithful picture of a period, in which the noble Lord appeared the principal figure on the canvass *.

With respect to the Speeches in Parliament, it is proper to inform the reader, that those marked M.S. in the margin, are now first printed from the Editor's notes; or from those of particular friends, who have obligingly assisted him. The rest are copied from various publications, in England, Holland and America. No pains have been spared to gain the best and fullest account of each speech. But it is not within the compass of one man, or of a first attempt, though neither crudely designed, nor precipitately executed, to obtain perfection. There are doubtless omissions; though it is hoped not many. But if any Gentleman is in possession of any papers, or notes of any speeches, which may elucidate, or contribute to the advantage of this work, the writer will think himself honoured by the communication of them, for the benefit of a future edition; if the public favour should make one necessary.

The reader's candour is solicited for some errors in the printing, which are obvious without the distinction of errata. The work was principally written at a considerable distance from the metropolis, in which situation the writer could not revise the press.

---

* It was the opinion of the great Lord Somers, "That the bent and genius of the age "is best known in a free country, by the pamphlets and papers which daily come out, as "containing the sense of parties, and sometimes the voice of the nation."———The authority may be seen in the front of Lord Somers's Tracts.———If these anecdotes had been printed in the fugitive periodical papers of the times, they must undoubtedly have classed under his Lordship's description. It is presumed, that neither the delay, nor the form of printing, will diminish the judgment of so respectable a recommendation.

CONTENTS of the FIRST VOLUME.

CHAP. I.——Introduction. Mr. Pitt's birth. Placed at Eton. Sent to Oxford. Mr. Warton's compliments to Mr. Pitt. Latin verses by Mr. Pitt. Goes abroad. Made a coronet of horse. Elected as a member of Parliament. Honoured by the Prince of Wales. His commission taken from him by Sir Robert Walpole. Verses to him by Mr. Lyttleton. Patronised by Lord Cobham. His accomplishments. Complimented by Thompson; by Hammond. His conduct in Parliament attacked by the Gazetteer; defended by the Craftsman. The Prince dismissed from St. James's. - - - - - 1

CHAP. II.——Mr. Pitt's speech in favour of a reduction of the army. On the convention with Spain. On Admiral Haddock's instructions. On Sir Charles Wager's bill for the encouragement of seamen. Reply to Mr. Horace Walpole. Reply to Mr Winnington. On the motion for an address to remove Sir R. Walpole. 13

CHAP. III.——A new Parliament. Mr. Pitt re-elected. The Minister loses several questions. Resigns, and is created Earl of Orford. Parliament adjourns. Secret negociation with Mr. Pulteney. That affair truly stated. Lord Cobham and his friends excluded. The new arrangement settled by the Earl of Orford. Stanzas of Sir Charles Hanbury Williams explained;. and the condition upon which Sir R. Walpole became minister. Duke of Argyll's expression to Mr. Pulteney. The nation dissatisfied. - - - - - 30

CHAP. IV.——The new Ministry charged with having bargained for the safety of the Earl of Orford. Motion for an inquiry into the Earl of Orford's conduct. Mr. Pitt's speech in support of that motion. Motion lost. Second motion, limiting an inquiry to the last ten years. Mr. Pitt's speech in support of this motion. The inquiry defeated by a Parliamentary manœuvre. - - 34

CHAP. V.——Lord Carteret's ascendancy in the closet. Enters into the German measures. Takes the Hanoverian troops into British pay. Mr. Pitt's speech against that measure. Death of Lord Wilmington, and Mr. Pelham's accession to the Treasury. Mr. Pitt's speech against the Address, at the commencement of the session, after the battle of Dettingen. Mr. Pitt's speech against voting money for a British army to serve in Flanders. The whole kingdom applauds his opposition in Parliament. The Duchess Dowager of Wales leaves him a handsome legacy.

CHAP. VI.——State of the Ministry. Lord Carlisle disappointed of the Privy Seal. Lord Cobham joins the Pelhams. Lord Granville opposed in Council, and resigns. The Broad Bottom Ministry appointed. Mr. Pitt's reply to Sir F. Dashwood, on the Address. Mr. Pitt's reply to Mr. Hume Campbell, on the noblemen's new-raised regiments. - - - - - 88

CHAP. VII.——Errors of history. Lord Bath at Court. His overtures to Lord Cobham. Duke of Newcastle asks the place of Secretary at War for Mr. Pitt, and is refused. Ministry resign. Lord Granville appointed Secretary of State. Lord Granville resigns, and the late Ministry restored. Mr. Pitt made Vice Treasurer of Ireland, and afterwards Paymaster. Makes no private use of the public money in his hands. Refuses to accept the perquisite of office on the Sardinian subsidy. 95

CHAP. VIII.——Lord Granville and Mr. Pelham reconciled. The Prince's claims in the Cornish boroughs. New Opposition formed. Mr. Pitt's speech on the Glasgow petition. On the mutiny bill, concerning the Westminster election. On Dunkirk. On the treaties with Bavaria and Spain. Death and character of the Prince of Wales. - - - - - 102

CHAP. IX.

CONTENTS.

CHAP. IX.——Regency appointed. The Bedfords turned out. Mr. Pitt's treatment of the Duke of Newcastle. Mr. Pitt's bill for the relief of the Chelsea pensioners. 116

CHAP. X.——Death of Mr. Pelham. Mr. Fox wishes to be made Secretary of State, and Minister of the House of Commons. Explanation of Minister of the House of Commons. Mr. Pitt expects to be made Secretary of State. Sir Thomas Robinson appointed. General dissatisfaction. Party at Leicester House. State of the nation. - - - - - 121

CHAP. XI.——Causes of the disagreements at Leicester House. Lord Harcourt and Dr. Hayter resign their posts of governor and preceptor to the Prince. Duke of Bedford's motion upon this subject in the House of Lords. Farther explanation of the principles inculcated at Leicester House. - - - 125

CHAP. XII.——Subsidiary treaties with Hanover, Hesse, and Russia. Payment to Russia refused. Duke of Newcastle sends Mr. York to Mr. Pitt. Mr. Fox offers to join Mr. Pitt. Debate on the subsidiary treaties. Mr. Pitt turned out. His balances found in the Bank. The Duke's Ministry appointed. Further debate on the treaties. France menaces an invasion of Great Britain. Hessians and Hanoverians arrive in England. France takes Minorca. Mr. Pitt and Mr. Fox explain the cause of that capture. Another cause. Convention with Prussia. - 131

CHAP. XIII.——Further account of Leicester House. The two Princesses of Brunswick in England. Observation. Mr. Fox resigns. Charte blanche offered to Mr. Pitt. Ministry changed. Mr. Pitt appointed Secretary of State. The King and Duke wished to have kept Mr. Fox. 141

CHAP. XIV.——Mr. Pitt's first Administration. Raises two thousand Highlanders. Refuses to support the Duke of Cumberland. Commanded to resign. Presented with the freedom of several cities and corporations. The King's distresses. Mr. Pitt made Minister upon his own terms. His triumph over Mr. Fox. The correspondence of the Admiralty given to Mr. Pitt. - - - 146

CHAP. XV.——Failure of the Duke of Cumberland. Expedition against Rochefort. Distresses of the King of Prussia. Hanover plundered. Mr. Pitt's two propositions; one, to send a fleet into the Baltic; the other, to cede Gibraltar to Spain. Anecdote of the treaty of peace made in 1783. Effects of Mr. Pitt's first Administration. Miscarriage of the expedition against Louisbourg. Union of Russia, Sweden, and Denmark, for the neutrality of the Baltic. Taking of the Dutch ships. Mr. Pitt opposes the proposition of sending the British fleet to the assistance of the Duke of Cumberland. - - - 153

CHAP. XVI.——The battle of Rosbach and its consequences. Its influence upon the British Council. Sudden prorogation of Parliament. Union of the King and Mr. Pitt. The King of Prussia's recommendation. Hanoverians resume their arms under Duke Ferdinand. Observations on the German war. 162

CHAP. XVII.——Meeting of Parliament. Mr. Alderman Beckford's explanation of the new principle of the German war. Mr. Pitt's speech on the Rochefort expedition. Effects of that speech. Successes of 1758. - - - 167

CHAP. XVIII.——Meeting of Parliament. Successes of 1759. Lord Bute's first interference. He goes to the Duke of Newcastle, and demands Lord Besborough's seat at the Treasury Board for Sir Gilbert Elliot. He also demands the representation of the county of Southampton for Sir Simeon Stuart. - - 171

CHAP. XIX.——Death of George II. Accession of George III. Lord Bute made a Privy Counsellor—Made Ranger of Richmond Park, in the room of the Princess Amelia. Views of the new King's party. Methods taken to accomplish those views. A number of writers hired at an enormous expence, to abuse the late King, the Duke of Cumberland, Mr. Pitt, and all the Whigs; to represent the war as ruinous,

CONTENTS.

ruinous, unjuſt, and impracticable. Parliament diſſolved. Mr. Legge turned out. Lord Holderneſſe reſigns upon a penſion. Lord Bute made Secretary of State in his room. The King's marriage. General Græme's merits on this occaſion. French anecdotes. Obſervations on royal marriages with foreigners. Negotiation with France—Breaks off. Martinico taken. Mr. Pitt prepares for a war with Spain. His deſign of attacking the Havannah. - - - 174

CHAP. XX.——State of France. Mr. Pitt oppoſed in his deſign to ſend ſome ſhips to Newfoundland. That place taken—Retaken. Mr. Pitt oppoſed in his deſign to attack the Spaniſh flota. Mr. Pitt and Lord Temple oppoſed in their advice to recall Lord Briſtol from Madrid. Three councils upon it. Mr. Pitt and Lord Temple reſign. Deſign againſt Panama and Manilla. Aſſertions of Lord Temple and Lord Bute. The Gazette account of Mr. Pitt's reſignation. His letter to the City of London. All the Spaniſh treaſure arrived in Spain. Explanatory note. Mr. Pitt greatly applauded in the city of London. War declared againſt Spain. Epitome of Mr. Pitt's adminiſtration. - - - - 185

CHAP. XXI.——Situation of Great Britain. Farther particulars concerning Mr. Pitt's reſignation—and the Princeſſes of Brunſwick. Union of Lord Bute with Lord Bath and Mr. Fox. Mr. Grenville wiſhes to be made Speaker. Mr. Pitt deſires all the papers relative to Spain to be laid before Parliament. He ſupports the motion of a ſupply for Portugal. Lord Tyrawley ſent to Liſbon. - 201

CHAP. XXII.——Reſolution of the Britiſh Cabinet to make peace. Subſidy to Pruſſia refuſed. Negotiation with the Court of Peterſburgh, and with the Court of Vienna. Both made known to the King of Pruſſia. Negotiation with the Court of Turin. Anecdote of the peace of Aix la Chapelle. Penſion granted to the Sardinian Miniſter. Privy purſe and ſecret ſervice. Alterations in the Britiſh Miniſtry. Lord Bute miniſter. His brother at Court. Intereſting particulars of the negotiation between Great Britain and France. Lord Bute's wealth. Examination of Dr. Muſgrave. Union of the Duke of Bedford and Mr. Grenville. Diſmiſſion of the Duke of Devonſhire. Anecdote of the Duke of Newcaſtle and Lord Granville. - - - - - 213

CHAP. XXIII.——Extraordinary preparations for the meeting of Parliament. Preliminary articles of peace laid before Parliament. Mr. Pitt's ſpeech againſt them 236

CHAP. XXIV.——Addreſſes on the peace. Mr. Pitt againſt the exciſe on cyder. Lord Bute tampers with the City of London. Denies it in the Houſe of Lords. Proved at Guildhall. A Portrait. Lord Bute reſigns. - - 249

CHAP. XXV.——Interview between Mr. Pitt and Lord Bute—Conferences between the King and Mr. Pitt. Treaty of connivance. Mr. Pitt at Court. His remark. Lord Hardwick's conduct - - - - - 258

CHAP. XXVI.——Meeting of Parliament. Servility of the Commons—of the Speaker. Verſatility. Vote away their own privilege. Royal apothgm. The North Briton. Mr. Pitt's ſpeech againſt the ſacrifice of privilege - 266

CHAP. XXVII.——Prince of Brunſwick viſits Mr. Pitt at Hayes. Queſtion concerning General Warrants. Mr. Pitt's ſpeech againſt them - 271

CHAP. XXVIII.——Sir William Pynſent leaves his fortune to Mr. Pitt. Similar intention of Mr. Hollis. Preſent and note from Wareham. Pitt's diamond. The Regency. American ſtamp act. Lord Bute reſolves to diſmiſs the Miniſters. Gets an audience of the Duke of Cumberland. The Duke ſends for Lord Temple. Conference between them. The Duke goes to Mr. Pitt. Applies to Lord Lyttelton. Lord Temple and Mr. Grenville reconciled. Obſervation. Mr. Stuart Mackenzie diſmiſſed. The King ſends for Mr. Pitt. Lord Temple ſent for. They refuſe the King's offers. Obſervation. King's friends. Conduct of the Duke of Bedford and Mr. Jenkinſon. The Duke forms a new miniſtry - 275

CHAP. XXIX.

CONTENTS.

CHAP. XXIX.——New ministry blamed for accepting. Lord Bute's influence not diminished. Their apology. Mr. Pitt's speech against the American stamp act. He compliments Mr. Burke. - - - - 286

CHAP. XXX.——Lord Bute resolves to change the ministry again. Disregards the Duke of Bedford. Tries to gain Lord Temple. Meeting at Lord Eglintoun's. Amuses Lord Temple. Lord Strange's assertion. Lord Rockingham's request. Affair of Dunkirk. Negotiation with Mr. Wilkes. Proposition for the government of Canada. Disapproved by the Chancellor, who advises the King to send for Mr. Pitt. - - - - - 300

CHAP. XXXI.——Lord Northington opens his negotiation with Mr. Pitt. Duke of Grafton resigns. Several persons refuse places. An eighteen days Journal. Mr. Pitt sees the King. Lord Temple sent for, and goes to the King. Conference between Mr. Pitt and Lord Temple at Hampstead. They differ, and separate. Lord Temple has an audience of the King, Returns to Stowe. Mr. Pitt created Earl of Chatham. His extraordinary grants. Mr. Townshend Manager of the House of Commons. Several persons refuse places. Lord Rockingham refuses to see Lord Chatham. Mr. Stuart Mackenzie restored. Lord Chatham not united with Lord Bute. - - - - - 313

CHAP. XXXII.——Embargo on the exportation of corn. State of parties. Conference between Lord Chatham and the Duke of Bedford at Bath. Conference between Lord Chatham and Lord Edgcumbe. Its consequences. The Admiralty offered to Lord Gower. Conduct of the Court. Second conference with the Duke of Bedford. Breaks off - - - - 326

CHAP. XXXIII.——Further arrangements. Lord Chatham regrets the loss of Lord Temple. Seized with the gout at Bath, and at Marlborough. Comes to Hampstead. Another change meditated. General Conway wishes to resign. Lord Northington wishes to resign. King's message to Lord Chatham. Duke of Newcastle is very anxious to preserve the union of the opposition. Application to Lord Rockingham. Declaration of the Duke of Bedford. Declaration of the Duke of Newcastle. Conference at Newcastle-house. Breaks off. Importance of the Minister of the House of Commons. America the true cause. Second conference at Newcastle-house. Anecdotes of Mr. Lownds's tickets, and of the Judges tickets. Lord Rockingham waits on the King. Lord Holland advises the King - - - - - 334

CHAP. XXXIV.——Mr. Townshend resolves to be Minister. Dies. Lord North appointed. Lord Chatham goes into Somersetshire. The Bedford interest join the Ministry. Duke of Bedford's apology to Mr. Grenville, and Mr. Grenville's answer. Lord Chatham returns to Hayes. French purchase Corsica. Difference between the Duke of Bedford and Lord Shelburne. Lord Rochford resigns. Lord Shelburn resigns. Fine diamond ring presented to his Majesty. Lord Rochford made Secretary of State—with the reasons. Lord Chatham resigns. Lord Townshend continued in Ireland. - - - 349

SPEECHES

SPEECHES
AND
ANECDOTES.

CHAP. I.

Introduction.—Mr. Pitt's Birth.—Placed at Eton.—Sent to Oxford.—Mr. Warton's Compliment to Mr. Pitt.—Latin Verses by Mr. Pitt.—Goes abroad.—Made a Cornet of Horse.—Elected as a Member of Parliament.—His Friends.—His first Speech in Parliament---Honoured by the Prince of Wales.---His Commission taken from him by Sir Robert Walpole.----Verses to him by Mr. Lyttelton.----Patronized by Lord Cobham.----His accomplishments.---Complimented by Thomson; by Hammond.---His Conduct in Parliament attacked by the Gazetteer; defended by the Craftsman.---The Prince dismissed from St. James's.

THE lives of Eminent Men afford useful lessons of instruction, as well as great examples for imitation. No native of the British Island stands higher in the judgment of the present age, for either the magnificence of his talents as a Senator and Statesman, or the virtue of his Conduct in both private and public Life, than the late EARL OF CHATHAM. Nor will the Character of any man, however flattered it may have

<small>Chap I. Introduction.</small> have been in defcription, or however fuperior he may have been in ftation, go down to pofterity with purer honour. Other men's names are remembered by the aid of biography: his will be revered by the glories of his actions, which illumined the political hemifphere, during the fplendid æra in which the reins of government were in his hands. The archives of the various nations of the world, at that period of his life, though written in different languages, will unite in raifing a pyramid to his name, which Time cannot deftroy.

The Memoirs of fuch a man fhould be written by the firft Hiftorian of the Age. This work affumes an humbler rank in literature. It goes forth with no other claim to public notice, than, that of being A Collection of Fugitive Papers and Anecdotes; many of them known to feveral perfons, now living, but all of them to very few. In fine, the prefent publication is the effect of induftry, not of ability.

<small>Birth.</small> THE EARL of CHATHAM was born on the fifteenth of November, 1708 in the Parifh of St. James's, Weftminfter. <small>Placed at Eton.</small> He received the firft part of his education at Eton; where he was placed upon the Foundation. His co-temporaries, at this fchool, were GEORGE LYTTELTON, afterwards LORD LYTTELTON, HENRY FOX, afterwards LORD HOLLAND, SIR CHAR-<small>Sent to Oxford</small> LES HANBURY WILLIAMS, HENRY FIELDING, author of Tom Jones, &c. At the age of eighteen he was fent to Trinity College, Oxford. This laft circumftance appears by the following Extract from the Regifter in the Burfary in Trinity College, fol. 258.

"Ego GULIELMUS PITT, filius ROBERTI PITT, armigeri
"de Old Sarum, natus Londini in Parochia Sancti Jacobi;
annorum

" annorum circiter 18 admiſſus ſum commenſalis primi ordi-
" nis ſub tutamine Magiſtri Stockwell Jan. die 10, 1726 *."

In the Oxford Verſes upon the Death of George the Firſt, which were publiſhed the year after he went to College, we find the following by Mr. PITT.

Angliacæ vos O præſentia numina gentis
Libertas, atque Alma Themis! Neptune Britanni
Tu Pater Ocean.! ſi jam pacata Georgi
Imperio tua perlabi licet æquora) veſtro
(Triſte miniſterium!) pia ſolvite munera Regi.
At teneri planctus abſint, molleſque querilæ
Herois tu nulo. quas mors deflenda requirit,
Geſta vetant lacrymas, juſtæque ſuperbia laudis.
  Inſtare horribiles longe latèque tumultus;
Hic ſuper Hiſpanos violenta tumeſcere campos
Belli diluvies, illic ad flumina Rheni
Ardentes furibundus equos immittere Mavors:
Heu quam in ſe miſeri cladem ſtrageſque cierent!
Quot fortes caderent animæ! quot gurgite torquens

* In reference to his having been a Member of Trinity College, are the following Lines in Mr. Warton's Addreſs to him, upon the Death of George the Second.

———— Nor thou refuſe
This humble preſent of no partial Muſe
From that calm Bower †, which nurs'd thy thoughtful Youth
In the pure precepts of Athenian truth:
Where firſt the form of Britiſh liberty
Beam'd in full radiance on thy muſing eye;
That form, whoſe mien ſublime, with equal awe,
In the ſame ſhade unblemiſh'd Somers ſaw.

† Trinity College, Oxford, in which alſo Lord Somers was educated.

Sanguineo

Chap. I. Sanguineo fluvius morientia corpora in altum
Volveret Oceanum ! ni Te fuccurrere fœclo
Te folum, vifum fuperis, Augufte, labenti.
Tu miferans hominum pacem fuper aftra volantem,
Imperio retines, terrafque revifere cogis.

    Dextera quid potuit, primis ubi fervor in armis
Impulit ulcifci patriam, populofque gementes,
Turcarum dicant acies, verfifque cohortes
Turbatæ fignis ; dicat perterrita Buda,
Invitaque Tuos prætollat laude triumphos,
Fulmina cum attonitum contra torquenda tyrannum
Vidit, et intremuit. Rerum at jam lenior ordo
Arrifit, gladiumque manus confueta rotare
(Majus opus!) gratæ prætendit figna quietis.

    Quare agite, O Populi, tantarum in munere laudum
Sternite humum foliis. Sed vos ante omnia Mufæ
Cæfarem ad aftra feretis ; amavit vos quoque Cæfar
Veftraque cum placida laurus concrevit Oliva.

    Felix, qui potuit mundi cohibere tumultus!
Fortunatus et illi, ægri folamen amoris
Qui fubit Angliacis, tanti audit nominis hæres.
Aufpice Te, cives agitans difcordia, ludo
Heu fatiata nimis! furias amnemque feverum
Cocyti repetat, propriofque perhorreat angues.
At fecura quies, metuens et gratia culpæ
Te circumvolitent. Themis hinc Cæleftis, et illinc
Suftentet folium clementia. Tu quoque magnam
Partem habeas opere in tanto, Carolina labore
Imperii recreans feffum : nam Maximus Ille
Te colit, atque animi Senfum Tibi credit opertum
Curarum conforti, et multo pignore junctæ.

                                                   Inclyta

Inclyta Progenies! Tibi quam dilecta Tonanti
Latona invideat, quam vel Berecynthia Mater
Centum enixa Deos; fi qua Hæc fint Dona Britannis
Propria, fintque Precor, referant et Utrumque Parentem.
GUL. PITT, e Coll. Trin.
Socio Commens.

Before he left Eton he was afflicted with the Gout, which encreafed during his refidence at Oxford; and which at length obliged him to quit the Univerfity, without taking a degree. It was Hereditary.

He afterwards made the Tour of part of France, and part of Italy. But his diforder was not removed by it. He, however, conftantly employed the leifure, which this painful and tedious malady afforded, in the cultivation and improvement of his mind. Lord Chesterfield, who rather envied than admired his fuperiority, fays " that thus he acquired a great " fund of premature and ufeful knowledge."

He came firft into Parliament in the month of February 1735, for the Borough of Old Sarum, in the room of his brother; who, being elected for Old Sarum and Oakhampton, made his election for the latter. His brother-in-law, Robert Nedham Efq. was his coadjutor. Having five Sifters, and an elder brother, his fortune was not very confiderable; his friends therefore obtained for him a Cornet's commiffion in the Blues, in addition to his income.

In March 1735, George Lyttelton, Efq; (eldeft Son of Sir Thomas Lyttelton of Hagley, who married Lord Cobham's Sifter) afterwards Lord Lyttelton, was elected member of parliament for Oakhampton, by the interest of Thomas Pitt Efq. in the room of Mr. Northmore, who died a little time before.

At

CHAP. I. At the General election in 1734. RICHARD GRENVILLE Efq. (the late EARL TEMPLE, whofe mother was LORD COBHAM's eldeſt Siſter) came firſt into parliament, being elected for Buckingham. Mr. W. PITT, Mr. GRENVILLE, and Mr. LYTTELTON, became affociates; and for feveral years always fat next to each other in the Houſe of Commons.

Mr. PITT had not been many days in Parliament, when he was felected for a teller. It appears by the Journals Vol. 22, page 535, upon a motion to refer the Navy eſtimates to a felect Committee, that the houfe divided, and that Mr. WILLIAM PITT, and Mr. SANDYS, afterwards LORD SANDYS, were appointed tellers of the minority, upon that queſtion.

1736. Mr. PITT's firſt Speech in Parliament was on the 29th of April 1736, upon feconding a motion made by his friend Mr. LYTTELTON; viz.

"That an humble addrefs be prefented to His Majeſty, to congratulate His Majeſty upon the nuptials of His Royal Highneſs the Prince of Wales· and to exprefs the fatisfaction and great joy. of his faithful Commons on this happy occafion, which they look upon with unfpeakable Comfort, as the means, under the divine Providence, of giving an additional ſtrength to the Proteſtant Intereſt, and of fecuring to all future ages, the laws and liberties of this nation, in the full manner we now happily and thankfully enjoy them, under the protection of his Majeſty's juſt and mild Government over his People."

When Mr. LYTTELTON fat down, Mr. PITT rofe, and

Mr. Pitt's firſt Speech. fpoke in fubſtance, nearly as follows.

"That he was unable to offer any thing that had not been faid by his Honourable friend who made the motion, in a manner much more fuitable to the dignity and importance of the ſubject.—But faid he, as I am really affected with the profpect of the bleſſings, to be derived to my Country. from this fo defirable and long defired meaſure, the marriage of his Royal Highneſs the Prince of Wales; I cannot

forbear

forbear troubling you with a few words, to exprefs my joy, and to mingle my humble offering, inconfiderable as it is, with this oblation of thanks and congratulation, to his Majefty.

How great fo-ever the joy of the Public may be, and very great it certainly is, in receiving this benefit from his Majefty, it muft be inferior to that high fatisfaction, which he himfelf enjoys, in beftowing it: And if I may be allowed to fuppofe, that to a Royal mind any thing can tranfcend the pleafure of gratifying the impatient wifhes of a loyal people, it can only be the paternal delight of tenderly indulging the moft dutiful application, and moft humble requeft of a fubmiffive obedient fon. I mention, Sir, his Royal Highnefs's having afked a marriage becaufe fomething is, in juftice, due to him, for having afked what we are fo ftrongly bound, by all the ties of Duty and Gratitude, to return his Majefty our moft humble acknowledgements for having granted.

The marriage of a Prince of Wales Sir, has at all times, been a a matter of the higheft importance to the public welfare, to prefent and to future Generations; But at no time has it been a more important, a more dear confideration, than at this day; if a Character, at once amiable and refpectable, can embellifh and evendignify the elevated rank of a Prince of Wales. Were it not a fort of prefumption to follow fo great a Perfon through his hours of retirement, to view him in the milder light of domeftic life, we fhould find him engaged in the noble exercife of humanity, benevolence, and of every focial virtue. But Sir, how pleafing, how captivating fo ever fuch a fcene may be, yet as it is a private one, I fear I fhould offend the delicacy of that Virtue, I fo ardently defire to do Juftice to, fhould I offer it to the confideration of this Houfe: But, Sir, filial duty to his Royal Parents, a generous love of liberty, and a juft reverence for the Britifh Conftitution; thefe are public Virtues, and cannot efcape the applaufe and benedictions of the public: They are Virtues, Sir, which render his Royal H'ghnefs not only a noble ornament, but a firm fupport, if any could poffibly be neceffary, of that throne fo greatly filled by his Royal Father.

I have been led to fay thus much of his Royal Highnefs's Character, becaufe, it is the confideration of that Character, which above all things, enforces the Juftice and goodnefs of his Majefty in the meafure now before us, a meafure which the nation thought could never come

too

CHAP. I.
1736

too soon, becaufe it brings with it the promife of an additional ftrength to the Proteftant fucceffion in his Majefty's illuftrious and Royal Houfe. The fpirit of liberty dictated that fucceffion, the fame fpirit now rejoices in the profpect of its being perpetuated to lateft pofterity. It rejoices in the wife and happy choice which his Majefty has been pleafed to make of a princefs, fo amiably diftinguifhed in herfelf, fo illuftrious in the merit of her family; the glory of whofe great anceftor it is, to have facrificed himfelf to the nobleft caufe for which a Prince can draw his fword, the caufe of liberty and the Proteftant Religion. Such, Sir, is the marriage, for which our moft humble acknowledgements are due to his Majefty; and may it afford the comfort of feeing the Royal Family (numerous as I thank God it is) ftill growing and rifing up in a third generation; a Family, Sir, which I muft fincerely wifh may be as immortal as thofe liberties, and that conftitution it came to maintain; and therefore I am heartily for the motion."

The motion was unanimoufly agreed to.

The fpeeches of both Gentlemen, being what are called maiden, or firft fpeeches, were not only heard with great indulgence, but pleafure; and were honoured with the warmeft approbation of every auditor. The extraordinary merit of thefe young Gentlemen, induced his ROYAL HIGHNESS to beftow upon them, the moft gracious and flattering marks of his diftinction and countenance.

Upon every queftion, Mr. PITT divided with his friends, againft the Minifter; and appeared, on every occafion, a firm and determined opponent of the Minifter's meafures. Sir ROBERT WALPOLE was not a little irritated by this conduct; and being in the habit of difmiffing military officers for their conduct in Parliament, and having, particularly, a fhort time before, broke Lord COBHAM and others, he made no hefitation of breaking Mr. PITT. This imprudent, violent, and unconftitutional meafure, fo far from diminifhing Mr. PITT's confequence in the eyes of his patrons, or the public,

public, very confiderably encreafed it in both. His friend Mr. LYTTELTON wrote the following lines on the occafion.

CHAP. I.
1736.

To WILLIAM PITT Efq. on his lofing his Commiffion in the year 1736.

Long had thy virtues mark'd thee out for fame,
Far, far fuperior to a Cornet's name;
This gen'rous WALPOLE faw, and griev'd to find
So mean a poft difgrace that noble mind.
The Servile Standard from the freeborn hand
He took, and bad thee lead the Patriot band.

Lord COBHAM, the revered Patron of Virtue and Genius, whofe character was in fuch high eftimation, that his fmile alone conferred honour; was among the foremoft to offer him his fervices and friendfhip. An acquaintance thus formed on a congeniality of fentiment and principle, foon ripened into affection; and Mr. PITT's fociety was ever after reckoned by his Lordfhip, among the greateft pleafures of his life. It is no wonder, indeed, that a Nobleman poffeffing the knowledge, the virtue, and the difcernment of Lord COBHAM, fhould be fo captivated with, and attached to his young friend: for to brilliancy of talents, to a high fenfe of honour, and to the moft exalted principles of public and private virtue, Mr. PITT had united every elegant accomplifhment; and his manners and addrefs were as irrefiftible as his eloquence. His character was, indeed, fuch as to form a fitter fubject of poetic praife than hiftoric defcription; and the following extracts will prove that the firft Poets of his time, Thomfon and Hammond, did not lofe the oppertunity of painting from fo rare a model.

The fair majeftic Paradife of Stowe.....
And there, O PITT, thy Country's early boaft,
There let me fit beneath the fhelter'd flopes;
Or in that Temple* where, in future times

* Temple of Virtue in Stowe Gardens.

VOL. I.   C   And

Thou well shalt merit a distinguish'd name;
And with thy converse blest, catch the last smiles
Of Autumn beaming o'er the yellow woods.
While there with thee th' enchanted round I walk,
The regulated wild, gay fancy then
Will tread in thought the groves of Attic land;
Will from thy Standard taste refine her own,
Correct her pencil to the purest truth
Of Nature; or th' unimpassioned shades
Forsaking, raise it to the human mind.
Or if hereafter she with juster hand,
Shall draw the tragic scene, instruct her thou,
To mark the varied movement. of the heart,
What ev'ry decent character requires,
And ev'ry passion speaks: O, through her strain
Breathe thy pathetic eloquence! that moulds
Th' attentive senate, charms, persuades, exalts,
Of honest zeal th' indignant light'ning throws,
And shakes corruption on her venal throne. *Thomson's Autumn.*

Nor does the elegant and pathetic Hammond fall short of Thomson in the following lines

To Stowe's delightful scenes I now repair,
In COBHAM's smile to lose the gloom of care.....
There PITT in manners soft, in friendship warm,
With mild advice my listening grief shall charm,
With sense to Counsel, and with wit to please,
A Roman's virtue with a. courtier's case.

On the 23d of February 1737 Mr. PULTENEY (afterwards EARL of BATH) moved for an address to the King, humbly beseeching his Majesty to settle 100,000l. per annum on the Prince of Wales.

The minister, Sir ROBERT WALPOLE, opposed this motion with all his strength. The PRINCE being in opposition to him, he was sensible that a compliance with the motion, would as infallibly encrease the power of his Royal Highness, as it would dimimish his own. Mr. PITT is said to have spoken very ably in support of the motion; as did Mr. GRENVILLE, and Mr. LYTTELTON, on the same side; but their speeches are no where distinctly preserved. The substance of the debate on both sides, is stated only in the form of a general argument, *for* and *against* the motion.

The political papers of the time, however, very clearly evince, that the minister smarted under the lash of Mr. PITT's eloquence; for in one of the numbers of the Gazetteer, a paper avowedly written in support of the minister, and published soon after the close of the session, Mr. PITT is characterized in terms, which are as illiberal as they are unjust. And which occasioned the Opposition-paper of those times, the Craftsman, to defend him, in reply to the Gazetteer.

" Should a young man, says the Gazetteer, just brought into the House of Commons, endeavour to rank himself with the first in reputation and experience, would he not render himself ridiculous by by the attempt, and even destroy the degree of fame which he might otherwise deserve? A young man of my acquaintance, through an overbearing disposition, and a weak judgment, assuming the character of a great man, which he is no way able to support, is become the object of ridicule, instead of praise. My young man has the vanity to put himself in the place of Tully. But let him consider, that every one who has the same natural imperfections with Tully, has not therefore the same natural perfections; though his neck should be as long, his body as slender, yet his voice may not be as sonorous, his action may not be as just. . . . . Such-a-one may be deluded

Chap. II. luded enough, to look upon himfelf as a perfon of real confequence, and not fee that he is raifed by a party, as a proper tool for their prefent purpofes, and whom they can at any time pull down, when thofe purpofes are ferved."

1737.

In anfwer to the preceding, the Craftfman, No. 596, fays,

"That he is not addicted to panegyric, but roufed by an honeft zeal to refent the blackeft perfonal calumny, by expofing the heart and intention of the wretched author, in brow-beating iifing virtue, and flandering a certain young gentleman in the groffeft manner; one, who, in every fituation, hath conducted himfelf, in the niceft and difcreeteft manner; and by his thirft after learning, hath given reafon to expect actions, fuitable to fo happy and fingular a beginning. The Gazetteer pretends to an acquaintance of the gentleman; but furely no man of the leaft honour would offer to fall fo foul on his friend; neither would an acquaintance, of any value, or worth, advife him thus publickly, and thereby endeavour to expofe him to the world. To fhew how prejudicial to the good of one's country fuch treatment of rifing merit may be, let us confider, the great Demofthenes returning from the bar, difcontented at his own performances, meeting fuch an advifer as this, perfuading him, already too much prejudiced againft his own imperfections, not to attempt to eftablifh his reputation as an orator, for which he was no way defign'd by nature. Such advice, in the fituation he was in, might perhaps have had its fatal effect; and what, Oh Athenians, would you have loft in this cafe? not only the reputation of producing one of the brighteft orators that ever lived, but the boldeft defender of your liberties; and the greateft check to the Macedonian Monarch? a man of whom Philip, by his own confeffion, ftood more in awe, than of all the Grecian States, he fought to opprefs."

The Prince being this year deprived of his apartments at St. James's and excluded from Court, feveral of his houfhold refigned their places, and were fucceeded by others; in this Revolution Mr. Pitt was appointed Groom of the Bedchamber, and Mr. Lyttelton private Secretary.

CHAP.

CHAP. II.

Mr. Pitt's Speech in favour of a Reduction of the Army—On the Convention with Spain—On Admiral Haddock's Instructions—On Sir Charles Wager's Bill for the Encouragement of Seamen.---Reply to Mr. Horace Walpole.---Reply to Mr. Winnington.---On the Motion for an Address to remove Sir Robert Walpole.

MR. PITT's Speeches during the remaining period of Sir ROBERT WALPOLE's Administration, which have been preserved, are the Seven following*.

On the 4th of February 1738, on the report of the number of land forces, Mr. PITT spoke in favour of a reduction, in reply to Sir THOMAS LUMLEY SAUNDERSON, afterwards EARL of SCARBOROUGH, who had spoken in support of the number proposed by the Minister.

Sir THOMAS had said, that he was surprised to hear any Placemen arguing in favour of a reduction of the army, which Sir JOSEPH JEKYL, Mr. LYTTELTON, &c. had done.

Mr. PITT began with saying, " That as to what the Honourable Gentleman had said, respecting those whom he calls placemen, he would agree with him, that if they were to be directed in their opinions by the places they held, they might unite for the support of each other, against the common good of the nation; but I

---

* They are taken from Chandler's Collection of Parliamentary Debates. The authority is not very good; but there is no other account of the Parliamentary Debates during this period. It must likewise be observed, that none of Lord CHATHAM's Speeches prior to 1760, are to be wholly depended upon. And the only apology that can be made, for giving them a place in this work, is, that they are generally supposed to contain a part, at least, of his argument.

CHAP. II.
1738.

hope, said he, none of them are under any such directions, I am sure the Hon. Gentleman himself is not, and therefore I am convinced he is not serious, when he talks of being surprized at any placeman's declaring for a reduction of our army; for, of all men, those who enjoy any places of profit under our government ought to be the most cautious of loading the public with any unnecessary tax or expence; because as the places they possess generally bring them in more than their share of our taxes can amount to, it may be properly said, that by consenting to any article of public expence, they lay a load upon others which they themselves bear no share of.

"I must look upon myself as a placeman as well as the Hon. Gentleman who spoke last. I am in the service of one of the branches of the Royal Family, and think it my honour to be so; but I should not think it, if I were not as free to give my opinion upon any question that happens in this House, as I was before I had any such place, and, I believe from the behaviour of Gentlemen, upon this very occasion, it will appear that all those who are in the service with me, are in the same state of freedom, because I believe they will, upon the question now before us, appear to be of different opinions. But there is another set of placemen, whose behaviour surprizes me not a little, because upon every question respecting public affairs they are always unanimous; and I confess it is to me a little astonishing that two or three hundred Gentlemen should, by an unaccountable sort of unanimity, always agree in opinion upon the many different questions which occur annually. I am convinced this surprizing unanimity does not proceed from any effect of the places they hold under the Crown; for if it did, a man's being possessed of any place under the Crown would in such a case, I am sure, be an infallible reason for the people not to trust him with the preservation of their liberties, or the disposal of their properties in Parliament.

"Then, as to the Tories, and suspected Jacobites, I am surprized to hear any comparison made between them and the fat man in the crowd. There are so few of either in the kingdom that I am sure they can give no man an occasion for being afraid of them, and therefore there is not the least shadow of reason for saying they are the occasion of our being obliged to keep such a numerous standing army.

"Our large army may properly be compared to the fat man in the crowd; for the keeping up of such an army is the first cause of our discontents,

discontents, and those discontents, now we find, are made the chief pretence for keeping the army. Remove therefore the army, or but a considerable part of it, and the discontents complained of will cease.

"I come now to the only argument the Hon. Gentleman made use of, which can admit a serious consideration; and if our army were intirely or but generally composed of veterans inured to the fatigues and the dangers of war, and such as had often ventured their lives against the enemies of their country, I confess the argument would have a great weight; but considering the circumstances of our present army, I can hardly think my Hon. Friend was serious when he made use of such argument. As for the Officers of the army they are quite out of the question; for in case of a reduction there is a handsome provision for every one of them: no man can doubt, nor would any man oppose, their being put upon half-pay; and I must observe that our half-pay is better, or as good as full pay, I believe, in any other country in Europe: for in the method our army is now kept up, I could shew by calculation that it costs the nation more than would maintain three times the number of men either in France or Germany. And as for the soldiers I believe it may be said of at least three fourths of them, that they never went under any fatigue except that of a review, nor were ever exposed to any danger except in apprehending smugglers, or dispersing mobs; therefore I must think they have no claim for any greater reward than the pay they have already received, nor should I think we were guilty of the least ingratitude if they were all turned adrift to-morrow morning.

"But suppose, Sir, the soldiers of our army were all such who served a campaign or two against a public enemy; is it from thence to be inferred that they must for ever after live idly, and be maintained at the expence of their country, and that in such a manner, as to be dangerous to the liberties of their country? At this rate if a man has but once ventured his life in the service of his country, he must for ever be, not only a burthen, but a terror to his country. This would be a sort of reward which I am sure no brave soldier would accept of, nor any honest one desire. That we should shew a proper gratitude to those who have ventured their lives in the service of their country, is what I shall readily acknowledge, but this gratitude ought to be shewn in such a way as not to be dangerous to the liberties nor too burthensome to the people;

people; and therefore after a war is at an end, if a soldier can provide for himself, either by his labour or by the means of his own private fortune, he ought not to expect, and if he is not of a mercenary disposition, he will scorn to receive, any other rewards than those which consists in the peculiar honour and privileges, which may and ought to be conferred upon him.

" That we ought to shew a proper gratitude to every man who has ventured his life in the cause of his country, is what, I am sure, no Gentleman will deny: yet as the laws now stand an old Officer, who has often ventured his life, and often spilt his blood in the service of his country, may be dismissed and reduced, perhaps to a starving condition, at the arbitrary will and pleasure, perhaps at the whim of a Minister; so that by the present establishment of the army, the reward of a soldier seems not to depend upon the services done to his country, but upon the services he does to those who happen to be Ministers at the time. Must not this be allowed to be a defect in the present establishment? And yet when a law was proposed for supplying this defect, we may remember what reception it met with, even from those who now insist so highly upon the gratitude we ought to shew the Gentlemen of the army."

1739.

On the 8th of March, 1739, Mr. H. WALPOLE having moved that an Address of Thanks be presented to the King, on the convention with Spain, this motion brought on a long debate; in which Mr. PITT followed Mr. HOWE (afterwards created LORD CHEDWORTH) who spoke for the Address, Mr. PITT against it, viz.

Speech upon the Spanish Convention.

" I can by no means think that the complicated question now before us is the proper, the direct manner of taking the sense of this Committee. We have here the soft name of an humble Address to the Crown proposed, and for no other end but to lead Gentlemen into an approbation of the Convention. But is this that full deliberate examination which we were with defiance called upon to give? Is this cursory blended disquisition of matters of such variety and extent, all we owe to ourselves and our country? When trade is at stake it is your last retrenchment; you must defend it, or perish, and whatever is to decide that deserves the most distinct consideration, and the most direct undisguised sense of Parliament. But how are we now proceeding? Upon an artificial, ministerial question: here is all the confidence, here is the conscious sense of the greatest service that ever was done to this country; to be complicating questions, to be lumping sanction and approbation like a Commissary's accompt; to be covering and taking sanctuary in the Royal name, instead of meeting openly and standing fairly the direct judgment and sentence of Parliament upon the several articles of this Convention.

"You have been moved to vote an humble Address of Thanks to his Majesty for a measure which (I will appeal to Gentlemen's conversation in the world) is odious throughout the kingdom: such thanks are only due to the fatal influence that framed it, as are due for that low, unallied condition abroad, which is now made a plea for this Convention. To what are Gentlemen reduced in support of it? First try a little to defend it upon its own merits; if that is not tenable, throw out general terrors, the House of Bourbon is united, who knows the consequence of a war? Sir, Spain knows the consequence of a war in America; whoever gains it must prove fatal to her; she knows it, and must therefore avoid it; but she knows England does not dare to make it, and what is a delay, which is all this magnified Convention is sometimes called, to produce? Can it produce such conjunctures as those you lost, while you were giving kingdoms to Spain, and all to bring her back again to that great branch of the House of Bourbon which is now thrown out to you with so much terror? If this union be formidable, are we to delay only till it becomes more formidable by being carried further into execution, and more strongly cemented? But be it what it will, is this any longer a nation, or what is an English Parliament, if with more ships in your harbours than in all the navies of Europe, with above two millions of people in your American colonies, you will bear to hear of the expediency of receiving from Spain an insecure, unsatisfactory, dishonourable Convention? Sir, I call it no more than it has been proved in this debate; it carries fallacy or downright subjection in almost every line. It has been laid open and exposed in so many strong and glaring lights that I can pretend to add nothing to the conviction and indignation it has raised.

"Sir, as to the great national objection, the searching your ships, that favourite word, as it was called, is not omitted, indeed, in the preamble to the Convention, but it stands there as the reproach of the

CHAP. II.
1739.

whole, as the strongest evidence of the fatal submission that follows: on the part of Spain an usurpation, an inhuman tyranny claimed and exercised over the American seas; on the part of England an undoubted right by treaties and from God and nature, declared and asserted in the resolutions of Parliament, are referred to the discussion of Plenipotentiaries, upon one and the same equal foot. Sir, I say this undoubted right is to be discussed and regulated. And if to regulate be to prescribe rules (as in all construction it is) this right is, by the express words of this Convention, to be given up and sacrificed; for it must cease to be any thing, from the moment it is submitted to limits.

"The Court of Spain has plainly told you (as appears by papers upon the table) you shall steer a due course, you shall navigate, by a line to and from your plantations in America; if you draw near to her coasts (though from the circumstances of that navigation you are under an unavoidable necessity of doing it) you shall be seized and confiscated. If then upon these terms only she has consented to refer, what becomes at once of all the security we are flattered with in consequence of this reference? Plenipotentiaries are to regulate finally the respective pretentions of the two Crowns with regard to trade and navigation in America; but does a man in Spain reason that these pretentions must be regulated to the satisfaction and honour of England? No, Sir, they conclude, and with reason, from the high spirit of their administration, from the superiority with which they have so long treated you, that this reference must end, as it has begun, to their honour and advantage.

"But, Gentlemen, say, the treaties subsisting are to be the measure of this regulation, Sir, as to treaties, I will take part of the words of Sir William Temple, quoted by the Hon. Gentleman near me, *It is vain to negociate* and make *treaties*, if there is not dignity and vigour to enforce the observance of them; for under the misconstruction and misrepresentation of these very treaties subsisting, this intolerable grievance has arisen; it has been growing upon you, treaty after treaty, through twenty years of negociation, and even under the discussion of Commissaries to whom it was referred. You have heard from Captain Vaughan at your bar, at what time these injuries and indignities were continued; as a kind of explanatory comment upon the Convention, Spain has thought fit to grant you; as another insolent protest, under

the

the validity and force of which she has suffered this Convention to be proceeded upon. We'll treat with you, but we'll search and take your ships; we'll sign a Convention, but we'll keep your subjects prisoners, prisoners in Old Spain; the West Indies are remote, Europe shall be witness how we use you.

"As to the inference of an admission of our right not to be searched, drawn from a reparation made for ships unduly seized and confiscated, I think that argument is very inconclusive. The right claimed by Spain to search our ships is one thing, and the excesses admitted to have been committed in consequence of this pretended right, is another, but surely, Sir, reasoning from inferences and implication only, is below the dignity of your proceedings, upon a right of this vast importance. What this reparation is, what sort of composition for your losses, forced upon you by Spain, in an instance that has come to light, where your own Commissaries could not in conscience decide against your claim, has fully appeared upon examination; and as for the payment of the sum stipulated (all but seven and twenty thousand pounds, and that too subject to a drawback) it is evidently a fallacious nominal payment only. I will not attempt to enter into the detail of a dark, confused, and scarcely intelligible accompt, I will only beg leave to conclude with one word upon it in the light of a submission, as well as of an adequate reparation. Spain stipulates to pay to the Crown of England ninety-five thousand pounds; by a preliminary protest of the King of Spain, the South Sea Company is at once to pay sixty-eight thousand of it: If they refuse, Spain, I admit, is still to pay the ninety-five thousand pounds; but how does it stand then? The Assiento contract is to be suspended: you are to purchase this sum at the price of an exclusive trade, pursuant to an national treaty, and of an immense debt of God knows how many hundred thousand pounds due from Spain to the South Sea Company. Here, Sir, is the submission of Spain by the payment of a stipulated sum; a tax laid upon subjects of England under the severest penalties, with the reciprocal accord of an English Minister, as a preliminary that the Convention may be signed; a condition imposed by Spain in the most absolute, imperious manner, and received by the Ministers of England in the most tame and abject. Can any verbal distinctions, any evasions whatever, possibly explain away this public infamy? To whom would we disguise it? To ourselves

CHAP. II. selves and to the nation: I wish we could hide it from the eyes of every
1739 Court in Europe: they see Spain has talked to you like your master, they see this arbitrary fundamental condition, and it must stand with distinction, with a pre-eminence of shame, as a part even of this Convention.

"This Convention, Sir, I think from my soul is nothing but a stipulation for national ignominy; an illusory expedient to baffle the resentment of the nation; a truce without a suspension of hostilities on the part of Spain; on the part of England a suspension; as to Georgia, of the first law of nature, self-preservation and self-defence, a surrender of the rights and trade of England to the mercy of Plenipotentiaries, and in this infinitely highest and sacred point, future security, not only inadequate, but directly repugnant to the resolutions of Parliament, and the gracious promise from the Throne. The complaints of your despairing Merchants, the voice of England has condemned it; be the guilt of it upon the head of the adviser. God forbid that this Committee should share the guilt by approving it!"

The Address was agreed to.

1740. On a motion made by Mr. WALLER, on the 24th of
On Adm. Haddock's Instructions, January, 1740, for copies of letters and orders sent to ADMIRAL HADDOCK, and others, Mr. PITT made a short speech in support of the motion in reply to Sir ROBERT WALPOLE, who opposed it. Sir ROBERT concluded with saying, "that the "time which would be taken up with such a fruitless enquiry "might be more usefully employed." Which brought up r. "PITT, who said,

"It is my opinion, that our time cannot be more usefully employed during a war, than examining how it has been conducted, and settling the degree of confidence that may be reposed in those to whose care are entrusted our reputations, our fortunes, and our lives.

"There is not any enquiry, Sir, of more importance than this; it is not a question about an uncertain privilege, or a law, which if found inconvenient may hereafter be repealed; we are now to examine whether it is probable that we shall preserve our commerce and our independence,

dence, or whether we are sinking into subjection to a foreign power.

"But this enquiry, Sir, will produce no great information, if those whose conduct is examined, are allowed to select the evidence, for what account will they exhibit but such as have often already been laid before us, and such as they now offer without concern. Accounts obscure and fallacious, imperfect and confused; from which nothing can be learned; and which can never entitle the Minister to praise, though they may screen him from punishment."

In the same session, on the 10th of March, 1740, on the Bill brought in by Sir CHARLES WAGER for the encouragement of seamen, and speedier manning the royal navy, Mr. PITT spoke against the Bill.

"It is common for those to have the greatest regard to their own interest who discover the least for that of others. I do not, therefore, despair of recalling the advocates of this Bill from the prosecution of their favourite measures by arguments of greater efficacy than those which are pretended to be founded on reason and justice.

"Nothing is more evident, than that some degree of reputation is absolutely necessary to men, who have any concern in the administration of a government like ours; they must either secure the fidelity of their adherents by the assistance of wisdom, or of virtue; their enemies must either be awed by their honesty, or terrified by their cunning. Mere artless bribery will never gain a sufficient majority to set them entirely free from apprehensions of censure. To different tempers different motives must be applied: some, who place their felicity in being accounted wise, are in very little care to preserve the character of honesty; others may be persuaded to join in measures which they easily discover to be weak and ill-concerted, because they are convinced that the authors of them are not corrupt but mistaken, and are unwilling that any man should be punished for natural defects or casual ignorance.

"I cannot say which of these motives influence the advocates for the Bill before us; a Bill in which such cruelties are proposed as are yet unknown among the most savage nations, such as slavery as not yet nor borne, or tyranny invented, such as cannot be heard without resentment nor thought of without horror.

" It is perhaps not unfortunate, that one more expedient has been added rather ridiculous than shocking, and that these tyrants of administration, who amuse themselves with oppressing their fellow subjects, who add, without reluctance, one hardship to another, invade the liberty of those whom they have already overborne with taxes, first plunder and then imprison, who take all opportunities of heightening the public distresses, and make the miseries of war the instruments of new oppressions, are too ignorant to be formidable, and owe their power not to their abilities, but to casual prosperity, or to the influence of money.

" The other clauses of this Bill, complicated at once with cruelty and folly, have been treated with becoming indignation; but this may be considered with less ardour and resentment, and fewer emotions of zeal, because, though not perhaps equally iniquitous, it will do no harm; for a law that can never be executed can never be felt.

" That it will consume the manufacture of paper, and swell the book of statutes, is all the good or hurt that can be hoped or feared from a law like this; a law which fixes what is in its own nature mutable, which prescribes rules to the seasons and limits to the wind.

" I am too well acquainted, Sir, with the disposition of its two chief supporters, to mention the contempt with which this law will be treated by posterity; for they have already shewn abundantly their disregard of succeeding generations; but I will remind them, that they are now venturing their whole interest at once, and hope they will recollect, before it is too late, that those who believe them to intend the happiness of their country will never be confirmed in their opinion by open cruelty and notorious oppression; and that those who have only their own interest in view, will be afraid of adhering to those leaders, however old and practised in expedients, however strengthened by corruption, or elated with power, who have no reason to hope for success from either their virtue or abilities.

Mr. H. Walpole. This speech produced an answer from Mr. WALPOLE; who, in the course of it, said, " Formidable sounds and furious

furious declamation, confident affertions and lofty periods, may affect the young and unexperienced; and perhaps the Hon. Gentleman may have contracted his habits of oratory, by converfing more with thofe of his own age, than with fuch as have had more opportunities of acquiring knowledge, and more fuccefsful methods of communicating their fentiments:" And made ufe of fome expreffions, fuch as vehemence of gefture, theatrical emotion, &c. applying them to Mr. PITT's manner of fpeaking. As foon as Mr. WALPOLE fat down, Mr. PITT got up and replied.

Reply to Mr. H. Walpole.

" The atrocious crime of being a young man, which the Hon. Gentleman has with fuch fpirit and decency charged upon me, I fhall neither attempt to palliate, nor deny, but content myfelf with wifhing that I may be one of thofe whofe follies may ceafe with their youth, and not of that number who are ignorant in fpite of experience.

" Whether youth can be imputed to any man as a reproach, I will not affume the province of determining; but furely age may become juftly contemptible, if the opportunities which it brings have paft away without improvement, and vice appears to prevail when the paffions have fubfided. The wretch that, after having feen the confequences of a thoufand errors, continues ftill to blunder, and whofe age has only added obftinacy to ftupidity, is furely the object of either abhorrence or contempt, and deferves not that his grey head fhould fecure him from infults.

" Much more is he to be abhorred who as he has advanced in age, has receded from virtue, and becomes more wicked with lefs temptation; who proftitutes himfelf for money which he cannot enjoy, and fpends the remains of his life in the ruin of his country.

" But youth is not my only crime, I have been accufed of acting a theatrical part—a theatrical part may either imply fome peculiarities of gefture, or a diffimulation of my real fentiments, and an adoption of the opinions and language of another man.

" In the firft fenfe the charge is too trifling to be confuted, and deferves only to be mentioned, that it may be defpifed. I am at liberty, like every other man, to use my own language; and though I may, perhaps, have some ambition, yet to please this Gentleman, I shall not lay myself under any restraint nor very solicitously copy his diction, or his mien, however matured by age, or modelled by experience. If any man shall by charging me with theatrical behaviour imply that I utter any sentiments but my own, I shall treat him as a calumniator and a villain, nor shall any protection shelter him from the treatment which he deserves I shall, on such an occasion, without scruple, trample upon all those forms with which wealth and dignity intrench themselves, nor shall any thing but age restrain my resentment; age, which always brings one privilege, that of being insolent and supercilious without punishment.

"But with regard to those whom I have offended, I am of opinion, that if I had acted a borrowed part, I should have avoided their censure; the heat that offended them is the ardour of conviction, and that zeal for the service of my country, which neither hope nor fear shall influence me to suppress. I will not sit unconcerned while my liberty is invaded, nor look in silence upon public robbery. I will exert my endeavours, at whatever hazard, to repel the aggressor, and drag the thief to justice, whoever may protect them in their villainy, and whoever may partake of their plunder. And if the Honourable Gentleman——"

[Here he was called to order by Mr. WINNINGTON, who reprehended him in very illiberal terms, and was proceeding in the same strain when Mr. PITT in turn called Mr. WINNINGTON to order] and said,

"If this be to preserve order, there is no danger of indecency from the most licentious tongue; for what calumny can be more attrocious, or what reproach more severe, than that of speaking with regard to any thing but truth. Order may sometimes be broken by passion, or inadvertency, but will hardly be re-established by monitors like this, who cannot govern his own passion, whilst he is restraining the impetuosity of others.

"Happy would it be for mankind if every one knew his own province; we should not then see the same man at once a criminal and a judge

judge; nor would this Gentleman assume the right of dictating to others what he has not learned himself.

"That I may return in some degree the favour which he intends me, I will advise him never hereafter to exert himself on the subject or order, but whenever he finds himself inclined to speak on such occasions, to remember how he has now succeeded, and condemn in silence what his censures will never perform."

On the 13th of February, 1741, Mr. SANDYS (afterwards Lord SANDYS) moved an Address to the King, requesting his Majesty to remove Sir ROBERT WALPOLE from his presence and councils for ever.

Mr. PITT spoke in support of this motion, *viz.*

"As it has been observed that those who have formerly approved the measures of the Gentleman into whose conduct we are now inquiring, cannot be expected to disavow their former opinions, unless new arguments are produced of greater force, than those which have formerly been offered; so the same steadiness must be expected in those who have opposed them, unless they can now hear them better defended.

"It is an established maxim, Sir, that as time is the test of opinions falshood grows every day weaker, and truth gains upon mankind. This is most eminently just in political assertions, which often respect future events, and the remote consequences of transactions; and therefore never fail to be by time incontestably verified or undeniably combated. On many occasions it is impossible to determine the expediency of measures otherwise than by conjecture; because almost every step that can be taken, may have a tendency to a good as well as to a bad end: and as he who proposes, and he who promotes, may conceal their intentions, till they are ripened into execution, time only can discover the motives of their demands, and the principles of their conduct.

"For this reason it may easily be expected that bad measures will be condemned by men of integrity, when their consequences are fully discovered; though, when they were proposed, they might by plausible declarations and specious appearances, obtain their approbation and applause. Those, whose purity of intention and simplicity of morals exposed

Chap. II.
1741.

exposed them to credulity and implicit confidence, must resent the arts by which they were deluded into a concurrence with projects detrimental to their country; but of which the confequences were artfully concealed from them, or the real intention steadily denied.

"With regard to those Gentlemen, whose neglect of political studies have not qualified them to judge of the questions when they were first debated; and who, giving their suffrages, were not so much directed by their own conviction as by the authority of men, whose experience and knowledge they knew to be great, and whose integrity they had hitherto found no reason to distrust; it may be naturally expected that when they see those measures which were recommended, as necessary to peace and happiness, productive only of confusion, oppression and distress, they should acknowledge their error and forsake their guides; whom they must discover to have been either ignorant or treacherous; and by an open recantation of their former decisions, endeavour to repair the calamities, which they have contributed to bring on their country.

"The extent and complication of political questions is such, that no man can justly be ashamed of having been sometimes mistaken in his determinations, and the propensity of the human mind to confidence and friendship is so great, that every man, however cautious, however sagacious, or however experienced, is exposed sometimes to the artifices of interests and the delusions of hypocrisy; but it is the duty and ought to be the honour of every man to own his mistake whenever he discovers it, and to warn others against those frauds which have been too succefsfully practiced upon himself.

"I am, therefore, inclined to hope that every man will not be equally pre-determined in the present debate, and that as I shall be ready to declare my approbation of integrity and wisdom, though they should be found where I have long suspected ignorance and corruption; as others will with equal justice censure wickedness and error, though they should have been detected in that person, whom they have been long taught to reverence as the oracle of knowledge, and the pattern of virtue.

"In political debates, time always produces new lights; time can in these inquiries never be neutral, but must always acquit or condemn. Time indeed may not alway produce new arguments against bad conduct, because all its consequences might be originally foreseen

and

and expofed; but it muft always coufirm them, and ripen conjectures into certainty. Though it fhould therefore be truly afferted, that nothing is urged in this debate which was not before mentioned and rejected, it will not prove that becaufe the arguments are the fame, they ought to produce the fame effect; becaufe what was then only foretold, has now been feen and felt, and what was then but believed is now known.

" But if Time has produced no vindication of thofe meafures, which were fufpected of imprudence or of treachery; it muft be at length acknowledged that thofe fufpicions were juft, and that what ought then to have been rejected ought now to be punifhed.

" This is for the moft part the ftate of the Queftion. Thofe meafures which were once defended by fophiftical reafoning, or palliated by warm declamations of fincerity and difinterefted zeal for the public happinefs, are found to be fuch as they were reprefented by thofe who oppofed them. It is now difcovered that the Treaty of Hanover was calculated only for the advancement of the Houfe of Bourbon; that our armies are kept up only to multiply dependence, and to awe the nation from the exertion of its rights; that Spain has been courted only to the ruin of our trade; and that the Convention was little more than an artifice to amufe the people with an idle appearance of a reconciliation, which our enemies never intended.

" Of the ftipulation which produced the memorable Treaty of Hanover, the improbability was often urged, but the abfolute falfhood could be proved only by the declaration of one of the parties. This declaration was at length produced by Time, which was never favovrable to the meafures of our Minifter. For the Emperor of Germany afferted, with the utmoft folemnity, that no fuch article was ever propofed; and that his engagements with Spain had no tendency to produce any change in the government of this kingdom.

" Thus it is evident, Sir, that all the terrors which the apprehenfion of this Alliance produced, was merely the operations of fraud upon cowardice; and that they were only raifed by the artful French, to difunite us from the only power with which it is our intereft to cultivate an infeparable friendfhip. This difunion may therefore be juftly charged upon the Minifter, who has weakened the intereft of this country, and endangered the liberties of Europe.

"If it be asked, Sir, how he could have discovered the falshood of the report, before it was confuted by the late Emperor? It may easily be answered, that he might have discovered it by the same tokens which betrayed it to his opponents, the impossibility of putting it into execution. For it must be confessed, that his French informers, well acquainted with his disposition to panic fears, had used no caution in the construction of their imposture, nor seem to have had any other view, than to add one error to another, to sink his reason with alarms, and to overbear him with astonishment.

"When they found he began to be disordered at the danger of our trade from enemies without naval forces, they easily discovered, that to make him the slave of France nothing more was necessary, than to add, that these bloody confederates had projected an invasion; that they intended to add slavery to poverty; and to place the Pretender upon the Throne.

"To be alarmed into vigilance had not been unworthy of the firmest and most sagacious Minister; but to be frighted by such reports into measures which even an invasion could scarcely have justified, was at least a proof of a capacity not formed by nature for the administration of government; and which it is therefore the interest of the motion to reduce to its proper sphere, and to mingle with the rest of the community.

"If it be required, what advantage was granted by this Treaty to the French, and to what inconveniencies it has subjected this nation? an answer may very justly be refused, till the Minister or his apologists shall explain his conduct in the last war with Spain; and inform us why the plate fleet was spared, our ships sacrificed to the worms, and our Admiral and his sailors poisoned in an unhealthy climate? Why the Spaniards in full security laugh'd at our armaments, and triumphed in our calamities.

"The lives of Hozier and his forces are now justly to be demanded from this man; he is now to be charged with the murder of those two unhappy men, whom he exposed to misery and contagion, to pacify, on one hand, the Britons who called out for war, and to gratify, on the other, the French, who insisted that the Spanish treasures should not be seized.

"The Minister who neglects any just opportunity of promoting the power, or increasing the wealth of his country, is to be considered as
an

an enemy to his fellow subjects; but what censure is to be passed upon him who betrays that army to a defeat, by which victory might be obtained; impoverishes the nation, whose affairs he is entrusted to transact, by those expeditions which might enrich it; who levies armies only to be exposed to pestilence, and compels them to perish in sight of their enemies, without molesting them? It cannot surely be denied, that such conduct may justly produce a censure more severe than that which is intended by this motion; and that he who has doomed thousands to the grave; who has co-operated with foreign powers against his country; who has protected its enemies, and dishonoured its arms, should be deprived not only of his honours, but his life; that he should at least be stripped of those riches which he has amassed during a long series of successful wickedness; and not barely be hindered from making new acquisitions, and increasing his wealth by multiplying his crimes.

"But no such penalties, Sir, are now required; those who have long stood up in opposition to him, give a proof by the motion, that they were not incited by personal malice; since they are not provoked to propose any arbitrary censure, nor have recommended what might be authorized by his own practice, an Act of Attainder, or a Bill of Pains and Penalties. They desire nothing further, than that the security of the nation may be restored, and the discontent of the people pacified, by his removal from that trust which he has so long abused.

"The discontent of the people is in itself a reason for agreeing to this motion, which no rhetorical vindicator of his conduct will be able to counterbalance; for since it is necessary to the prosperity of the government, that the people should believe their interest favoured, and their liberties protected; since to imagine themselves neglected, and to be neglected in reality, must produce in them the same suspicions, and the same distrust, it is the duty of every faithful subject whom his station qualifies, to offer advice to his Sovereign, to persuade him, for the preservation of his own honour and the affection of his subjects, to remove from his councils that man, whom they have long considered as the author of pernicious measures, and a favourer of arbitrary power.

Upon a division, the motion was negatived by 290 against 106.

CHAP.

CHAP. III.

A New Parliament—Mr. Pitt re-elected—The Minister loses several Questions—Resigns, and is created Earl of Orford—Parliament adjourns—Secret Negotiation with Mr. Pulteney—That affair truely stated—Lord Cobham and his Friends excluded—The new Arrangement settled by the Earl of Orford—Stanza of Sir Charles Hanbury Williams explained; and the condition upon which Sir Robert Walpole became Minister—Duke of Argyll's expression to Mr. Pulteney—The Nation dissatisfied.

THE Minister having become exceedingly unpopular, and the leaders of several parties having united against him, he had not character and interest sufficient to secure a majority in the new Parliament, which was elected in the spring of 1741.

In this Parliament, which met on the 4th of December 1741, Mr. PITT was re-elected for Old Sarum. The first question which the Minister lost, was that of Chairman of the Committee of Privileges and Elections; Dr. LEE being chosen by a majority of four, against Mr. EARLE, who had been supported by himself. After losing some questions upon the decisions of the contested elections, he saw that there was a confirmed majority against him; and therefore, on the 3d of February 1742, he resigned his employments, and was created EARL of ORFORD. At the same time the Parliament, by the King's Command, adjourned to the 18th of the same month.

Although the Minister was personally departed, his influence was not extinguished: he still possessed power sufficient to enable him to capitulate with his opponents for his safety.

With his usual penetration, he prudently selected from amongst his opponents those who were the most eager for power, to commence his negotiation with. His view in making this selection was judicious. Those chiefs, or heads of opposition, to whom he made no communication of his designs, the moment they heard of the negotiation, became jealous of their friends; and a schism amongst them was thereby created; which was the thing Sir ROBERT WALPOLE most wished; because in their united state, they had power to crush him, but when divided, he knew they could not hurt him.

The negotiation began by the DUKE of NEWCASTLE requesting to see Mr. PULTENEY *privately* at Mr. STONE's (his Grace's secretary) at Whitehall. Mr. PULTENEY replied, That he would rather see the Duke at his own house in Piccadilly; and desired his Grace to fix the time; and added, that Lord CARTERET must be present at the conference. The same evening was agreed upon: and the DUKE of NEWCASTLE, with Lord HARDWICKE, went to Mr. PULTENEY's, where they found him with only Lord CARTERET. They said, they came from the King with proposals; that it was His Majesty's desire, Mr. PULTENEY should be placed at the head of the Treasury. Mr. PULTENEY excused himself, and proposed Lord CARTERET for that situation. The conference ended, however, without any thing being settled. But information of the meeting was in a few hours spread all over the town. A thousand conjectures were formed.

It was this *private* meeting, and *another* which happened two days afterwards, of the same persons, at the same place, which *caused* the *division* in the opposition. Between Lord CARTERET and Lord COBHAM there was no intimacy; but the contrary. The selection of Lord CARTERET for these *private* conferences, which were to lay the foundation of, and to fix the boundaries of, the new arrangement, was therefore a sort of *marked exclusion* of Lord COBHAM, whose Parliamentary friends

friends (Mr. PITT, Mr. LYTTELTON, the three GRENVILLES, [*Richard, George and James*] Mr. WALLER, and several others) deserved consideration; whose personal character was high, and whose reputation had been assailed, in being turned out of the army. Lord COBHAM was not of a temper to see these transactions with indifference. His friends felt their share of the contempt which was shewn to him; they gave him the most cordial assurances of attachment; and they immediately formed a separate party. They were in a short time joined by the DUKE of ARGYLL, who, though he had taken the Ordnance in the first moments of the change, he quickly resigned it; and returned to his old friends; who were, in a few weeks, joined by all those who saw that the change of the Ministry was only to be partial, inadequate and imperfect; that the nation, as well as themselves, had been deceived.

Sir ROBERT WALPOLE, now EARL of ORFORD, did not approve of the nomination of Lord CARTERET for his successor at the Treasury; and as Mr. PULTENEY had declined that post, he managed the KING to insist upon Lord WILMINGTON for it. Lord WILMINGTON had been Sir ROBERT's President of the Council from 1732 *. It was some triumph to the opponents,

---

* To this appointment Sir CHARLES HANBURY WILLIAMS alludes in a beautiful stanza. Lord WLMINGTON had, upon the *Accession* of GEORGE the SECOND, been offered the Treasury; *if* he would undertake to *encrease* the Civil List from 700,000l. to 800,000l. but he was timid, and declined the offer; upon which the offer was next made to Sir ROBERT WALPOLE, who accepted it; and became Minister from that circumstance alone.

> Why did you cross God's good intent?
> He made you for a President:
>   Back to that station go;
> Nor longer act this farce of pow'r,
> We know you miss'd the thing before,
>   And have not got it now.

to see him so soon baffled in his arrangement. The DUKE of ARGYLL observed to him on the occasion at a large meeting of their friends at the *Fountain Tavern* in the Strand *, " That a Grain of Honesty was worth a Cart-load of Gold."

The EARL of HARRINGTON, who had been Sir ROBERT's Secretary of State, was made President of the Council. Lord CARTERET accepted of Lord HARRINGTON's Seals; and Mr. SANDYS was made Chancellor of the Exchequer, with a new Board of Treasury. A new Board of Admiralty, with the EARL of WINCHELSEA at the head, were all the alterations of any consequence that were made.

The disappointment of the nation at this trifling change of a few men, was greater than can be described. Many of the most respectable parts of the community were provoked and exasperated to the use of the bitterest language, which could express their execration and abhorrence of the junction that was thus formed between Mr. PULTENEY and the friends of the late Minister.

offer; upon which it was next made to Sir ROBERT WALPOLE, who accepted it; and from that circumstance alone became Minister.

> Why did you cross God's good intent?
> He made you for a President:
> Back to that station go;
> Nor longer act this farce of pow'r,
> We know you miss'd the thing before,
> And have not got it now.

* This meeting was held on the 12th of February, 1742. There were near 300 Members of both Houses of Parliament present. Amongst them were the following:—Dukes of *Bedford* and *Argyll*—Marquis of *Caernarvon*—Earls of *Exeter*, *Berkshire*, *Chesterfield*, *Carlisle*, *Aylesbury*, *Shaftsbury*, *Litchfield*, *Oxford*, *Rockingham*, *Halifax*, *Stanhope*, *Macclesfield*, *Darnly*, *Barrimore*, *Granard*—Viscounts *Cobham*, *Falmouth*, *Limerick*, *Gage*, *Cherwynd*—Lords *Ward*, *Gower*, *Bathurst*, *Talbot*, *Strange*, *Andover*, *Guernsey*, *Quarendon*, *Percival*—Sir *Edward Seymour*, Sir *Charles Mordaunt*, Sir *Erasmus Philips*, Sir *Robert Grosvenor*, Sir *Edward Dering*, Sir *Roger Burgoyne*, Sir *John Hind Cotton*, Sir *Henry Northcote*, Sir *William Carew*, Sir *Miles Stapylton*, Sir *Hugh Smithson*, Sir *William Morris*, Sir *John Rushout*, Sir *Michael Newton*, Sir *Roger Twisden*, Sir *Robert Long*, Sir *Charles Wyndham*, Sir *Jermyn Davers*, Sir *James Dashwood*, Sir *Watkyn Williams Wynne*, Sir *Cordel Firebrace*, Sir *Edward Thomas*, Sir *Francis Dashwood*, Sir *Jacob Bouverie*, Sir *John Chapman*, Sir *Abraham Elton*, Sir *John Peachy*, Sir *William Courtney*, Sir *James Hamilton*—Mr. *Pulteney*, Mr. *Sandys*, Mr. *Gybbon*, Mr. *Doddington*, Mr. *Waller*, Mr. *Shippen*, Mr. *Fazakerley*, Mr. *Mellish*, Mr. Alderman *Heathcote*, Mr. *Bance*, &c.

The purpose of the meeting was to consider of what was expedient to be done in the present critical conjuncture. But it was too late; the arrangements were settled before the meeting was called.

It is to *this* Meeting that Sir Charles Hanbury Williams alludes, in one of his Odes to Mr. Pulteney; where, invoking the Muse to display his Hero's merit, he says:

> Then enlarge on his Cunning and Wit;   Say, how the Old Patriots were bit,
> Say, how he harangued at the Fountain;   And a Mouse was produc'd by a Mountain.

CHAP. IV.

CHAP. IV.
1742.
The new Ministry charged with having bargained for the safety of the Earl of Orford—Motion for an Enquiry into the Earl of Orford's Conduct—Mr. Pitt's Speech in support of that Motion—Motion lost—Second Motion, limiting the Enquiry to the last ten Years—Mr. Pitt's Speech in support of this Motion.—The Enquiry defeated by a Parliamentary Manœuvre.

AN important charge was brought against the new Ministry by their opponents, who affirmed, in most direct and positive terms, that Mr. PULTENEY had first, and that his friends had afterwards, *bargained* with the Court, for the safety of the EARL of ORFO D; that it was expresly on that *condition* they were admitted into office; and upon that tenure *only*, that they held their employments; that such bargain was a sale of the public confidence, and a total dereliction of principle; that there was a treason against the people as well as against the Crown, and that this was the superlative degree of that treason. And in order to put these assertions to the test, *Motion for an Enquiry into Sir R. Walpole's Conduct.* a motion was made in the House of Commons, on the 9th of March 1742, by Lord LIMERICK (whose son was created EARL of CLANBRASSIL) for an Enquiry into the conduct of the late Administration, during the last *twenty* years. In support of this motion, Mr. PITT spoke in reply to Mr. PELHAM, who had opposed it, and said, " that it would considerably shorten " the debate, if Gentlemen would keep close to the argument, " and not run out into long harangues and flowers of rhetorick, " which might be introduced upon any other subject, as well " as the present;" to which Mr. PITT replied:

" What the Gentlemen of the other side mean by long harangues, or flowers of rhetorick, I shall not pretend to guess; but if they make

use

use of nothing of that kind, it is no very good argument of their sincerity; for a man who speaks from his heart, and is sincerely affected with the subject he speaks on, as every honest man must be when he speaks in the cause of his country; such a man, I say, falls naturally into expressions which may be called flowers of rhetorick, and therefore deserves as little to be charged with affectation as the most stupid serjeant at law that ever spoke for half a guinea a fee. For my part, I have heard nothing in favour of the question, but what I thought very proper, and very much to the purpose. What has been said, indeed, on the other side of the question, especially the long justification that has been made of our late measures, I cannot think so proper upon this occasion, because this motion is founded upon the present melancholy situation of affairs, and upon the general clamour without doors against the late conduct of our public servants; and either of these with me, shall always be a sufficient reason for agreeing to a parliamentary enquiry; for without such an enquiry I cannot, even in my own mind, enter into the disquisition, whether our public measures have been right or not, because I cannot otherwise be furnished with the necessary lights for that purpose.

" But the Hon. Gentlemen who oppose this motion seem to mistake, I shall not say wilfully, the difference between a motion for an impeachment, and a motion for an enquiry. If any Member of this House were to stand up in his place, and move for impeaching a Minister, he would be obliged to charge him with some particular crimes or misdemeanors, and produce some proof, or to declare that he was ready to prove the facts: but any Gentleman may move for an enquiry, without any particular allegation, and without offering any proof, or declaring that he is ready to prove, because the very design of an enquiry is to find out particular facts and particular proofs. The general circumstances of things, or general rumours without doors, are a sufficient foundation for such a motion, and for the House agreeing to it when it is made. This, Sir, has always been the practice, and has been the foundation of almost all the enquiries that were ever set on foot in this House, especially those that have been carried on by Secret and Select Committees. What other foundation was there for the Secret Committee appointed in the year 1694 (to go no further back) to enquire into and inspect the books and accounts of the East India Company and Chamber of London?

don?—Nothing but a general rumour that some corrupt practice had been made use of. What was the foundation of the enquiry in the year 1714? Did the Hon. Gentleman who moved for appointing that Secret Committee charge the former Administration with any particular crimes? Did he offer any proofs, or declare that he was ready to prove any thing? It is said, the measures pursued by that Administration were condemned by a great majority of that House of Commons. What, Sir, were those Ministers condemned before they were heard? Could any Gentleman be so unjust as to pass sentence, even in his own mind, upon a measure, before he had enquired into it. He might perhaps dislike the Treaty of Utrecht, but upon enquiry it might appear to be the best that could be obtained; and it has since been so far justified, that it is as least as good, if not better than any treaty we have made since that time.

"Sir, It was not the Treaty of Utrecht, nor any measure that Administration openly pursued that was the foundation or the cause of an enquiry into their conduct. It was the loud complaints of a great party against them, and the general suspicion of their having carried on treasonable negotiations in favour of the Pretender, and for defeating the protestant succession; and the enquiry was set on foot, in order to detect those practices, if there were any such, and to find proper evidence for convicting the offenders. The same argument holds with regard to the enquiry into the management of the South Sea Company in the year 1721. When that affair was first moved in the House by Mr. NEVILLE, he did not, he could not charge those Directors, or any of them, with any particular proofs. His motion, which was, That the Directors of the South Sea Company should forthwith lay before the House an Account of their Proceedings, was founded upon the general circumstances of things, the distress brought upon the public credit of the nation, and the general and loud complaints without doors. This motion, indeed, reasonable as it was, we know was opposed by our courtiers at that time, and in particular by two doughty brothers, who have been courtiers ever since; but their opposition raised such a warmth in the House, that they were glad to give it up, and never afterwards durst directly oppose that enquiry. I wish I could now see the same zeal for public justice. I am sure, the circumstances of affairs deserve it. Our public credit was then indeed brought into distress; but now the nation

itself,

itself, nay not only this nation, but all our friends upon the Continent are brought into the most imminent danger.

"This, Sir, is admitted even by those who oppose this motion; and if they have ever lately conversed with those that dare speak their minds, they must admit, that the murmurs of the people against the conduct of the Administration are now as general and as loud as ever they were upon any occasion; but the misfortune is, that Gentlemen who are in office seldom converse with any but such as are in office, or want to be in office; and such men, let them think what they will, will always applaud their superiors; consequently, Gentlemen who are in Administration, or in any office under it, can rarely know the voice of the people. The voice of this House was formerly, I shall grant, and always ought to be, the voice of the people. If new Parliaments were more frequent, and few placemen, and no pensioners admitted, it would be so still; but if long Parliaments be continued, and a corrupt influence should prevail, not only at elections but in this House, the voice of this House will generally be very different from, nay often directly contrary to, the voice of the people. However, as this is not, I believe, the case at present, I hope that there is a majority of us who know what is the voice of the people; and if it be admitted by all, that the nation is at present in the utmost distress and danger, and admitted by a majority, that the voice of the people is loud against the late conduct of our Administration, this motion must be agreed to, because I have shewn, that these two circumstances, without any particular charge, have been the foundation of almost all Parliamentary Enquiries.

"I shall readily admit, Sir, that we should have very little to do with the character or reputation of a Minister, but as it does and always must affect our Sovereign; as the people may become disaffected as well as discontented, when they find the King continues obstinately to employ a Minister, who they think oppresses them at home, and betrays them abroad. We are therefore, in duty to our Sovereign, obliged to enquire into the conduct of a Minister, when it becomes generally suspected by the people, in order that we may vindicate his character, if he appears innocent as to every thing laid to his charge, or that we may get him removed from the councils of our Sovereign, and condignly punished, if he appears guilty.

"After

Chap. IV.
1742.

"After having said thus much, Sir, I have no great occasion to answer what has been said, that no Parliamentary Enquiry ought ever to be set up, unless we are convinced that something has been done amiss. Sir, the very name given to this House of Parliament shews the contrary. We are called, The Grand Inquest of the Nation; and as such, it is our duty to enquire into every step of public management, either abroad or at home, in order to see that nothing has been done amiss. It is not necessary upon every occasion to establish a Secret Committee. This is never necessary, but when the affairs to be brought before them, or some of those affairs, are supposed to be of such a nature as ought to be kept a secret; but as experience has shewn, that nothing but a special enquiry is ever made by a General Committee, or a Committee of the whole House, I wish that all Estimates and Accounts, and many other affairs, were respectively referred to Select Committees. Their enquiries would be more exact, and the receiving of their Reports would not take up so much of our time as Is represented; but if it did, as it is our duty to make strict enquiries into every thing relating to the Public; as we assemble here for that purpose, we ought to do our duty before we break up; and I am sure, His present Majesty would never put an end to any session, till both Houses had fully performed their duty to their country.

"It is said by some Gentlemen, that by this enquiry we shall be in danger of discovering the secrets of our government to our enemies. This argument, Sir, by proving too much, proves nothing at all. If it were admitted, it would always have been, and for ever will be, an argument against our enquiring into any affair, in which our Government can be supposed to have a concern. Our enquiries would then be confined to the conduct of our little Companies, or of inferior Custom-House Officers, or Excisemen; for if we should be so bold as to offer to enquire into the conduct of Commissioners of great Companies, it would be said, the Government had a concern in their conduct, and the secrets of Government must not be divulged. Every Gentleman must see that this would be the consequence of admitting such an argument; but besides, it is false in fact, and contrary to experience. We have had many Parliamentary Enquiries into the conduct of Ministers of State, and yet I defy any one to shew, that any State Affair was thereby discovered, which ought to have been concealed, or that our public affairs,

affairs, either abroad or at home, ever suffered by such a discovery. There are methods, Sir, for preventing papers of a very secret nature from coming into the hands of the servants attending, or even of all the Members of our Secret Committee. If His Majesty should, by message, acquaint us, that some of the papers sealed up and laid before us required the utmost secrecy, we might refer them to our Committee, with an instruction for them, to order only two or three of the number to inspect such papers, and to report from them nothing but what they thought might be safely communicated to their whole number. By this method I hope, the danger of a discovery would be effectually removed; therefore this danger cannot be a good argument against a Parliamentary Enquiry.

" The other objection, Sir, is really surprizing, because it is founded upon a circumstance, which in all former times has been admitted as a strong argument for an immediate enquiry. The Hon. Gentlemen are so ingenuous, as to confess that our affairs, both abroad and at home, are at present in the utmost distress; but say they, you ought to free yourselves from this distress, before you enquire how or by what means you was brought into it. Sir, according to this way of arguing, a Minister that has plundered and betrayed his country, and fears being called to an account in Parliament, has nothing to do but to involve his country in a dangerous war, or some other great distress, in order to prevent an enquiry into his conduct; because he may be dead before that war is at an end, or that distress got over. Thus, like the most villainous of all thieves, after he had plundered the House he had nothing to do but to set it in a flame, that he may escape in the confusion. It is really astonishing to hear such an argument seriously urged in this House; but, say these Gentlemen, if you found yourself upon a precipice, would you stand to enquire how you was led there, before you considered how to get off? No, Sir, but if a guide had led me there, I should very probably be provoked to throw him over, before I thought of any thing else; at least I am sure, I should not trust to the same guide for bringing me off; and this, Sir, is the strongest argument that can be used for an enquiry.

" We have been for these twenty years under the guidance, I may truly say, of one man, of one single Minister. We now at last find ourselves upon a dangerous precipice. Ought not we then immediately to

enquire,

CHAP. IV.
1742

enquire, whether we have been led upon this precipice by his ignorance or wickedness; and if by either, to take care not to trust to his guidance for bringing us off? This is an additional, and a stronger argument for this enquiry than ever was for any former; for if we do not enquire, we shall probably remain under his guidance; because, though he be removed from the Treasury Board, he is not from the King's Courts, nor probably will, unless it be by our advice, or by sending him to a lodging at the other end of the town, where he cannot do so much harm to his country. Sir, the distress we are in at home, is evidently owing to bad œconomy, and to our having been led into many needles expences. The distress and danger we are in abroad are evidently owing to the misconduct of our war with Spain, and to the little confidence put in our councils by our natural and antient allies. This is evident, that I should not have thought it necessary to have entered into any particular explanation, if an Hon. Gentleman on the other side had not entered into a particular justification of most of our late measures, both abroad and at home; but as he has done so, though not, in my opinion, quite to the purpose of the present debate; yet, I hope I shall be excused making some remarks upon what he has said on that subject, beginning, as he did, with the measures taken for punishing the South Sea Directors, and restoring public credit, after the terrible shock it met with in the year 1720.

" As those measures, Sir, were among the first exploits of our late, and I fear still, our present Prime Minister, at least his first since he came last into Administration; and as the Committee proposed, if agreed to, will probably consist of one and twenty, I wish the Motion had been for one year further back, that the number of years might have been equal to the number of enquirers, and that it might have comprehended the first of those measures; for as it stands, it will not comprehend the methods taken for punishing the Directors, nor the first regulation made for restoring public credit; and with regard to both, some practices might be discovered, that would deserve a much severer punishment than any of those Directors met with. Considering the many tricks and frauds made use of by the Directors and their agents for drawing people into their ruin, I am not a little surprized to hear it now said, that their punishment was ever thought too severe. Justice by the Lump was an epithet given it, not because it was thought too severe, but because

cause it was a piece of cunning made use of to screen the most heinous offenders, who, if they did not deserve to be hanged, deserved at least to have that total ruin brought upon them, which they had brought upon many unthinking men; and therefore they very ill deserved those allowances which were made them by Parliament.

Then, Sir, as to the restoring of public credit, its speedy restoration was founded upon the conduct of the nation, and not upon the wisdom or justice of the measures taken to restore it. Was it a wise method to remit to the South Sea Company the whole seven millions, or thereabouts, which they had solemnly engaged to pay to the public? It might as well be said, that a private man's giving away a great part of his estate to those who no way deserved it, would be a wise method of reviving or establishing his credit; If these seven millions had been distributed among the poorer sort of annuitants, it would have been both generous and charitable; but to give it among the proprietors in general was neither generous nor just, because most of them deserved no favour from the public; for as the proceedings of the Directors were authorized by general courts, those who were then the proprietors were in some measure accessary to the frauds of the Directors, and therefore deserved to have been punished, rather than rewarded, as they really were, because every one of them who continued to hold stock in that company got near 50 per cent. added to his capital, most part of which arose from the high price annuitants were by Act of Parliament obliged to take stock at, and was therefore a most flagrant piece of injustice done to the annuitants. But we need not be at a loss for the true cause of this act of injustice, when we consider that a certain gentleman had a great many friends among the old stockholders, and few or none among the annuitants.

Another act of injustice which, I believe, we may ascribe to the same cause, relates to those who were engaged in heavy contracts for stock or subscriptions, many of whom groan under the load to this very day; for after we had by Act of Parliament quite altered the nature, though not the name of the stock they had bought, and made it much less valuable than it was when they engaged to pay a high price for it, I must think it an act of public injustice to leave them liable to be prosecuted at law for the whole money they had engaged to pay; and I am sure it was not a method of restoring private credit, upon which our trade and navigation

navigation very much depend. If the same regulation had been made with regard to them, as had been made with regard to those who had borrowed money of the Company, or a sort of *uti possidetis* enacted, by declaring all such contracts void, so far as related to any future payments, it would not have been unjust, and was extremely necessary for quieting the minds of the people, for preventing their ruining one another at law, and of restoring credit between man and man, which is so necessary in a trading country; but there is reason to suppose, that a certain gentleman had many friends among the sellers in those contracts, and very few among the buyers, which was the reason why the latter could obtain little or no relief or mercy, by any public law or regulation.

" Then, Sir, with regard to the extraordinary grants made to the civil list, the very reason given by the Hon. Gentleman, for justifying those grants, is a strong reason for an immediate enquiry. If there have arisen any considerable charges upon that revenue, let us see what those charges are; let us examine whether or no they were necessary. We have the more reason to do this, because the Revenue settled upon his late Majesty's Civil List was at least as great as was settled either upon King William or Queen Anne, and yet neither of them asked any extraordinary grant, but on the contrary, the latter gave out of her civil list revenue 100,000l. yearly towards the support of the war; and yet there was as great hospitality in the Royal Palace during her time as ever has been since. Besides, there is a general rumour without doors, that the civil list is now greatly in arrear, which, if true, renders an enquiry absolutely necessary; for it is inconsistent with the honour and dignity of the crown of these kingdoms, to be in arrear to its tradesmen and servants; and it is the duty of this House, to take care that the revenue which we have settled for supporting the honour and dignity of our Crown, shall not be squandered or misapplied. If former Parliaments have failed in this respect, they must be blamed, though they cannot be punished; but we ought now to attone for their neglect, and we may punish those, if they can be discovered, who were the cause of it.

" I come now in course to the Excise Scheme, which the Hon. Gentleman says ought to be forgiven, because it was easily given up. Sir, it was not easily given up. The promoter of that scheme did not easily give it up; he gave it up with sorrow, with tears in his eyes, when he saw, and not till he saw it impossible to carry it through the House. Did not

not his majority decreafe every divifion? It was almoft certain, that if he had pufhed it any further, the majority would have turned againſt him. His forrow fhewed his difappointment; and his difappointment fhewed, that his defign was higher than that of preventing frauds in the Cuſtoms. He was at that time as fenfible of the influence of excife laws and excifemen, with regard to elections, and of the great occafion he would have for that fort of influence at the next general election, which was then approaching, that it is impoffible to fuppofe he had not that influence in view; and if he had, it was a moft wicked attempt againſt our conftitution; therefore he deferved the treatment he met with from the people. Perhaps there were none but what Gentlemen are pleafed to call Mob concerned in burning him in effigy; but as the mob confifts chiefly in children, journeymen and fervants, who fpeak the fentiments of their parents and mafters, we may thence judge of the fentiments of the better fort of people.

" The Hon. Gentleman faid, thefe were all the meafures of a domeſtic nature that could be found fault with, becaufe none other were mentioned in this debate. Sir, he has already heard a reafon why no other wrong meafures fhould be particularly mentioned in this debate. If it were neceffary, many others might be mentioned. Is not the keeping up fo numerous an army in time of peace, to be found fault with? Is not the fitting out fo many expenfive fquadrons for no purpofe, to be found fault with? Are not the encroachments made upon the finking fund, the reviving the falt duty, the rejecting many ufeful bills and motions in Parliament, and many other domeftic meafures, to be found fault with? The weaknefs or wickednefs of thefe meafures has been often demonftrated. Their ill confequences were at the refpective times foretold, and thofe confequences are now become vifible by our diftrefs.

" Now, Sir with regard to the foreign meafures which the Hon. Gentleman has attempted to juftify. The Treaty of Hanover deferves indeed to be firft mentioned, becaufe from thence fprings the danger which Europe is now expofed to; and it is impoffible to affign a reafon for our entering into that treaty, without fuppofing that we then refolved to be revenged on the Emperor for refufing to grant us fome favour in Germany. It is in vain now to infift upon the fecret engagements entered into by the Courts of Vienna and Madrid, as the caufe of that treaty. Time has fully fhewn, that there never were any fuch engage ments; and his late Majesty's speech from the Throne cannot here be admitted as any evidence of the fact. Every one knows, that in Parliament the King's Speech is always confidered as the Speech of the Minifter; and furely a Minifter is not to be allowed to bring his own fpeech as an evidence of a fact in his own juftification. If it be pretended, that his late Majefty had fome fort of information, that fuch engagements had been entered into; that very pretence furnifhes an unanfwerable argument for an enquiry; for as the information now appears to have been groundlefs, we ought to enquire into it; becaufe, if it appears to be fuch information as ought not to have been believed, that Minifter ought to be punifhed who advifed his late Majefty to give credit to it, and who has precipitated the nation into the moft pernicious meafures, in confequence of it.

" At the time this treaty was entered into, we wanted nothing from the Emperor upon our own account. The abolition of the Oftend Company was a demand we had no right to make, nor was it effentially our intereft to infift upon it, becaufe that Company would have been more prejudicial to the interefts of both the French and Dutch Eaft India trades than to ours; and if it had been a point that concerned us much, we might probably have gained it, by acceding to the Vienna Treaty between the Emperor and Spain, or by guaranting the pragmatic fanction, which we afterwards did in the moft abfolute manner, without any confideration at all. We wanted nothing from Spain but a departure from the pretence fhe had juft begun, or I believe hardly begun, to fet up, in an exprefs manner, with regard to fearching and feizing our fhips in the American Seas; and this we did not obtain, or perhaps did not defire to obtain, by the Treaty of Seville. By that treaty we obtained nothing; but we made another ftep towards bringing in that danger which Europe is now involved in, by uniting the Courts of France and Spain, and laying a foundation for a new breach between the Courts of Spain and Vienna.

" I fhall grant, Sir, our minifters appear to have been fond and diligent enough in negociating, and writing letters and memorials to the Court of Spain; but by all I have looked into, it appears they never rightly underftood, or perhaps would not underftand, the point they were negotiating about; and, as they fuffered themfelves to be amufed, as they fay, with fair promifes, for ten years together, whilft in the mean time

time our merchants were plundered, and our trade interrupted, we ought to enquire into this affair; for if it should appear they allowed themselves to be amused with such answers, as no man of honour in such circumstances would have taken, nor any man of common sense been amused with, they must have had some secret motive for allowing themselves to be thus imposed upon; this secret motive we may perhaps discover by an enquiry; and as it must be a wicked one, if it can be discovered, they ought to be severely punished.

" But, in excuse for their conduct, it is said our ministers had a laudable shyness of involving their country in a war. Sir, This shyness could not proceed from any regard to their country. It was involved in a war: Spain was carrying on a war against our trade, and that in the most insulting manner too, during the whole time of their negotiations. It was this very shyness, or at least making the Court of Spain too sensible of it, that at last made it absolutely necessary for us to begin a war on our side. If they had at first insisted properly and peremptorily upon an explicit answer, Spain would have expressly given up the pretence she had just set up; but by the long experience we allowed her she found the fruits of that pretence so plentiful and savory, that she thought them worth risking a war for; and the damage we had sustained became so considerable, that it was worth contending for. Besides, the Court of Spain was convinced that whilst we were under such an Administration, nothing could provoke us to begin the war on our side; or if we did it, would be managed weakly and pusillanimously; and have we not since found, that they formed a right judgment? Nothing, Sir, ever demanded more a Parliamentary enquiry than our conduct in the war. The only branch of it we have enquired into, we have already censured and condemned. Is not this a good reason for enquiring into every other branch? disappointment and ill success have always, till now, occasioned a Parliamentary Enquiry. Inactivity of itself is a sufficient cause for an enquiry. We have now all these reasons concurring. Our admirals abroad desire nothing more; because they are conscious, that our inactivity and ill success would appear not to be owing to their conduct, but to the conduct of those that sent them out.

" I cannot conclude, Sir, without taking notice of the two other foreign measures mentioned by the Hon. Gentleman. Our conduct in the year 1734, with regard to the war between the Emperor and France, may

Chap. IV.
1742.

may be easily accounted for, though not easily excused. Ever sincethe last accession of our late minister to power, we seem to have had an enmity to the House of Austria. Our guaranty of the pragmatic sanction was an effect of that enmity, because we entered into it, when, as has since appeared, we had no mind to perform our engagement; and by that false guaranty induced the Emperor to admit the introduction of the Spanish troops into Italy, which he would not otherwise have done. The preparations we made in that year, the armies we raised, and the fleet we fitted out, were not to guard against the event of the war abroad, but against the event of the ensuing election at home. The new commissions, the promotions, and the money laid out in these preparations, were of excellent use at the time of a general election, and in some measure attone for the loss of the Excise Scheme; but France and her allies were well convinced, that we would in no event declare against them, otherwise they would not have dared to attack the Emperor at that time; for Muscovy, Poland, Germany and Britain would have been by much an over-match for them. It was not our preparations that set bounds to the ambition of France, but her getting all she wanted at that time for herself, and all she desired for her allies. Her own prudence directed her, that it was not then a proper time to push her views further; because she did not know, but that the spirit of this nation might get the better, as it has since done with regard to Spain, of the spirit of our Administration; and if this should have happened, the House of Austria was then in such a condition, that our assistance, even though late, would have been of effectual service.

" I am surprized, Sir, to hear the Hon. Gentleman now say, that. we gave up nothing, or got any thing by an infamous convention with Spain. Did we not give up the freedom of our trade and navigation, by submitting it to be regulated by plenipotentiaries? Can freedom be regulated, without being confined, and consequently in some part destroyed? Did not we give up Georgia, or some part of it, by submitting to have new limits settled by plenipotentiaries? Did we not give up all the reparation of honour we had so just a title to insist on? Did we not give up all reparation of the damage we had suffered, amounting to five or six hundred thousand pounds, for the paltry sum of twenty-seven thousand pounds. For this was all that Spain promised to pay, after deducting the sixty-eight thousand pounds, which we, by the declaration

annexed

annexed to that treaty, allowed her to infist on having from our South Sea Company, under the penalty of stripping them of the Assiento Contract, and all the privileges they were thereby entitled to. Even this sum of twenty-seven thousand pounds, or more, they had before acknowledged to be due, on account of ships they allowed to have been unjustly taken, and had actually sent orders for their restitution: so that by this infamous treaty we got nothing, and gave up every thing; and therefore, in my opinion, the honour of this nation can never be retrieved, unless the advisers and authors of it be censured and punished, which cannot regularly be done without a Parliamentary Enquiry.

"By these and the like wicked, or weak and pusillanimous measures, we are become the ridicule of every Court in Europe, and have lost the confidence of all our antient allies. By these we have encouraged France to extend her ambitious views, and now at last to attempt carrying them into execution. By bad œconomy and extravagance in our domestic measures, we have brought ourselves into such distress at home, that we are almost utterly incapable of entering into a war. By weakness or wickedness in our foreign measures, we have brought the affairs of Europe into such distress, that it is almost impossible for us to avoid entering into a war. By these means we have been brought upon a dangerous precipice, on which we now find ourselves; and shall we trust our being led safely off to the same guide who has led us on? Sir, it is impossible for him to lead us off; it is impossible for us to get off, without first recovering that confidence among our antient allies, which this nation formerly used to have. This we cannot do, as long as they suppose that our councils are influenced by our late minister; and this they will suppose as long as he has access to the King's Closet, and his conduct remains unenquired into, and uncensured. It is not, therefore, a revenge for past sufferings, but a desire to prevent future, that makes me so sanguine for this enquiry. His punishment, let it be ever so severe, will be but a small attonement to his country for what is past. But his impunity will be the source of many future miseries to Europe, as well as to his native country. Let us be as merciful as we will, as any man can reasonably desire, when we come to pronounce sentence; but sentence we must pronounce; and for this purpose we must enquire, unless we are resolved to sacrifice our own liberties, and the liberties of Europe, to the preservation of one guilty man."

The House divided. For the Motion 242—against it, 244.

The

Chap. IV.
1742.

The fate of this motion was called a confirmation of the veracity of the charge brought againſt the new Miniſtry, that they had compounded for the ſafety of the late Miniſter. Mr. PULTENEY was extremely mortified at this miſcarriage. And as ſoon as Mr. SANDYS, and ſome others, were returned from their re-elections, the motion was made again on the 23d of March by Lord LIMERICK; but it was confined to only the laſt *ten* years of the late Adminiſtration. Mr. PITT ſpoke in ſupport of this motion, although altered to half the period. His ſpeech on this occaſion was in reply to Mr. GEORGE COOKE of Harefield, who was juſt come into Parliament. He began with ſaying,

" AS the Hon. Gentleman who ſpoke laſt againſt the motion, has not been long in the Houſe, one ought in charity to believe there is ſome ſincerity in the profeſſions he makes, of his being ready to agree to a Parliamentary Enquiry, when he ſees cauſe, and a convenient time for it; but if he knew how often thoſe profeſſions have been made by thoſe, who, on all occaſions, have oppoſed every kind of enquiry, he would ſave himſelf the trouble of making any ſuch, becauſe they are believed to be ſincere by very few, within doors or without. He may, it is true, have no occaſion upon his own account, to be afraid of an enquiry of any ſort; but when a Gentleman has contracted a friendſhip, or any of his near relations have contracted a friendſhip for one, who may be brought into danger by an enquiry, it is very natural to ſuppoſe, that ſuch a Gentleman's oppoſition to an enquiry does not proceed entirely from motives of a public nature; and if that Gentleman follows the advice of ſome of his friends, I very much queſtion if he will ever ſee cauſe, or a convenient time, for an enquiry into the late conduct of our public affairs. As a Parliamentary Enquiry muſt always be founded upon ſuſpicions, as well as facts, or manifeſt crimes, it will always be eaſy to find reaſons or pretences for averring thoſe ſuſpicions to be groundleſs; and upon the principle that a Parliamentary Enquiry muſt neceſſarily lay open the ſecrets of our government, no time can ever be proper or convenient for ſuch an enquiry, becauſe it is impoſſible to
ſuppoſe

suppose a time when our government can have no secrets of importance to the nation.

"This, Sir, would be a most convenient doctrine for Ministers, because it would put an end to all Parliamentary Enquiries into the conduct of our public affairs; and therefore when I hear it urged, and so much insisted upon, by a certain set of Gentlemen in this House, I must suppose their hopes to be very extensive. I must suppose them to expect that they and their posterity will for ever continue to be ministers, which, if possible, would be more fatal to it, than their having so long continued to be so. But this doctrine has been so often contradicted by experience, that I am surprized to hear Gentlemen insist upon it. Even this very session has afforded us a convincing proof how little foundation there is for saying that a Parliamentary Enquiry must necessarily discover the secrets of our Government. Surely, in a war with Spain, which must be carried on chiefly by sea, if our Government have any secrets, the Lords of the Admiralty must be intrusted with the most important of them; yet we have in this very session, and without any Secret Committees, made an enquiry into the conduct of the Lords Commissioners of our Admiralty. We have not only enquired into their conduct, but we have censured it in such a manner as hath put an end to the same Commissioners being any longer entrusted with that branch of the public business. Has that enquiry discovered any of the secrets of our Government? On the contrary, the Committee found they had no occasion to dive into any of the secrets of Government. They found cause enough for censure without it; and none of the Commissioners pretended to justify their conduct by papers, containing secrets which ought not to be discovered.

"This, Sir, is so late, and so strong a proof of there being no necessary connection between a Parliamentary Enquiry and a discovery of secrets which it behoves the nation to conceal, that I hope Gentlemen will no longer insist upon this danger, as an argument against the enquiry now proposed, which of all others is the least liable to objection. The first Commissioner of the Treasury has nothing to do with the application of secret service money: He is only to take care, that it be regularly issued from his office, and that no more shall be issued upon that head, than according to the then conjuncture of affairs, may seem to be necessary. As to the particular application, it properly belongs to the Secretaries of State, or such other persons as his Majesty shall employ; so that we cannot suppose the enquiry proposed will discover any secrets relating to the application of that money, unless the Noble Lord has acted as Secretary of State as well as First Commissioner of the Treasury; or unless a great part of the money, drawn out for secret services, has been delivered to himself, or to persons employed by him, and applied by him or them towards gaining a corrupt influence in Parliament, or at elections. Both these, indeed, he is most grievously suspected of, and both are secrets which it behoves him very much to have concealed; but it equally behoves the nation to have them both revealed. His country and he are, I grant, in this cause, equally, though oppositely, concerned; for the safety or ruin of one or the other depends upon the fate of the question; and, in my opinion, the violent opposition made to this motion adds great strength to the suspicion.

" I shall admit, Sir, that the Noble Lord, whose conduct is now proposed to be enquired into, was one of His Majesty's Most Hon. Privy Council, and that consequently he must have had a share at least in advising all the measures we have pursued, both abroad and at home; but I cannot admit, that therefore an enquiry into his conduct must necessarily occasion a discovery of any secrets that may be of dangerous consequence to the nation; because we are not to enquire into the measures themselves, or into the wisdom and uprightness of them, and consequently can have no call to look into any of the Government's secrets relating to them. This has nothing to do with an enquiry into his conduct; but there are several suspicions spread abroad, relating to his conduct as a Privy Counsellor, which, if true, would be of the last importance to the nation to have discovered. It has been strongly asserted, that he was not only a Privy Counsellor, but had usurped the whole and sole direction of his Majesty's Privy Council. It has been asserted, that he gave the Spanish Court the first hint of the unjust claim they afterwards set up against our South Sea Company, which was one of the chief causes of the war between the two nations. And it has been asserted, that this very Minister has given advice to the French, what measures to take upon several occasions, in order to bring our Court into their measures; particularly, that he advised them to send the numerous army they have this last summer sent into Westphalia. What truth there is in these assertions, I shall not pretend to answer. The

facts

facts are of such a nature, and they must have been perpetrated with so much caution and secrecy, that it will be difficult to bring them to light, even by a Parliamentary Enquiry; but the very suspicion is ground enough for setting up such an enquiry, and for carrying it on with the utmost strictness and vigour; which leads me to consider the cause we now have for an enquiry.

"Upon this subject, Sir, I must say I am a good deal surprized to hear the Representatives of the People make so light of the sentiments or suspicions of the people. That there are suspicions and complaints among the people, and among the generality of the best sort of people is, 'tis true, a fact we cannot easily prove against one that denies it, no more than we could do, that the generality of our people are of a fair or a brown complexion; but if I should say, that the majority of our people are Whites, I could not prove what I asserted; and yet I should look upon him as a very whimsical or a very disingenuous Gentleman that would deny it, and assert the majority of our people were Blackamoors. Such facts it is impossible to prove any other way but by the opinion of those who are the best judges; and surely a Country Gentleman who lives most part of his time among the people, and has no court favours to bestow as a temptation, for those he converses with to disguise their sentiments, is a better judge than one who seldom stirs out of the purlieus of a Court, and converses with none but such as expect places or preferment by his favour. Therefore if we judge of this fact according to the only evidence that can be had, that is, according to the opinion of those who are the best judges, we must conclude, that the suspicions and complaints of the people were never more general than they are against the late conduct of our public affairs; and this by me shall always be deemed a sufficient reason for a Parliamentary Enquiry.

"Whatever my opinion of past measures may be, I shall never be so vain, or bigotted to my own opinion as, without any enquiry, to determine against the majority of my countrymen. If I found the public measures generally condemned, let my private opinion of them be never so favourable, I should be for an enquiry, in order to convince the people of their error, or at least to furnish myself with the most authentic arguments for the opinion I have embraced. The desire of bringing other people into our sentiments is so natural to mankind, that

CHAP. IV.
1742.

I shall always suspect the candour of those, who, in politicks or religion, are against a free enquiry. Besides, Sir, when the complaints of the people are general against an Administration, or against any particular Minister, an enquiry is a duty we owe to our Sovereign as well as the people. We meet here to communicate to our Sovereign the sentiments of his people. We meet here to redress the grievances of the people. By performing our duty in these two respects, we shall always be able to establish the throne of our Sovereign in the hearts of his people, and to prevent the people's being led into insurrections or rebellions by misrepresentations, or false surmises. When the people complain, they must be in the right or in the wrong. If they are in the right, we are in duty bound to enquire into the conduct of the Ministers, and punish those who shall appear to have been the most guilty. If the people are in the wrong, we ought to enquire into the conduct of our Ministers, in order to convince the people that they have been misled. We ought not therefore, in any question about an enquiry, to be governed by our own sentiments. We must be governed by the sentiments of our constituents, if we are resolved to perform our duty, either as true representatives of the people, or as faithful messengers to our Sovereign. I will agree with the Hon. Gentleman, that if we are convinced or suspect the public measures to be wrong, we ought to enquire into them, even though they are not much complained of by the people without doors; but I cannot agree with him in thinking, that notwithstanding the Administration, or a Minister's being complained of by the people in general without doors, we ought not to enquire into his conduct, unless we are ourselves convinced that his measures have been wrong. Without an enquiry we can no more determine this question, than a judge can declare a man innocent of any crime laid to his charge, without a previous trial or inquisition. Common fame is a sufficient ground for an inquisition at common law; and, for the same reason, the general voice of the people of England ought always to be looked on as a sufficient ground for a Parliamentary Enquiry.

" But, say Gentlemen, What is this Minister accused of? What crime is laid to his charge? For unless some misfortune is said to have happened, or some crime to have been committed, no enquiry ought to be set on foot. Sir, the ill posture of our affairs, both abroad and at home; the melancholy situation we are in; the distress we are now

reduced

reduced to, is of itself a sufficient cause for an enquiry, even supposing he were accused of no particular crime or misconduct. The nation lies a bleeding, perhaps expiring. The balance of power has received a deadly blow. Shall we acknowledge this to be the case, and shall we not enquire whether it has happened by mischance, or by the misconduct, perhaps the malice prepence, of our Minister here at home. Before the Treaty of Utrecht, it was the general opinion, that in a few years of peace we should be able to pay off most of our debts. We have now been very near thirty years in profound peace, at least we have never been engaged in any war but what we unnecessarily brought upon ourselves, and yet our debts are near as great as they were when that treaty was concluded. Is not this a misfortune, and shall we make no enquiry how this misfortune has happened.

" I am surprized to hear it said, that no enquiry ought to be set on foot, unless some public crime be known to have been committed. The suspicion of any crime's having been actually committed, has always been deemed a sufficient reason for setting up an enquiry. Is there not a suspicion that the public money has been applied towards gaining a corrupt influence at elections? Is it not become a common expression to say, " The floodgates of the Treasury are opened against a General Election?" I shall desire no more than that every Gentleman who is conscious of this having been done, either for or against him, would give his vote in favour of this motion. Will any Gentleman say this is not a crime, when even private corruption has such high penalties inflicted upon it by express statute? A Minister that commits this crime, and makes use of the public money for that purpose, adds thieving and breach of trust to the crime of corruption; and as the crime, when committed by him, is of much more dangerous consequence than when committed by a private man, it becomes more properly the object of a Parliamentary Enquiry, and ought to be more severely punished. The Hon. Gentleman may much more reasonably tell us that PORTEUS was never murdered by the mob at Edinburgh, because no discovery of his murderers could ever yet be made, notwithstanding the high reward, as well as pardon offered; than to tell us, we cannot suppose our Minister ever, by himself or his agents, corrupted an election, because no information has as yet been brought against him; for nothing but a pardon on conviction the offender has ever yet been offered in this cafe; and how could any informer expect fuch a pardon, much lefs a reward, when he knew the very man againft whom he was to inform had not only the diftribution of all public rewards, but the packing of a jury or Parliament againft him? Sir, Whilft fuch a Minifter preferves the favour of the Crown, and thereby the exercife of its power, we can never expect fuch an information. Even malice itfelf can never provoke fuch an information; becaufe, like all other forts of impotent malice, it will rebound upon the heart that conceived it.

" This fhews the infignificancy of the Act mentioned by the Hon. Gentlemen, with regard to that fort of corruption which is called Bribery; and with regard to the other fort of corruption, which confifts in giving or taking away thofe pofts, penfions, or preferments which depend upon the arbitrary will of the Crown, this Act is ftill more infignificant, becaufe it is not neceffary; it would even be ridiculous in a minifter to tell any man, that he gave or refufed him a poft, penfion or preferment, on account of his voting for or againft any minifterial meafure in Parliament, or any minifterial candidate at an election. If he makes it his conftant rule never to give a poft, penfion or preferment but to thofe who vote for his meafures and his candidates, and makes a few examples of difmiffing thofe who vote otherwife, it will have the fame effect as when he declares it openly. Will any Gentleman fay, that this has not been the practice of the Minifter whofe conduct is now propofed to be enquired into? Has he not declared in the face of this Houfe, that he will continue to make this his practice? And will not this have the fame effect as if he went feparately and diftinctly to every particular man, and told him in exprefs terms: " Sir, If you vote for fuch a meafure, or fuch a candidate, you fhall " have the firft preferment in the gift of the Crown; if you vote other- " wife, you muft not expect to keep what you have." Gentlemen may deny the fun fhines at noon-day; but if they have any eyes, and do not wilfully fhut them, or turn their backs towards him, I am fure no man will believe they are ingenuous in what they fay; and therefore I think the Hon. Gentleman was in the right, who endeavoured to juftify this practice. It was more candid than to deny it; but as his arguments have been already fully anfwered, I fhall add nothing upon that fubject.

" Gentlemen cry out, What! Will you take from the Crown the power of preferring or cafhiering the officers of our army? No, Sir.

This

This is neither the design, nor will it be the effect of our agreeing to this motion. The King has at present an absolute power of preferring or cashiering the officers of our army. It is a prerogative he may make use of, for the benefit or safety of the public; but, like other prerogatives, it may be made a wrong use of; and the Minister is answerable to Parliament when it is. When an officer is preferred or cashiered upon the motive of his voting for or against any court measure or candidate, it is a wrong use of this prerogative, for which the Minister is answerable. We may judge from circumstances or outward appearances. From these we may condemn; and I hope we have still a power to punish any minister that will dare to advise the King to prefer or cashier upon such a motive. Whether this prerogative ought to remain as it is without any limitation, is a question that has nothing to do in this debate; but I must observe, that the argument made use of for it, might with equal weight be made use of for giving our King an absolute power over every man's property; for a large property will always give the possessor a command over a great number of men, whom he may arm and discipline if he pleases. I know of no law for restraining it. I hope there never will be any such; and I wish our Gentlemen of Estates would make more use of this power than they do, because it would contribute towards keeping our domestic as well as our foreign enemies in awe. For my part, I think a Gentleman who has earned his commission by his services, (in his military capacity I mean) or bought it with his money, has as much a property in it as any man has in his estate, and ought to have it as well secured by the laws of his country. Whilst it remains at the absolute will of the Crown, he must be a slave to the Minister, unless he has some other estate to depend on; and if the officers of our army long continue in that state of slavery in which they are at present, I am afraid it will make slaves of us all.

" The only method we have for preventing this fatal consequence, as the law now stands, is to make the best and most constant use of the power we have, as Members of this House, to prevent any Minister's daring to advise the King to make a bad use of his prerogative; and as there is such a strong suspicion that this Minister has done so, we ought certainly to enquire into it, not only for the sake of punishing him, if guilty, but as a terror to all future Ministers.

" This,

CHAP. IV.
1742.

"This, Sir, may therefore be justly reckoned among the many other sufficient causes for the enquiry proposed: and the suspicion of the Civil List's being greatly in debt is another; for if it is, it must either have been misapplied or profusely thrown away, which it is our duty both to prevent and punish. It is inconsistent with the honour of this nation to have our King stand indebted to his servants or tradesmen, who may be ruined by a delay of payment. The Parliament has provided sufficiently for preventing this dishonour's being brought upon the nation; and if the provision we have made should be misapplied or lavished, we must supply the deficiency; we ought to do it, whether the King makes any application for that purpose, or no; and the reason is very plain, because we ought first to enquire into the management of that revenue, and punish those who have occasioned the deficiency. They will certainly chuse to leave the creditors of the Crown and the honour of the nation in a state of suffering, rather than advise the King to make an application which will bring their conduct into question, and themselves, probably, to condign punishment. Beside this, Sir, there is at present another reason still stronger for promoting an enquiry. As there is a great suspicion that the public money has been applied towards corrupting voters at elections, and in Parliament, if the Civil List be in debt, it gives reason to presume that some part of this revenue has, under the pretence of secret service money, been applied to that wicked purpose.

"I shall conclude, Sir, with a few remarks upon the last argument made use of against the enquiry proposed. It has been said, that the Minister delivered in his accounts annually; that those accounts have been annually passed and approved of by Parliament; and that therefore it would be unjust to call him now to a general account, because the vouchers may now be lost, or many expensive transactions have slipt out of his memory. 'Tis true, Sir, estimates and accounts have been annually delivered in. The forms of proceeding made that necessary; but were any of those estimates or accounts ever properly enquired into? Were not all questions for that purpose rejected by the Minister's friends in Parliament? Has not the Parliament always taken them upon trust, and passed them without examination? Can such a superficial passing, to call it no worse, be deemed a reason for not calling him to a new and general account? If the steward to an infant's

estate

estate should annually, for twenty years together, deliver in his accounts to the guardians; and if the guardians through negligence, or for a share of the plunder, should annually pass his accounts without any examination, or at least without any objection; would that be a reason for saying, that it would be unjust in the infant to call his steward to an account when he came of age? Especially if that steward had built and furnished sumptuous palaces, and had, during the whole time, lived at a much greater expence than his visible income could afford, and yet nevertheless had amassed great riches. The public, Sir, is always in a state of infancy; therefore no prescription can be pleaded against it, nor even a general release, if there appears the least cause to suspect that it was surreptitiously obtained. Public vouchers ought always to remain upon record; nor ought there to be any public expence without a proper voucher; therefore the case of the public is still stronger than that of any infant. Thus the Hon. Gentleman who made use of this objection must see of how little avail it can be in the case now before us; and consequently I hope, we shall have his concurrence in the question.

This motion was indeed agreed to, and a Committee was appointed; but the measure was rendered abortive by a Parliamentary manœuvre. Several of the persons brought before the Committee to be examined, refused to answer, urging, that by their answers they might possibly criminate themselves. This objection being reported to the House, a Bill was immediately brought in and passed, to indemnify all persons for the discoveries they made before the Committee. When this Bill came into the House of Lords, Lord CARTERET opposed it most violently, and the Bill was thrown out. Some of the ministerial party in the House of Commons affected to be very angry; but all proceedings dropt. And the EARL of ORFORD continued undisturbed during the remainder of his life.

CHAP. V.

Lord Carteret's Afcendancy in the Clofet—Enters into the German Meafures—Takes the Hanoverian Troops into Britifh Pay— Mr. Pitt's Speech againft that Meafure—Death of Lord Wilmington, and Mr. Pelham's Acceffion to the Treafury—Mr. Pitt's Speech againft the Addrefs, at the Commencement of the Seffion, after the battle of Dettingen—Mr. Pitt's Speech againft voting Money for a Britifh Army to ferve in Flanders—The whole Kingdom applauds his Oppofition in Parliament—The Dutchefs Dowager of Marlborough leaves him a handfome Legacy.

CHAP. V.
1742.
Lord Carteret's Adminiftration.

LORD CARTERET, by adopting the politics of the clofet, became a favourite in it. He entered warmly into the meafures of the Continent, particularly thofe in fupport of the Houfe of Auftria againft France, for which purpofe he took 16000 Hanoverian troops into Britifh Pay, and marched them into the Low Countries. Upon the motion for granting the money for the payment of thefe troops on the 10th of December 1742, there was a long debate, in which Mr. PITT fpoke againft the motion, in reply to Mr. HENRY FOX, at that time Surveyor of the Board of Works, and afterwards Lord HOLLAND, who had fpoken for the motion:

Mr. Pitt's Speech againft the Hanoverian Troops.

"If the Gentlemen, who have fpoke in fupport of this motion, are, as they pretend, determined to abandon their prefent fentiments as foon as any better meafures are propofed, the Miniftry will quickly be deprived of their ableft defenders: for I think the meafures which have hitherto been purfued, fo weak and pernicious, that fcarcely any alteration can be propofed, that will not be for the advantage of the nation.

"They

"They have already been informed, there was no necessity of hiring auxiliary troops, since it does not yet appear, that either justice or policy required us to engage in the quarrels of the Continent, that there was any need of forming an army in the Low Countries, or that in order to form an army, auxiliaries were necessary.

"But not to dwell upon disputable questions, I think it may be justly concluded, that the measures of our ministry have been ill concerted, because it is undoubtedly wrong to squander the public money without effect, and to pay armies only to be a shew to our friends, and a jest to our enemies.

"The troops of Hanover, whom we are now expected to pay, marched into the Low Countries indeed, and still remain in the same places; they marched to the place most distant from the enemy, least in danger of an attack, and most strongly fortified, if any attack had been designed; nor have any claim to be paid, but that they left their own country for a place of greater security.

"It is always reasonable to judge of the future by the past, and therefore it is probable, that the services of these troops will not, next year, be of equal importance with that for which they are now to be paid: And I shall not be surprized, though the opponents of the Ministry should be challenged, after such another glorious campaign, to propose better men, and told, that the money of this nation cannot be more properly employed than in hiring Hanoverians to eat and sleep.

"But to prove yet more particularly, that better measures may be taken, and that more useful troops may be retained, and that therefore the Hon. Gentlemen may be expected to quit those to whom they now adhere, I shall shew, that in hiring the forces of Hanover, we have obstructed our own designs; that we have, instead of assisting the Queen of Hungary, withdrawn part of the allies from her, and that we have burthened the nation with troops, from which no service can be reasonably expected.

"The advocates for the Ministry have on this occasion affected to speak of the balance of power, the pragmatic sanction, and the preservation of the Queen of Hungary, not only as if they were to be the chief care of Great Britain, which, though easily controvertible, might perhaps, in compliance with long prejudices, be admitted; but as if they were to be the care of Great Britain alone; as if the power of France

CHAP. V.
1742.

France were formidable to no other people; as if no other part of the world would be injured, by becoming a prey to an univerfal monarchy, and being fubjected to an arbitrary government of a French Deputy; by being drained of its inhabitants, only to extend the conquefts of its mafters, and to make other nations equally miferable; and by being oppreffed with exorbitant taxes, levied by military executions, and employed only in fupporting the ftate of its oppreffors. They dwell upon the importance of public faith, and the neceffity of an exact obfervation of treaties, as if the pragmatic fanction had been figned by no other Potentate than the King of Great Britain; or as if the public faith were to be obligatory to us only.

" That we fhould inviolably obferve our treaties, and obferve them, though every other nation fhould difregard them; that we fhould fhew an example of fidelity to mankind, and ftand firm, though we fhould ftand alone, in the practice of virtue, I fhall readily allow; and therefore I am far from advifing, that we fhould recede from our ftipulations, whatever we may fuffer by performing, or neglect the fupport of pragmatic fanction, however we may be at prefent embarraffed, or however inconvenient it may be to affert it.

" But furely, that for the fame reafon we obferve our own ftipulations, we ought to excite other powers likewife to the obfervation of theirs; or at leaft not to contribute to hinder it. But how is our prefent conduct agreeable to thefe principles? The pragmatic fanction was confirmed not only by the King of Great Britain, but by the Elector likewife of Hanover, who is therefore equally obliged, if treaties conftitute obligation, to defend the Houfe of Auftria againft the attacks of any foreign power, and to fend in his proportion of troops to fupport the Queen of Hungary.

" Whether thefe troops have been fent, thofe whofe province obliges them to have fome knowledge with foreign affairs, can better inform the Houfe than I; but fince we have not heard them mentioned in this debate, and have found by experience that none of the merits of that Electorate are paffed over in filence, it may, I think, fairly be concluded, that the diftreffes of the illuftrious Queen of Hungary have yet received no alleviation from her alliance with Hanover; that her complaints have moved no compaffion at that Court, nor the juftice of her caufe obtained any regard.

" To

"To what can be imputed this negligence of Treaties, this difregard of juftice, this defect of compaffion, but to the pernicious counfels of thofe men who have advifed his Majefty to hire to Great Britain thofe troops which he fhould have employed in the affiftance of the Queen of Hungary; for it is not to be imagined that his Majefty has more or lefs regard to juftice as King of Great Britain than as Elector of Hanover; or that he would not have fent his proportion of troops to the Auftrian army, had not the temptation of greater profit been induftrioufly laid before him.

"But this is not all that may be urged againft this conduct: For can we imagine, that the power of France is lefs, or that her defigns are lefs formidable to Hanover than to Great Britain; nor is it lefs neceffary for the fecurity of Hanover, that the Houfe of Auftria fhould be reeftablifhed in its former grandeur, and enabled to fupport the liberties of Europe againft the bold attempts for univerfal monarchy.

"If therefore our affiftance be an act of honefty, and granted, inconfequence of treaties, why may it not equally be required of Hanover? And if it be an act of generofity, why fhould this nation alone be obliged to facrifice her own intereft to that of others? Or why fhould the Elector of Hanover exert his liberality at the expence of Great Britain?

"It is now too apparent, that this great, this powerful, this formidable kingdom, is confidered only as a province to a defpicable Electorate; and that, in confequence of a fcheme formed long ago, and invariably purfued, thefe troops are hired only to drain this unhappy nation of its money. That they have hitherto been of no ufe to Great Britain or to Auftria, is evident beyond controverfy; and therefore it is plain, that they are retained only for the purpofe of Hanover.

"How much reafon the tranfactions of almoft every year have given for fufpecting this ridiculous, ungrateful and perfidious partiality, it is not neceffary to mention. I doubt not but moft of thofe who fit in this Houfe can recollect a great number of inftances, from the purchafe of part of the Swedifh dominions, to the contract which we are now called upon to ratify. I hope few have forgotten the memorable ftipulation for the Heffian troops; for the forces of the DUKE of WOLFEMBUTTLE, which we were fcarcely to march beyond the verge of their own country or th ever memorable treaty, of which the tendency is dif-

CHAP. V. covered in the name*. The treaty by which we difunited ourſelves
1742. from Auſtria, deſtroyed that building which we may perhaps now endeavour, without ſucceſs, to raiſe again; and weakened the only power which it was our intereſt to ſtrengthen.

" To dwell upon all the inſtances of partiality which have been ſhewn; to remark the yearly viſits that have been made to that delightful country; to reckon up all the ſums that have been ſpent to aggrandize and enrich it, would be at once invidious and tireſome; tireſome to thoſe who are afraid to hear the truth, and to thoſe who are unwilling to mention facts diſhonourable or injurious to their country. Nor ſhall I dwell any longer on this unpleaſing ſubject, than to expreſs my hopes, that we ſhall no more ſuffer ourſelves to be deceived and oppreſſed; that we ſhall at length perform the duty of the Repreſentatives of the people; and, by refuſing to ratify this contract, ſhew, that however the intereſt of Hanover has been preferred by the Miniſters, the Parliament pays no regard but to that of Great Britain.

The motion was agreed to upon a diviſion of 260 againſt 193.

More Changes in the Miniſtry. In July 1743, Lord WILMINGTON died, and Mr. PELHAM ſucceeded him at the Treaſury, and Mr. WINNINGTON ſucceeded Mr. PELHAM in the office of Paymaſter. On the 22d of December 1743, Mr. SANDYS being created a peer, Mr. PELHAM was made Chancellor of the Exchequer.

On the 1ſt of December 1743 Parliament met. The King's Speech recited the affairs of the Continent, which, from the late battle at Dettingen, and other events, had engaged the public attention. The uſual motion for an Addreſs, in anſwer

* In the debate upon the Hanover Treaty (Anno 1725) it was alleged by Mr. HORATIO WALPOLE, " That the Treaty between the Emperor and the " King of Spain might probably be cemented by a match between the eldeſt " daughter of the former (now Queen of Hungary) and the Infant Don " Carlos."

to the King's Speech, brought on a long debate, in which Mr. Pitt spoke against the motion; *viz.*

CHAP. V.
1743.

"From what is now proposed, we may see, that whatever change we have got or may get, with respect to foreign measures, by the late change in our Administration, the nation is to expect no change with respect to our domestic affairs. In foreign affairs I shall grant we have felt a very remarkable change. From one extreme, our Administration have quite run to the verge of another. Our former Minister betrayed the interest of his country by his pusillanimity; our present Minister (meaning Lord CARTERET) sacrifices it by his Quixotism. Our former Minister was for negotiating with all the World; our present is for fighting against all the World. Our former Minister was for agreeing to every treaty, though never so dishonourable; our present will give ear to no treaty, though never so reasonable. Thus both appear to be extravagant, but with this difference, that by the extravagance of our present, the nation will be put to a much greater charge than ever it was by the extravagance of our former.

Mr. Pitt's Speech against the Address.

"It must therefore be allowed, Sir, that by a change of a few men in our Administration, we have got a change of measures, so far as relates to foreign affairs; but with respect to our domestic affairs, we have met with no change in our measures; we can now, I think, expect none. The same screening, the same plundering, the same prodigal spirit prevails. The same criminal complaisance, we may depend on it, the same corrupt, extravagant and dangerous measures will be made use of. They have, I am convinced, been already practised; otherwise no Minister would expect, that a British House of Commons would cram their address to their Sovereign, with so many fulsome panegyrics upon the conduct of his Ministers. I say, Sir, no minister would expect such complaisance; for I hope the Hon. Gentleman who made the motion will excuse me, if I suppose it was put into his hands by the Minister; and if he thinks he has acquired honour by making such a motion, I promise him I shall never envy him the acquisition.

"The Hon. Gentleman who spoke last was in the right, when he said, in the beginning of the session we could know nothing in a Parliamentary way of the measures that had been pursued. I believe we shall know as little in that way at the end of the session as we do at the beginning;

CHAP. V.
1743.

ning; for I am perſuaded our new Miniſter will in this, as well as in every other ſtep of his domeſtic conduct, follow the example of his predeceſſor, by getting a negative put upon every motion that may tend towards our acquiring any Parliamentary Knowledge of our late meaſures. But if we have no knowledge of them, ſurely it is as ſtrong an argument for our not approving, as it can be for our not anſwering; and if nothing relating to our late meaſures had been propoſed to be inſerted in our Addreſs upon this occaſion, I ſhould not have taken the leaſt notice of them; but whether I have any Parliamentary Knowledge or no, when an approbation is propoſed, it lays me under a neceſſity to make uſe of the knowledge I have, whatever it may be, in order to determine whether I am to join or not in the approbation propoſed. Suppoſe I had no knowledge of any of our late meaſures but what I have gathered from foreign and domeſtic newſpapers, even that knowledge I muſt make uſe of when I am obliged to give my opinion of them; and if from that knowledge I think them wrong, I ought ſurely to refuſe joining in any thing that may look like an approbation. Nay, this refuſal I ought to perſiſt in, till the Miniſter be pleaſed to furniſh me with ſuch Parliamentary Knowledge as may convince me that I have been miſinformed. This, I ſay, ought certainly to be my conduct, when, from the knowledge I have, I find more reaſon to condemn than approve of any late meaſure; but ſuppoſe that from the knowledge I have, I find more reaſon to approve than condemn; yet even in that caſe I ought not to approve, unleſs my knowledge be ſuch as may authorize that approbation; and as no ſort of knowledge but a Parliamentary knowledge can warrant a Parliamentary Approbation, for this reaſon alone I ought to refuſe it; ſo that if what is now propoſed contains any ſort of approbation, our refuſing to agree to it, is not a cenſure upon any paſt meaſure; it is only a declaration, that we have not ſuch a knowledge of paſt meaſures, as may be a ſufficient foundation for our approving them in a Parliamentary Way; which is a declaration none but thoſe who are admitted into the inmoſt receſſes of the Cabinet can refuſe to make; and as we have not now, I believe, any ſuch in this Houſe, therefore every Gentleman here ought to join in ſuch a declaration, by giving his negative to this propoſition now before us, if it be ſuch an one as contains an approbation of our late

meaſures

measures; and that it is so, no Gentleman who attends to the words of it, can make the least doubt of.

CHAP. V.
1743.

" Sir, It is not only an approbation of all that our Ministers have advised, but an acknowledgement of the truth of several facts, which, upon enquiry, may appear to be false; or at least they are such as we have seen no proof of, nor have any proper authority to assert. Suppose it should appear, that his Majesty was exposed to few or no dangers abroad, but what he is daily exposed to at home, such as the overturning of his coach or the stumbling of his horse, would not the Address proposed be an affront and an insult upon our Sovereign, instead of being a compliment? Suppose it should appear, that our Ministers have shewn no regard to the advice of Parliament, and that they have exerted their endeavours, not for the preservation of the House of Austria, but for involving that House in dangers which it might otherwise have avoided, and which, I believe, it will hardly be possible for us to avert; suppose it should appear, that though a body of Dutch troops marched to the Rhine, they never joined our army; suppose it should appear, that the Treaty with Sardinia is not yet ratified by all the parties concerned, or that it is such a one as cannot be performed. If these things should appear upon an enquiry, would not such an Address as this appear very ridiculous? What assurance have we that all these facts may not appear to be as I have supposed? For as the King's Speech from the Throne is always, in this House, considered as the Speech of the Minister, it can never be allowed to be a proof upon which we ought to found any resolution.

" What I have said, Sir, will shew, that even though we had reason to conclude from such knowledge as we may have accidentally acquired, that all our late measures were right, and that all the facts to be mentioned in our Address were exactly true, yet we ought not to express any sort of approbation, because we have as yet no Parliamentary Knowledge that can authorize a Parliamentary Approbation. But when the contrary happens to be the case; when we have great reason to conclude from every sort of knowledge we have hitherto acquired, that our late measures were fundamentally wrong; that facts have been misrepresented to us; and that we may, very probably, have reason to condole what we are now desired to congratulate, how cautious ought we to be of saying any thing in our Address that may look like an ap-

VOL. I.   K   probation

CHAP. V. probation either of the measures or the methods that have been taken to prosecute them.

1743.

"In order to shew, Sir, that this is really the case, I must begin with the turn which the affairs of Europe took upon the death of the late Emperor. Upon that emergency I shall grant, that it was the interest of this nation to have had the Queen of Hungary established in the possession of her father's dominions, and her Husband, the Duke of Lorrain, chosen Emperor. This was our interest, because it would have been the best security for the preservation of the balance of power; but this was our only interest, and it was an interest we had in common with all the powers of Europe, except France. We were not therefore to take upon us the sole support of this interest; and therefore, when the King of Prussia attacked Silesia and the King of Spain, the King of Poland and the Duke of Bavaria laid claim to the late Emperor's succession; we might then have seen that the establishment of the Queen of Hungary in all her father's dominions was become impossible, especially as the Dutch refused to interfere any other way than by good offices. What then ought we to have done? Since we could not preserve the whole, is it not evident that, in order to engage some of the claimants on our side, we ought to have advised her to yield up a part? This we ought to have insisted on, and the claimant whom we ought first to have thought of taking off was the King of Prussia; both because his claim was the smallest, and because he was one of the most neutral, as well as one of the most powerful allies we could treat with. For this reason we ought certainly to have advised the Queen of Hungary to have accepted of the terms offered by the King of Prussia when he first invaded Silesia. Nay, we ought to have insisted on it, as the condition of our assisting her against any of the other claimants. If we had done this, the Court of Vienna must and would have agreed to it; and in this case, whatever protestations the other claimants might have made, the Queen of Hungary would, to this day I believe, have remained the undisturbed possessor of all the rest of her father's dominions; and her husband, the Duke of Lorrain, would now have been in possession of the Imperial Throne.

"Did we at that time pursue this salutary measure? No, Sir, the contrary appears not only from our Gazettes, but from our Parliamentary Knowledge; for from the papers that have been, either accidentally

or

or necessarily laid before Parliament, it appears, that instead of insisting upon the Court of Vienna agreeing to the terms offered by Prussia, we rather encouraged them in their obstinacy, not only by our memorials, but by his Majesty's Speech to his Parliament, the Addresses of both Houses thereupon, and by flaming speeches made by our courtiers against the King of Prussia. What I mean, is his Majesty's Speech on the 8th of April 1741; the famous Addresses made upon that occasion for guarantying the dominions of Hanover, and the grant of 300,000l. for enabling his Majesty to support the Queen of Hungary. Every one must remember the flaming speeches made upon that occasion by some favourites at Court against the King of Prussia; and every one must remember, that the Queen of Hungary was not then, nor for some months after, attacked by any one Prince in Europe, except the King of Prussia; therefore the Court of Vienna could not but suppose that both the Court and Nation of Great Britain were resolved to support her, not only against the King of Prussia, but *contra omnes mortales*; and consequently we have no reason to be surprized at that Court's shewing an unwillingness to part with such a plentiful country as those Lordships of Silesia claimed by the King of Prussia.

"This I say, Sir, was sufficient to confirm the Queen of Hungary in her obstinacy; but this was not all. We had not only promised her our assistance against the King of Prussia, but we had actually begun a negotiation for a powerful alliance against that Prince, and for parcelling out his dominions amongst the allies. We had solicited not only the Queen of Hungary, but also the Dutch and Muscovites to enter into this alliance; and we had been at the expence to take both Danes and the Hessians into the pay of Great Britain, for the use of this alliance. Nay, even Hanover put itself to a great expence upon this occasion, by making an augmentation of near one third to the army it had on foot, which I believe was the first extraordinary expence it was put to since its happy conjunction with England, notwithstanding the great acquisitions it has since made, and the many expensive broils England has been involved in upon the sole account of that Electorate. Therefore, if the Queen of Hungary shewed any thing like obstinacy with regard to the claims of Prussia, we may easily perceive at whose door that obstinacy ought to be laid; and to them only the misfortunes which afterwards befel that Princess ought most justly to be

Chap. V.
1743.

be imputed. Whilst the French seemed resolved not to interfere in the affairs of Germany, it was easy to promise her our assistance. It was safe to engage in schemes that might contribute to her support as well as to the enlargement of the dominions of Hanover, because Prussia was certainly not an equal match for the Queen of Hungary alone, and much less for the Queen of Hungary supported by Hanover and the whole power of Great Britain. During this posture of affairs, I say, it was safe for us, that is to say it was safe for Hanover, to promise, and to concert schemes for the support of the Queen o Hungary; but as soon as France began to appear, our schemes were all dropt, and our promises forgot, because it began then to be unsafe for Hanover to engage in the affair, and England surely is never to mind any promises, or engage in any schemes, that may possibly bring Hanover into any danger or distress.

" From this time, Sir, we thought no more of assisting the Queen of Hungary, except by those grants which were made to her by Parliament. These indeed our Ministers did not oppose, because they are sure of making, some way or other, a job of every grant made by Parliament: but from the use that was made, or rather the no use that was made, of the Danish and Hessian troops, notwithstanding their being continued in British pay, and from the insult tamely suffered by our squadron in the Mediterranean, we cannot conclude that our Ministers, from the time the French began to interfere, resolved, and were perhaps afterwards engaged, to give the Queen of Hungary no assistance either by sea or land. Thus, after having led that Princess upon the ice by our promises, we left her there to shift for herself; by which means the Duke of Bavaria came to be chosen Emperor, and the House of Austria was stripped of a great part of its dominions, and in the utmost danger of being stript of all, if France had inclined. it should have been so; but this was what saved the House of Austria, France had a mind to have the power of that House reduced, but had no mind to see it absolutely ruined; because the power of the Duke of Bavaria, then Emperor, would have been raised to a higher pitch than was consistent with the French scheme, which was to make the Princes of Germany ruin one another as much as possible, and then to make such a partition as should render the Houses of Bavaria, Austria, Saxony and Prussia, pretty near equal; in which case it is highly probable,

bable, and the French have not since scrupled to say, that the King of Prussia's share would not have been so large as it has been since made.

" This prevented the French from sending such a powerful army into Germany as they might have done; and by the bad conduct of the generals they sent there, and the good conduct of the Queen of Hungary's generals, together with the bravery of her troops, her affairs in Germany took a new turn just about the time of the late change in our Administration; which brings me to the origin of the measures that are now carrying on; and therefore I must consider the posture of the affairs of Europe at that particular time, that is in February 1742. But before I begin I must lay this down as a maxim, which this nation ought always to observe, that though it be our interest to preserve a balance of power in Europe, yet, as we are the most remote from danger, we ought always to be the least susceptible of jealousy, and the last to take the alarm; and with regard to the balance of power, I must observe, that this balance may be supported, either by having one single Potentate capable of opposing and defeating any ambitious design of France, or by having a well connected confederacy sufficient for the same purpose. Of these two I shall grant, that the first is the most eligible, when it can be had, because it may be most securely depended on; but when this cannot be had, the whole address of our ministers and negociators ought to be employed in establishing the second.

" The wisdom of my first maxim, Sir, must be acknowledged by every one who considers, that when the powers upon the Continent apply to us to join with them in a war against France, we may take what share and what sort of share in the war we think fit; whereas, when we apply to them, they will prescribe to us in both; and whatever art some gentlemen may make use of to frighten themselves, or to frighten others, when it serves their purpose, with the dependency of all the powers of Europe upon France, we may rest secure, that as often as they are in any real danger of being brought under such a dependency, they will unite among themselves to prevent it, and will call upon us for assistance; nay, if they should be imperceptibly brought under such a dependency, they would as soon as they perceived it, unite amongst themselves, and call upon us to join with them, in a

confe-

confederacy against France, in order to enable them to shake off that dependency; so that we can never be obliged to stand single and alone, in supporting the balance of power, nor shall we ever have occasion to call upon our neighbours on the Continent to join with us for such a purpose, unless when our Ministers, for some bye-ends of their own, pretend dangers which have no real foundation; for Europe is now in a very different situation from what it was in the time of the Romans. Every country then was divided into so many sovereignties, that it was impossible for the people of any one country to unite among themselves, and much more for two or three large countries to unite in a general confederacy against the overgrown power of the Romans; whereas this is now practicable, and always may be practised as often as France, or any other power in Europe, discovers a real design to enslave the rest.

"This brings me, Sir, to what I have already observed, that the balance of power in Europe may be preserved by a confederacy, almost as securely as it can be by setting up any one power as a rival to the power of France. And now let me examine, which of these two methods we ought to have thought on in February 1742. The Imperial Diadem was then gone from the House of Austria; and though the Queen of Hungary's troops had met with some success in the Winter, she was still stript of a great part of the Austrian dominions; so that the power of the House was much inferior to what it was at the time of the late Emperor's death, and still more inferior to what it was in the year 1716, when we thought it necessary to add Naples and Sicily to its former acquisitions, in order to make it a match for the power of France. Beside this, there was then a most powerful confederacy against that House, and no jealousy subsisting against the powers of Europe of the ambitious designs of France; for though that Court had assisted in pulling down the House of Austria, they had discovered no design of encreasing their own power or dominions; but on the other hand, by the haughty behaviour of the Court of Vienna, and the height that House had been raised to, a jealousy had arisen amongst the Princes of Germany, of the overgrown power of that House; which jealousy had first manifested itself in the House of Hanover, and was at this very time subsisting not only in the House of Hanover, but also in most of the Sovereign Houses of Germany. In these circumstances

stances it was impossible for our Ministers, however wrong-headed we may suppose them, to think of restoring the House of Austria to its former grandeur and power, or of setting that House up again as a match for the power of France; because in such a scheme, they must have seen that they would not be cordially assisted by any power in Europe, and that they would be opposed, not only by France and Spain, but by all the Princes of Germany and Italy who were jealous of the power of the House of Austria.

" In these circumstances, what was this nation to do? What ought our Ministers to have done? Since it was impossible to establish the balance of power in Europe upon the single power of the House of Austria, surely, Sir, it was our business to think of restoring the peace of Germany as soon as possible, by our good offices, in order thereby to establish a confederacy sufficient for opposing France, in case that Court should afterwards discover any ambitious views. It was not now so much our business to prevent the lessening of the power of the House of Austria, as it was our business to bring about a speedy reconciliation among the Princes of Germany, and to take care that France should get as little by the Treaty of Peace, as she said she expected by the War. This, I say, ought to have been our chief concern, because the preservation of the balance of power was now no longer to depend upon the sole power of the House of Austria, but upon the joint power of a confederacy then to be formed; and till the Princes of Germany were reconciled among themselves, there was scarcely a possibility of forming such a confederacy. If we had made this our scheme, the Dutch would have joined heartily in it. The Germanic body would have joined in it; and the peace of Germany might have been restored, without putting this nation to any expence, or diverting us from the prosecution of our just and necessary war against Spain, in case our differences with that nation could not have been adjusted by the Treaty for restoring the peace of Germany. But our new Minister, as I have said, ran into an extreme quite opposite to that of the old. Our former Minister thought of nothing but negotiating when he ought to have thought of nothing but war; and this Minister thought of nothing but war, or at least the resemblance of it, when he ought to have thought of nothing but negotiation. A resolution was taken, and preparations were made, for sending a body of our troops to Flanders, even before

we

CHAP. V.
1743.

we had any hopes of the King of Prussia's deserting his alliance with France, and without our being called on to do so by any one power in Europe: I say, Sir, by any one power in Europe; for I defy our Ministers to shew, that even the Queen of Hungary desired any such thing before it was resolved on. I believe some of her Ministers were free enough to declare, that the money those troops cost would have done her much more service; and I am sure, we were so far from being called on by the Dutch to do so, that it was resolved on without their participitation, and the measures carried into execution, I believe, expresly contrary to their advice.

"This Resolution, Sir, was so far from having any influence on the King of Prussia, that he continued firm to his alliance with France, and fought the battle of Crotska, after he knew it was taken; and if he had continued firm in the same sentiments, I am very sure our troops neither would nor could have been of the least service to the Queen of Hungary; but the battle of Crotska fully convinced him, that the French designed chiefly to play one German Prince against another, in order to weaken both ; and perhaps he had before then discovered, that, according to the French scheme, his share of Silesia was not to be so considerable as he expected. These considerations, and not the eloquence or address of any of our Ministers, inclined him to come to an agreement with the Queen of Hungary; and as she was now convinced, that she could not depend upon our promises, she readily agreed to his terms, though his demands were now much more extravagant than they were at first; and what is worse, they were now unaccompanied with any one promise or consideration, except that of a neutrality; whereas his first demands were made palatable, by the tender of a large sum of money, and by the promise of his utmost assistance, not only in supporting the Pragmatic Sanction, but in raising her husband, the Duke of Lorrain, to the Imperial Throne. Nay, he even insinuated, that he would embrace the first opportunity to assist in procuring her House an equivalent for whatever part of Silesia she should yield up to him.

"This accommodation between the Queen of Hungary and the King of Prussia, and that which soon after followed between her and the Duke of Saxony, produced a very great alteration in the affairs of Europe; but as they promised nothing but a neutrality, and as the Dutch absolutely refused to join, either with the Queen of Hungary or us, us, in any offensive measures against France, it was still impossible for us to think of restoring the House of Austria to such power, as to render it a match for the power of France; therefore we ought still to have thought of nothing but negotiation, in order to restore the peace of Germany, by an accommodation between her and the Emperor; and the distresses which the Bavarian and French armies in Germany were drove to, furnished us with such an opportunity, as we ought by all means to have embraced, and to have insisted on the Queen of Hungary's doing the same, under the pain of being entirely deserted by us. A peace was offered both by the Emperor and the French, upon the moderate terms of *Uti Possidetis*, with respect to Germany; but, for what reason I cannot comprehend, we were so far from advising the Queen of Hungary to accept, that I believe we advised her not to accept of the terms offered.

" This, Sir, was a conduct in our Ministers so very extraordinary, so directly opposite to the interest of this nation, and the security of the balance of power, that I can suggest to myself no one reason for it, but their being resolved to put this nation to the expence of maintaining 16,000 Hanoverians; and this, I am afraid, was the true motive our new Ministers had at first for all the warlike measures they resolved on. Nothing will now satisfy us but a conquest of Alsace and Lorrain, in order to give them to the Queen of Hungary, as an equivalent for what she had lost; and this we resolved on, or at least pretended to resolve on, at a time when France and Prussia were in close conjunction; at a time when no one of the powers of Europe could assist us; at a time when none of them entertained any jealousy of the ambitious designs of France; and at a time when most of the Princes of Germany entertained such a jealousy of the power of the House of Austria, that we had great reason to apprehend the whole Germanic Body, at least the most considerable Princes of Germany, joining against us, in case we should meet with any success.

Sir, If our Ministers were really serious in this scheme, it was one of the most romantic that ever entered into the head of any English Don Quixote; and if they made this only a pretence for putting this nation to the expence of maintaining 16,000 Hanoverians, or of acquiring some new territory for the Electorate of Hanover, I am sure no British House of Commons ought to approve of their conduct.

CHAP. V.
1743.

"It is ridiculous to say, Sir, that we could not advise the Queen of Hungary to accept of the terms offered by the Emperor and France, when their troops were cooped up in the city of Prague, because those terms were offered with a view only to get their troops at liberty, and to take the first opportunity to attack her with more vigour. This, I say, is ridiculous, because if she had accepted of the terms offered, she might have had them guarantied by the Dutch, by the Germanic Body, and by all the powerful Princes of Germany, which would have brought all these powers into a confederacy with us against the Emperor and France, if they had afterwards attacked her in Germany; and all of them, but especially the Dutch and the King of Prussia, would have been ready to have joined us, if the French had attacked her in Flanders. It is equally ridiculous to say, that she could not accept of these terms, because they contained nothing for the security of her dominions in Italy; for suppose the war had continued in Italy, if the Queen of Hungary had been safe upon the side of Germany, she could have poured in such a number of troops into Italy, as would have been sufficient for opposing and defeating all the armies that both the French and Spaniards could have sent to, and maintained in that country, since we could, by our superior squadrons, have made it impossible for the French and Spaniards to maintain great armies in that country.

"No reason can therefore be assigned for the Queen of Hungary's refusing the terms offered her for restoring the tranquility of Germany, but this alone, that we had promised to assist her so effectually as to enable her to conquer a part of France, by way of equivalent for what she had lost in Germany and Italy; and such an assistance as is neither our interest, nor in our power to give, as the circumstances of Europe stand at present. I am really surprized how the Queen of Hungary came to trust a second time to our promises; for I may venture to prophecy, that she will find herself a second time deceived. We shall only put ourselves to a vast needless expence, as we did when she was first attacked by Prussia, and may give France a pretence for conquering Flanders, without raising any jealousy in the other powers of Europe, which otherwise she would not have done; or we may bring the Queen of Hungary a second time to the verge of destruction, and leave her there; for that we certainly shall do, as soon as Hanover comes to be a second time in danger. From all which I must conclude, that our

present

present scheme of politics is fundamentally wrong, and that the longer we continue to build upon such a foundation, the more dangerous it will be for us. The whole fabric must crush this unfortunate nation in its ruins.

"But now, Sir, let us see how we have prosecuted this scheme, bad, as it is, during the last campaign, As this nation must bear the chief part of the expence, it was certainly our business to prosecute the war with all possible vigour, to come to action as soon as possible, and to push every advantage to the utmost. Since we soon found we could not attack the French upon the side of Flanders, why were our troops so long marching into Germany? Or indeed I should ask, why our army was not first assembled in that country? Why did they continue so long inactive upon the Maine? If our army was not numerous enough for attacking the French, why were the Hessians left behind for some time in Flanders? Why did we not send over 20,000 of those regular troops that were lying idle here at home? How to answer all these questions, I cannot tell; but it is certain, we never thought of attacking the French army in our neighbourhood, and I believe expected very little to be attacked. Nay, I doubt much if any action would have happened during the whole campaign, if the French had not, by the misconduct of some one or other of our generals, caught our army in a hose-net, from which it could not have escaped, if the French generals had all observed the directions of their Commander in Chief, and had thought only of guarding and fortifying themselves in the defiles, and marching up to attack our troops. Thank God, the courage of some of the French generals got the better of their discretion, as well as their military discipline. This made them attack, instead of waiting to be attacked; and by the bravery of the English foot, and the cowardice of their own, they met with a severe repulse, which put their whole army into confusion, and obliged it to retire with precipitation over the Maine, by which our army escaped the snare they had been led into, and got free liberty to pursue their retreat to Hanau.

"This, Sir, was a signal advantage; but did we push this advantage? Did we pursue the enemy in their precipitate retreat over a great river, where many of them must have been lost, had they been closely pursued? Did we endeavour to take the least advantage of the confusion

CHAP. V.
1743.

they had been thrown into by their unexpected repulse? No, Sir, the ardour of our British troops was restrained by the cowardice of the Hanoverian; and instead of pursuing the enemy, we ourselves ran away in the night-time, and in such haste, that we left all our wounded to the mercy and care of the enemy, who had likewise the honour of burying our dead as well as their own. This action may therefore, on our side, be called a lucky escape; but I shall never give my consent to honour it with the name of a victory.

" After this escape, Sir, our army was joined by a very large reinforcement. Did this revive our courage, or give us any better stomach for fighting? Not a bit, Sir. Though the French continued for some time upon the German side of the Rhine, we never offered to attack them, or to give them the least disturbance. At last, upon Prince Charles's approach with the Austrian army under his command, the French not only re-passed the Rhine, but retired quite out of Germany; and as the Austrian army and the allied army might then have joined and might both have passed the Rhine without opposition at Mentz, or almost any where in the Palatinate, it was expected that both armies would have marched together into Lorrain, or in search of the French army, in order to force them to a battle; but instead of this, Prince Charles marched up the German side of the Rhine—to do what? To pass that great river, in the sight of a French army equal in number to his own, which, without some extraordinary neglect in the French, was impracticable; and so it was found by experience. So that the whole campaign, upon that side, was consumed in often attempting, what as often appeared to be impracticable.

" On the other side, I mean that of the allied army, was there any thing done of consequence? I know of nothing but that of sending a party of Hussars into Lorrain with a manifesto. The army, indeed, passed the Rhine at Mentz, and marched up to the French lines upon the frontier of Alsace, but never offered to pass those lines until the French had abandoned them, I believe with a design to draw our army into some snare; for upon the French returning again towards those lines, we retired with much greater haste than we had advanced, though the Dutch auxiliaries were then come up, and pretended at least to be ready to join our army; though, as I have heard, they found a pretence for never coming into the line; and I doubt much if they would have

marched

marched with us to attack the French army in their own territories, or
\n eftany of their fortified places; for I muſt obſerve, that the French lines upon the Queick were not, as to ſome part of them, within the territories of France. But ſuppoſe this Dutch detachment had been ready to march with us to attack the French in their own territories, or to inveſt ſome of their fortified places, it could have given me no joy; and therefore I cannot join in any congratulations upon that event; for a ſmall detachment of Dutch troops can never enable us to execute the vaſt ſcheme we have undertaken. The whole force of that Republic would not be ſufficient for that purpoſe; becauſe we ſhould have the majority of the Empire againſt us; and therefore if the Dutch had joined *totis viribus* in our ſcheme, inſtead of congratulating, I ſhould have bemoaned their running mad by our example, and at our inſti-

" Having now briefly examined our conduct during the laſt campaign, from the few remarks I have made, I believe, Sir, it will appear, that ſuppoſing our ſcheme to be in itſelf poſſible or practicable, we have no reaſon to hope for ſucceſs, if it be not proſecuted with more vigour and better conduct than it was during laſt campaign. While we continue in the proſecution of this ſcheme, the Hanoverians indeed will be conſiderable gainers, let whoever will be the loſer, becauſe they will draw 4 or 500,000l. yearly from this nation, over and above what they have annually drawn from us ever ſince they have had the good fortune to be united with us under the ſame Sovereign. But we ought to conſider, even the Hanoverians ought to conſider, that this nation is not now in a condition to carry on an expenſive war, for ten or twelve years, as it did in the reign of Queen Anne. We may fund it out for a year, two or three, but we are now ſo much in debt, that if we go on for a few years, adding millions to it every year, our credit will certainly at laſt, I am afraid, ſooner than ſome amongſt us imagine, be undone; and if this misfortune ſhould happen to us, neither Hanover nor any other foreign ſtate would be able to draw a ſhilling more from us. A ſtop to our public credit would put an end to our paper currency. An univerſal bankruptcy would enſue, and all the little ready money left amongſt us would, by the happy poſſeſſors, be locked up in iron cheſts, or hid in bye-corners. It would then be impoſſible to raiſe our taxes, and conſequently impoſſible to maintain either

fleets

CHAP. V.
1743.

ficets or armies. Our troops abroad would be obliged to enter into the service of any prince that could maintain them, and our troops at home would be obliged to live upon free quarter. Nay, this they could not do long; for the farmer would neither fow nor reap, if he found his produce taken from him by the ftarving foldier. In thefe circumftances I muft defire the real friends of our prefent happy eftablifhment to confider what might be the confequence of the Pretender's being landed amongft us at the head of a French army. Would not he be looked upon by moft as a third Saviour? Would not the majority of the people join with him, in order to refcue the nation from thofe that had brought it into fuch confufion?

" This danger, Sir, is I hope one of thofe that may be called imaginary; but I am fure it is far from being fo imaginary, as that we have been frightened with in this debate, of all the powers of the Continent of Europe being brought under fuch a flavifh dependence upon France as to join with that nation in conquering this ifland, or in bringing it under the fame flavifh dependence with themfelves.

" I had almoft forgot, Sir, to take notice of the famous Treaty of Worms; and I wifh after ages may never take notice of it. I wifh it could be erafed out of our annals, as well as records, fo as never to be hereafter mentioned! for that treaty with its appendix, the convention that followed it, is one of the moft deftructive, unjuft and ridiculous treaties we ever made. By that treaty we have taken upon ourfelves a burthen which I think impoffible for us to fupport; and we have engaged in fuch an act of injuftice towards Genoa, as muft alarm all Europe, and give the French a fignal advantage; for from thence all the princes of Europe will fee what regard we have to juftice, where we think we have power; and therefore moft of them will probably join with France in curtailing our power, or at leaft in preventing its increafe. The alliance of Sardinia and his affiftance may, I admit, be of great ufe to us in defeating the defigns of the Spaniards in Italy; but gold itfelf may be bought too dear; and I am afraid we fhall find the purchafe we have made, to be at leaft but a precarious bargain, efpecially if Sardinia fhould be attacked by France as well as Spain, which will be the certain confequence of the fcheme of politics we are now purfuing. For thefe reafons, Sir, I hope no Gentleman, nor even any

Minifter,

Minister, will expect that I should declare my satssfaction at that treaty's being concluded.

" It is very surprising, Sir, to hear Gentlemen talk of the great advantage of unanimity in our proceedings, when at the same time they are doing all they can to prevent unanimity. If the Hon. Gentleman had intended, that what he proposed should be unanimously agreed to, he would have returned to the antient custom of Parliament, which some of his new friends have so often upon former occasions recommended. It is a new doctrine, to pretend that we ought, in our Address, to return some sort of answer to every thing mentioned in his Majesty's Speech. It is a doctrine that has prevailed only since our Parliaments began to look more like a French than an English Parliament; and now we pretend to be such enemies to France, I suspected we should have laid aside this doctrine. The very method of proceeding in Parliament must shew this doctrine to be false. His Majesty's Speech is not now so much as under our consideration, but upon a previous order for that purpose; therefore we cannot now properly take notice of its contents, any further than to determine whether we ought to return thanks for it or no; for even this is what we may refuse, without being guilty of any breach of duty to our Sovereign; but this I believe no Gentleman would have thought of, if the Hon. Gentleman who made this motion had not tacked to it a long and fulsome panegyric upon the conduct of our Ministers. I am convinced no Gentleman would have objected against our expressing our duty to our Sovereign, and our zeal for his service, in the most strong and affectionate terms; nor would any Gentleman have refused to congratulate his Majesty upon any fortunate event happening to the Royal Family; and the Hon. Gentleman would have desired no more, if he had intended that his motion should be unanimously agreed to; but as Ministers are generally the authors and drawers up of the motion, they always have a greater regard for themselves than for the service of their Sovereign; and this is the true reason why such motions seldom meet with an unanimous approbation.

" As for the danger, Sir, of our returning, or not returning to our national custom upon this occasion, I think it lies wholly upon the side of our not returning. I have shewn, that the measures we are now pursuing are fundamentally wrong, and that the longer we do pursue them,

CHAP. V.
1743.

CHAP. V.
1744.

them, the heavier our misfortunes will be. Unless some signal Providence intervenes, Experience, I am sure, will confirm what I say. By the immediate intervention of Providence, we may, it is true, succeed in the most improbable schemes; but Providence seems to be against us. The sooner therefore we repent, the better it will be for us; and unless repentance begins in this House, I shall expect it no where else, 'till dire experience has convinced us of our being in the wrong.

"For this reason I hope, and I wish that we may now begin, to put a stop to the farther prosecution of these destructive and dangerous measures, by refusing them our approbation. If we put a negative upon this question, it may awaken our Ministers out of their deceitful dream. If we agree to it, they will dream on, till they have dreamed Europe and their country, as well as themselves, into perdition. If they stop now, the nation may recover; but if by such a flattering Address we encourage them to go on, it may soon become impossible, for them to retreat; and therefore, for the sake of Europe, as well as my country, I shall most heartily join in putting a negative upon this question.

The Address was agreed to.

1744.

On the 12th of January 1744, the Report from the Committee of Supply being made to the House, viz. "That 634,344 l. "be granted, for defraying the charge of 21,358 effective men, "to be employed in Flanders in 1744;" Mr. PITT spoke against agreeing with the Committee, in this Resolution, to the following purport:

Speech against sending Troops to Flanders.

"As it is not the custom, at this time, to lay before Parliament, any information of our public measures, which, as well as the motives for adopting them, are too great secrets to be communicated to this House, I protest I know nothing of them; nor can I, from any public appearances, judge of them. No man can, who has not an intimate correspondence with some of our Ministers of the Closet; which, I thank God! I have not; and therefore, if I mistake or misstate our late or present measures, I hope the Gentlemen, who think themselves happy in having such a correspondence, will excuse me.

"There are two points, Sir, which ought to be considered, and fully discussed, before we agree to the Hon. Gentleman's motion; and that is, the end of our giving affiftance to the Queen of Hungary, and the manner in which we are to give that affiftance. If the French ftill infift upon taking a great part of the Queen of Hungary's dominions in Germany from her, and giving them to the Emperor, in order to induce him to agree to their taking Flanders, or fomething elfe to themfelves, I think we ought to endeavour, *totis viribus*, to prevent fuch a fcheme's taking effect; becaufe I am, and always have been of opinion, that the the Monarchy of France is already more powerful than is confiftent with the fafety of Europe. I thought fo even before they made the acquifition of Lorrain, which they were permitted to do, by a moft criminal connivance of our Minifters, at a time when we had a better opportunity than, I am afraid, we fhall ever have again, for reducing the power of the Houfe of Bourbon. If this, therefore, were the end of our giving affiftance to the Queen of Hungary, I fhould approve of our giving her our utmoft affiftance; yet, even in this cafe, I fhould not agree to the Hon. Gentleman's motion, becaufe I do not approve of the manner he propofes for giving her our affiftance.

" But, Sir, if the French have entirely departed from this fcheme; if they departed from it as foon as they found themfelves abandoned by Pruffia and Saxony; if they were then willing, as I believe they were, to reftore the peace of Germany, upon the fingle condition of the Queen of Hungary's reftoring to the Emperor his hereditary dominions, I think, we ought not to have encouraged her, by our affiftance, to have continued the war in Germany, and much lefs ought we to encourage her, which I am afraid we do, to think of procuring, by our affiftance, an equivalent from France, for what fhe has yielded to Pruffia and Saxony in Germany. If this be the end of our affifting her, I difapprove of the end as much as I do of the manner; and I difapprove of it, not becaufe I fhould not be glad to fee the power of France reduced, but becaufe I think the prefent a very improper time, either for the Queen of Hungary or us to think of it. There is a certain fpirit which prevails, and by which courts as well as private men are governed. This fpirit a wife and confiderate Minifter will always have great regard to, and will take his meafures accordingly; for the World is not to be directed by every whim that may enter into the head of an ignorant, though enterprifing Minifter. The ambitious fchemes of the late

CHAP. V.
1743.

late King of France had raised a spirit of jealousy against that Monarchy, in almost every Court of Europe, which produced several confederacies against it, and one at last which brought it to the brink of perdition. Since his death, the Court of France, being made sensible by experience of the danger of raising such a spirit, have guarded against doing so as much as possible, so that there is now no such spirit in any Court in Europe; but, on the contrary, there is a spirit of jealousy among all the Princes of Germany against the power of the House of Austria; therefore no one Court in Europe will join with us and the Queen of Hungary, in this project against France.

" When I say so, Sir, I mean humanly speaking; for the race, I know, is not to the swift, nor the battle to the strong. Suppose then that Providence should work miracles in our favour, and give us unexpected success against France in the execution of this design. Suppose their armies, like that of the Midianites, should set every man his sword against his fellow, and their walls, like those of Jericho, fall down flat before us; yet can we suppose, that the Princes of Germany, who are so jealous of the power of the House of Austria, especially such of them as have lately got hold of some part of the Austrian territories; I say, can we suppose, that those Princes would sit still and see the power of the House of Austria vastly increased, and the Monarchy of France very much reduced, when it is so evident, that the preservation of the possessions they have so lately acquired, and perhaps their future independency, must depend chiefly upon the friendship and assistance of France? It is, I think, almost certain, that in case of our success, they would all unite together for putting a stop to it

" Thus, Sir, if the procuring the Queen of Hungary an equivalent from France, be the end or design of our maintaining an army in Flanders, it is so evidently impracticable, that I am convinced it cannot be the true end. It must be a pretence made use of for covering some hidden design, which our Ministers dare not own, and which would certainly cost some of them their heads, if it should be proved upon them. I mean that of lavishing the blood and treasure of England, for the sake of getting an opportunity to maintain 16,000 Hanoverians, or for the sake of getting some little territories added to the dominions of that Electorate. And if the end be to defeat the French in their scheme of taking a great part of the Queen of Hungary's dominions

from

from her, and giving them to the Emperor, that he may consent to some additions being made to their Monarchy, we ought to be well convinced, that there is still some such scheme *in petto*, before we agree to load our country with so great an expence; because from the public accounts we have great reason to believe, that, if ever the French had such a scheme, they have now given it up; and because we have no reason to believe, that the French would embark in a scheme which must be attended with great danger, difficulty and expence to them, when unassisted by any of the Princes of Germany. The only hopes they can now have of being able to execute such a scheme, must arise from our encouraging the Queen of Hungary to be immoderate in her demands, which may raise the jealousy of the German Princes to such a height, as may force them to join again in an alliance with France, for reducing her power, and putting an end to her ambitious views.

" In all I have yet said, Sir, I have not mentioned Italy, because I believe no one is so ignorant as to suppose, that in order to assist the Queen of Hungary to preserve her dominions in Italy, the best method is to form an army in Flanders, or to attempt to make an impression upon France on that side, where every one knows their Monarchy is the best guarded, and the least susceptible of an impression; therefore, no one surely will pretend, that this is the end of our forming or maintaining an army in Flanders.

" I shall now, Sir, consider the manner in which we ought to assist the Queen of Hungary; and let the end be what it will, I am very sure the manner proposed is in every respect wrong. I must lay it down, and I shall always consider it as a certain maxim, that we ought never to think of assisting any of our allies upon the Continent with a great number of troops. If we send any of our troops to their assistance, it ought always to be, rather with a view to give our Gentlemen an opportunity to improve themselves in the military art, than with a view to assist our allies. They have no occasion for our men, and the Queen of Hungary less than any other. She has men, and brave men too, in abundance. She only wants money to arm and support them. Therefore, the only manner in which we ought to think of supporting her, or any other of our allies upon the Continent, is with our money and our navy. And my reason for laying this down as a maxim is, not only because the sea is our natural element, but because it is dan-

CHAP. V.
1743.

gerous to our liberties, as well as destructive to our trade, to encourag great numbers of our people to make the profeſſion of arms their trade, ſo as to depend upon that alone for their livelihood. A farmer, a day-labourer, a cobler, may be a good ſoldier, if you take care to have him properly diſciplined, and always will be ready to defend his country, in caſe of an attack; but as he has another way of living, he may be a good ſubject; whereas a man who has no other way of living, can never be a good ſubject, eſpecially in a free country; and for this reaſon we ought to have as few of them as poſſible, either abroad or at home. At leaſt, they ought never to be kept long in the ſervice; for after a long diſuſe, there are very few of them can afterwards turn to any induſtrious employment for their ſupport.

" Another reaſon is, Sir, becauſe cuſtom has made our troops more expenſive than thoſe of any other country; and therefore our money will always be of more ſervice to our allies, becauſe it will enable them to raiſe and maintain a greater number of troops than we can furniſh them with for the ſame ſum of money. This, Sir, I ſhall prove by figures, which are ſuch ſtrange obſtinate things, that they will not twiſt and wind at the pleaſure of a Miniſter, or any of his orators. By the motion now made to us, our own troops in Flanders are to coſt us for next year, 634,344l. and, I ſuppoſe, the 16,000 Hanoverians will coſt us near 400,000l. To theſe two ſums I ſhall add 200,000l. for waggon money, dry and green forage, douceurs, and the like; for I believe we ſhall find, that this article for laſt year amounts to a much larger ſum. Theſe three articles make 1,234,344l. I ſhall call it the even ſum of 1,200,000l. which we muſt pay next year, for maintaining an army of 37,000 men, one third part of which I ſhall ſuppoſe to be horſe or dragoons. Now, if we had ſent this ſum to the Queen of Hungary, let us ſee what an additional number of men ſhe might have maintained with it. By ſeveral treaties, and particularly by the acceſſion of the States-General to the Vienna Treaty of 1731, the charge of 1000 foot is fixed at 10,000 guilders per month: which in ſterling money, at the rate of 10 guilders 16 ſtivers per pound ſterling, is 926l. and the charge of 1000 horſe is fixed at 30,000 guilders for the ſame time, which is 2778l. ſo that 1,200,000l. would have maintained near 108,000 foot for the Queen of Hungary, or near 36,000 horſe; or it would have maintained an army for her of 54,000 foot, and
18,000

18,000 horse for the ensuing year; and I must ask even our Ministers, if they do not think, that an additional army of 72,000 men, to be employed wherever she pleased, would have been of more service to her and the common cause, as they are pleased to call it, than our 37,000 men in Flanders? For though I will not allow that any of her troops are better than the British, yet I may take upon me to say, that the worst of her troops are better than the Hanoverians were ever yet supposed to be.

"But now, Sir, suppose we could think it of advantage to the common cause to assist the Queen of Hungary with troops instead of money, the very worst place we could think of sending these troops to, or employing them in, is Flanders. If we had formed no army there, the French would have formed no army there, nor would they have attacked any place there, for fear of provoking the Dutch to declare against them. Whereas, if we form an army next summer in Flanders, though we do not begin to act offensively with that army, as I firmly believe we do not intend to do, it may furnish the French with an excuse for attacking the Queen of Hungary in that country, and that excuse may be admitted by the Dutch, who seem at present to have no sort of jealousy of France; and for that, as well as several other reasons, they seem resolved not to enter into any of our romantic schemes. If we must assist the Queen of Hungary with troops, why did they not stay and take winter quarters in Germany, or upon the Rhine, by which we might have secured a passage for Prince Charles in the Spring? If it be alledged, that the Princes and circles of the Empire would not admit of our troops taking winter quarters within the Empire, this of itself alone was a good reason for our calling home our troops, dismissing our mercenaries, and resolving to assist the Queen of Hungary for the future, as we ought to have done from the beginning, solely with our money, and our squadron in the Mediterranean.

"In short, Sir, as I could at first see no reason for sending our troops to Flanders, unless it was to furnish our Ministers with a pretence for loading us with the maintenance of 16,000 Hanoverians, I can now see no reason for our keeping them there, unless it be to furnish a pretence for continuing that load upon us; and as I think our keeping them there may be attended with infinite danger to the cause of the Queen of Hungary, I cannot therefore agree with the report of the Committee."

CHAP. V. The Report was agreed to.

1744.
Explanation.

Some apology or explanation is necessary, for inserting the preceding speeches, under the name of Mr. PITT.—The Reader has undoubtedly observed, that the style in which they are written, does not seem to preserve Mr. PITT's language, or phrase; but they have been printed in the Parliamentary Debates of this period; and it has not come to the Editor's knowledge that there is any better, or even any other account of them. They were written by a Mr. *Gordon*, a Minister of the Church of Scotland, originally for the London Magazine—when Dr. *Samuel Johnson* ceased to write the speeches for the Gentleman's Magazine; or rather when *Cave*, the printer of that miscellany, was punished for printing them;—*Gordon* continued some sketches of them, with less accuracy, and in *inferior* language, but with more attention to the argument, until the death of FREDERICK Prince of Wales, in 1751. His practice was to go to the Coffee-houses contiguous to Westminster Hall; where he frequently heard the Members conversing with each other, upon what had passed in the House; and sometimes he gained admission into the gallery; and as he was known to a few of the gentlemen, two or three of them, upon particular occasions, furnished him with some information.

The vigorous opposition which Mr. PITT had made in Parliament, to the measures pursued for the defence of Hanover, raised him very high in the esteem of the English nation. He had for some years been admired as an orator,—he was now revered as a patriot. The spirit and energy which distinguished his Parliamentary conduct, evinced that he was actuated by principle, not by an illiberal passion, to display the superiority

of

of his talents; that his oppofition was the refult of conviction, not of pique; that it was not founded in a perſonal confideration of the men who held the offices of government, but in an indignant abhorrence of the meafures, which, he faid, infulated Great Britain, from a participation of the advantages her money was voted to procure, and gave her a right to demand.

CHAP. V.
1744.

Amongſt the many perfons of elevated rank, who honoured this conduct of Mr. PITT with the warmeſt approbation, was the late SARAH Duchefs Dowager of Marlborough. This lady, by a codicil to her will, dated on the 11th of Auguſt 1744, gave to Mr. PITT a legacy, in thefe words:*

Duchefs of Marlborough's Legacy.

" I alfo give to WILLIAM PITT, of the parifh of St. James, within the liberty of Weſtminſter, Efq. the fum of Ten Thoufand Pounds, upon account of his merit, in the noble defence he has made for the fupport of the laws of England, and to prevent the ruin of his country."

* She died in October following, and the money was paid.

CHAP.

CHAP. VI.

State of the Ministry—Lord Carlisle disappointed of the Privy Seal—Lord Cobham joins the Pelhams—Lord Granville opposed in Council, and resigns—The Broad Bottom Ministry appointed—Mr. Pitt's reply to Sir Francis Dashwood, on the Address—Mr. Pitt's reply to Mr. Hume Campbell, on the Noblemens' new raised Regiments.

FROM the time that Sir ROBERT WALPOLE had been compelled to relinquish the Government, the British Councils had not been influenced by the principles of any system, plan, or regulation. It was a government of expedients, proceeding fortuitously; too cowardly to act upon a bold measure, and too ignorant to frame a wise one. The members of the Cabinet being composed of Deserters from all parties, became a faction, without confidence in each other. Lord BATH, who had been their creator, was the only cement which held them together.

It has been observed, that Lord CARTERET, who had been made Secretary of State by Lord BATH, had gained an ascendancy in the closet, by favouring the predilections of the King, respecting Hanover. This ascendancy alarmed the other members of the Cabinet. They beheld, with jealousy, Lord CARTERET's encreasing influence with the King. There was however, a manly firmness and constitutional dignity in Lord CARTERET's conduct. His German measures were always communicated to the British Cabinet in the *first* instance; nor was there any attempt ever made to carry them into execution, until they had been proposed to, and adopted by, his colleagues in office. But had the King concerted them *secretly*, and not communicated

municated the information to his British Ministers, until it was necessary to involve his British dominions in the expence, and when it was too late to make any alteration; it is more than probable, that there was not a gentleman, either in out of Court, at that time, who, if he had been Secretary of State, would not, in such a case, have laid the Seals at his Majesty's feet.

It has long been seen clearly, and said by wise and honest men, that the foundation of all other factions, is the faction at Court. The Court faction, which had been lately formed by Lord BATH, gave rise to several factions. During these disputes, Lord COBHAM and his friends, kept aloof.

The unsettled state of the Ministry was made apparent to the whole kingdom, by the contention amongst them for the Privy Seal, which Lord GOWER had resigned.—Lord BATH, who interfered upon this occasion, and affected to act by the authority of the King, sent for Lord CARLISLE, and assured his Lordship he should be appointed Privy Seal; and Lord CARLISLE thought himself so certain of the place, that he informed his friends the appointment was made. The PELHAMS resisted this scheme of Lord BATH's with all their might; and the Duke of NEWCASTLE went to the King, and demanded the place for Lord CHOLMONDELEY. Those who knew the King, said his Majesty was taken by surprise, and consented with reluctance. Several other alterations were made, by which the power of Lord BATH's friends was decreased, and that of the PELHAMS advanced. This arrangement, however, was but of short duration. The two parties continued to struggle for superiority.

A war with France was the favourite measure of the King at this time, on account of his German dominions; which were

CHAP. VI. exposed to the enmity of France, by his alliance with the Court
1744. of Vienna; and Lord CARTERET, now Earl GRANVILLE, by
the death of his mother, entering fully into his Majesty's views
respecting this war, became a favourite in the closet.

The circumstance of a favourite in that situation, was a matter of great alarm to those, who could not endure a rival. Sixteen thousand Hanoverian troops were last year taken into British pay. This measure was extremely obnoxious to the nation. Lord GRANVILLE avowed the measure, and being secure, as he thought of the King's support, he treated his colleagues with some hauteur, in a debate in Council upon it.

Lord Cobham joins the Pelhams.

The PELHAMS were now convinced, that Lord GRANVILLE was both their rival and enemy; and therefore they resolved, to remove, if possible, so dangerous a competitor. In order to carry this point, their first step was to strengthen their party. They made overtures to Lord COBHAM, who, at the request of the Duke of NEWCASTLE, met his Grace at Lord HARRINGTON's. At this meeting, the accession of Lord COBHAM was settled. The principal terms were, that the expence of the Hanoverian measures should be diminished, and that his Lordship's friends should be included in the next change of the Ministry. With respect to his Lordship, and the GRENVILLE's, the matter was easy—all the difficulty was concerning Mr. PITT. The King had entertained a violent prejudice against him, on account of his opposition to German measures. This prejudice, Lord GRANVILLE was supposed to have encreased, by stating in the closet, more than once, Mr. PITT's Parliamentary conduct, in the most unfavourable light. The Duke of NEWCASTLE promised to remove this prejudice from the King's mind,

and

and to accommodate Mr. PITT at a future period, which, he affured Lord COBHAM, fhould not be far diftant.

The junction of Lord COBHAM with the PELHAMS, influenced feveral others to follow his example; fuch as Sir JOHN HIND COTTON, Mr. WALLER, Mr. DODDINGTON, and many more; fo that this junction had the effect of a coalition of parties. Indeed it muft be confeffed, that all parties, except Lord BATH's, joined in oppofing Lord GRANVILLE.

This union was negociated, and completed, during the fummer and autumn of 1744. The firft effects of it were felt by Lord GRANVILLE, in a Council, called on the affairs of Hanover, previous to the meeting of Parliament; when his Lordfhip propofed to *continue* the fixteen thoufand Hanoverian troops in Britifh pay, for the year 1745. This propofition was ftrongly oppofed, and the Council divided upon it. Four and himfelf were for it, and eleven againft it. Eight thoufand only was the number agreed upon.

Upon this defeat, Lord GRANVILLE took his refolution to refign; and accordingly waited on his Majefty on Tuefday, the fourteenth of November, 1744, and refigned the Seals.

A new Adminiftration was immediately formed, or perhaps, had been already formed; which, from the circumftance of its having arifen out of the coalition of parties, already mentioned, was commonly denominated *the Broad Bottom*. [The particulars of this change, the reader will find in the General Lift of Changes, at the end of the work.]

Parliament met in November 1744, and exhibited fuch a fcene of unanimity, as had not been feen fince the King's acceffion. The feffion clofed on the fecond of May 1745; immediately after

Chap. VI.
1745.

after which, the King went to Hanover; having first added Lord Cobham to the list of Lords Justices, for the administration of Government during his absence, created him Field Marshall, and given him a regiment of horse (late *Neville's*.)

In October 1745, Parliament met, on account of the Scots rebellion. There was a short debate upon the Address, in answer to the King's Speech, occasioned by an amendment offered by Sir Francis Dashwood, afterwards Lord Le Despencer, expressing, " That for the firmer establishment of his Majesty's " throne on the solid basis of his people's affections, it shall be " our speedy care to frame such bills, as may effectually secure to " his Majesty's subjects the perpetual enjoyment of their un- " doubted right, to be freely and fairly represented in Parlia- " ments, frequently chosen, and exempted from undue influence " of every kind."

The motion was seconded by Sir John Phillips.

Mr. Pitt's reply.

M.S.

Mr. Pitt opposed the motion.—The amendment, he said, being offered at a time so extremely improper as the present, was fraught with a dangerous tendency. There was only one motive to which this motion could be ascribed; and it was, to make Ministers odious in the eyes of the people, if they put a negative upon it. But the contrary, however, he would venture to say would be the fact; for, although motions of this kind are always popular, yet in this hour of distress and difficulty, when rebellion raged in the kingdom, and an invasion from France was expected, when the people were seriously intent upon measures of the highest consequence, they could not think favourably of those, who attempted to draw off their attention from subjects of alarm, to points of speculation. In such circumstances shall we, he asked, employ ourselves in contriving bills to guard our liberties from corruption, when we are in danger of losing them, and every thing else that is dear to us, by the force of arms? Would not this be like a man's amusing himself with making regulations to prevent his servants cheating him, at the very time that thieves were breaking into his house?

But

But why are we to introduce this subject into the address?—No county, no city, nor corporation have requested their representatives to bring in any such bills,—the people are every where engaged in making subscriptions, and forming associations, for defending their Sovereign, and themselves, against those, who have traiterously conspired to rob him of his crown, and them of their liberties. Do gentlemen wish to give a turn to the spirit of the people, to create a contention about the Constitution, that the kingdom may fall an easy prey to the enemy? —" If, Sir, I did not know the Honourable Gentlemen, who made and seconded this motion, I should really suspect their having some such design; and however much I may, from my own personal knowledge, be convinced, that they have no such design, they may be assured, that if they do not withdraw their motion, the suspicion will be strong against them, amongst those persons who have not the honour of their acquaintance."

The motion was negatived, without a division.

On the fourth of November, 1745, the Hon. ALEX. HUME CAMPBELL,* brother to Lord MARCHMONT, moved, That an address be presented to his Majesty, most humbly to beseech his Majesty, that the officers in the new † regiments, now raising, or already raised, may not be allowed any rank, after those regiments are broke.

* This gentleman had been brought into Parliament on purpose to oppose Mr. PITT. Some time after, he left his friends, and was appointed Solicitor General to the Prince of Wales; but on the second of February, 1746, he was dismissed from that Prince's service.

† Several Noblemen having raised regiments on account of the Scots Rebellion, for the service of his Majesty, these new regiments were:

HORSE.
Duke of Montagu's,
Duke of Kingston's.
FOOT.
Duke of Bolton's,
Duke of Bedford's,
Duke of Montagu's,
Duke of Ancaster's,
Marquis of Granby's,
Earl of Cholmondeley's,
Earl of Halifax's,
Lord Viscount Falmouth's,
Lord Viscount Harcourt's,
Lord Gower's,
Lord Herbert's,
Lord Edgecumbe's.

Mr.

CHAP. VI.   Mr. PITT reprobated this motion with warmth and indignation. He said, that a commission, and the rank implied by it, were inseparable. A commission contained a power conferred by the King, by which the person who received it, became subordinate to some, and superior to others. The motion, he contended, was irrational, contrary to common sense, and impracticable, as well as impolitic; by tending to discourage those noble persons, who were exerting their utmost influence in the service of their country. The officers who are to be employed under them, are, by this motion, he said, to be stigmatized, as unworthy of rank. These gentlemen are not driven into the army by necessity; but are offering themselves to serve their country in the day of distress, from motives of the warmest zeal. And shall we disgrace these men? Shall we check their noble and generous ardour in the hour of danger? Those who desire the House to agree to this motion, cannot be serious, or if serious, cannot be aware of the obvious construction of their conduct.— Is this the time, he asked, that loyalty ought to be stigmatized, instead of being rewarded with honour? Are gentlemen endeavouring to obtain that object by oblique paths, from which they are restrained in the direct way? The motion at best is suspicious; it is paradoxical.

The argument in support of the motion, is an insult upon the whole army; for it is this, That the army will behold with discontent this new promotion of officers. The very assertion is an impeachment of the allegiance of the army. It would be a reproach to the dignity of this House, if our deliberations here, were to be influenced by the views of any class of men. The right of deciding what measures are most conducive to the public interest and security, belongs not to the army, but to this House.

Those who advise us to deny rank to the new officers, advise us to deny what the King has already granted, and what he had an undoubted right to grant;—they advise us to vacate his commissions, and to break his promises;—they advise us to weaken him, at the time that he wants the most assistance; and to shew to our enemies, that he is at variance with his Parliament.

The motion was negatived.

CHAP.

CHAP. VII.

Errors of History—Lord Bath at Court—His overtures to Lord Cobham—Duke of Newcastle asks the place of Secretary at War for Mr. Pitt, and is refused—Ministry resign—Lord Granville appointed Secretary of State—Lord Granville resigns, and the late Ministry restored—Mr. Pitt made Vice Treasurer of Ireland, and afterwards Paymaster—Makes no private use of the public money in his hands—Refuses to accept the perquisite of office on the Sardinian Subsidy.

THE versatility of Courts has been the popular theme of writers, during several of the latter centuries. It would have been more to the honour of history, had the causes of such mutability been explained. But it has been the misfortune of the public, that few of the modern historians have been in situations in which they might obtain true information. This has more than once occasioned Lord MANSFIELD, and other great men to say, that nothing is so false as *history*. *Tindall, Smollet, Goldsmith,* and a long train of others, have stated, that about this time a very extraordinary change took place in the British Ministry. That Lord GRANVILLE was made Minister, and the PELHAMS resigned;—that in a few days afterwards Lord GRANVILLE resigned, and the PELHAMS were restored. The London Gazette furnishes them with the *appointments* and the *dates*, which are the only facts to be depended upon: all the rest being of their own invention. Dr. *Newton* says, that Lord BATH wrote an account of these transactions, at the desire of GEORGE the SECOND; but that on the death of his son, Lord PULTENEY, in the reign of GEORGE the THIRD, his Lordship burned it—

File

CHAP. VII.
1745.

Fide indignus. If it had been written at the defire of the King, it is more than probable, that it would have been publifhed.—However, if it was not more true, than the account of the great change in the Miniftry in the year 1742, written by the fame hand, and given us by Dr. *Newton*, the lofs is not important nor worthy of regret.

Upon the King's return from Hanover, Lord COBHAM claimed of the Duke of NEWCASTLE, the performance of his promife, refpecting Mr. PITT. The Duke wifhed to poftpone the matter; but Lord COBHAM infifted upon it. At length his Grace undertook to lay the affair before the King. A more unfavourable period could not have been chofen. The King was at this time diffatisfied with the conduct of his Minifters. The difmiffion of the eight thoufand Hanoverians, he imputed to their perfonal diflike of Lord GRANVILLE; and the rapid progrefs of the Rebellion, he imputed to their negligence, while he was abroad. He fufpected that the PELHAMS were averfe to war, which was true; and he had conceived an idea, probably from Lord GRANVILLE, when Minifter, that war at this time, was his only refource. It was an omiffion in the *Broad Bottom* treaty, that Lord BATH had not been profcribed; for foon after the King's return from the continent, his Lordfhip appeared at Court feveral times—and was each time honoured with an audience. His own friends have faid, that in thefe audiences, he did not fail to exaggerate the caufes of the King's difguft with his fervants, and to flatter the abilities of his friend, Lord GRANVILLE, and to warmly reprefent his zeal for his Majefty. The French war was Lord GRANVILLE's favourite meafure. It was alfo the King's. On this great point, as well as in fome leffer

Lord Bath at Court.

ones,

ones, there was a co-incidence of sentiment, which naturally led to a partiality in favour of Lord GRANVILLE.

CHAP. VII.
1745.

During the time that Lord BATH was thus improving his interest in the closet, he made overtures to Lord COBHAM, with a view to form a new Administration; in which he offered to include Mr. PITT. But Lord COBHAM returned an answer importing, that Lord BATH had deceived him in 1742, and he should not dupe him in 1745. This refusal of Lord COBHAM, gave his Lordship a stronger claim upon the Duke of NEWCASTLE. The common language of Lord BATH's and Lord GRANVILLE's friends at this time, was, that the King was surrounded by a faction; that he was a prisoner upon his throne; and that an Administration on a *broader bottom* ought to be formed, for the interest of the country, and for the *emancipation* of the King.

Lord Bath's offers to Lord Cobham.

At length the PELHAMS took the alarm; and whether, from the apprehension of losing Lord COBHAM, or of losing their places, or both; the Duke of NEWCASTLE resolved to lay before his Majesty, a list of some alterations in the inferior departments of Government, which they intended to make, in order to introduce Mr. PITT; who, in this arrangement, they proposed for Secretary at War, in the room of Sir WM. YONGE, to be made one of the Vice Treasurers of Ireland. But when the King came to Mr. PITT's name, he gave an immediate and positive refusal to the whole list. The Duke stated to his Majesty his engagement with Lord COBHAM; the King angrily replied, *then he must break his engagement.*

Mr. Pitt intended for Secretary at War.

Lord BATH and Lord GRANVILLE instantly seized this opportunity of improving their influence in the closet. Their friends

VOL. I.   O

friends applauded in the warmeſt terms of panegyrick, the ſpirit which the King had ſhewn in the rejection of Mr. PITT; and they added, "that Lord BATH had adviſed his Majeſty to "ſtand ſteady, and be true to his own intereſt."

In conſequence of the King's negative on the propoſed employment of Mr. PITT, the Duke of NEWCASTLE met Lord COBHAM again at Lord HARRINGTON'S. After ſome converſation on the neceſſity of *reſigning*, and the Duke ſaying, that Lord HARDWICKE was decidedly of that opinion, and had both ſuggeſted and warmly recommended it, the Duke put this queſtion, —" Will Lord COBHAM, and his friends, adhere to us (the PELHAMS) in and out of Court, if we engage, never to negociate with the Court, without including Lord COBHAM and all his friends?" Lord COBHAM confeſſed, the propoſition was ſo handſome, he could not, as a man of honour, refuſe giving it his moſt hearty aſſent. This compact being made, and the union thus cemented, between the great Parliamentary intereſts, and the great Parliamentary abilities, the PELHAMS now conſidered themſelves ſtrong enough to combat any faction, however favoured and ſupported it might be in the cloſet.

The meaſure of a *general reſignation* was immediately adopted. Accordingly, on the next day, Feb. 10, 1746, the Duke of NEWCASTLE and Lord HARRINGTON reſigned. The King immediately gave the Duke's Seals to Lord GRANVILLE. But the following day, Mr. PELHAM, Lord HARDWICKE, Lord PEMBROKE, Mr. LEGGE, Mr. GEORGE GRENVILLE, and ſeveral others, all went to Court, and reſigned their employments. Neither the King, nor Lord BATH were prepared for this ſtroke. They had not the leaſt expectation of it. And they were informed, that ſeveral Noblemen and Gentlemen, who held commiſſions in the

the army, were preparing to resign in a few days. The King, Lord BATH, and Lord GRANVILLE, were alarmed beyond expression at these resignations. It was upon this occasion only, that the King discovered his own insignificancy. He found, that the assurances of men, without alliances, were no support to a Sovereign; and that if a King would be maintained in his royalty, he must take those into his service, who have the greatest influence amongst his subjects. It is a maxim, that a King without his people, is either more than he ought to be, or less than he should be. Lord GRANVILLE saw the storm gathering round the political hemisphere; and having no other support than his great friend, Lord BATH, who had lost all esteem with the nation, by his treacherous conduct in 1742, he resolved to desert his own chimerical enterprize, and resign also.

If it was cruel, or unhandsome, in the Whigs to leave the King, when he had given his confidence to their enemies; it was infinitely more cruel and inhuman in those new favourites, to abandon their Sovereign, whom they first deceived with promises, which they knew they could not perform, and next betrayed to the mercy of his late servants; whose return to office they now barbarously obliged him to solicit, without making one effort to accomplish that pretended *emancipation*, with which they affected to colour the motive of their presumption.

But the Whigs took no advantage of the distresses of the King. When his Majesty sent for them to resume their offices, they only stipulated for leave to fulfil their engagements. They asked no peerages, they secured no reversions, they demanded no pensions; and above all, however odious the royal attachment to Hanover was become, they offered no illiberal resentment

resentment to the royal mind upon that account, by which they might have obtained an unlimited popularity. They did not leave the King, until he had withdrawn himself from them; nor did they with-hold their support, the moment he was disposed to receive it. They all returned to office on the fourteenth of February, 1746; so that Lord GRANVILLE's Administration lasted three whole days. In the new arrangement, Mr. PITT was made a Vice Treasurer of Ireland. The rest of the changes, the reader will find at the end of the work. And upon the death of Mr. WINNINGTON, which happened in May following, Mr. PITT was appointed Paymaster in his room. In his office of Paymaster, he was early distinguished by his disinterested integrity, and incorruptible virtue. There are two Facts related, of his conduct, while in this office, which reflect the highest honour upon his character. They have already been published in these words:

" When he was appointed to the Office of Paymaster of the Forces, he found it had been customary to have 100,000l. by advance, generally lie in the hands of the Paymaster, which, in the time of some of those that presided before him in that office, used to be subscribed in Government Securities, which brought 3 or 4000l. per ann. more or less, into their private purses.—And in our memory there happened a conjuncture, when this money so subscribed into the land-tax, was called for, upon an extraordinary emergency, for the use of the army:—but being locked up in the Exchequer, and all public funds bearing a large discount, it could not be sold but at such a great loss, as would have been of the utmost damage to the subscriber. What was the consequence—The payment of the army, in the time of war and rebellion, was stopped, when there was the greatest occasion

for

for public credit, and punctuality in the payment of those troops, on whom our *whole* depended.

"But when Mr. PITT went into that department, he placed whatever sums of money belonged to the office, in the Bank, where they might be ready for the public service, without ever appropriating any part of it to his private use, as had been the custom of former times; he never subscribed one shilling into the funds, nor ever availed himself of any interest arising from public monies at his disposal, but was satisfied with, and touched no more than the *legal appointment*.

"The next fact is—that when the Parliament granted Subsidies to the King of Sardinia, and Queen of Hungary, payable at his office, half per cent. or more, used to be taken on the whole subsidy, in the most reputable times, and by those of the most approved characters—as a *perquisite of office*:—this Mr. PITT refused, which would have come to a large sum, as the grants at that time to both those powers, were very considerable. —When the King of Sardinia was told this, he could not help expressing his surprize, at such an instance of greatness of mind, and disinterestedness, and therefore ordered his agent to offer the same sum, as a royal present to Mr. PITT, who had before refused it as a perquisite. His answer to this was, that as the Parliament had granted those sums for such uses, he had no right to any part of the money;—that he did no more than his duty in paying it *entire*; and hoped the refusal of the King's present upon that occasion, would not give offence. When his Sardinian Majesty heard this, he said, surely this Englishman was somewhat more than a man."

CHAP.

CHAP. VIII.

Lord Granville and Mr. Pelham reconciled—The Prince's claims in the Cornish boroughs—New Opposition formed—Mr. Pitt's speech on the Mutiny Bill, concerning the half-pay officers—On the Glasgow petition—On the Mutiny Bill, concerning the Westminster election—On Dunkirk—On the treaties with Bavaria, and Spain—Death and character of the Prince of Wales.

THE same unanimity which distinguished the two last sessions of Parliament, continued until the peace of Aix la Chapelle, in 1748. Even Lord GRANVILLE became reconciled to the Minister. This extraordinary reconciliation was effected by ROBERT NUGENT, Esq. afterwards Earl NUGENT, as he himself related it in the House of Commons, in the year 1784. " He appointed them, he said, to meet at his house, and their meeting was to be kept a profound secret. One repaired to his house quite muffled up, so that it was impossible for any one who saw him to know him. He just introduced them to one another, and left them to themselves. He took care, in the mean time to have a good supper ready for them, of which they partook; they drank heartily after it: the wine put an end to the reserve on which they had acted: they spoke freely: confidence was established between them: they became sincere friends, and remained so; and cared not the next day, who knew the story of this interview."

When the rebellion was effectually crushed, the Ministry resolved to dissolve the Parliament. The PRINCE of WALES having been informed of this resolution, he held a Stannary Court,

Court, in his capacity of Duke of Cornwall. In this Court some claims, attached to that honour, were revived; which, had they been admitted, would have given the PRINCE a considerable influence in some of the Cornish boroughs. Lord BOLINGBROKE was supposed to have been the PRINCE's adviser in this affair. When the King heard it, he sent the Duke of NEWCASTLE to the PRINCE, with a message, declaring the claims set up by the Court of Stannary, to be wholly inadmissible.

CHAP. VIII.
1747.

The new Parliament met in November 1747; but although it was obvious the PRINCE's friends were joined by the Tories, there was no opposition made to the measures of Government, and the session passed over with the same unanimity as before. But during the prorogation, a strong opposition was formed, and it was resolved to act with vigour. The PRINCE put himself publicly at the head of it. Mr. PITT, Mr. Fox, (afterwards Lord HOLLAND) Mr. MURRAY, (afterwards Lord MANSFIELD) and several other gentlemen of distinguished abilities, adhered to Mr. PELHAM.

1747.

New Opposition formed.

One the 29th of November 1748, commenced the second session of the new Parliament. But although the treaty of Aix la Chapelle had been concluded, and published in the preceding month of October, no copy of it was laid before Parliament. The King mentioned the treaty in his speech, and the terms of it were severely reprobated in the debate upon the address. But Mr. PITT did not speak on the subject.

1748.

When the Mutiny Bill was brought in, there appeared to be some fresh clauses added, particularly one, subjecting officers upon half-pay, to the penalties of the bill. This was warmly opposed, as being dangerous to the Constitution.

CHAP. VIII.
1749.

Mr. Pitt's speech on the mutiny bill.

Mr. PITT defended the clause. What danger, he asked, could arise, from obliging a half-pay officer to continue upon the military establishment? It is admitted on all hands, that while he is in full pay, he must employ his time, his study, and even his sword, as his superiors shall direct. There may possibly be danger in this, but it never can happen until the direction becomes wicked, nor prevented but by the virtue of the army. It is to that virtue we even at this time trust, small as our army is; it is to that virtue we must have trusted, had this bill been modelled as its warmest oppposers could have wished; and without this virtue, should the Lords, the Commons, and the people of England, entrench themselves behind parchment up to the teeth, the sword will find a passage to the vitals of the Constitution.

A petition from the city of Glasgow, praying to be re-imbursed the sum of ten thousand pounds, extorted from that city, by the Pretender, during the late rebellion, occasioned a debate in a Committee of Supply, on the 12th of April 1749; when it was moved to grant the said sum. The motion was opposed by Mr. BOWES; other towns, he said, deserved the same favour; and if this sum was granted to Glasgow, other places having the same claim, would expect the like.

Mr. Pitt's speech on the Glasgow petition.

He was answered by Mr. PITT, who said, * I shall not enter into a dispute with the Honourable Gentleman, whether there are not many places, both in England and Scotland, that have an equal pretence to loyalty as the city of Glasgow, and that shewed as much zeal for the support of the Government during the late rebellion, as that city; but this I will aver, that there was no city, town, or place in Great Britain, that suffered so much, or that shewed greater zeal in the same circumstances. And without derogating from the merit of any one, I may say, that there are not many cities in the united kingdom, that have so often, or so remarkably distinguished themselves in the cause of liberty. It was this, Sir: It was the whole tenor of this city's conduct, from the time of the reformation, that drew the resentment of the rebels upon it,

and

* This speech was also written by Gordon.

and made them resolve upon the extravagant demand they at first made upon that city. If they had insisted upon their first demand, the city must have been ruined; because it would have been impossible for the inhabitants to have raised such a sum. Of this they had the good fortune to convince the chiefs of the rebels; and even the rebels shewed, that they had no inclination to ruin such a flourishing city, though the inhabitants appeared generally to be their enemies. Shall a British Parliament, Sir, shew less regard to their friends, than the rebels shewed to their enemies? The rebels gave them 10,000l. that is to say, they passed from 10,000l. of their first demand, rather than ruin the city; and this I may the more justly call giving them 10,000l. because, if the rebels had plundered the city, they would have found three times the value of that sum among the inhabitants. If then, the rebels gave that city 10,000l. rather than expose it to ruin, shall a British Parliament refuse to give it 10,000l. to preserve it from ruin?

It really shocks me, Sir, to see such a question stand a debate in a British House of Commons. If the rebels had succeeded in their flagitious attempt, and had called a Slavish Parliament, for they would never have called a free one, I should not have wondered to see such a question opposed in a House of Commons assembled by their authority; but it astonishes me to see such a question opposed in a House, where every member present professes his friendship for that city, and acknowledges the gratitude due to it from the public, for its behaviour. The Hon. Gentleman told us, he did not intend to depreciate the real merit of the city of Glasgow: I do not know what he intended; but he endeavoured to shew, that the behaviour of that city was not so meritorious as represented, because they attempted nothing in favour of Government, till after the rebels had marched into England, from whence they had reason to expect that none of them would ever return. This, Sir, was certainly an insinuation, that the people of Glasgow never did any thing in favour of the Government, as long as they thought the Government in any danger from the rebellion; and if this had really been the case, I should have had no great opinion of their merit. But I shall shew, that before the rebel army entered England, it was not in the power of the people of Glasgow to do any thing in favour of the Government; and that they had not then the least reason to imagine that Government was out of all danger from the rebellion.

When we consider, Sir, that the rebels marched through one half of England, without any opposition from the militia: When we consider, that even in their retreat back again, though pursued by the Duke and the regular forces, they met with no obstruction from the militia; we cannot with any justice blame the south or west parts of Scotland, for not opposing them with their militia. And as to the city of Glasgow, it had neither time to provide for its defence, nor was it capable of making a resistance, had it had time: The town is an open town, without so much as a wall round it, and the inhabitants had neither arms, ammunition, nor any sort of military discipline among them; so that it was impossible for them to think of opposing an army of Highlanders, who are by the care of their chiefs, bred up to arms and military discipline from their infancy. Besides, they had no time for such an undertaking; for the rebels came down upon them in a very few weeks after first appearing in arms; and, till the battle at Preston, every one had reason to believe, that General Cope, with the forces under his command, would have given a good account of them.

The case was very different, Sir, both with regard to Newcastle and Carlisle, because both being surrounded with a wall, may, in a few days, be so fortified, as to be able to resist a flying party. Yet how little resistance did the latter make? For though they had many weeks to prepare for their defence, though they had hopes of being relieved in a few days by the army then assembled at Newcastle, under Marshal Wade, they gave up their city the very next day after they found the rebels were preparing for a general assault; and yet that city, or at least the castle might have held out much longer against the rebels, who had no battering cannon along with them; for a small party of the rebels held out the castle afterwards for some days against the Duke, and would probably have held out much longer, if they had not heard that some battering cannon were upon the road from Whitehaven, to be employed against them.

Now, Sir, as to the opinion the people of Glasgow might have of the safety of the Government, or the event of the rebellion, at the time the rebel army marched into England, they could not have such thoughts of either

either as the Hon. Gentleman was pleased to represent; for as to the small number of that army, the people in Scotland had from thence reason to fear, that the rebels were well assured of being joined by great numbers in England, or that there was treachery both in his Majesty's councils and armies; for without some such well-grounded hopes, no one could suppose, that men of common sense would think of invading England with an army of 5 or 6000 Highlanders. At the time of the Revolution, when it was at first said, that the Prince of Orange was to invade England with an army of 30,000 men, and many of the King's friends seemed to be frightened at the news, a noble Lord, who was known to be a firm friend, seemed to make light of the news, and said, he apprehended no danger from such an army; but when it was afterwards reported, that the Prince was to bring 20,000, he began to be afraid; and when he heard that the Prince was to come with 14,000 only, then, cries he, "We are undone!" When they asked him the reason, why he was so much afraid of 14,000 when he seemed no way afraid of 30,000, he answered, "An army of 30,000 could not conquer England; but no man would come here with an army of 14,000, if he was sure of not finding a great many traitors amongst ourselves."

This, Sir soon appeared to be a just way of thinking; and though the event shewed, that if the rebels had any such hopes, those hopes were very ill grounded; yet this the people of Glasgow could not foresee; therefore, from the small number of the rebel army, they had, according to the same way of thinking, rather cause to dread the event, than to suppose that none of that army would ever return: Nor could they suppose this from the spirit that appeared in England in favour of the Government; for though I am very well convinced, that this spirit was sincere and true, yet I am afraid, that if the rebel-leader could have persuaded his people to have ventured a battle against the Duke in Staffordshire, or to have given him the slip, marched towards London, and fought a battle near this city, the fate of England would have depended upon the issue of that battle; for if they had obtained a victory, and made themselves masters of London, I question much, if the spirit of the populace would not soon have taken a very different turn.

I must therefore conclude, Sir, that when the rebel army marched to England, the people of Glasgow could form no judgment with any certainty, about the event of the rebellion; and consequently, that what

CHAP. VIII.
1749.

they did afterwards, could proceed from nothing but their steady attachment to this Government; and I must add, that their zeal was much the more meritorious, as it was manifested after they had severely smarted for it, in having such a large sum of money extorted from them by the rebels, merely on account of the zeal they had formerly shewn for supporting the liberties of their country. A burnt child, they say dreads the fire; and if the people of Glasgow, after having smarted so sensibly for their loyalty, had resolved to lie quiet, and wait the event of things, their conduct, would have been excusable: By holding such a conduct, they would have been considerable gainers, even though we should grant the money now moved for. But they honestly and bravely resolved not to be idle spectators of the confusions of their country. They resolved to be active in putting a happy end to them as soon as possible; and with this view, as soon as they had an opportunity, they put themselves to very great expence.

To say, Sir, that this expence was attended with no success or effect, is what no man can say with any certainty; for the regiment they raised and sent to Stirling, with two more, so effectually guarded that pass, that no reinforcement ever did march that way to the rebels; and the regiment they kept at home, very probably prevented any reinforcement being sent by the way of Glasgow. And though our army was unfortunate at the affair of Falkirk, yet if the the Glasgow regiment had not been there, it might have been much more unfortunate, and the victory of the rebels more complete; for though that regiment was engaged in the action, it is evident, that it was not defeated and dispersed, because if it had, the men would have run home, whereas it retreated in good order to Edinburgh, without the loss of a man, except those that were killed, wounded, or taken prisoners at the battle.

As to the behaviour of the Northern counties, and that of Newcastle in particular, comparisons are odious, Sir, and I should have avoided making any, if I had not been forced to it by the Honourable Gentleman who spoke last. I shall readily acknowledge, and gratefully own the dutiful zeal of all these places for the support of his Majesty's Government; and I must likewise confess, that those who do not desire from the public any reimbursement of the expence they were at upon that occasion, have more merit than those that do; but at the same time

must

must observe, that before the rebels left Edinburgh, all those places were secured against any visit from them, not only by the strong town of Berwick, but by an army equal to that of the rebels encamped near Newcastle, and commanded by one of the best Generals in the service; whereas the inhabitants of Glasgow shewed their zeal for his Majesty, even when the rebels were masters of their country. And as to the expence, it must be acknowledged, that over and above the relief now prayed for, that city was, either voluntarily, or by compulsion, at a much greater expence, in proportion, than any of the places mentioned; for, from what was said by the Gentleman at your bar, it appears, that over and above the two fines extorted from them by the rebels, their expence amounted to above 8000l. which is greater than what the town of Newcastle is said to have been put to; and is, I am sure, more in in proportion, for the single city of Glasgow alone, than 30,000l. is for the whole county of York. Besides, Sir, none of those places suffered any interruption in their trade or manufactures, whereas the trade and manufactures of Glasgow were at full stop, almost during the whole time of the rebellion. To which I must add, that the expence of the former was voluntary, whereas a great part of the latter's expence was by compulsion, which makes a very great difference; for people may generously contribute more to the assistance of Government, as all those places did, but they will never voluntarily contribute more than they can spare; whereas a people may be forced to contribute what would infallibly prove their ruin, should they meet with no retribution; which is the he case now before us.

Then, Sir, as to the city of Carlisle, the rebels might perhaps raise the taxes there; as they did in many other places; but I cannot think they imposed any fine upon that city: I am rather inclined to think they favoured it, because the people absolutely refused to support his Majesty's commanding officer there in making a stout resistance, which was the cause of the city and castle's being surrendered. I therefore think, we have no need to be afraid of an application for relief from any of those places; at least, I am sure that if any such application should be made, it cannot be so well supported as the application now under our consideration; and consequently, our complying with this, can be no precedent for our complying with any future.

But

CHAP. VIII.
1749.

But that of introducing a bad precedent, is not, it seems, Sir, the only danger we are to expose ourselves to by agreeing to this motion: we are besides threatened with the danger of exciting a rebellion in England. This, Sir, is so imaginary a danger, that I cannot think there is any one Gentleman in this House that is really afraid of it. If there should be no future application of this kind, we can be in no such danger; because no man can be disobliged at the Parliament's not granting him relief, if he does not apply for it; and I have good reason to hope, that that there will be no such future application. I hope all gentlemen and bodies politic in Great Britain, will follow the example of the city of Glasgow, and desire no relief for what they voluntarily contributed towards the support of his Majesty's Government, nor for what they suffered in being obliged to give free quarters to the rebels; and if we have no application upon either of these heads, I believe we can have no application made to us upon any other. But suppose we should have some applications, we shall then have an opportunity to consider their merit; and if the circumstances of the petitioners should appear to be same with those of the petitioners now before us, I do not question their meeting with the same success. If their circumstances should appear to be different, and not near so meritorious, we may refuse their petition with safety; because, however partial they may be in their own favour, the rest of the nation will judge impartially, and approve our refusal; and if the rest of the nation approve it, we can be in no danger of its exciting a rebellion in this part of the kingdom.

Another danger we are threatened with upon this occasion is, that if we agree to this motion, it will encourage people not to be active in defending themselves against any future invasion or insurrection, or perhaps, under the pretence of force, to contribute to its support. This I shall grant, Sir, might be the consequence of laying it down as a general principle, that all who suffer by an invasion or insurrection, shall have their loss made good by the public; and therefore it would be wrong to lay down such a general principle. But if the laying down a principle would surely be wrong, it would be much more so, to lay the contrary down as an unalterable maxim of state. It would be unjust, as well as imprudent, to lay it down as a principle, that those who honestly and bravely risk their lives and fortunes in opposition to an invasion or insurrection, and have suffered severely on account of that
opposition

opposition, should meet with no relief from the public, especially when their preservation or ruin depends upon that relief, which appears to be the case now before us. And if we consider this, we must allow, that if we think of the justice due to the public creditors, or of relieving our poor labourers and manufacturers, we must agree to this motion, because the the public revenue will suffer a great deal more by the ruin of such a trading town as Glasgow, than it can suffer by granting the relief desired by the petitioners for preventing that ruin.

This relief, Sir, they cannot have from the produce of the forfeited estates in Scotland. It would be like prescribing a remedy to a sick man, which could not be got ready till after his distemper had put an end to his life. It will be several years before any thing can be made of those estates; and in the mean time, the city of Glasgow must be ruined with law charges, by their creditors suing for their money, which they will certainly do, if their interest be not regularly paid. This it is impossible for the Corporation to do out of their present income, and at the same time support their necessary annual expence; therefore their ruin must be inevitable, or the relief now moved for must be granted.

The motion was agreed to.

The session ended the 13th of June, 1749.

Nothing material happened during the summer.

On the 16th of November, 1749, Parliament met again; when it appeared, that the party in Opposition had increased considerably in number; and being under the patronage of the Prince of Wales, who was highly popular at this time; they were, from that circumstance, favourably judged of by the public. The address, and many other points, were warmly debated; but Mr. Pitt did not speak upon any of them.

When the mutiny bill was brought in, (January 1750) Col. George Townshend, afterwards Marquis Townshend, proposed a clause, by way of rider, for preventing any non-commissioned

CHAP. VIII. missioned officer's being broke, or reduced to the ranks, or any
1750. soldier's being punished, but by the sentence of a Court Martial. He informed the House, that his clause was founded upon indubitable facts. He said he had witnesses at the door, to prove, that a serjeant and corporal were reduced to the ranks, because some of their party in the rear, as they were going upon duty to the play-house, happened to say in the street, *Vanaeput for ever!*—for this heinous offence, which they could not prevent, the two non-commissioned officers were, without trial, reduced to the ranks. There was a long debate.

Mr. PITT (who was still Paymaster) spoke against the clause.—

Mr. Pitt's speech on the Mutiny Bill, concerning the Westminster election.

I never will agree, he said, to call officers and soldiers to the bar of this House, to traduce and impeach each other. If they once learn the way to come here with their complaints, they will next come with their petitions. Our business is to consider of the number of forces necessary

M.S.

for the defence of this kingdom, and our possessions, and to grant the money for the maintaining that number. We have no business with the conduct of the army, or the officers or soldiers complaints; those are subjects which belong to the King, or to such as shall be commissioned by him to hear them. If we give ear to them, we shall not only destroy the discipline of the army, but make Parliament detestable; for it will be impossible to give satisfaction to both parties; besides causing great trouble and neglect of duty, in coming from distant parts of the kingdom. Therefore, I hope, Sir the House will not permit any enquiry to be made into the complaint that has been offered. There is not the least pretence for saying that it relates to the freedom of election; nor to the particular election for Westminster now going on. It relates singly to the duty of two non-commissioned officers, sent out with a party, upon duty, and it was the serjeant's duty to have made report of this circumstance, if it happened, and he knew of it, to his commanding officer. Why he did not, is not for us to enquire; nor is it a question for this House to determine, whether the commanding officer has punished his serjeant and corporal with unmerited severy. It belongs to a Court Martial, or Board of Officers,

The

The clause was withdrawn.

On the 5th of February, 1750, Lord EGMONT moved for copies of all letters and papers, relative to the demolition of Dunkirk, according to the late treaty of Aix la Chapelle. *

Mr. PITT opposed this motion. He said it was not only impolitic but dangerous; as tending to involve the nation in another war with France, when it was notorious we were in no situation adequate to bear the expence. It was a very good answer to the motion, to say it was premature; for since the conclusion of the treaty, there had not yet been opportunity to execute all the articles of it: that the cost of the work being to be defrayed and performed by the French, they may say, " our finances are reduced, we cannot afford the money at present, but shall in a little time." At all events, the motion, he said, was highly improper at that moment. It was an affront to the French Court, and as we were not in a condition to support it, by any strong measures, it was exhibiting our petulance and impotence. At a future period, with a recruited finance and repaired marine, the motion may be proper, if the terms of the treaty have not been complied with. But if the motion is carried, and it should come out, that Dunkirk is now in the state that it was in by the treaty of Utrecht, explained in the year 1717, which he believed to be the fact, would any Gentleman say, this was a crime in the present Ministry? or a sufficient reason for a quarrel with France?]

Mr. Pitt's speech on Dunkirk.

M.S.

The motion was negatived by 242 to 115.

On the 17th of January 1751, the Parliament met. The King in his speech informed them, that he had concluded a treaty with Spain, and another with the Elector of Bavaria. The address was moved in the usual stile, *approving* of these treaties, although they had not then been laid before the House; which occasioned a long debate.

* Lord MELCOMBE says, (in his Diary) that this motion originated with the Prince; and when the inutility of it was represented to his Royal Highness, he said, "that making the motion would make the Ministry feel they had *la Corde au Col*.

Chap. VIII.
1751.

Mr. Pitt's speech on the treaties with Bavaria and Spain.

M.S.

Lord EGMONT moved to leave out all the words of *approbation* in the addrefs. He was anfwered by

Mr. PITT; who faid, the treaty with Bavaria was founded in the beft political wifdom; it was a wife meafure, as tending moft effectually to preferve the balance of power in Germany; and of courfe to preferve the tranquility of Europe. The Elector of Bavaria was taken off from the French intereft by it; which, as it contributed to weaken the Houfe of Bourbon, it contributed to the continuation of peace. The treaty with Spain, was a wife and advantageous meafure. The Court of Spain had agreed to many conceffions; they had agreed to pay a large fum to the South Sea Company; to the re-eftablifhment of the Britifh trade in Spain; that Britifh fubjects were to pay no other duties on merchandize, than what the King of Spain's own fubjects were to pay. Lord EGMONT had obferved; that the claim of *no fearch* had not been revived in the treaty; and not being even mentioned in it, this effential point had been totally abandoned. To this part of Lord EGMONT's fpeech, Mr. PITT anfwered, that he had once been an advocate for that claim; it was when he was a young man; but now he was ten years older; had confidered public affairs more coolly; and was convinced, that the claim of *no fearch*, refpecting Britifh veffels near the coaft of Spanifh America, could never be obtained unlefs Spain was fo reduced, as to confent to any terms, her conqueror might think proper to impofe.

Lord EGMONT's motion was negatived, by 203 againft 74.

Death of the Prince of Wales

On the 20th of March the Prince of WALES died.

It is not the defign of this work to ftate the particulars of any event, which have been already related in other books, unlefs fuch relation is very erroneous. This event is no otherwife neceffary to mention here, than as it annihilated the plan of a regular and fyftematic Oppofition that was forming, and when completed, was intended to act under his Royal Highnefs's protection and controul. Lord MELCOMBE's printed account admits this fact, in part. But there are letters from perfons of the firft confide-
tion,

ration, which may perhaps, in some future day be printed, which state this and other traits of the Prince's character, stronger, and with more truth than Lord MELCOMBE has done.

CHAP. VIII.
1751.

The printed accounts of the Prince's character, are not very exact. Perhaps they were written soon after his death, when an impartial writer, might be influenced by caution.

There was a caprice in his Court, which a dignified mind, like that of Mr. PITT, could not approve. After his death, this caprice was succeeded by a partiality to two or three persons; which laid the foundation of a Faction of the most singular and extraordinary kind, and of an Influence in the succeeding reign, as disgraceful as it was unfortunate.

CHAP.

CHAP. IX.

The Regency appointed—The Bedford's turned out—Mr. Pitt's treatment of the Duke of Newcastle—Mr. Pitt's Bill for the Relief of the Chelsea Pensioners.

CHAP. IX.
1751.

THE death of the PRINCE of WALES filled the Opposition with the greatest consternation and confusion. Several thought of making terms with the Minister—others of seceding—and some were for remaining with the Princess, and taking the chance of events.

The Regency appointed.

The first measure of Government was the settlement of a Regency; which was done upon fair and liberal terms. The *Princess Dowager* was made Regent, and guardian of the minor, as well as of her other children. Being a female, there was a Council of Regency appointed, consisting of the great Officers of State, and the Duke of CUMBERLAND was placed at the head of it. This compliment to the Duke, occasioned some invidious speeches in Parliament, from Gentlemen who were not acquainted with the Duke's real character. Time has shewn that the analogies they offered in the way of prophecy, had not the least foundation in truth. The Duke had, in the judgment of these Gentlemen, treated the Scot's rebels with too much severity. But this was a justifiable severity. And those who had latent designs, forgave not the disappointment.

The debate was upon the clause respecting the Council. Mr. PITT defended the bill; but by something he said concerning the Council, Mr. Fox thought he hinted at the Duke of CUMBERLAND, and began defending the Duke; but Mr. PITT explained

plained in such terms, that Mr. Fox went away without dividing. The debate being in a Committee, the *Speaker* (ONSLOW) made a very able speech against the clause; which he deprecated, as fraught with great and probable evils; he dreaded no improper ambition in the DUKE, nothing he was confident, was farther from his Royal Highness's heart; but his apprehension was, that the DUKE and PRINCESS would not *coalesce* in measures; and he insinuated in delicate terms, his anxiety upon the misunderstanding which subsisted between the PRINCESS Dowager and the Princess AMELIA; and the warm affection between the latter Princess and her brother. This speech gave Mr. PELHAM a great deal of uneasiness; and he often mentioned it.

The Regent was not impeded in her just authority, by any harsh conditions; nor were there any limitations of her power introduced, that implied the least suspicion of her integrity or rectitude. The King himself treated her with every mark of respect, attention, and affection. He frequently visited her; and 12,500l. were immediately paid her; and notwithstanding the war, which quickly followed, demanded greater supplies than the war of any former period, yet her money was always actually paid; and when the Prince of WALES (GEORGE III.) arrived at the age of eighteen, the King ordered him a separate allowance, (over and above what was given to the Princess) of 40,000l per annum, from his Civil List.

The Party which had arranged themselves under the late Prince of WALES, being now without head, or cement, the PELHAMS saw they had an opportunity of encreasing the number of their supporters, by embracing the fugitives, and turning out the Duke of BEDFORD and his friends; who had never acted cordially

CHAP. IX. cordially with them, not even during the war. In June 1751, the Duke of BEDFORD was difmiffed from the office of Secretary of State, and Lord SANDWICH from the poft of Firft Lord of the Admiralty, Lord TRENTHAM, (fince created Marquis of Marquis of STAFFORD) from the fame Board, and fome others of his Grace's friends, from other offices. Thefe Noblemen and Gentlemen being joined by thofe, of the late Prince's party, who had not united with the PELHAMS, they formed a frefh oppofition; and though they were not eonfiderable in number, yet they were fuppofed to be privately countenanced by the Duke of CUMBERLAND, and to have a fecret communication with Mr. Fox. Lord HOLDERNESSE fucceeded the Duke of BEDFORD, and Lord ANSON was placed at the Admiralty.

1752.

The feffion clofed in June, and nothing material happened during the fummer.

Parliament met again on the 14th of November 1751, but there were no debates; and the feffion clofed on the 25th of March 1752. Five days after the Parliament rofe, the King went to Hanover. During his Majefty's abfence, there was a great deal of intriguing and negociating, amongft the parties; in all which, Mr. PITT and the GRENVILLES were totally omitted. The encreafing weight and confequence of Mr. PITT in the Houfe of Commons, excited the jealoufy of the principal perfons in office, as well as of thofe in Oppofition. He was not ignorant of the clandiftine projects of both parties; but he defpifed them. In one conference he had with the Duke of NEWCASTLE, he treated that Nobleman in fuch a manner, that if he had not dreaded him, he would have difmiffed him; for he ftill held the poft of Paymafter. The fubject of the conference was,

the

the measures the King was taking in Germany, to secure the election of a King of the Romans: In which Mr. PITT told him, he engaged for subsidies without knowing the extent, and for alliances without knowing the terms. The Duke complained of Mr. PITT's hauteur, to his confidential friend, Mr. STONE, who advised his Grace to overlook it, saying it would be most prudent.

In the succeeding session, which began on the 11th of January 1753, and ended the 7th of June, in the same year, Mr. PITT took no part in any of the debates.

And he was also totally silent in the next session, which commenced on the 15th of November 1753, and closed on the 6th of April 1754.

In 1754 Parliament was dissolved.

The new Parliament met on the 14th of November 1754. Mr. PITT was still in his office of Paymaster. The next day, (the 15th) as soon as the address was reported, Mr. PITT moved for leave to bring in a bill, which will be an everlasting monument of his humanity. He prefaced this motion with a melancholy description of the hardships to which the out Pensioners of Chelsea-hospital were exposed, by the present improper mode of paying their pensions. The poor disabled veterans, he said, who were entitled to this excellent charity, were cruelly oppressed, by a number of wretches, who supplied them with money in advance. By the present method, the poor man can receive no money, until he has been twelve months upon the list. This was extremely unjust; because the poor veteran's merit,

and

and claim to the charity, [commenced from the moment of his difability in the fervice. But by this delay of the firſt payment, he was under the neceſſity of borrowing money, upon the cir‑tificate of his admiſſion upon the liſt. He was fupplied with a pittance, by one of the people called ufurers; who compelled the poor wretch to allow him a moſt exorbitant intereſt. The practice continuing a few years, the penſioner had nothing to ſubſiſt on; the whole of his penſion being fwallowed up in ufury. To remedy this grievance, he propoſed, by his bill, that when the penſioner was admitted upon the liſt, half a year's penſion ſhould be advanced, and paid him; with fome other re‑gulations on the ſame humane principle, and the bill to com‑mence on the 25th of December, 1754. The bill was imme‑diately brought in, and unanimouſly paſſed both Houſes, with uncommon expedition.

Mr. PITT took no part in the debates during the feſſion; which ended on the 25th of April, 1755; and three days after, the King ſet out for Hanover.

CHAP.

CHAP. X.

Death of Mr. Pelham—Mr. Fox wishes to be made Secretary of State, and Minister of the House of Commons—Explanation of Minister of the House of Commons—Mr. Pitt expects to be made Secretary of State—Sir Thomas Robinson appointed—General dissatisfaction—Party at Leicester House—State of the nation.

IN March 1754 Mr. PELHAM died. This event proved as fatal to the Ministry, as the death of the Prince of WALES had been to the Opposition.

Mr. Fox, who was Secretary at War, wished to succeed to Mr. PELHAM's situation, and the Opposition offered to act under him, if he was appointed; but the Duke of NEWCASTLE said, " he had been *second* Minister long enough; that he would not have acted in that capacity under any body but his brother; and now his brother was gone, he would be at the head of the Treasury himself." Mr. Fox then solicited the Duke, to succeed his Grace in the office of Secretary of State: and it is very probable, that this request would have been granted, had he not insisted upon having the management of the House of Commons; which the Duke peremptorily refused; and upon that point the negociation broke off.

The management of the House of Commons, as it is called, is a confidential department, unknown to the Constitution. In the public accounts, it is immerfed under the head of Secret Service. It is usually given to the Secretary of State, when that post is filled by a Commoner. The business of the department

VOL. I.   R   is

[122]

CHAP. X.
1754.

is to diftribute, with *art* and *policy*, amongft the members, who have no oftenfible places, fums of money; for their fupport during the feffion; befides contracts, lottery tickets, and other douceurs. It is no uncommon circumftance at the end of a feffion, for a gentleman to receive five hundred or a thoufand pounds, for *his ferviccs.* *

Mr. Pitt expects to be Secretary of State.

When it was known, that the Duke of NEWCASTLE intended the Treafury for himfelf, Mr. PITT expected, that the Seals of Secretary of State would have been offered to him. It is certain,

* Mr. Fox was fo confident his negotiation with the Duke would fucceed, that while it was pending, he fent the following letter to his friends:

" SIR,

" The King has declared his intention to make me Secretary of State, and I (very unworthy as I fear I am of fuch an undertaking) *muft take the conduct of the Houfe of Commons.* I cannot therefore well accept the office, till after the firft day's debate, which may be a warm one. A great attendance that day of my friends, will be of the greateft confequence to my future fituation, and I fhould be extremely happy, if you would for that reafon, fhew yourfelf amongft them, to the great honour of, &c. &c.

H. F O X."

In the memoirs of the Marchionefs of Pompadour, (vol. I. pages 57, 58, 59, Eng. Tranf. 1766.) we are prefented with a very interefting anecdote, written to Cardinal Fleury, by *an Englifh Minifter* of that time.

" I penfion (writes the Minifter) *half* the Parliament, to keep it *quiet*. But as the King's money is not fufficient, they, to whom I give none, clamour loudly for a war; it would be expedient for your Eminence to remit me three millions of French livres, in order to filence thefe barkers. *Gold* is a metal which here corrects all ill qualities in the blood. A penfion of 2000l. a year will make the moft impetuous warrior in Parliament, as *tame as a lamb*."

By the help of this anecdote, we are enabled to comprehend the *myftical* meaning of a Minifter's *planning* of a Parliament, and of a Minifter's *conducting a Houfe of Commons.*—The former phrafe we find ufed by Mr. Tindal, in the octavo edition of his hiftory of England. vol. 21ft, page 439—It runs thus:
" Mr. P——, before his death, had fettled the *plan* of the new Parliament."
——and fame vol. page 510, he fubjoins—" As to the elections they went much in the fame track *that had been laid out by* Mr. P——."

tain, that he did not aſk for them, but he expected them without aſking. This diſappointment was in ſome degree palliated, by making Mr. GEORGE GRENVILLE, Treaſurer of the Navy; who at that time lived in the utmoſt intimacy with Mr. PITT; and they were become relations, by Mr. PITT having lately married his ſiſter. Mr. LEGGE was appointed Chancellor of the Exchequer, and Sir THOMAS ROBINSON Secretary of State, and ſome other alterations were made. But notwithſtanding this arrangement, there was a general diſſatisfaction throughout all parties. Some diſliked the meaſures, others diſliked the men; in fine, nobody was pleaſed; neither thoſe in office, nor thoſe out: and there was a new party forming, that ſeemed to menace more danger to their views, than their own differences. This was the party of Leiceſter-houſe; which threw a general alarm, and conſternation over the whole. No one was quite certain of whom this party conſiſted. Several individuals in office, and in Oppoſition, were ſuſpected of ſecretly belonging to it.

The flame of war had been kindled in North America, and it was preparing to burſt out in Europe. Great Britain was every day more cloſely rivetted to the continent, by freſh engagements; while her own proper buſineſs was totally neglected. Her fleet was rotting in ordinary; her army, except ſuch corps as were under the eye of the Duke of CUMBERLAND, relaxed in diſcipline. Her Miniſters were timid by diſunion, and their meaſures were enervated by ignorance. However unpleaſing the fact may be to relate, it is a fact, which the beſt informed perſons will not contradict, that the principal, if not only attention of all deſcriptions of men, was employed at this time in intriguing and negotiating for places. But in this general aſſertion, it is not to be underſtood, that all parties were influenced by the ſame motives.

CHAP. X.
1754.

There is no doubt that some persons were actuated by the passion of self interest; but it is equally true, that there were many who were governed by a sincere desire to serve the country; that offices were no otherwise their objects, than as they gave them power and situation to do good. This distinction it is not only proper, but necessary to make; because it was a principle laid down in the next reign, and the votaries of the Court disseminated it with uncommon art and industry, that all mankind were knaves alike; that the subjects of all Kings, ought to look for honesty in the royal bosom; they said it resided no where else. This political blasphemy, came with unpardonable effrontery from the followers of a Court, which owed its elevation to the true orthodox principles of the Constitution.

CHAP.

CHAP. XI.

Causes of the disagreements at Leicester-house—Lord Harcourt and Dr. Hayter resign their posts of Governor and Preceptor to the Prince—Duke of Bedford's motion upon this subject in the House of Lords—Further explanation of the principles inculcated at Leicester-house.

UPON the death of FREDERICK Prince of Wales, the education of the Prince (GEORGE III.) had been committed to Lord HARCOURT as Governor; to Dr. HAYTER, Bishop of Norwich, as Preceptor; and to ANDREW STONE, Esq. brother to the Primate of that name, as Sub-Governor; recommended by the Duke of NEWCASTLE; and to Mr. SCOTT, as Sub-preceptor; recommended by Lord BOLINGBROKE. In about a year and a half, a disagreement broke out amongst them, of a very interesting nature. It was said by the friends of Leicester-house, that the Governor and Preceptor did not discharge the duties of their trust with alacrity, But it came out afterwards, that this complaint lay deeper than was at first supposed. There were two persons concerned in this affair, whom it is proper to mention particularly. Mr. STONE, was the most particular friend and adviser of the Duke of NEWCASTLE. The other, Mr. MURRAY, afterwards Lord MANSFIELD, was in precisely the same situation, and degree of credit, with Mr. PELHAM. Between Mr. STONE and Mr. MURRAY there subsisted the warmest intimacy; not only their friendships; but their principles and politics were perfectly congenial. Lord BUTE, who had been Lord of the Bedchamber to the late Prince, and was continued in the family, gained a superiour influence, by assiduity

and

CHAP. XI. attention. He was moreover favoured by the Princefs. The
1753. referve of Lord HARCOURT, and the very orderly demeanour
of the BISHOP, gave great advantage, as well as opportunity, to
Lord BUTE, who excelled in the affumption of theatrical grace and
gefture; which, added to a good figure, rendered his converfation particularly pleafing, and at length created a partiality in his
favour. The Duke of NEWCASTLE and Mr. PELHAM, had information of every circumftance at Leicefter-houfe. In a little
time, the BISHOP found fome very improper books put into the
hands of the PRINCE. He complained of this matter to the
Duke of NEWCASTLE. And in a few days Lord HARCOURT
Lord Harcourt and the BISHOP refigned. From the period of making this *counter*
and Dr. Hayter
refign. complaint, it became a ftruggle between the party of *Leicester-
houfe*, and the *Pelhams*, which fhould have the power of educating
the PRINCE. While this difpute was going on, a third party (the
Bedfords) interfered for the fame purpofe; by attacking STONE
and MURRAY. Thefe gentlemen were charged with being *Jacobites*. Lord RAVENSWORTH brought the charge. A Committee
of the Privy Council was directed to enquire into it. The Committee fat feveral times upon it: but the two Confidents had the
addrefs to acquit themfelves; though Mr. FAWCETT, Recorder
of Newcaftle, fwore to their having drank the Pretender's health
feveral times.

On the 22d of March 1753, the Duke of BEDFORD made the
Duke of Bed- following motion in the Houfe of Lords: " That an humble
ford's motion.
addrefs be prefented to his Majefty, that he would be gracioufly
pleafed to give orders, that there be laid before this Houfe. the
feveral examinations of the Lord *Ravenfworth*, the Dean of *Durham*, Mr. *Fawcett*, the Lord Bifhop of *St. Afaph*, the Lord Bifhop of *Gloucester*, the Honourable Mr. *Murray*, his Majefty's
Solicitor

Solicitor General; *Andrew Stone*, Efq. and fuch other examinations upon oath, as have been taken before the Lords appointed by his Majefty to enquire into informations of a very material nature, relating to a perfon in the fervice of their Royal Highneffes the Prince of WALES and Prince EDWARD; and the other perfons mentioned in the courfe of the faid examinations, likewife all letters and papers relative thereto, and the report made by their Lordfhips to his Majefty thereupon." But the Duke of NEWCASTLE, and the reft of the Miniftry were againft the motion; and therefore it was negatived. Lord HARCOURT faid in the debate, that he found he had no authority over the Prince's education; nor could he be of any fervice, unlefs the Sub-governor and others (Scott and Creffet*) were difmiffed, all of whom he had ftrong reafons to believe, were *Jacobites*, and therefore he had refigned. The PELHAMS thought they had gained their point, in the protection of STONE and MURRAY, and in appointing Lord WALDEGRAVE and the PRIMATE to fucceed the refigners; while the fact was, they were deceived and betrayed by their own people. By this fecret manœuvre, the influence and afcendancy of Lord BUTE were completely eftablifhed. At that time was circulated by the *Bedford party* a remarkable paper, which the reader will find in the note.† And in the

CHAP. XI.
1753.

---

* Creffet was Secretary to the Princefs; and upon her recommendation, was appointed Treafurer to the Prince.

† *A Memorial of feveral Noblemen and Gentlemen of the firft rank and fortune.*

The Memorialifts reprefent,

THAT the education of the Prince of Wales, is of the utmoft importance to the whole nation: that it ought always to be entrufted to Noblemen of the moft unblemifhed honour, and to Prelates of the moft diftinguifhed virtue, of the moft accomplifhed learning, and of the moft unfufpected principles, with regard to government

CHAP. XI the weekly paper, called the *Protester*, (printed in small folio, like
1753. the *North Briton*, *Auditor* &c. and which seems to be the paper
alluded to by Lord MELCOMBE, in his Diary, pp. 235 and 236)
number fifteen, September 8, 1753, after saying a good dea labout
STONE, are these words, " And whatever may be the misgivings
and repinings of those who expected a kingdom of their own,
and who now see themselves for ever excluded, *Those* who have
the forming of the *Youth*, have reason to promise themselves a
like ascendancy over the *Man*."

This business being settled, Leicester-house went on as it
pleased. STONE and MURRAY, and Lord BUTE, were in perfect
union; not indeed ostensibly, but confidentially: And in a very
little time, (that is before the war broke out) Lord BATH paid
his Court to Lord BUTE, and was admitted of his Cabinet. From
this time may be dated that unhappy and dangerous idea, which
Lord BUTE had imbibed, of forming a *double* Cabinet: He
had

vernment both in Church and State: That the misfortunes which the nation
formerly suffered, or escaped, under King Charles I. King Charles II.
and King James II. were owing to the bad education of those Princes, who
were early initiated in maxims of arbitrary power: That for a faction to engross
the education of the Prince of Wales to themselves, excluding men of probity
and learning, is unwarrantable, dangerous, and illegal: That to place men about
the Prince of Wales, whose principles are suspected, and whose belief in the
mysteries of our faith is doubtful, has the most mischievous tendency, and ought
justly to alarm the friends of their country, and of the Protestant succession:
That for a Minister to support low men, who were originally improper for the
high trust to which they were advanced, after complaints made of dark, suspicious,
and unwarrantable methods made use of by such men, in their plan of education,
and to protect and countenance such men in their insolent and unheard of behaviour to their superiors, is a foundation for suspecting the worst designs in such
Ministers: That, it being notorious that books *, inculcating the worst maxims
of government, and defending the most avowed tyrannies, have been put into the
hands

* Father Orleans's Revolutions of the House of Stuart.—Ramsays travels of Cyrus.—Sir Robert
Filmer's Petriarch, and other books inculcating the same principles.

had it from Lord BATH, who told him, the *official* men ought never to be trusted with information of any measure, until it was given them to execute. They were the *servants*, he said, of the executive power; not the power itself. This extraordinary doctrine will appear more fully, if the letters at Fonthill are are printed; for Mr. Alderman BECKFORD was one of those, who at this time, paid their devoirs at Leicester-house.

After hands of the Prince of Wales, it cannot but affect the memorialists, with the most melancholy apprehensions, when they find that the men who had the honesty and resolution to complain of such astonishing methods of instruction, are driven away from Court†, and the men, who have dared to teach such doctrines, are continued in trust and favour. That the security of this Government, being built on Whig principles, is alone supported by Whig zeal. That the establishment of the present Royal Family being settled in the timely overthrow of Queen Anne's last Ministry, it cannot but alarm all true Whigs, to hear of schoolmasters of very contrary principles, being thought of for preceptors ; and to see none but the friends and pupils of the late Lord Bolingbroke entrusted with the education of a Prince, whose family that Lord endeavoured, by his measures, to exclude, and by his writings to expel, from the throne of these kingdoms: That there being great reason to believe, that a noble Lord has accused one of the Preceptors of Jacobitism, it is astonishing that no notice has been taken of a complaint of so high a nature; on the contrary, the accused person continues in the same trust, without any enquiry into the grounds of the charge, or any step taken by the accused, to purge himself of a crime of so black a dye: That no satisfaction being given to the Governor and Preceptor, one of whom, though a Nobleman of the most unblemished honour, and the other a Prelate of the most unbiassed

† Alluding to the resignations of Lord Harcourt and Dr. Hayter, who were succeeded by Lord Waldegrave and Dr. Stone.
The following lines were written under Dr. Hayter's portrait, published at this time:

  Not gentler virtues glow'd in Cambray's breast,
  Not more his young Telemachus was bless'd ;
  'Till Envy, Faction, and ambitious rage,
  Drove from a guilty Court the pious Sage.
  Back to his flock with transport, he withdrew,
  And but one sigh, an honest one, he knew !
  O guard my royal Pupil, Heaven ! he said !
  Let not his youth be, like my age, betray'd !
  I would have form'd his footsteps in thy way,
  But Vice prevails, and impious men bear sway !

VOL. I.   S

CHAP. XI.
1753.

After STONE and MURRAY had been acquitted by the Privy Council, very little attention was paid to Leicester-house, or its concerns, by the PELHAMS, or their Whig friends. In a very few years, the ideas of a separate interest, and of a separate party, were become perfectly visible at Leicester-house.

CHAP.

unbiassed virtue, who have both been treated in the grossest terms of abuse, by a menial servant of the family; it is derogatory to his Majesty's authority, under which they acted; is an affront to the Peerage; and an outrage to the dignity of the Church. That whoever advised the refusal of an audience to the Bishop of Norwich, who was so justly alarmed at the wrong methods which he saw taken in the education of the Prince of Wales, is an enemy to this country, and can only mean, at least, to govern by a faction, or is himself influenced by a more dangerous faction, which intends to overthrow the Government, and restore that of the exiled and arbitrary House of Stuart. That to have a Scotchman [*Murray*] of a most disaffected family, and allied in the nearest manner, to the Pretender's first Minister, consulted in the education of the Prince of Wales, and intrusted with the most important secrets of Government, must tend to alarm and disgust the friends of the present Royal Family, and to encourage the hopes and attempts of the Jacobites. Lastly, the Memorialists cannot help remarking, that the three or four low, dark, suspected persons, are the only men whose station is fixed and permanent; but that all the great offices and officers, are so constantly varied and shuffled about, to the disgrace of this country, that the best affected persons apprehend, that there is a settled design in these low and suspected people, to infuse such jealousies, caprices, and ficklenefs, into the two Ministers, whose confidence they engross, as may render this Government ridiculous and contemptible, and facilitate the revolution, which the Memorialists think they have but too much reason to fear is meditating.

GOD PRESERVE THE KING.

CHAP. XII.

Sufidiary treaties with Hanover, Hesse and Russia—Payment to Russia refused—Duke of Newcastle sends Mr. Yorke to Mr. Pitt—Mr. Fox offers to join Mr. Pitt—Debate on the subsidiary treaties—Mr. Pitt turned out—His balances found in the Bank—The Duke's Ministry appointed—Further debate on the treaties—France menaces an invasion of Great Britain—Hessians and Hanoverians arrive in England—France takes Minorca—Mr. Pitt and Mr. Fox explain the causes of that capture—Another cause—Convention with Prussia.

ON the 15th of September, 1755, the King returned from Hanover, with a subsidiary treaty he had concluded with Hesse, for 12,000 thousand men, for the defence of Hanover or Great Britain. Another treaty with Russia, which he had negotiated abroad, for 40,000 men, for the defence of Hanover, in case that Electorate should be invaded, was *finished*, and signed at Kensington on the 30th of the same month.

In the month of October, a draft from Petersburgh, was presented to the British Exchequer for 100,000l. in consequence of the Russian treaty. Mr. LEGGE consulted Mr. PITT. They united in refusing payment, until the treaty had been approved by Parliament.

While the King was at Hanover, the Duke of NEWCASTLE received information of the negotiations carrying on there; and being sensible of the disapprobation with which the treaties with Hesse and Russia, would be received in England, he endeavoured, by negotiations at home, to strengthen his ministerial power.

CHAP. XII.
1755.

Mr. Yorke sent to Mr. Pitt.

Of all his opponents, he reckoned Mr. PITT the most formidable: to him, therefore, he first applied. He sent the Hon. CHAS. YORKE to him, to *found him*, as he called it. When Mr. YORKE had opened his business, and began to make a tender of the Duke's sincere friendship for Mr. PITT, his Grace's unlimited confidence in ——— Mr. PITT stopped him short, and said, " that as to friendship and confidence, there were none between them; if ever there had been any, they were now entirely destroyed: that he (Mr. PITT) laboured under the King's displeasure, which the Duke of NEWCASTLE ought to have removed; the Duke perfectly knew, that the royal displeasure arose from misrepresentation, and until that proscription was taken off, he would enter into no conversation whatever, either with his Grace, or with any body from him."

Mr. Fox offers to join Mr. Pitt.

Mr. Fox having been informed of this difference between the Duke of NEWCASTLE and Mr. PITT, made a proposal to join Mr. PITT against the Duke of NEWCASTLE. Mr. PITT rejected the proposal. It is easy to see Mr. PITT's motive for this. Mr. Fox was the favourite of the Duke of CUMBERLAND; and his Royal Highness had differed with the Duke of NEWCASTLE, concerning the preparations for war, in which he thought the Minister negligent and backward; and he had in contemplation the appointment of a new Ministry;—if Mr. PITT had accepted Mr. Fox's proposal, he must have taken a subordinate situation; which he would never think of under Mr. Fox.

The Prince's party at Leicester-house, was encreasing, and Mr. PITT was supposed to belong to them; but it was not true; he was their friend, but not their coadjutor.

Parties

Parties were in this state when Parliament met, on the 13th of November, 1755.

CHAP. XII.
1755.

The treaties with Russia and Hesse were mentioned in the King's speech. And an insinuation of an engagement to approve of them, was introduced in the Address of each House.

Mr. PITT and Mr. LEGGE condemned them in the strongest terms.

Mr. PITT said they were advised, framed, and executed, not with a view to the defence of Great Britain, in case she should be invaded by France: not with a view to protect the allies of Great Britain, if they should be attacked by France: but purely and entirely for the preservation of Hanover, against the attempts of France and her confederates; which I believe to be so entirely the only object of the treaties, that I am convinced they would not have been made, had not that Electorate belonged to the Sovereign of this island.

Mr. Pitt's speech against the treaties with Hesse, and Russia.
M.S.

They must be considered as parts of a vast comprehensive system, to gather and combine the powers of the European continent into a defensive alliance, of magnitude sufficient to withstand the utmost efforts of France and her adherents against the Electorate; and all this to be effected at the single expence and charge of Great Britain.

I conceive this whole system and scheme of politics, to be absolutely impracticable.

This unsizable project, impracticable and desperate as it is, with respect to all human probability of success, will, if fully pursued, bring bankruptcy upon Great Britain.

The three last wars with France cost Britain above one hundred and twenty millions of money, according to the best of my information; which sum amounts to the rate of more than forty millions each war. If I were to be provided with materials to be more exact, I should not think it worth while to consult them for the sake of accuracy, the immensity of the sum being such by any calculation, that a mistake of a few millions can produce no sensible abatement in the argument; for whether forty or thirty millions be the medium of our former expence in the three wars with

CHAP. XII. with France, the present system of politics, if carried roundly into execution, presents us with an effusion of treasure still more enormous, because in the first place, the maintenance of our just and necessary war, in North America, an object which had no place in the times of King William and Queen Anne, and did not run very high in the late war, will prove a very inflammatory article in our account; and in the next place, the expence of paying and feeding those military multitudes which fought the former wars, was divided between the English, the Dutch, and other nations, in the alliance. All which expence is by the system of these treaties prepared for Britain alone; and when we consider, that such immense issues of money, outmeasuring any experiment of past time, are to be supplied by new loans, heaped upon a debt of eighty millions, who will answer for the consequence, or insure us from the fate of the decayed States of antiquity.

1755

We are are pressed into the service of an Electorate. We have suffered ourselves to be deceived by names and sounds, the balance of power, the liberty of Europe, a common cause, and many more such expressions, without any other meaning, than to exhaust our wealth, consume the profits of our trade, and load our posterity with intolerable burthens. None but a nation, that had lost all signs of virility would submit to be so treated.*

The

* Mr. PITT spoke a second time in this debate. It is not at present known, that any notes have been preserved of this second speech. But it is certain, that the argument of it was prefectly similar to the following Protest.

HOUSE OF LORDS, *November 13, 1755.*

It was moved to leave out these words in the motion for an address—
" Or against any other of his dominions, although not belonging to the Crown
" of Great Britain, in case they shall be attacked on account of the part taken by
" his Majesty, for the support of the essential interests of Great Britain."

After debate,

The question was put, " whether those words shall stand part of the question?"
It was resolved in the affirmative.

Dissentient,

1st. Because the words of the address objected to, pledging the honour of the
nation

The address, however, was agreed to. But next day the Duke's negotiations for a new Ministry being finished, and his arrangements ready, Sir THOMAS ROBINSON resigned, upon a pension for three lives, and the Wardrobe. Mr. Fox was on the same day, appointed Secretary of State in his room.

CHAP. XII.
1755.

On the 20th of November 1755, Mr. PITT and Mr. LEGGE were

Mr. Pitt dismiss'd.

nation to his Majesty in defence of his Electoral dominions, at this critical conjuncture, and under our present encumbered and perilous circumstances, tend not only to mislead his Majesty into a fallacious and delusive hope, that they can be defended at the expence of this country, but seem to be the natural and obvious means of drawing on attacks upon those Electoral dominions; thereby kindling a ruinous war upon the continent of Europe, in which it is next to impossible that we can prove successful, and under which Great Britain and the Electorate itself may be involved in one common destruction.

2dly. Because it is, in effect, defeating the intention of that part of the act of Settlement (the second great charter of England), whereby it is enacted, ' That in case the crown, and imperial dignity of this realm shall hereafter come to any person not being a native of this kingdom of England, the nation be not obliged to engage in any war for the defence of any dominions or territories, which do not belong to the crown of England, without the consent of Parliament." For if, at this juncture, under all the circumstances of our present quarrel with France, to which no other prince in Europe is a party, and in which we do not call for, **or** wish to receive, the least assistance from the Electorate of Hanover, it shall be deemed necessary in justice and gratitude, for this nation to make the declaration objected to, there never can be a situation, or point of time, the same reasons may not be pleaded, and subsist in full force; nor can Great Britain ever engage in a war with France, in the defence of her most essential interests, her commerce, and her colonies, in which she will not be deprived of the most invaluble advantages of situation, bestowed upon her by God and Nature, as an island.

3dly. Because, without any such previous engagement, his Majesty might safely rely upon the known attachment of this House to his sacred person, and upon the generosity of this country, famous and renowned in all times, for her humanity and magnanimity, that we should set no other bounds to an object so desirable, but those of absolute necessity and self-preservation, the first and great law of nature. TEMPLE."

CHAP. XII. dismissed from their offices, as were also Messrs. GEO. and JAMES
1755. GRENVILLE.

It is proper to remark, not only because the circumstance is peculiar, and exhibiting a prominent feature in Mr. PITT's character; but as it is an example worthy the imitation of all honest statesmen, That when Mr. PITT was turned out, all the balances belonging to his office, were lodged in the Bank. Those who encouraged the many attempts which were made to throw a shade upon his moral character, were the discoverers of this fact, to their utter mortification.

New ministry. Sir GEO. LYTTELTON, afterwards Lord LYTTELTON, was made Chancellor of the Exchequer, Lord BARRINGTON, Secretary at War, Lord DARLINGTON and Lord DUPPLIN joint Paymaster, Mr. DODDINGTON, afterwards Lord MELCOMBE, Treasurer of the Navy; and many other alterations took place, which the reader will find in the general list of Administrations, at the end of the work.

The new Administration were called the *Duke's Ministry*; because his Royal Highness had recommended the principal persons who composed it. Notwithstanding the respectability of the recommendation, yet there never was an Administration more unpopular and odious:

The first measure was to vote the 100,000l. for Russia, which Mr. PITT and Mr. LEGGE had refused to pay: also 54,000l. to the Landegrave of Hesse.

Mr. Pitt's speech against foreign subsidies. M.S. Mr. PITT opposed these votes. He contended, that a naval war, we could and ought to support; but a continental war, upon this system, we could not. He admitted, that regard ought to be had to Hanover; but it should be secondarily. If Hanover was made our *first* object, and

we

we proceeeded upon this fyſtem, it would lead us to bankruptcy. It was impoſſible to defend Hanover by fubſidies. An open country could not be defended againſt a neighbour, who could march 150,000 men into it, and fupport them by as many more. If Hanover ſhould be attacked on account of her connection with Great Britain, we ought not to make peace, until we had procured her full and ample fatisfaction, for every injury and damage ſhe may have fuſtained. But the idea of defending Hanover by fubſidies, he ridiculed, as prepoſterous, abfurd, and impracticable. This fyſtem, he ſaid, would, in a few years, coſt us more money than the fee fimple of the Electorate was worth; for it was a place of fuch inconfiderable note, that its name was not to be found the map. He ardently wiſhed to break theſe fetters, which chained us, like Prometheus, to that barren rock.

In the months of January and February, 1756, France began to march large bodies of her troops towards the fea coaſt, particularly into Picardy, and to Dunkirk; and threatened to invade Great Britain. Theſe prepartions overwhelmed our timid Cabinet with alarm and defpair. The Miniſtry thought it was "wifeſt and beſt" to defend Great Britain with an army. Accordingly in the month of March, the King fent a meſſage to Parliament, acquainting them, that he had made a requiſition for a body of Heſſian troops, purfuant to the treaty lately made with the Landgrave of Heſſe Caſſel, to be brought forthwith hither.— Both Houſes thanked the King for his meſſage.

The unanimity with which theſe addreſſes of thanks had been carried, encouraged Mr. Fox to move another addreſs to the King; which was, befeeching his Majeſty, that for the more effectual defence of this iſland, and for the better fecurity of the religion and liberty of his fubjects againſt the threatened attack by a foreign enemy, he would be graciouſly pleaſed to order twelve battalions of his Electoral troops, together with the ufual detachment of artillery, to be forthwith brought into this kingdom.

CHAP. XII.

1755.

There

CHAP. XII. There was some debate upon this motion; but people in ge-
1755. neral were afraid to oppose it; because they foresaw it would
be immediately said they were Jacobites, and meant to favour a
design of bringing in the Pretender again; and Mr. Fox threw
out this idea, when he made the motion.

Mr. Pitt is against bringing in foreign troops. Mr. PITT however declared his disapprobation of the measure; the natural force of the nation, he said, was sufficient to
repel any attack of the enemy. That state alone is a Sovereign
state *qui suis stat viribus, non alieno pendet arbitrio*, which subsists
by its own strength, not by the courtesy of its neighbours.

Accordingly next month both Hessians and Hanoverians arrived in England, and were encamped in different parts of the
kingdom.

The people hearing their danger from authority, and seeing
these foreigners brought over to defend them, were panic struck,
and gave themselves up to despair.

This conduct of the Court of France, in menacing an invasion upon England, was no other than a feint to conceal her
real design; which was an attack upon Minorca, or Gibraltar.
The French Cabinet had formed this design with a view to induce Spain to join in the war; but they did not communicate
their design to the Court of Madrid, until it was too late. For
the King of Great Britain in his memorials to the Spanish ministry, presented by the British minister at Madrid, complained of
the conduct of the French in America, and of their hostile designs
in Europe; of which the King takes notice in his speech at the
opening of the session, and says, that the King of Spain had assured him he would observe a strict neutrality.

In

In the month of December 1755, it was deliberated in the French Cabinet, whether they should attack Gibraltar, or Minorca. The former was determined upon; and that when it was conquered, it should be given to Spain, if Spain would join France in the war against Great Britain. The King of Spain rejected the proposal, on account of the pacific assurance abovementioned, which he had so recently given. So the French changed their plan, and attacked Minorca. They might have taken Gibraltar at that time, for it was almost defenceless. It is not probable, that it would have held out so long as fort St. Philip did. However, some months before the French landed upon Minorca, our Ministry received repeated information of the preparations making at Toulon, for equipping a fleet, and embarking an army, with all the implements necessary for a siege, and the most positive assurances, that Minorca was the object of attack; but they were so thoroughly frightened by the French menaces of an invasion of Great Britain, that they gave neither attention nor credit to the information concerning Minorca; although it came in streams from all parts of Italy, the south of France, and other places. In March they believed the intelligence, and not before. The fate of Minorca, and all the circumstances attending it, are very well known. Lord ANSON was the person most in fault.

Mr. PITT upon his legs in the House of Commons, charged the loss of Minorca upon Lord ANSON, and the Duke of NEWCASTLE; and added, with respect to Lord ANSON particularly, that he was not fit to command a cock-boat upon the river Thames. [But in his speech, on the 22d of Jan. 1770, which see in the second volume, he said the loss of Minorca was owing to the want of four battalions.]

CHAP. XII.
1755.

Mr. Fox said, the loss of Minorca was owing to the Dutch refusing the six thousand men, he demanded, according to the treaty of 1674; for had they been granted, he could have relieved Minorca. There may be something in this; but the Dutch were justifiable in their refusal: if they had complied, the French would have treated them as principals in the war. The great error was in the Admiralty not sending a larger fleet, and not sending it sooner. Mr. BYNG's only fault was, acting with too much prudence. He was sacrificed, through the management of Lord H——, to screen Lord ANSON; and so determined were this party upon the measure, that they had provided a Naval Officer upon whom they could rely, for *President* of the Court-Martial; had not Lord TEMPLE prevented it. It is one of the worst features in the character of GEORGE the SECOND, that he yielded to this manœuvre; and he was highly offended with Lord TEMPLE for defeating it. Mr. PITT said afterwards in the House of Commons, that more honour would have accrued to the King and nation, from a pardon to the unhappy Admiral, than from his execution.

Admiral Byng sacrificed.

Convention with Prussia.

In order the more effectually to provide for the security of Hanover, early in the month of January 1756, a convention was made with the King of Prussia; the main object of which was, to keep all foreign troops out of Germany; and Parliament voted 20,000l. to make good this treaty. Thus the treaty with Russia was virtually renounced.

CHAP.

CHAP. XIII.

Further account of Leicester House---The two Princesses of Brunswick in England---Observations---Mr. Fox resigns---Carte-blanche offered to Mr. Pitt---Ministry changed---Mr. Pitt appointed Secretary of State---The King and Duke wished to have kept Mr. Fox.

THE nation was highly incensed by the losses of Minorca, of the fort of Oswego in America, and by some other defeats and miscarriages. The appearance of the Hessians and Hanoverians in England, served but to encrease the public indignation. A spirit of resentment, and of detestation of the Ministers, pervaded every part of the kingdom.

CHAP. XIII.
1756.

Besides the frowning aspect of public affairs, there was another of a private, but not less alarming nature to the Ministry. This was the party at Leicester-house. The Prince's levees were crouded. Mr. PITT, Lord TEMPLE, and the GRENVILLES, and many others, were frequently seen there. This gave the Lord *Chancellor (Hardwicke)* and the Duke of NEWCASTLE much concern. *Their wish now was to get possession of the Prince.* Accordingly they advised the King to send a message to his Royal Highness, offering him a suite of apartments at St. James's and Kensington palaces. Had this step been taken in the year 1752, it might have been productive of the happiest emancipation. There would have been wisdom in the measure at that time: and it must have succeeded. But in 1756 it was too late: the blossom was off, and the fruit was set. Upon the receipt of this message Leicester-house was thrown into

Leicester-house Party

into the deepest consternation. The two Princesses of Brunswick, whom the King had last year invited to Hanover, were now in England.

We are yet too near the time, to relate with safety, all the circumstances of this interesting affair.

Observations. There is such a delicacy prevails in England, greater than in some arbitrary monarchies, concerning the conduct of the Royal Family, that truth of them is usually suppressed, until it is forgotten. The justice of History is thereby perverted; and the Constitution, in this important point, is literally and efficiently destroyed. The King of England is no more than the first Magistrate. It is an office held in trust. And although the maxim is, that he can do no wrong, which is founded upon the presumption, that every Privy Counsellor, according to the Act of Settlement, signs the advice he gives; yet this law is not always observed; and if it were, all important matters are transacted in the King's name, and he assents to them. In whose name then are they to be scrutinized, examined, and canvassed? The adviser is seldom known. The nation has unquestionably as deep an interest in the conduct of the Royal Family, as in the conduct of the Ministry. Will any body now say, that the German measures in the reign of *George the Second*, were not the *favourite* measures of that King, or that they did not *originate* with him? If the free spirit of the Constitution was fairly recognized, it must appear, that the conduct of the Royal Family, is, in every part of it, a proper subject for public disquisition. The people are interested in it; the welfare of the country is concerned in it. Even the *female*

branches

branches are called the *children of the nation*; and when they marry, their portions are taken out of the public purse. But lawyers say, the people can only know, and speak, by their representatives. If this legal opinion is well founded, the liberty of the press, which Englishmen sometimes esteem, but oftener betray, is a shadow, an *ignis fatuus*. Certain it is, that *time-serving* judges and *timid* juries, have made a deeper incision in the liberties of England, than all the arms of all the STUARTS. Some years ago it was a notion in Westminster-hall, that no person out of Parliament, had a right to make observations upon the speech delivered by the King to his Parliament. But after a little reflection and examination, this law-notion was exploded; it was insupportable: it tended to establish a privileged vehicle of imposition upon the whole nation: than which nothing could be more unjust, nor more foreign to the British Constitution. The people have a right to examine the conduct of every man in a public situation; and it will hardly be contended, that they have no interest in that of the Royal Family. Therefore in those cases, where the party is not only in the highest state of elevation, but possesses the greatest extent of power, does not the *exercise* of this right become most essentially their concern? To this delicacy, or something worse, is to be ascribed, the general falsification of all *modern* history. If the Reader will give himself the trouble to compare the anecdotes of this work, with the histories of the times, he will see a manifest difference; and yet the writer declares, that he has not inserted a single word, which, in his judgment, is not founded in the purest veracity.

We

CHAP. XIII. We will return to the fact before us. All that can with
1756. prudence, or impunity, be added at prefent is, the offer was not
accepted*. Upon which fomething elfe was talked of. But
Lord TEMPLE and Mr. PITT *" ſtood in the gap, and* SAVED
LEICESTER-HOUSE †."

The Miniſters having failed in their defign; and being
frightened at the ſtorm of public indignation, which was ready
to burſt upon their heads, determined to refign. The Duke of
NEWCASTLE applied to Mr. PITT. His Grace affured him,
the King was perfectly agreeable to take him into his fervice.
Mr. PITT anfwered him fomewhat abruptly, that he would
accept of no fituation under his Grace. This was on the 20th
of October 1756. The King then defired the Duke of DEVON-
SHIRE to go to Mr. PITT, who was at Hayes, in Kent, and offer
Carte-blanche him a *carte-blanche*, except as to Mr. Fox, whom the King
offered to Mr.
Pitt. wifhed to keep in his fervice. Mr. PITT gave a pofitive refufal
as to Mr. Fox.

Miniſtry refign. When Mr. Fox heard this, he immediately refigned: His re-
fignation threw the Miniſtry into confufion; and diſtreſſed the
King extremely. The Duke of NEWCASTLE and the reſt of his
Majeſty's fervants refigned alfo.

New Miniſtry. At the earneſt requeſt of the King, the Duke of DEVONSHIRE
took the Duke of NEWCASTLE's place at the Treafury; and

* A Princefs of the Houfe of Saxe Gotha was in the contemplation of the
Princefs of Wales. But the intention was difapproved by a Higher Perfon.

† Thefe are the concluding words of one of Lord T——'s letters, in
which the particulars of this affair are ſtated; and which, may, in a future day
be publifhed, to fhew the *gratitude* of certain people.

again

again waited on Mr. PITT at Hayes, with a meſſage from his Majeſty, requeſting to know the terms upon which he would come into office. Mr. PITT gave his arrangement. Himſelf to be Secretary of State. Lord TEMPLE firſt Lord of the Admiralty. Mr. LEGGE Chancellor of the Exchequer. The Great Seal to be in Commiſſion. G. GRENVILLE Treaſurer of the Navy. J. GRENVILLE a Lord of the Treaſury, &c. &c.—The whole were accepted.

CHAP. XIII.
1756.

While this change of Miniſters was in agitation, the King gave orders for the return of the Hanoverians to Germany. It was the King's reſolution, to aſſemble an army for the defence of Hanover, early in the ſpring, and to give the command of it to the Duke of CUMBERLAND. It was with this view, that the treaty with Heſſe had been made; and that the Duke of CUMBERLAND had formed the laſt Miniſtry, as conſiſting of thoſe perſons in whom his Royal Highneſs thought he could beſt confide; and that was the reaſon the King wiſhed to keep Mr. Fox in place, becauſe he knew the Duke had a great partiality for him. But the tide of public odium having ſet ſo ſtrong againſt Mr. Fox, and his coadjutors, the Court were obliged to ſurrender; and to admit Mr. PITT. The King, however, continued his reſolution to purſue the plan he had laid down, for the protection of his German dominions.

On the 28th of November, 1756, the Prince of WALES's houſhold being eſtabliſhed, he held his firſt levee at Savile-houſe.*

* The principal perſons of his Royal Highneſs's houſehold were,
    Earl of Bute, groom of the ſtole,
    Earl of Huntingdon, maſter of the horſe.
    Earl of Suſſex, Lord Down, and Lord Robert Bertie, with the Earls of Pembroke and Euſton, and Lord Digby, lords of the bed-chamber.
    Meſſrs. Schutz and Peachy, with Hon. S. Marſham, Hon. G. Monſon, C. Ingram, and E. Nugent, grooms of the bed-chamber.
    Lord Bathurſt, Treaſurer.
    Hon. James Brudenell, privy purſe.——S. Fanſhaw, comptroller.

CHAP. XIV.

Mr. Pitt's first administration—Raises two thousand Highlanders—Refuses to support the Duke of Cumberland—Commanded to resign—Presented with the freedom of several cities and corporations—The King's distresses---Mr. Pitt made Minister upon his own terms---His triumph over Mr. Fox---The correspondence of the Admiralty given to Mr. Pitt.

ON the second of December, 1756, Parliament met. The first measure of Government, after sending away the Hessian troops, was the establishment of a national militia.

On the first of January 1757, orders were given, for raising two thousand men in the Highlands of Scotland, for the British service in America. This measure reflected the greatest honour upon Mr. PITT's wisdom and penetration; and whether he adopted it from the paper, which the reader will find in the note, or whether it originated with himself, it equally shewed the superiority of his mind, to all vulgar and local prejudices.* He sent a squadron to the East Indies, under Admiral *Stevens,* and

* The following plan, for carrying on the war, was submitted to his Royal Highness the Duke of CUMBERLAND in May 1756, and was by his Royal Highness's command, delivered to Mr. PITT, by the Earl of ALBEMARLE, in December 1756:—

"France constantly keeping numerous armies in pay, is always prepared for war. Wars of a short duration, for the most part, have proved advantageous to that kingdom; but wars of long continuance, very detrimental, and ruinous to the people. If the present war is well conducted, before the next year ends, that nation will be filled with complaints of losses, and his Majesty's subjects joyful for the successes against their enemies.

"The land forces in Great Britain and Ireland, may be put on a better establishment, by raising more infantry. Two thousand horse of all denominations, are

and another to the West Indies, under Admiral *Cotes*. His resolution was to employ the whole British fleet.

CHAP. XIV.
1757.

The debates in Parliament were few, and inconsiderable this session. Although Mr. PITT delivered a message from the King, requesting a sum of money for the army that was forming in Germany, he did not support the motion.

The are sufficient for the services in Great Britain; and one thousand dragoons for Ireland. The troopers and dragoons reduced, will form several companies of grenadiers.

" The British regiments of foot would appear nobly, if they contained twelve companies in each; two of them grenadiers.

" Improvement in agriculture, fisheries, multiplying and enlarging manufactures, the increase of buildings, &c. give so much employment, that workmen are wanted in most parts of England.

" Therefore it is expedient to procure out of Germany, some regiments, for the service of America, and reward them with lands, at the conclusion of the war.

" *Two regiments, a thousand men in a corps, may be raised in the North of Scotland for the said service, and on the same terms. No men on this island are better qualified for the American war, than the Scots Highlanders.*

" Certainly the Scots regiments in the Dutch service, ought immediately to be recalled. Better it will be for them to serve their own country, than perish in sickly garrisons.

" In the North of Ireland two thousand brave Protestants, or more, if necessary, might be raised with celerity, and facility; upon the promise of having lands assigned to them, when the war is finished.

" It ought not to be supposed, that the French really intend to invade Great Britain or Ireland; the difficulties and dangers which must attend the enterprize, are more than enough to deter them; nevertheless, the report of an invasion, made such an impression on the minds of some men in power, or they would have it so believed, that this idle rumour or feint, occasioned the loss of Minorca, and the neglect of sending so many ships as were necessary in the West Indies.

" The naval forces of Great Britain, being more than twice as strong as the French, and this kingdom so well provided with conveniences, for constructing ships of war, that three may be built here, as soon as one in France; the British cruisers and squadrons, may always exceed the French by a third in all parts; which must distress their commerce to a high degree, ruin their fisheries, and starve the inhabitants in the French sugar colonies. The war continuing three

CHAP. XIV.   The late Cabinet faw, that the King was very far from being
~~~~~~~
1757.   reconciled to Mr. PITT. They employed every fecret whif-
perer, to widen the breach, and filled every private channel to
to the royal ear, with prejudices againſt him. An enquiry was
inſtituted into the cauſes of the loſs of Minorca, which, if poſſible, encreaſed their diſapprobation. But the circumſtance which
offended his Majeſty moſt, was Mr. PITT's refuſal to ſupport
the army in Germany; in which refuſal he was joined by Mr.
LEGGE. The DUKE was preparing to ſet out for Germany;
and the royal *requeſt*, at firſt, was to have an immediate ſupply of
money, without waiting for the approbation of Parliament. The
Mr. Pitt refuſes
to ſupport the D. King and Duke, finding the new Miniſters hoſtile to their plan
of Cumberland.
of German meaſures, determined to remove them. The Duke
declared, he would not go to Germany unleſs Mr. PITT was
removed.

three or four years, France muſt inevitably be greatly diſtreſſed; her merchants
bankrupted; and her manufactures brought to ruin; others obliged to ſeek their
food in foreign countries; whereas, in England, the manufactures, more eſpecially, the woollen, ſell at higher rates, when at war with France, than in times
of peace.

" When the French perceive, this nation takes proper means for maintaining
a war, and THAT THEIR SECRET FRIENDS ARE DEPRIVED OF DIRECTING
AND ADMINISTERING THE AFFAIRS OF THIS GOVERNMENT, (a) they will uſe
every artifice and device, that fraud and cunning can ſuggeſt, *to make an inſiduous
peace*; but it is earneſtly recommended, that the war may endure, until the enemy
is entirely ſubdued in America, and ſo totally diſabled, as not to become trouble-
ſome to this kingdom in future times."

NOTE, by the Author of the preceding:—

(a) When his Royal Highneſs formed the Adminiſtration, of which Mr. Fox had the lead, the
French perceived this influence of their SECRET FRIENDS ſomewhat abridged; and although they
ſtill had a ſhare of power; yet they were obliged to act very cautiouſly. Upon the Adminiſtration
being put into the hands of Mr. PITT, theſe SECRET FRIENDS were WHOLLY EXCLUDED from the
Cabinet. While he guided, Great Britain was IN HER OWN HANDS. When in the next reign, peace was
reſolved upon, thoſe SECRET FRIENDS came forward again, to conduct the negotiation. Then Mr.
PITT was forced out of Adminiſtration. He then felt the Secret Influence of the Cloſet. Our allies
were deſerted; and peace was made with the enemies of the nation, who were the friends of THESE
SECRET FRIENDS.

removed. On the 5th of April, 1757, the King commanded Mr. PITT to resign; and on the ninth the Duke set out for Germany. Lord TEMPLE was also turned out; and Lord WINCHELSEA put at the head of the Admiralty; Mr. LEGGE was turned out, and Lord MANSFIELD was appointed to succeed him; no successor was appointed to Mr. PITT; Lord HOLDERNESSE, the other Secretary of State, executed the duties of both offices.

<small>CHAP. XIV.
1757.
Commanded to resign.</small>

This change of the Ministry, operated like a convulsion on the nation. The people were exasperated beyond measure, at the dismissions of Mr. PITT and Mr. LEGGE; whom they now joined together, as the political saviours of the kingdom. These dismissions were universally ascribed to the secret influence, which it was believed, the late Ministers still possessed in the King's closet.

It was judged unconstitutional to address the throne upon these changes; therefore another method was adopted to convince the King of the sentiments of the nation. This was to send addresses of thanks to the dismissed Patriots, expressing the highest approbation of their conduct; with presents of their freedom of most of the principal corporations, in gold, and other boxes, of great value, and curious workmanship.

<small>Presented with the freedom of several places.</small>

This intestine commotion alarmed the Court exceedingly. They saw the danger of permitting the ferment to encrease. The Duke of NEWCASTLE, though at this time not in office, was the first person who went to the King, and advised his Majesty to recall Mr. PITT. The Monarch wept: He complained of all his servants. He thought none of them had acted with fidelity towards him, since the time of Sir R. WALPOLE. At length,

<small>King's distresses</small>

CHAP. XIV.
1757.

length, he confented to give the Duke of NEWCASTLE full power to negociate with Mr. PITT, and all his friends. The Duke of NEWCASTLE faw Mr. PITT and Lord TEMPLE privately: for although the ftream of popularity run in favour of Mr. PITT and Mr. LEGGE, yet in all meafures of confequence Mr. PITT folely confided in Lord TEMPLE. The Duke informed Mr. PITT, that he was commiffioned by the King, to agree to Mr. PITT's terms; and he hoped, and trufted, that fuch condefcenfion in his Majefty, would meet with the moft favourable interpretation. Mr. PITT's reply was full of gratitude and humility to the King. The Duke then faid, that it was his Majefty's wifh, to form an healing Adminiftration, and he had left it entirely to the Duke of NEWCASTLE and Mr. PITV, to fettle every arrangement, in the moft amicable manner.

Mr. Pitt made Miniftev upon his own terms.

Mr. PITT's firft propofition, was the exclufion of Lord ANSON from the Cabinet. The Duke of NEWCASTLE pleaded earneftly to have Lord HARDWICKE in the Cabinet. He faid it was the King's requeft. Mr. PITT confented, on condition that Sir ROBERT HENLEY had the Great Seal: this ftipulation was defired by Leicefter-houfe. Lord TEMPLE to be Privy Seal. Himfelf Secretary of State, as before. The Duke of NEWCASTLE offered Lord TEMPLE the Treafury. Mr. PITT interpofed, and faid, " that could not be; his Grace muft go there himfelf.* But, if at any time hereafter, he fhould think proper to

---

* There were two reafons for this. The firft was, the Houfe of Commons had been chofen by Mr. PELHAM; at whofe death, his *pocket lift* (as it is called) was given to the Duke of NEWCASTLE, and this circumftance made *another* ftipulation in the arrangement; which *was*, that the Duke fhould *transfer his majority* to Mr. PITT. Mr. PITT himfelf defcribed this fact, on a fubfequent occafion, in thefe words, " I borrowed the Duke of NEWCASTLE's majority to carry on the Public bufinefs."

The

to retire, Lord TEMPLE should succeed him." Having gone on some time, in making the arrangements, the Duke said, what shall we do with Mr. Fox? Mr. PITT replied, " he may have the Pay-office." This was a triumph to Mr. PITT—to put Mr. Fox *below* him, and into the office he had left. But it was a triumph too diminutive for the dignity of Mr. PITT's mind. However, he enjoyed it; which shews the influence of little passions in men of the first abilities. Lord ANSON was proposed for the Admiralty. Mr. PITT declared, that Lord ANSON should never have the Correspondence. The Duke replied, that would be such an alteration of the Board, as could not be made without his Majesty's consent. Here the conference broke off. Mr. PITT had an audience of the King. He laid before his Majesty, the difference between the Duke of NEWCASTLE and himself, concerning the Admiralty. The King consented, that the Correspondence with the naval officers, usually in the Board of Admiralty, should be given to Mr. PITT, and that the Board should only sign the dispatches, without being privy to their contents.* It was at this audience that the following remarkable words were spoken, which Lord NUGENT repeated

CHAP. XIV.
1757.

His triumph over Mr. Fox.

The other was—Lord TEMPLE would have had his brother, Mr. GEORGE GRENVILLL, for his Chancellor of the Exchequer; and in that case what could have been done with Mr. LEGGE? the public would not at that time have approved of any other person in that situation. Mr. PITT also knew, that there had been a *private* understanding between the Duke of NEWCASTLE and Mr. LEGGE, for some time past.

* The rule, or custom is, The Secretary of State sends all the orders respecting the navy, which have been agreed to in the Cabinet, to the Admiralty, and the Secretary to the Board writes those orders again, in the form of instructions, from the Admiralty, to the Admiral, or Captain of the fleet, expedition, &c. for whom they are designed: which instructions *must* be signed by three of the Board. But during Mr. PITT's Administration, he wrote the Instructions himself

CHAP. XIV. repeated in the House of Commons, in the year 1784; Mr.
1757. Pitt said, " Sire, give me your confidence, and I will deserve it." The King replied without hesitation, " Deserve my confidence, and you shall have it." Lord NUGENT added, "that Mr. PITT at last so won upon the King, that he was able to turn his very partialities in favour of Germany to the benefit of his country." Lord ANSON took the Admiralty, under Mr. PITT's limitation; and Mr. Fox took the Pay-office. Mr. LEGGE had the Exchequer. All the arrangements being settled, the parties all kissed hands in July 1757; and the nation was thereby restored to tranquility and satisfaction.

CHAP.

self, and sent them to their Lordships to be signed; always ordering his Secretary to put a sheet of white paper over the writing. Thus they were kept in perfect ignorance of what they had signed. And the Secretary and Clerks of the Board, were all in the same state of exclusion.

CHAP. XV.

Failure of the Duke of Cumberland---Expedition against Rochefort ---Distresses of the King of Prussia---Hanover plundered---Mr. Pitt's two propositions; one, to send a fleet into the Baltic; the other, to cede Gibraltar to Spain---Anecdote of the treaty of peace made in 1783---Effects of Mr. Pitt's first administration--- Miscarriage of the expedition against Louisbourg--Union of Russia, Sweden and Denmark, for the neutrality of the Baltic---Taking of the Dutch ships---Mr. Pitt opposes the proposition of sending the British fleet to the assistance of the Duke of Cumberland.

THE Duke of CUMBERLAND failed on the Continent. His Royal Highness attributed his failure to the want of British troops and money. His army was not only inferior to the enemy in number, but consisted entirely of Germans. The French pursued him almost to the sea coast. The King of Denmark commiserated his situation; and under that Monarch's mediation, a convention was signed, in the month of September 1757, between the Duke and Marshal *Richlieu*, the French General; by which the allied army were to retire to their respective countries.

The King of Prussia was driven out of Bohemia this summer, and an account arrived, of the suffocation at Calcutta.

Under all these discouraging circumstances, Mr. PITT had to commence his new Administration. His first measure was, an attempt to make a descent upon the coast of France. His view

CHAP. XV. in this, was to oblige the French to recall their troops from Hanover to protect their own kingdom. A fleet and an army were assembled. The destination was kept a profound secret. Sir EDW. HAWKE was commander of the fleet, and Mr. PITT corresponded with him. It is not a little remarkable, that when Mr. PITT ordered the fleet to be equipped, and appointed the period for its being at the place of rendezvous, Lord ANSON said, it was impossible to comply with the order; the ships could not be got ready in the time limited; and he wanted to know where they were going, in order to victual them accordingly. Mr. PITT replied, that if the ships were not ready at the time required, he would lay the matter before the King, and impeach his Lordship in the House of Commons. This spirited menace, produced the men of war and transports, all ready, in perfect compliance with the order. They sailed on the 8th of Sept. 1757, from Spithead. The force was considerable; and had it succeeded, must have made a deep impression. After lying some time before Rochefort, the fleet returned. The cause of the miscarriage was not precisely ascertained. Mr. PITT ascribed it to the inactivity of Sir JOHN MORDAUNT, who had the command of the troops. The friends of that officer ascribed it to the plan; which, in derision, they called *one of Mr. Pitt's visions*.

Mr. Pitt's two propositions. The distresses of the *King of Prussia* daily encreased. The Russians quickened their march against him. His territories were invaded on every side; and the French were plundering Hanover. In this situation of affairs, the Minister framed two propositions. The first was, to send a fleet into the Baltic, as early in the spring of 1758, as the season would permit; to overawe the Swedes and Russians, particularly the latter; and

To find a fleet to the Baltic.

to

to support the King of Prussia. The most formidable powers against the King of Prussia, were Austria and Russia. Against Austria he was able to defend himself; but Russia being a naval as well as military power, he could not oppose her with equal facility. Her vessels carried provisions, military stores, and reinforcements to her armies in Pomerania and Ducal Prussia; and thereby supported their operations with the most essential assistance. An alliance between the two Imperial Courts of Vienna and Petersburgh, is dangerous to the liberties of Europe. The King of Prussia is a barrier between them; but if either of them should be able to annex the Prussian power to her own, the independence of the other states would be in a critical situation. Upon this ground the proposition was made to the Court of Copenhagen, who at first seemed to approve of it.

The other proposition was to the Court of Madrid. The Sovereignty of the Mediterranean being lost to Great Britain with the island of Minorca, our ships having no port in that sea, wherein they could lie, or refit, it was become almost impossible to keep any fleet there, and absolutely impracticable, in time of war with the House of Bourbon, to carry on any considerable trade in the Levant. For these reasons Gibraltar was become of less importance to this country than formerly; while the expence to maintain and defend it, in case of war, must be encreased; therefore the proposition was, *to cede Gibraltar to Spain*, if the Court of Madrid would undertake to detach France from the war against Prussia and Hanover. The fact is important, and may surprise those who never heard it. But it is to be found in a dispatch to Sir BEN. KEENE, who at that time was the British Ambassador at Madrid: and to Gibraltar was added, the

CHAP. XV.
1757.

To cede Gibraltar to Spain.

CHAP. XV. British settlements on Honduras and the Musquito shore. Mr.
1757. PITT was not partial to Gibraltar. He would have ceded it to Spain in 1761, if he could thereby have dissolved the Bourbon family compact. In the negotiations for peace in 1783, the Spa-

Anecdote of the peace of 1783. nish minister at London, for some time insisted on the cession of Gibraltar; but having no equivalent to give, the Earl of SHELBURNE (since Marquis of LANSDOWN) firmly refused it; and the whole negotiation for peace was on the point of breaking off entirely, when the Spanish minister received instructions from his Court, to give up the point. Every reader will make his own comments on these facts. The objects intended to have been gained by the proposed cession, were, in their day, of the first importance.

Mr Pitt's first Administration. The effects of Mr. PITT's short, or first Administration, soon began to appear; and to confirm and encrease that confidence, which the nation had reposed in his wisdom and integrity. Admiral *Cotes*, whom he had dispatched to the West Indies, had recovered the honour of the British flag; and the East India Company felt themselves perfectly easy under the protection of Admiral *Stevens*, who at the same time had been dispatched to the East Indies. Nor were the effects of his being removed from Administration less conspicuous; for he had also, during the short time he was in office, ordered, and to a considerable degree prepared, a third fleet, which he designed for North America, the

Miscarriage of the expedition against Louisbourg. command of which he proposed for Admiral *Hawke*; which fleet was intended to co-operate with the army assembled at New York, under Lord LOUDON, in an attack on Louisbourg: but his successors had not his activity; they changed the command of the fleet to Admiral *Holbourne*; nor did the fleet sail from England until some months after the proper time; and instead

of

of joining the army at New York, Lord Loudon was waiting at Halifax, when Admiral *Holbourne* appeared on the American coast. The consequence of this delay was, the expedition was rendered abortive. The French at Louisbourg were prepared to receive them. Upon which the army returned to New York, and the fleet was dispersed in a storm. Had this expedition proceeded upon the plan it was originally formed, according to the time prescribed, and under the officers first named, there is the strongest reason to believe, the war in North America would have been of short duration; at most, it could have lasted but one campaign more; because the French could not have reinforced Quebec, and Canada would therefore have fallen a much easier conquest, than it afterwards proved. And to this consideration, may be added, that great part of that force, which was afterwards employed against Canada, would, in such case, have been employed *elsewhere*. It is impossible to state the extent of the misfortunes, which this abortive expedition brought after it, or the extent of the advantages, which might have flowed from it, had the plan been carried into execution by the person who formed it.

Before the conclusion of 1757, the unsound and unwise politics of 1755 and 1756, appeared in a new and unexpected manner. The convention with Prussia made in 1756, *for the keeping all foreign troops out of the Empire*, destroyed the treaty with Russia, made in 1755, for the defence of Hanover, because the *Russians* are *foreign troops*. After this example the Court of Copenhagen acted. The Danish minister communicated the British proposition of sending a fleet into the Baltic, to the Courts of Stockholm and Petersburgh. The last Court resented it highly, because her alliance with the Court of Vienna was concluded.

And

CHAP. XV.
1757.

And though she did not wish to go to war with England; yet sooner than break her faith with the Empress Queen, she would have done it. She therefore suggested an *expedient*; which was an imitation of the conduct of the British Court, who had first made a subsidiary treaty with her for troops, and afterwards rendered it ineffectual, by a convention with Prussia, *to keep all foreign troops out of the Empire*—She therefore proposed to to Sweden and Denmark, a maritime treaty of alliance, *to keep all foreign ships out of the Baltic*. Sweden being under the influence of French Counsels, entered into it immediately; and Denmark not chusing to incur the enmity of two such powerful neighbours, and being perhaps more under the influence of Russia than Great Britain, became a party to the treaty likewise.

Union of Russia, Sweden, and Denmark.

Thus the British fleet was excluded the Baltic, whatever the Prussian treaties may pretend (which will be seen in the *Appendix*). The Minister could not send a fleet into that sea, unless he made war upon those three powers; and he had too much penetration, not to see, that a war upon the Baltic, was synonimous to a war upon the British navy; which was supplied with naval stores from thence. Unless he sent a very powerful fleet, consisting of the largest and best ships, no effectual service could be expected; and if he did, the force against France must have been so essentially weakened by it, as to give the French a considerable superiority at sea. One fact only need be mentioned, that as soon as the season permitted the ports in the Baltic to be open, a fleet of twenty Russian, and ten Swedish ships of the line, appeared in the Baltic, to preserve the neutrality of that sea.

The

The French Minister was equally sensible of the sources of the Baltic, for the supply of his navy; and he bribed the Dutch, to become the carriers of his Baltic naval stores. But Mr. Pitt ordered the Dutch vessels, whenever laden with naval and military stores, to be constantly taken; which judicious and spirited resolution, contributed greatly to the successes of his Administration.*

CHAP. XV.
1757.

Taking of the Dutch ships.

Mr.

* When Mr. Pitt found the Dutch heartily inclined to assist the French with naval stores, he resolved to make them as heartily tired of doing it; for, without any ceremony, he gave orders that all Dutch ships with cargoes on on board, for the use of France, should be considered as the ships of enemies, not of neutrals. His orders were not without effect; and in consequence of the captures that ensued, the loudest clamours were raised in Holland against the English. The general cry there was for war. A memorial was presented to the States General in 1758, in the names of 269 of the principal Dutch merchants, who subscribed it; they complained that trade and navigation, the very sinews of the Republic, were in danger; that the Dutch flag was disregarded by the English, who had already taken 240 ships. They called upon the States General for the protection of their property. Nay, they offered to contribute each his contingent, and to arm at their own charge, for the support and protection of their navigation. The memorial concluded with this remarkable paragraph: " The petitioners flatter themselves, that the toils and the risks, to which their effects are exposed on the seas, will have their proper influence on the general body of the State; since the traders of this country, finding themselves left to discretion of a part of that nation with whom the State is most intimately connected, *will be forced to abandon it, to their great regret,* and *seek shelter and protection elsewhere*; which will give a mortal blow to the principal members of the State."

The Dutch, no doubt, must have been very severely handled, when they so far trespassed upon their love of money, as to offer to disburse and arm at their own charge, for the security of navigation; but what must we think of the provocation given to them by the British Minister, when we find the Dutch merchants ready to abandon their country, and become voluntary exiles in a foreign land!

The

CHAP. XV.
1757.

Mr. PITT laboured under many disadvantages, at the time of his restoration to the office of Secretary of State; his former plans had either been defeated, or rendered useless; and he was obliged to make great sacrifices, to correct the errors of others, before he could carry his future plans into execution. Nothing but the magnanimity of his spirit prevented the same interference, which had chilled the execution of his former measures, from extending its blighting influence over his future designs. When the fleet returned from Rochefort, a puerile scheme was proposed, by those whose impolitic measures had given birth to the Baltic alliance against us, to send the fleet to the assistance of the Duke of CUMBERLAND; who was flying before the French in Hanover. Mr. PITT alone resisted the proposal: upon which, the Duke of NEWCASTLE, and Lord HARDWICKE, who had pressed it, gave it up. Mr. PITT had not a thorough confidence in his coadjutors; and therefore he did not always assign his reasons for his opinion. On this occasion, he only said, that the assistance of a naval armament in the North had been frustrated; and therefore the scene, as well as the instrument of war, must be changed, before any hopes of success could be entertained; but if a contrary opinion

Mr. Pitt opposes sending the fleet to the assistance of the Duke.

The neutrality of the Dutch did not procure respect for their ports in America, as appears by a letter from St. Eustatia, published in the Amsterdam Gazette, April 9, 1758, wherein the writer declares, "that the depredations of the English are carried to the utmost height, and that the trade of St. Eustatia is at an end; the harbour being more closely blocked up than that of any enemy—that every vessel is stopped, carried off, and *confiscated*—that jealousy is the motive of the English; conveniency their right; and greediness their law; that the English had gone so far as to confiscate Dutch ships, merely for having entered French harbours, alledging, that as they paid the usual charges and customs in those harbours, they thereby became French property, &c."

nion prevailed, he would lay the Seals at his Majesty's feet, and retire from his situation. The Cabinet Ministers, from this time, resigned their judgment: in which they were influenced by two motives—One was, a dread of his superior abilities, which threw their minor talents into shade; the other was, an expectation, that, by permitting him freely to indulge in the exercise of his own opinions, he would precipitate his own exclusion from power, by drawing upon himself some capital disgrace; which they were confident, would, at the same time, restore to them the Administration of Government.*

The Duke of CUMBERLAND returned to England; and finding that his conduct had met with the disapprobation of the King, who disavowed the convention of Closter-Seven, he instantly resigned all his military employments, and retired to Windsor.

* At this period, and for several months past, there had issued from the press, a torrent of papers and pamphlets against Mr. PITT; condemning his plans, his measures, his principles, his politics, and even reviling his person; in which the King himself was not spared, for having taken him into his service, and for not dismissing him---all which were permitted to die unnoticed; he felt not the least smart from any of them. One day, when Mr. GRENVILLE mentioned some of them to him, he smiled, and only said, *the press is like " the air, a charter'd libertine."*

* Shakespeare—Henry V.

CHAP. XVI.

The battle of Rosbach, and its consequences—Its influence upon the British Councils—Sudden prorogation of Parliament—Union of the King and Mr. Pitt—The King of Prussia's recommendation—Hanoverians resume their arms under Duke Ferdinand—Observations on the German war.

CHAP. XVI.
1757.
Battle of Rosbach, and its consequences.

ALTHOUGH the operations of the war are foreign to this work; yet those events, from which important circumstances have arisen, and which having either been misrepresented by other writers, or been entirely omitted, it is necessary to mention. Of this nature was the *King of Prussia's* great victory at Rosbach, over the French and Germans, on the fifth of November 1757. No event during the war was attended with such interesting consequences. This victory may be said to have changed the scene, the plan, and the principle of the war. Besides the emancipation which it immediately gave to the King of Prussia, its effects were no less instantaneous and powerful on the Councils of Great Britain. The British Minister possessed an understanding to distinguish, and a genius to seize, a fortunate circumstance, and to improve it to the utmost advantage. Parliament had been appointed to meet on the 15th of November. Intelligence of this victory arrived at St. James's on the ninth in the morning. The moment the dispatches were read, the Minister resolved to prorogue the Parliament for a fortnight; notwithstanding every preparation had been made for opening the session on the fifteenth. The reason of this sudden prorogation was, to give time to concert a new plan of operations,

tions, and to write another speech for the King—undoubtedly the speech that had been designed, would not apply to this great and unexpected change of affairs. Whether there was any precedent for this extraordinary step, was not in the contemplation of the Minister. In taking a resolution, that involved concerns of the greatest magnitude, he was not to be influenced by precedents. Forty thousand Hanoverians, who had laid down their arms, but not surrendered them, composed such an engine of power and strength, as might, if employed *against* France, not *for* Hanover; or, to speak in more direct terms, if ordered to act *offensively*, instead of *defensively*, might *divide* her power; and thereby facilitate the conquest of her possessions, in America, Africa and Asia.

CHAP. XVI.
1757.

George the Second, though not possessed of brilliant talents, yet, to a strong firmness of mind, he added a long experience of men and public affairs, with a sufficient share of penetration to distinguish, even in his present short acquaintance with Mr. PITT, and particularly by his instant resolution of proroguing the Parliament, that he was a bold and intelligent Minister; qualities which were perfectly agreeable to the King—because personal courage was not amongst his defects. The King himself first suggested to his Minister the resumption of his Hanoverian troops. It was the very measure which Mr. PITT had resolved to propose, when he advised the prorogation of Parliament; and it was only by accident, or chance, that the proposition came first from the King. The King and his Minister, therefore, were in perfect unison upon the first mention of this important subject. From this moment, the King gave his confidence to Mr. PITT; and the latter, upon discovering the whole of the King's views, saw he could make them secondary, and subservient

Union of the King and Mr. Pitt.

CHAP. XVI.
1757.

vient to the interests of Great Britain. During the remainder of the reign, they acted together, under the influence of the same congeniality of sentiment, and thereby naturally fell into a perfect union and cordiality of opinion, upon all public measures.

The King of Prussia's recommendation.

Immediately after the battle of Rosbach, the *King of Prussia* wrote a letter to the *King of England*, in which he strongly recommended the resumption of the allied army, and *Duke Ferdinand* of Brunswick to the command of it: and he accompanied this letter with a plan of operations, in which he proposed to act in concert with the Duke. Independent of the policy of the measure, there were not wanting very fair and honourable reasons to support it. The French troops had repeatedly broken several articles of the convention; and had, in general, from the time they entered the electorate, conducted themselves in a manner, more like a banditti of Barbarians, than an army of disciplined soldiers.

Hanoverians resumed under D. Ferdinand.

Mr. PITT adopted the whole of the *King of Prussia*'s recommendation; but so modelled the German measures, as to make them co-operate with his own plans of attacking France, in every other quarter at the same time. The *King of Prussia* highly approved of Mr. PITT's alterations of his plan. Mr. PITT's plan was bold and comprehensive; but it should be remembered, that timidity in war, is as criminal as treachery; and therefore it is proverbially said, that the boldest measures are the safest. The *King of Prussia* saw it in this sense, and therefore he gave it his warmest approbation. In concert with the *King of Prussia*, the plan of operations was formed. Emden was secured,

cured, and the coast of France was annoyed, at his request.*— Duke Ferdinand drove the French out of Hanover; and pursued them with such rapidity, that France was presently under the necessity of preparing for the *defence* of her own frontiers. This sudden change of affairs, and the victories gained by the *King of Prussia* in Silesia, shewed, that a war upon the continent of Europe, conducted upon British principles, was highly serviceable to the interests of this country. France, so far from being able to invade Great Britain, could not send troops to strengthen her garrisons and settlements abroad: and in a few months her first object was, to provide a fresh army to stop the progress of *Duke Ferdinand*: while Mr. PITT, on the other hand, prepared expeditions against her coast, to co-operate with the Duke. In this situation, the Councils of France were distracted. Her whole force was kept at home. A German war, conducted upon this principle, against France, was the most advantageous war that Great Britain could make; and, notwithstanding the expence has been urged as the greatest objection to it, yet when it is recollected, that this war employed the armies of France, and prevented succours being sent to her settlements abroad, it was the most *œconomical* war, that the British Minister could carry on. The expence of transporting troops, forage, stores, &c. to a short distance, is infinitely less than to a great one. Whoever will be at the trouble to look over the charges of the American war, which commenced in 1775, and of the German war, which commenced under Mr. PITT's direction,

in

CHAP. XVI.
1757.

Observations on the Germ. war.

---

* The King of Prussia saw, and fully comprehended, the wisdom of the attempt upon Rochefort; and he adopted the idea of annoying the coast of France, from that measure. He conceived a very favourable opinion of Mr. PITT's political talents, from that circumstance; although it had not been successful.

CHAP. XVII. in 1758, will fee the fact indifputably confirmed. It need only
1757.   be added, that if the armies of France, had been to be conquered in Canada, in the Weſt Indies, in Africa, and in Aſia, the expence to this country, of tranſporting, and maintaining an adequate force to encounter them, in all thoſe places, muſt have been immenſe. Upon a ſubſequent occaſion, the Miniſter emphatically ſaid, "That America had been conquered in Germany." Experience hath ſince ſhewn, that the aſſertion was well founded.

CHAP.

CHAP. XVII.

Meeting of Parliament—Mr. Alderman Beckford's explanation of the new principle of the German war—Mr. Pitt's speech on the Rochefort expedition—Effects of that speech—Successes of 1758.

THE proceedings of Parliament, to which we will now return, were not diftinguifhed by any debates, during the remainder of Mr. PITT's adminiftration.

Both Houfes met on the firft of December 1757, according to the fingular prorogation, already mentioned. Mr. PITT delivered a meffage from the King, acquainting the Houfe, that he had put his army in motion in Hanover, to act in concert with the *King of Prufsia*, and requefting their fupport. An adequate fum was immediately voted, without a diffenting voice.

Mr. Alderman BECKFORD faid a few words upon this occafion; which, as they tend to explain the new principle of politics, they will not be improper to infert here. "If the Hanorian and Heffians, he faid, were to be entirely under the direction of Britifh Councils, the larger the fum that was granted, in order to render that army effectual, the more likely it would be to anfwer the end for which it was given; that is, to try the iffue of the war with France; than which, in his judgment, there never was fo favourable an opportunity as the prefent. But if the *Regency of Hanover* were to have the difpofal of the money, and the difpofition of the army, he would not give a fhilling towards its fubfiftence."

CHAP. XVII.
1757.

A new treaty was made with Prussia, which was approved by Parliament; and which the reader will find in the Appendix to this work.

Parliament was never known to be so unanimous, as at this time.

The fleet and army sent against Rochefort, having returned, without making the impression intended, Sir JOHN MORDAUNT, the commander of the army, was put under an arrest; and being a Member of Parliament, the King sent a message to the Commons, at the beginning of the session, acquainting them of the restraint put upon one of their Members. They thanked the King for his attention to their privileges.

Mr. Pitt's speech on the Rochfort expedition. M.S.

Mr. PITT reprehended, in terms of great warmth, the indolence, the caution, of those entrusted with the execution of the military operations, during the last campaign. He declared solemnly, that his belief was, that there was a determined resolution, both in the naval and military commanders, against any vigorous exertion of the national power. He affirmed, that though his Majesty appeared ready to embrace every measure proposed by his Ministers, for the honour and interest of his British dominions, yet scarce a man could be found, with whom the execution of any one plan, in which there was the least appearance of danger, could with confidence be trusted. He particularized, the inactivity of Lord LOUDON in America, from whose force the nation had a right to form great expectations; from whom there had been received no intelligence, except one small scrap of paper, containing a few lines of no moment. He further said, that with a force greater than ever the nation had heretofore maintained, with a King and Ministry ardently desirous of redeeming her glory, and promoting her true interest, a shameful dislike to the service every where prevailed. Nor was it amongst the officers alone, that indolence and neglect appeared; those who filled the other departments of military service, seemed to be affected with the same indifference: the victuallers, contractors, purvey-

ors,

purveyors, were never to be found, but upon occasions of their own personal advantage. In conversation they appeared totally ignorant of their own business. The extent of their knowledge, went only to the making of false accounts: In that science they were adepts.

_{CHAP. XVII.
1758.}

This detection of the abuses in the several departments, where they had long prevailed; and of the want of exertion in the Commanders in Chief, which had also been obvious; operated in a manner highly advantageous to the public service. Those Gentlemen, as well as the nation, now saw, that there was a Minister at the head of affairs, who not only knew the duties of his own office, but the duties of others: and therefore they might expect him to examine their conduct; to traverse all parts of it with a keen and penetrating eye. This apprehension rouzed them from their lethargy in an instant. They awakened as from a dream; and seemed to be electrified by the fire of his mind; they burned with fresh ardour in every subsequent enterprize. The British honour was recovered. The events of the war, placed the name of Great Britain upon the highest pinnacle of national honour.

_{Effects of the preceding speech.}

The Session closed on the 20th of June, 1758.

The British arms this year, were successful in every quarter of the globe.

_{1758.
Successes of the British arms in 1758.}

In Asia, owing to the reinforcement Mr. PITT sent by Commodore *Stevens*, when he was in office last year, the French were defeated at Massulipatam, and in two naval engagements.

In America, Louisbourg was taken, also the Isle of St. John, and the forts Du Quesne and Frontenac,

In Africa, Senegal surrendered.

CHAP. XVII.
1758.

In Europe, Admiral *Osborne* defeated, and took the French fleet from Toulon, deftined for the relief of Louifbourg; and Sir *Edward Hawke* drove another fleet upon the fand banks on the coaft of France, that was equipped at Rochefort, for the fame purpofe. A defcent was made on the coaft of France, near St. Malo, where all the fhips and veffels were deftroyed. Another was made at Cherbourg; where the fhips, mole, pier, bafon, and other works, were all deftroyed, and the cannon brought away. A third defcent was made in St. Lunar Bay, which being full of rocks, the fleet were obliged to go to St. Cas, and thus the army and fleet became feparated. In the re-embarkation at St. Cas, the rear guard, under General DRURY, were cut off, by a large body of French troops. However, thefe defcents kept the whole coaft of France in perpetual alarm; and prevented the French miniftry from fending any troops to reinforce their army in Germany. *Duke Ferdinand* drove the French army entirely out of Hanover, and acrofs the Rhine. The *King of Pruſsia* entirely fubdued Silefia, and entered Bohemia and Moravia.

All the terrors of invafion being now transferred, from Great Britain to France, the Britifh troops were all fent to fcenes of active and important fervice; and the defence of the Ifland was entrufted to a conftitutioual and well regulated militia; which had been raifed, difciplined, and officered, by the gentlemen of the country.

CHAP.

CHAP. XVIII.

Meeting of Parliament—Succeſſes of 1759*—Lord Bute's firſt interference—He goes to the Duke of Newcaſtle, and demands Lord Besborough's ſeat at the Treaſury Board, for Sir Gilbert Elliot— He alſo demands the repreſentation of the county of Southampton, for Sir Simeon Stuart.*

ON the 23d of November 1758, Parliament met. The ſame unanimity prevailed. All the ſupplies were voted, without the leaſt heſitation; and the ſeſſion cloſed on the 2nd of June 1759, without any debates.

The moſt ample preparations were made for another vigorous campaign. The ſucceſſes of the laſt campaign, had inſpired every individual, both in the army and navy, with a paſſion for glory, that was nothing ſhort of enthuſiaſm.

In America, Quebec and Niagara were taken. And in the Weſt Indies, Guadaloupe, and other iſlands.

In Europe, another ſquadron fitted out at Toulon, was defeated in the Mediterranean, by Admiral *Boſcawen*. Havre was bombarded by Sir *George Rodney*; and Breſt was blocked up by Sir *Edward Hawke*. Duke *Ferdinand* defeated the French at Minden: And the *King of Pruſſia*, though ſurrounded by his numerous enemies, maintained himſelf with aſtoniſhing ſkill and valour.

After the French had been defeated at Minden, they ſaw it was in vain to preſs forward their whole ſtrength in Germany; and therefore

CHAP. XVIII. therefore they resolved upon making their next effort by sea. For this purpose they equipped all the naval force they had at Brest, and other ports in the Atlantic; and, with an army, which were in readiness to embark, they intended to make a descent upon Ireland, with a view of diverting the attention of the British Cabinet from Germany, and the West Indies. Sir *Edward Hawke* lay off Brest, to intercept their sailing; and his squadron was reinforced from time to time. At length the French came out, and Sir *Edward Hawke* gained a compleat victory over them, on the twentieth of November, 1759.— This victory annihilated the naval power of France.

1759.

Lord Bute's first interference.

It was in this year of unanimity and victory, that the seeds were sown of those divisions, which appeared soon after the accession of *George the Third*. The patronage of places, that never-failing source of discord, was claimed by Lord BUTE. Upon Lord BESBOROUGH going to the Post-office, in the month of May 1759, in the room of Lord LEICESTER, deceased, there was a vacancy at the Treasury Board, and the Duke of NEW-CASTLE purposed to fill it, with Mr. JAMES OSWALD, from the Board of Trade, who was recommended by Lord HALIFAX; but Lord BUTE interfered;—he told the Duke of NEWCASTLE, " he came to him, in the name of all them on " that side of the Administration, who thought they had as " good a right to recommend as any other party whatever; " and it was their wish, that Mr. (afterwards Sir) GILBERT " ELLIOT, of the Admiralty, might be appointed." The Duke of NEWCASTLE finding himself impeded in his own wishes, and resolving not to comply with those of Lord BUTE, appointed Lord NORTH to fill the vacancy.

This was the first cause of difference.

The

The second related to Mr. LEGGE; and happened a few months afterwards in the same year. There being a vacancy in the representation of the county of Southampton, by the Marquis of WINCHESTER becoming Duke of BOLTON, it was the desire of the *Prince of Wales*, signified by Lord BUTE to Mr. LEGGE; that though Mr. LEGGE had been invited by a great majority of the gentlemen of the county, to represent them, yet that he must not accept of those invitations, but yield all pretentions in this matter to Sir SIMEON STUART, who had his (Lord B's) recommendation. Mr. LEGGE lamented, that he had not known the Prince's inclinations sooner; that his engagements were made, and he could not break them. Mr. LEGGE was elected. But when the Prince became King, although Mr. LEGGE had been made Chancellor of the Exchequer by the voice of the nation, and his conduct in office distinguished by the strictest integrity, yet *he was turned out*.

On the 13th of November 1759, Parliament met. The *Prince of Wales* took his seat on the first day. There were no debates upon any public measure this session; which ended on the 22d of May, 1760.

The war was carried on with unabating vigour; and the same uniformity of success attended the British arms, wherever they appeared.

CHAP.

CHAP. XIX.

Death of George II.—Accession of George III.—Lord Bute made a Privy Counsellor—Made Ranger of Richmond Park, in the room of the Princess Amelia—Views of the new King's party—Methods taken to accomplish those views—A number of writers hired at an enormous expence, to abuse the late King, the Duke of Cumberland, Mr. Pitt, and all the Whigs; to represent the war as ruinous, unjust, and impracticable—Parliament dissolved—Mr. Legge turned out—Lord Holdernesse resigns upon a pension—Lord Bute made Secretary of State in his room—The King's marriage—General Græme's merits on this occasion—French anecdotes—Observations on Royal marriages with Foreigners—Negotiation with France—Breaks off—Martinico taken—Mr. Pitt prepares for a war with Spain—His design of attacking the Havannah.

UNFORTUNATELY for the war, but more unfortunately for Great Britain, on the 25th of October 1760, the venerable *George the Second* died. The circumstances of his death are too well known to be repeated here. As to the Successor, the effects of the wickedness of his advisers have been, and are still, too deeply felt, to be described in any terms adequate to the injuries committed. Posterity, in a subsequent age, when truth may be spoken, and the motives of men laid open, will be astonished at the conduct of their ancestors at this period.

Two days after the King's accession, the Earl of BUTE was introduced into the Privy Council; and at the same time, the name

name of the Duke of CUMBERLAND was ſtruck out of the Liturgy. Another circumſtance not lefs remarkable, immediately ſucceeded; this was, Lord BUTE was made Ranger of Richmond park, in the room of the Princeſs AMELIA, who was turned out.

CHAP. XIX.
1760.
Ranger of Richmond Park.

It was the fixed deſign of the party, which the new King brought with him from Leiceſter-houſe, to remove the Miniſters and conclude the war;* but the tide of popularity ran ſo ſtrong in favour of both, they were obliged to poſtpone the execution of their deſign, until they had prepared the nation to receive it. For this purpoſe a great number of writers were employed, to calumniate the late King, the Duke of CUMBERLAND, Mr. PITT, and all the Whigs.

Writers engaged, to calumniate the late King, &c.

The late King was reviled for the affection he had ſhewn to his native country, for his love of female ſociety, † and for his attachment to the Whigs:

The Duke was charged with inhumanity; he was ſtiled " a Prince that delighteth in blood;" becauſe the Princeſs of WALES had ſometime ago conceived a jealouſy of his popularity. Nothing could be more unjuſt than this ſuſpicion: there was not a perſon in the kingdom more firmly attached to the rights of her ſon.

The

---

* The King is made to acknowledge in November 1763, in his ſpeech to Parliament, " The re-eſtabliſhment of the public tranquility, *was the* FIRST *great object of my reign*."

† After the death of Queen CAROLINE, he was fond of a game at cards in an evening, with the Counteſſes of PEMBROKE, ALBEMARLE, and other ladies.

Chap. XIX.
1760.

The Whigs were called Republicans, although many of them had exhausted their fortunes in support of the Monarchy.

But Mr. PITT was the principal object of their calumny. He was assailed in pamphlets, in news-paper essays, and in every other channel of conveyance to the public. The war upon the continent, was called *his* German war; his former opposition to German measures, was contrasted with his present conduct; the expences of former wars, were compared with the present war. The ruin of the country, the annihilation of all public credit, were predicted, and deplored, as the inevitable consequences of the present unjust, impolitic, and impracticable war; for although it was successful, yet they affirmed, that every victory, and every conquest, was a fresh wound to the kingdom. Mr. PITT's thirst for war, they said, was insatiable; his ambition knew no bounds. He was madly ruining the kingdom with conquests.

By the conquest of Canada, they affirmed, that all had been obtained, that justice gave us a right to demand; every subsequent conquest, they affirmed, was not only superfluous, but unjust; that it was now perfect suicide to go on conquering what must be surrendered; they wept over our victories. The nation, they said, was destroying itself. At the same time, they held out flattering and false pictures, of the enemy's strength and resources.

Smollett, *Mallett*, *Francis*, *Home*, *Murphy*, *Mauduit*, and many others were the instruments employed upon this occasion. It has been said, that the sum paid to these, and other hired writers, during

during the firſt three years of the reign of GEORGE *the Third*, exceeded thirty thouſand pounds. And the printing charges amounted to more than twice that ſum. In facilitating the views of the party, the money was well laid out; for the nation was completely duped. And as to the few, who might attempt to undeceive the public, there was a *political Judge* ready to puniſh their temerity.

A perſon at this time, (thirty years ſubſequent) may very rationally aſk, if there were any Engliſhmen weak enough to give credit to theſe baſe aſſertions. The queſtion indeed, is natural. And if the anſwer correſponds with truth, it muſt be confeſſed, that ſuch was the induſtry uſed in writing and circulating theſe doctrines, that the new King's faction, in a ſhort time, had their defenders in every town and village in the kingdom.

The war indeed went on; and though the conqueſts and victories were not leſs brilliant than heretofore, the expence was continually urged as a matter of more importance than the advantage.

The unanimity of Parliament was not yet diſturbed. As the enſuing ſeſſion was the laſt ſeſſion of the preſent Parliament, the King's party thought it moſt prudent to poſtpone any attacks, in either Houſe, until the new Parliament was elected. The ſeſſion commenced on the 18th of November, 1760, and cloſed on the 19th of March, 1761.

The Parliament was immediately diſſolved.

And on the ſame day, Mr. LEGGE was diſmiſſed.

CHAP. XIX.
1761.

Upon the difmiffion of Mr. LEGGE, the whole Miniftry ought immediately to have refigned. A meafure of fuch union and fpirit, muft have had the happieft effects. The new King's Favourite would have been checked in his defign of feizing upon the kingdom; and the K—— himfelf would have been convinced, that the Tory principles inculcated at Leicefter-houfe, though amufing in Theory, were mifchievous in Practice.

Lord Bute made Sec. of State; and Mr. Jenkinfon his Commis.

Two days after the difmiffion of Mr. LEGGE, Lord HOLDERNESSE refigned, upon condition of having a large penfion fecured to him, and the reverfion of the Cinque Ports. Lord BUTE, in whofe favour this refignation was purchafed, was inftantly appointed Secretary of State in his room: and he made Mr. CHARLES JENKINSON his *confidential commis.*

It was now obvious to every underftanding, that there was an end of that unanimity which had for fome years fo happily and fo honourably prevailed in Council, and in Parliament. The refolution of the new King's faction, to change the Miniftry, was now perceptible to every man, who had not loft his penetration, in that torrent of popularity, which was artfully managed to abforb all confiderations, in the moft extravagant eulogies on the found wifdom of the King, and the immaculate virtues of his mother.

King's marriage.

The faction further contrived to amufe the people, with *two* other circumftances this year. One was the King's marriage; the other, his coronation; which gave them opportunity to proceed in their meafures, unobferved by the nation.

The

CHAPTER XIX.
1761.

The Court had not for many years been adorned with the presence of a Queen. The novelty operated with the most powerful attraction. The whole nation caught the contagion. The Faction could not have contrived any measure more fortunate to engage the public attention; while unobserved, they pursued their own designs, with the utmost alacrity *.

However,

---

* Respecting the *choice* of the Princess, there was some years afterwards, an extraordinary controversy in the public prints, which merits more notice, than many of those fugitive papers usually deserve. We shall select only two, which contain the principal facts.

It should be previously observed, that in the first arrangement of the Queen's establishment, General Græme was made Secretary to the Queen; and in 1765, he was made Comptroller; but in February 1770, he was dismissed from her Majesty's service.

On the fourth day of October 1777, the following paragraph appeared in the public prints:

"It were to be wished, that in introducing General G——e to the public notice, a little more pains had been taken to explain the ease and independence that Gentleman was called from, as well as his appointment as Negociator and Ambassador. The world has hitherto had the misfortune of beholding this officer only in the light of a simple individual; bred in a foreign service: employed once as a *private* Agent, to find out where a negotiation might be set on foot, and rewarded liberally for the discovery. It remains also to know the independent patrimony he was originally seised of, and how he may have spent it in her Majesty's service. These, and other circumstances being cleared up, will have the effect of rescuing from oblivion, an illustrious character, whose merit has apparently not been enough considered.

A a 2
[*This*

[180]

CHAPTER XIX.
1761.

However, there were some persons who imagined, that they saw an analogy, between the sending back the Princess of BRUNSWICK

[*This paragraph, at the beginning, seems to allude to some prior publication; but notwithstanding a diligent search, nothing can be found, except a short paragraph, stating, that General Græme had resigned his employment.*]

To the Printer, &c.

I TAKE the earliest opportunity to comply with the wish of the Paragraph-writer in your paper of to-day, respecting General Græme. At the time he was first sent to Mecklenburgh, he was possessed of a family estate of six hundred pounds a year, and twenty thousand pounds in money. Your Correspondent, though he takes up the ludicrous stile, as master of his subject, is certainly very ill informed. General Græme was sent three several times to Germany; once as a private agent, and twice as a public one: First, *to find out a Princess*, then to bring her over; and lastly, to carry the Garter to the Prince, her brother. The expences of these journies were considerable: He gave in no bill of them—the others employed did. His liberal rewards were a regiment, which cost him seven thousand pounds in raising; the office of Secretary to the Queen, for which he drew only one *half* of the salary, *being rode for the other half*; and some time after he was made Comptroller of the Queen's Houshold; He retired from her Majesty's service with not one shilling of ready money, and his estate so much encumbered, that he has little more than his regiment to support him. Vice or extravagance he has never been accused of. Let common sense put all this together, and I defy the most obsequious Courtier to say, that he has been indemnified, much less rewarded. He went, when a boy; into the Scotch Brigade, in the service of the States of Holland, &c. then reckoned famous for their military discipline; and, I believe, had finished his first campaign, before Major Sturgeon (whom, from the phrase " seised of," I take to be the author of the paragraph) had finished, or broken, his apprenticeship to the attorney.

G. A. D.

October 4, 1777.

Brunswick and the fending back the Infanta of Spain, in the early part of the reign of Lewis the Fifteenth. But this

CHAPTER
XIX.
1761.

To the Printer, &c.

October 12, 1777.

TO refcue merit from obfcurity is highly laudable. This praife will defervedly belong to the Letter-writer, who celebrates the virtues and difappointments of General G———e, when he has thrown the neceffary light upon fome few points. He grants, that this gentleman was bred in the Dutch fervice, and that he was at firft a *private* agent—" to *find out* a Princefs:—(It were to be wifhed he had chofe another phrafe, for this will hardly be received as a compliment by the family it is applied to)—But then the fecond commiffion was *public,* " to bring her over." Here, either the Letter-writer, or the public, is in a great error : For the univerfal belief has been, that the late Lord Harcourt was the Minifter commiffioned to bring her over*. Again, the paying of feven thoufand pounds for a regiment, is a new fort of traffic, even in this commercial country, and merits a full illuftration ; yet, even admitting of its full extent, as this happened fo many years ago, the General muft, upon a moderate computation, be a very confiderable gainer upon that bargain, befides the very unufual favour, of being adopted from a foreign fervice over the heads of a multitude of brave and deferving officers in our own. Another point to be cleared up is, his having fpent in the public fervice, fo large a patrimony as his eftate of fix hundred pounds a year, and twenty thoufand pounds in money, befides the emoluments of a regiment, a *half Secretaryfhip,* *and a whole Comptrollerfhip.* The hungry Courtiers furely did not ride him

[* *It is well known, that Lord Harcourt was the perfon who went to Mecklenburgh in a* public character ; *but that circumftance does not invalidate the fact, of General Græme being the* confidential man ; *for, according to the maxims of Government, which the* Faction *had laid down for the new reign, there were always an* oftenfible man, *and* a confidential man, *in every* fituation: *and this anecdote fhews, the very early period at which the* theory *of* duplicity, *was brought into practice.*]

in

CHAPTER XIX.
1751.

this speculation was founded in a great mistake; for the cases differed materially, particularly in this point—the Princess of BRUNSWICK returned voluntarily; whereas the Infanta was sent back by force. And the French King was thereupon married to the daughter of STANISLAUS, King of Poland, who at the time of this marriage, was only a private gentleman. It is true, that eight years subsequent, he was, by the interest of France, raised to the throne of Poland; but in less than a month afterwards he was dispossessed of his kingdom, by his rival, the Elector of Saxony.

There is a further, and, if possible, a more important difference in this pretended analogy.—Several of the great families in France, disapproved of this union of their Sovereign with the daughter of a private gentleman; whereas, none of the Families in England, ever disapproved of the choice made for, or by the King of Great Britain: and although the Queen of France, by her placid demeanor, qualified the acidity, which her birth alone occasioned; yet her unexceptionable conduct, was not sufficient to prevent some harsh remarks on that policy, which, said they, sends our King's in quest of foreigners for wives, in whom their private happiness is as

in all of these—estate, and money and all: For, Germany (though it is a great gulph) could never have swallowed any thing like this in three journies. The bills, had they been given in, (which it is really pity they were not) could scarcely, we should think, have amounted to one-tenth part of the General's patrimony alone.

Your's, &c.

D.

little

little confulted, as the public welfare; and in which alliances, we fometimes import not the beft, but the worft blood on the Continent.

Chap. XIX.
1761.

There was likewife, a *third* circumftance this year, which commenced prior to either the King's Marriage or Coronation, and which claimed a confiderable fhare of the public attention. This was a negotiation for peace, defired by France; and carried on in London by M. Bussy, and in Paris by Mr. Hans Stanley. The reader will find in the Appendix, all the important documents of the negotiation. M. Bussy arrived in London, in May 1761, and Mr. Stanley at Paris in the fame month. This negotiation continued until Auguft; at which time the Court of France had prevailed on the King of Spain to join them in the war. Mr. Pitt had fufpected for fome time, that this junction was in contemplation; and upon the the delivery of a memorial by M. Bussy, on the interefts of Spain, (when there was a Spanifh Minifter at our Court) he was confirmed in his fufpicions. He faw, that a war with Spain was inevitable; and he immediately made preparation for it. He had ordered an attack to be made on the French ifland of Martinico, and the other iflands belonging to that power, in the Weft Indies. And it was now his refolution to haften thofe meafures, and to fend the fleet and army, as foon as thofe iflands were reduced, againft the Havannah, the key of the Spanifh Weft Indies; and alfo, to reinforce the army with the troops from North America, where the conquefts were completed.

Negotiation with France.

Martinico, St. Lucia, Grenada, and St. Vincent, were taken by his orders. The French power in the Eaft Indies, was totally deftroyed. And Belleifle, on the coaft of France, was taken.

Martinico, &c. taken.

The

CHAP. XIX. There was a very unaccountable negligence in equipping the expedition against the Havannah, under the subsequent Administration, who could not avoid attempting this conquest; because the plan of it was left to them by Mr. PITT. After taking the last of the French islands in the West Indies, the victorious troops remained idle a considerable time. Had they been sent immediately against the Havannah, as Mr. PITT intended, the Spaniards would have been attacked before they were prepared, and the place would have been taken, before the unhealthy season commenced. The misfortune was, that though the Ministry sent only four ships from England, to join the armament Mr. PITT had assembled in the West Indies; yet, these ships did not sail from England until the month of March 1762; at which time, according to Mr. PITT's plan, they would have been before the Havannah; for Martinico surrendered on the 12th of February. Our great loss of men at the Havannah, was more owing to the unhealthy season, than to the fire of the enemy.*

marginal note: 1764. M....'s design of taking the Havannah.

CHAP.

* There was a suspicion, and the coolest impartiality must allow, that it seems to have been founded on neither ordinary nor weak probability, that the Ministry would have rejoiced at a defeat before the Havannah. The officers were appointed upon the recommendation of the Duke of Cumberland, who was not less obnoxious to the faction, called the King's friends, than Mr. Pitt himself. They were sent in the manner above-mentioned. The advices of this important conquest arrived in England while the negociations for peace were on the tapis, which were in some measure impeded by it, because Ministers were obliged to encrease in their demands respecting the terms of peace; a circumstance that was quite opposite to their private wishes, which were to obtain peace upon any terms, rather than carry on the war.

CHAP. XX.

State of France—Mr. Pitt opposed in his design to send some ships to Newfoundland—That place taken—Re-taken---Mr. Pitt opposed in his design to attack the Spanish Flota—Mr. Pitt and Lord Temple opposed in their advice to recall Lord Bristol from Madrid—Three Councils upon it—Mr. Pitt and Lord Temple resign—Design against Panama and Manilla—Assertions of Lord Temple and Lord Bute—The Gazette account of Mr. Pitt's resignation—His Letter to the City of London—All the Spanish treasure arrived in Spain—Explanatory note—Mr. Pitt greatly applauded in the City of London—War declared against Spain—Epitome of Mr. Pitt's Administration.

FRANCE at this time, was reduced to the lowest ebb of distress and despondency. All her colonies were in the hands of Great Britain. Her arms had been discomfitted in every quarter. The payment of her public bills was stopped; and she might literally be called a bankrupt nation: She was reduced to a more distressed and humbled condition, in the three years Administration of Mr. PITT, than by the whole ten years war of the Duke of MARLBOROUGH.* Her navy was ruined: She

---

* France was never more pressed by England, than by Mr PITT's Administration. An Englishman might at this period, with some propriety ask, Where were now her 450,000 fighting men, which her Ministers boasted of in the reign of LOUIS the Fourteenth? and where were her sailors, who in the same reign, fought on board one hundred ships of war? It may be answered, that we had thousands of her sailors in prison; and that their number of land forces were sufficient for her purpose. But we know, that so reduced was her navy before November 1759, she was obliged to force the peasants into that service.

CHAP. XX. She had not at this time ten ships of the line fit for service;
1761. yet, with these, her Ministers resolved to make one more effort.
Their design was to obtain a share of the Fishery in the North
American Seas, at a cheaper rate than they could hope to gain it
by treaty. From a circumstance that happened during the late
negociation, Mr. PITT foresaw, that they would make this attempt. His dilligence and penetration were constant and uniform; and they were not less apparent on this, than they had
been on every former occasion. Immediately on the departure
of M. BUSSY, he proposed to send four ships of the line to
Mr. Pitt opposed in his design respecting Newfoundland: But to his great surprise, he was opposed in
this measure. The Cabinet put a negative upon his proposition. The consequence was, the French took Newfoundland.
Newfoundland taken.
As soon as Lord AMHERST, who was at New York, heard it, he
sent his brother and Lord COLVILLE to retake the island, which
Re-taken.
they accomplished, before the arrival of any orders from England.

Mr. PITT now saw, and felt, the strength of the new King's
party. He did not, however, resign upon this check; because
his grand object was Spain. His design was by an early and
vigorous exertion to cripple that power. He did not suspect
the House of Bourbon to have so many friends in England, as

service. We know, that however diminished her armies might be, compared
with the flourishing times of LOUIS the Fourteenth, still it was with the greatest
difficulty the Government could pay, and provide for those armies; and had
they resolved upon the augmentation of them, their revenues would have failed
to support them; and what is more, the augmentation itself was impracticable. The dregs of the people, and the lower artificers, were already swept
away by the recruiting serjeant; and the fields were in a manner abandoned.
Whoever travelled through France at that juncture, might see the women not
only drive, but hold the plough. And in some provinces, it was no uncommon
spectacle, to behold two women yoked with one cow, drawing the plough.

he

he afterwards found. The King of Spain had at this time, an immense treasure at sea, coming from America. He was sensible the King of Spain would not declare himself until that treasure had arrived. Mr. PITT's design was to intercept it, and bring it to England. He was confident of the hostile intentions of Spain. The plan of union, which had been negociating between the Courts of France and Spain, all the summer at Paris, was now completed, and Mr. PITT had been furnished with a copy of this treaty of alliance, which included all the branches of the House of Bourbon, and is commonly called the Family Compact. He communicated to the Cabinet his resolution of attacking Spain. Lord BUTE was the first person who opposed it; he called it rash and unadvisable. Lord GRANVILLE thought it precipitate, and desired time to consider of it. Lord TEMPLE supported Mr. PITT, which he had done uniformly from his coming into office. The Duke of NEWCASTLE was neuter. The Chancellor was absent. Lord TEMPLE and Mr. PITT submitted to his Majesty, their advice in writing, signed by themselves, to recall Lord BRISTOL, (the British Ambassador) from Madrid. This was on the 18th of September 1761.

CHAP. XX.
1761.

Mr. Pitt's design of attacking the Spanish Flota opposed.

Mr. Pitt and Lord Temple opposed in their advice to recall Lord Bristol.

A few days afterwards a second Cabinet was summoned upon the same subject. All the Cabinet Ministers were present. Mr. PITT asserted, that he did not ground his resolution of attacking Spain, upon what the Court of Spain had said, or might say; but upon what that Court had *actually done*. The majority said they were not yet convinced of the necessity or propriety of his measure. And the Cabinet broke up without coming to any resolution. In a few days more, a third Cabi-

B b 2   net

CHAP. XX. net was summoned upon this subject. Mr. PITT and Lord
1761. TEMPLE insisted upon the necessity of recalling Lord BRISTOL.
Every other member of the Cabinet now declared against the
measure; upon which Mr. PITT and Lord TEMPLE took their
leaves. Lord GRANVILLE (the Lord President) regretted that
they were going to lose Mr. PITT and his noble relation. He
spoke highly of Mr. PITT's penetration and integrity; but on
this occasion he thought him mistaken; for the best accounts
from Spain, justified a contrary opinion. His Majesty having
rejected the written advice of Mr. PITT and Lord TEMPLE,
they resigned on the fifth of October 1761.*

Mr. Pitt and
Lord Temple
resign.

But

* A few weeks previous to Mr. PITT's resignation, the following conversation, as nearly as it can be related from memory, happened between Mr. PITT and a GENERAL OFFICER:—

" Sir, says Mr. PITT, I find the Spaniards are determined to break with us. It may become a fortunate circumstance; for although we have taken the French Islands and colonies, they do not afford us ready money, which we want. You must take possession of Panama: How many regiments shall you want for such an expedition?—the ships can be provided for the purpose immediately—I have no doubt of making up 5,000 men, if necessary, from the British colonies, who are now secure. We have no reason to apprehend a disappointment—they may not be ready in time, but must be sent you as they are raised; rather as recruits than part of your command?"

GENERAL OFFICER—" Sir I shall not want a great number of disciplined troops—I know the exact force in that part of America—give me three or four regiments, with instructions to the middle and southern provinces to supply me with a few men accustomed to bush-fighting, and about two thousand negroes to work in the heat of the day. Give me powers to form an alliance, and a promise of protection in religion and commerce.—I'll answer for the the success, not only against Panama, but for a resignation of all Spanish America, in all matters which may be deemed beneficial to Great Britain."

Mr. PITT.—" Sir, get yourself in readiness—your commission shall be made out immediately."

Nor was this all——He meditated an attack upon the Phillipine Islands: and

But the most abandoned part of this business was in the House of Lords, on the commencement of the first session of the new Parliament, on the 6th of November 1761, when Lord TEMPLE said in the debate, "That their advice (meaning "Mr. PITT and himself) was not founded upon *suspicion* only, "although they had for *several months suspected* the views of "Spain, and would have been amply justified from the *just* "*grounds* of their *suspicions*, but upon positive and authentic "information of a treaty of alliance being signed between France "and Spain." Upon which Lord BUTE with astonishing and incredible effrontery got up, and pronounced these words:

"My Lords,

"I affirm, *upon my honour*, that there was NO intelligence of "such a fact so constituted, at that time."

This brought Lord TEMPLE up again, who affirmed also *upon his honour*, "That there WAS intelligence of the highest "moment; that he was not at liberty to publish that intelli- "in the House, but would refresh his Lordship's memory in "*private*." He beckoned Lord BUTE out of the House, and

and he consulted Lord ANSON upon the subject, on account of his knowledge of those seas. Mr. PITT's design was to have reduced Panama first; and next, to have made a detatchment from thence against Manilla. The reader has been already informed of his design against the Havannah; which, though it was afterwards executed by his successors, yet had he continued to direct the war, that conquest would have been accomplished much sooner; and consequently great part of the force employed there, would have been at leisure, perhaps to have co-opperated at Porto Bello, or some other place, with the expedition against Panama; or have been ready for any other service. His design against the Phillipine Islands was adopted by his successors; but materially altered, by joining the East India Company in the measure. Nor would this expedition have been undertaken, had not Lord ANSON, in the strongest terms, repeatedly recommended, and pressed it to Lord EGREMONT.

repeated

CHAP. XX. repeated to him the intelligence which had been laid before the
1761. Cabinet. In this conference Lord BUTE found himself under
the neceffity of acknowledging that he *recollected* it. The dates
will fhew the fact indifputably. The Family Compact was
figned on the 15th of Auguft 1761; it was ratified on the
eighth day of September, and the written advice to recall Lord
BRISTOL was given, and dated on the 18th of the fame month.

Mr. PITT's refignation was not publifhed in the London
Gazette until *five* days after it had taken place. The Miniftry
waited for fome of *their favourable* advices from Spain to con-
traft with it.

In the Gazette of October 10, 1761, thefe articles appeared
together:

Gazette account of the refigna- tion.
" *Madrid, September* 4. A report having been lately fpread here,
" upon the arrival of our late letters from France, as if there was rea-
" fon to apprehend an immediate rupture between our Court, and
" that of Great Britain; *we [who were meant by this pronoun?]* underftand,
" that the Spanifh Minifters, in a converfation which they had lately with
" the Earl of BRISTOL, Ambaffador Extraordinary from his Britannic
" Majefty, expreffed their concern thereat, and declared very explicitly
" to his Excellency, that on the part of their Court, there was not the
" leaft ground for any fuch apprenfions, as the Catholic King had, at no
" time been more intent upon cultivating a good correfpondence with
" England, than in the prefent conjuncture; and at the fame time,
" informed the Earl of Briftol, that orders had been fent to Monfieur
" MANSO, Governor of San Roque, to reprimand fuch of the inha-
" bitants under his jurifdiction, as had encouraged the illegal protec-
" tion given to the French privateer row-boats, under the cannon
" of a Spanifh Fort."

" *St. James's,*

" *St. James's, October* 9. The Right Honourable WILLIAM PITT,
" having refigned the Seals into the King's hands, his Majefty was this
" day pleafed to appoint the Earl of EGREMONT, to be one of his Ma-
" jefty's Principal Secretaries of State. And in confideration of the
" great and important fervices of the faid Mr. PITT, his Majefty has
" been gracioufly pleafed to direct, that a warrant be prepared for
" granting to the Lady HESTER PITT, his wife, a Barony of Great
" Britain, by the name, ftile, and title, of Baronefs of CHATHAM, to
" herfelf, and of Baron of CHATHAM to her heirs male; and alfo to
" confer upon the faid WILLIAM PITT, Efq. an annuity of three
" thoufand pounds fterling, during his own life, and that of Lady
" HESTER PITT, and their fon JOHN PITT, Efq."

" *St. James's, October* 9. This day Earl TEMPLE, Keeper of the
" King's Privy Seal, refigned the faid Seal into his Majey's hands."

The moment the preceding intelligence was publifhed, Mr. PITT's character was affailed with the moft ardent malignity, and favage phrenzy, that ever difgraced any age or country —— by all the hired writers in the fervice of the King's party. They branded him with the names of Penfioner, Apoftate, Deferter, and with every term of reproach, that Malice could apply, or Depravity fuggeft. Every news-paper was filled with their invectives. Pamphlets were written, and induftrioufly circulated, for the fame purpofe; and every art, and every method, were practifed, in order to effect a change of the public opinion, refpecting the glory of his meafures, and the purity of his conduct.

The King's Faction were perfectly fenfible, that the confidence of the Nation had been repofed in Mr. PITT; and they deprecated, by this criminal induftry, his return to power. They dreaded nothing fo much, as a difpofition in the people, fimilar to that fhewn in the year 1757, when the public voice

obliged

CHAP. XX.
1761.

Mr. Pitt's letter to the City of London.

obliged the late King to receive him. And it is certain, that they succeeded so far, as to occasion a temporary diminution of his character, in the public esteem. Mr. PITT himself was so thoroughly convinced of this truth, that he thought it necessary to state the cause of his resignation, in the following letter to the Town Clerk of the City of London.

"*Dear Sir,*

"FINDING, to my great surprise, that the cause and manner of my resigning the seals, is grosly misrepresented in the City, as well as that the most gracious and spontaneous marks of his Majesty's approbation of my services, which marks followed my resignation, have been infamously traduced, as a bargain for my forsaking the public, I am under a necessity of declaring the truth of both these facts in a manner which I am sure no gentleman will contradict; a difference of opinion with regard to measures to be taken against Spain, of the highest importance to the honour of the crown, and to the most essential national interests, and this founded on what Spain had already done,* not on what

---

* *What Spain had already done.*] At this distance of time, these words may require a little explanation.—Besides the Family Compact, which was Mr. PITT's principal object, there were the following facts:

A memorial of Mr. PITT's, in the name of the King of Great Britain, had been returned by the Spanish Minister at Madrid, *as wholly inadmissible.*—This memorial Mr. PITT wished to have had laid before Parliament; because having made, he said, the conduct of Spain, in this instance, the *precedent* for his refusal of the Spanish memorial, offered by M. BUSSY; he thought both the *matter* and the *expression* of the British memorial, ought to be made known. Mr. PITT's successors in office, however, put a negative upon his wishes.

And besides the points* in dispute, between the two Courts, there were the following reprehensible proceedings, on the part of Spain :—

At St. Lucar, about seven leagues from Cadiz, there were, in 1757, eleven sail of English ships in that harbour, which sailed with Spanish pilots, and at

* These points were three in number. They are given in the private memorial of France, dated July 15, 1761; which see in the Appendix.

the

what that Court may farther intend to do, was the cause of my refigning the feals. Lord TEMPLE and I fubmitted in writing, and figned by us, our moft humble fentiments to his Majefty, which being over-ruled by the united opinion of all the reft of the King's fervants, I refigned the feals on Monday the 5th of this month, in order not to remain refponfible for meafures, which I was no longer allowed to guide. Moft gracious public marks of his Majefty's approbation of my fervices followed my refignation: They are unmerited and *unfolicited*, and I fhall ever be proud to have received them from the beft of Sovereigns.

" I will now only add, my dear Sir, that I have explained thefe matters only for the honour of truth, not in any view to court return of confidence from any man, who with a credulity, as weak as it is injurious, has thought fit haftily to withdraw his good opinion, from one who has ferved his country with fidelity and fuccefs; and who juftly reveres the upright and candid judgment of it; little folicitous about the cenfures of the capricious and the ungenerous. Accept my fincereft acknowledgments for all your kind friendfhip, and believe me ever with truth and efteem,

My dear Sir,

Hayes, Your faithful friend,
Oct. 15, 1761. W. PITT."

A little the mouth of the river, between the two necks of land, and in fhoal water, they were followed by a French privateer; they were all taken, and brought back that into port. Sir BENJAMIN KEENE, our Ambaffador at that time at Madrid, remonftrated very ftrongly upon this fubject; but to no purpofe; they were deemed good prizes, though taken clofe to the land, in fhoal water.

The affair of the Antigallican and her prize, the Duc de Penthievre, is well known.

In the beginning of the year 1759, the Experiment, (a King'sfhip) was chafed off the coaft of Spain, by the Telemachus, a large French privateer, double the force of the Experiment: but the Britifh Captain not chufing to fuffer the difgrace, engaged the Frenchman and at length took him. The victor then ftood for the Spanifh coaft, when he fent his boat with his mafter and four men afhore, to land fome of the prifoners, and bring off fome neceffaries. The boat was immediately

CHAP. XX.
1761.

A little time after Mr. PITT's refignation the Miniftry received a difpatch from Lord BRISTOL at Madrid, containing the following interefting information:

Efcurial,

mediately detained, and the officer and crew thrown into prifon; the Governor alledging, that the French fhip was an illegal capture; though fhe came off from the land where fhe lay at anchor, and purfued the Experiment. And orders were fent to all the Spanifh ports, to detain the Experiment, if fhe put into any of them.

About June, 1760, the Saltafh floop of war chafed on fhore a French row-boat, a few leagues to the eaftward of Almeria Bay, and fome time after fhe took a French row-boat off Mahon, and put a midfhipman and fourteen men on board, and fome time in the following month came to anchor in that bay. The Spaniards detained her, and made the men prifoners: upon which, the Captain of the Saltafh, finding his prize not come out, fent his boat, with the Mafter and five men to know the reafon; who, on coming afhore, were threatened by the Spanifh foldiers to be fired at unlefs they hauled their boat afhore to a port a quarter of a mile from thence, which they refufed to do, infifting, as Britifh fubjects, they had a right to Spanifh protection; whereupon they feized the boat's crew, as well as the prize, and put them in the common prifon, where the mafter was ftruck and abufed by the foldiers, and all the reft ufed with great cruelty, and refufed the ufe of pen, ink and paper. The Saltafh was never able to get her men, to the number of 19. The Spaniards fent the mafter of a Catalan bark to prifon, for carrying a meffage from one of the prifoners to Gibraltar.

In 1761, the Speedwell cutter, commanded by Lieutenant ALLEN, was chafed into the harbour of Vigo, by the Achilles, a French man of war, and there made a prize of by her. Mr. ALLEN was tried at Spithead, for lofing his Majefty's cutter, and was honourably acquitted; but the Court declared their opinion, that fhe was an illegal prize, and taken contrary to the law of nations.

In Cadiz there were many French privateers manned and fitted out by Spaniards, built under the windows of the Governor's houfe, where they lay, and in his fight; when any Englifh veffel failed out of the harbour, would follow inftantly, and bring her in; though on the contrary, if any French fhip fhould fail out, no Englifh fhip of war dared to follow her, or fail out of the harbour in lefs than 24 hours; and the garrifon guns were always ready to protect a French fhip.

Escurial, November 2, 1761.

CHAP. XX.
1761.

" Two ships have lately arrived at Cadiz, with very extraor-
" dinary rich cargoes, from the West Indies. *So that* ALL *the*
" *wealth that was expected from Spanish America, is* NOW *safe in*
" *Old Spain.*" *

All the Spanish treasure arrived in Spain.

The triumphs of the Courts of London and Madrid, over Mr. PITT, were now complete. The first, in having compelled him to relinquish the direction of a war, by which he had nearly crushed one branch of the House of Bourbon, and was ready to pour its thunders upon another: The latter, in having supported the designs of his enemies, until that immense wealth was arrived, which they knew he meant to have intercepted; and which had he been permitted to accomplish, he must, by a

In the harbour of Vigo, in May 1761, there were upwards of thirty French row-boats; in which thirty boats, there were not above thirty Frenchmen, one in each boat, and the rest of the crews all Spaniards, and these fitted out by the Spaniards there, and at St. John de Luz.

At Cabaretta, a small town on the Spanish coast, in the Gut of Gibraltar, where there is a castle and some few guns, there was always a fleet of French row-boats at anchor under those guns, with not one Frenchman on board, mostly Spaniards and Genoese, but fitted out by Spaniards, who, in a piratical manner, watched and seized all English vessels which passed without a convoy, or happened to be becalmed. This was very detrimental to the garrison of Gibraltar, as many of those vessels were bound from Ireland, &c. with provisions.

About two months before Mr. Pitt resigned, Mr. R——, an eminent ship-builder in the King of Spain's service, quitted Spain, and returned to England. He knew authentically and exactly, the force and condition of every ship and vessel belonging to the King of Spain. Mr. Pitt saw him several times immediately after his arrival, and placed a proper value upon his information.

* See other extracts from the Spanish papers, with some explanatory notes, in the Appendix.

<small>Chap. XX.
1761.</small>

successes of such immense importance, at the beginning of the war, have speedily reduced Spain to the necessity of deprecating the rage of so potent and active an enemy. But to those few persons who were not duped by the artifices of the King's confidential servants, nor deceived by the hired writers of foreign and domestic enemies, these triumphs over a great Minister, were matters of the most sincere concern, regret, and anguish.

<small>Mr. Pitt applauded in the city.</small>

In a few weeks, however, the public prejudice began to dissipate. When he went into the City on the ensuing Lord Mayor's day, he was honoured in all the streets through which he passed, with unbounded marks of applause. The King and Queen honoured the city feast with their presence, (according to custom, on the first Lord Mayor's day after their coronation); and the courtiers said his Majesty betrayed some signs of disapprobation, that the applause given to Mr. Pitt, was greater than that shewn to himself.

This applause was, indeed, confined to the metropolis. But whatever doubts might have remained on the minds of men, whose residencies were remote from the source of information, respecting the propriety of Mr. Pitt's conduct, relative to Spain, they were all dispelled by the declaration of war against that power; which Mr. Pitt's successor's found themselves under the necessity of issuing on the second day of January, 1762, although they postponed that important measure, until the insults of the Spanish Court had become so notorious, that even Lord Bute confessed they could be no longer concealed.

Thus

Thus came by conftraint, and without dignity, and what is worfe than both, above three months after the opportunity had elapfed, that declaration of war, fneaking, and as it were by ftealth; which Mr. PITT would have iffued with eclat, in the month of Auguft laft, and illumined with the fplendour of his victories before the end of the year.

CHAP. XX.
1761.

EPITOME

CHAP. XX.
1761.

EPITOME

OF

MR. PITT's ADMINISTRATION.

MDCCLVII.

Epitome of Mr. Pitt's Administration.

THE Hanoverians and Hessians were sent home, and a well-regulated Militia established; by which the enemy saw, that we were so far from wanting foreign troops, to protect us, that we could afford to send the national troops abroad.

The foundations were laid of the subsequent conquests.

Fleets and armies were sent to Asia, Africa, and America.

MDCCLVIII.

Shipping destroyed at St. Malo.
Bason and shipping destroyed at Cherburg.
Emden recovered from the French.
Senegal taken.
Louisbourg, and the Isles of Cape Breton and St. John's taken.
Fort Frontenac taken.
Fort Du Quesne taken.
Fort and island of Goree taken.
Mussulipatam taken.
D'Ache's fleet defeated.
French army defeated at Crevelt.
French fleet under Du Quesne, taken by Admiral Osborne.
French fleet drove ashore at Rochefort, by Sir Edward Hawke.

MDCCLIX.

Guadaloupe, Marie Galante, Desirade, &c. taken.
Siege of Madras raised.
Surat taken.
Niagara taken.
Shipping destroyed at Havre.

French

French fleet under DE LA CLUE, taken by Admiral BOSCAWEN.   CHAP. XX.
Ticonderoga taken.   1761.
Crown Point taken.
Quebec taken.
Complete defeat of the French fleet in Quiberon Bay.
French army defeated at Minden.

MDCCLX.

THUROT killed and his three frigates taken.
French army defeated at Warburgh.
Montreal taken, and all Canada.
Frigates, stages and stores destroyed in Chaleur Bay.
Dumet taken.
Dominique taken.

MDCCLXI.

Pondicherry taken, and all the French power in India destroyed.
Belleisle taken.
French army defeated at Fellinghaufen.

MDCCLXII.

Martinico taken, and with it, the islands of Grenada, St. Lucia and St. Vincent. And

The Havannah taken; though after Mr. PITT's refignation, yet in consequence of his plans.

To these conquests must be added, the annihilation of the French Marine, Commerce and Credit. The loss to France of the following ships of war, which composed nine-tenths of her Royal Navy.

FRENCH KING'S SHIPS TAKEN OR DESTROYED.

Forty-four of the line, viz.—Four of 84; eleven of 74: two of 70; seventeen of 64; two of 60; two of 56; one of 54; and five of 50.

Sixty one frigates, viz.—Four of 44; two of 40; eighteen of 36; two of 34; fifteen of 32; one of 30; one of 28; two of 26; eight of 24; two of 22; six of 20.

Twenty

Twenty-fix floops of war, viz.—One of 18; nine of 16; fix of 14; two of 12; one of 10; feven of 8.

Befides the advantages derived from all thefe conquefts and captures, Mr. PITT left the late Thirteen Britifh Colonies in North America, in perfect fecurity and happinefs; every inhabitant there glowing with the warmeft affection to the Parent Country. At home, all was animation and induftry. Riches and glory flowed in from every quarter.

" Gods! what a golden fcene was this,
" Of public fame, of private blifs!‡"

‡ Ode by H. Seymour, Efq. late M. P. for Evefham.

CHAP. XXI.

Situation of Great Britain—Farther particulars concerning Mr. Pitt's resignation—and the Princesses of Brunswick—Union of Lord Bute with Lord Bath and Mr. Fox—Mr. Grenville wishes to be made Speaker—Mr. Pitt desires all the papers relative to Spain to be laid before Parliament—He supports the motion of a supply for Portugal.

THE situation of Great Britain at the end of Mr. Pitt's Administration, might not be improperly compared to that of Rome at the end of the Common-wealth. The Roman Empire extended from Britain to Media; and the British dominions included North America, and a great part of the Mogul Empire; with many islands and colonies in Europe, America, Africa and Asia. Both Empires at these periods, were in their zenith; and from these periods, both Empires declined in virtue, and diminished in extent.——The principal differences hitherto have been, that the servility of the British senate has exceeded that of the Roman; and the diminution of the British empire has been more rapid.

We have seen the end of this great man's brilliancy, as a Minister. We are now to view him in the character of a single member of the Legislature; dignified, indeed, by reputation, but accompanied by no influence, nor followed by one individual of that obsequious crowd of representatives, who had lately given him unlimited confidence, and unbounded praise. This sudden, but not surprising

Chap. XXI. surprising change of opinion, in the representatives of the na-
1761. tion, was occasioned by no alteration in his sentiments or prin-
ples, no relaxation of his promptitude or vigour, no impeachment of his conduct, his judgment or his virtue; nor was it to be ascribed to the usual versatility of mankind, particularly the natives of Great Britain, whose ruling passion is *novelty*; but it is to be attributed entirely, and exclusively, to the influence of Corruption, to the avarice and vanity of such men as are always eager to pay homage to the Distributor of rewards; whoever he may be, of whatever nation, or of whatever complexion.

The management of the House of Commons is become so perfectly mechanical, that it requires only a small knowledge of the principles of the machine, to be able to transfer the majority at almost any time, from the most able Statesman, to the Favourite of the Crown, or the Confident of the enemy; who may have no other recommendation, than the smiles of the first, or the money of the last; with the same facility, that an India bond, or any other negotiable property is transferred every day.

These observations may seem illiberal to the inexperienced, because they are unfavourable to the admirers of national glory. It is the misfortune of *Truth*, to be often disagreeable—the ancients very wisely painted her naked, to signify that those who were her enemies, were the enemies of nature. Notwithstanding the state of modern depravity, *Truth* will continue to have her worshippers; and it may be presumed, that they will in the present age, as they have in former ages, survive the advocates of Falshood. It is to them only, that Impartial History can

addrefs

address herself—from them only, she can expect protection. The Betrayer of his country, and the Destroyer of Public Liberty, whether supported by a Commodus, or protected by a Fauſtina, may endeavour by the aſſiſtance of the corrupt inſtruments of law, to intimidate and to ſtrangle her voice: But conſcious that ſhe has *Truth* for her ſhield, ſhe ventures upon a taſk that will give a new complexion to the public events, of one of the moſt intereſting periods, in the annals of Great Britain.

Mr. PITT's firſt care after his reſignation, was the diminution of his houſhold. Amongſt his other retrenchments were his coach horſes, which were ſold by public advertiſement in his own name. His enemies ſtigmatized this circumſtance with the appellations of parade and oſtentation;—his friends denominated the whole meaſure prudence and œconomy. Certain it is, that he had not, like many of his predeceſſors, amaſſed a fortune in his late ſituation. He retired from office an indigent man, with little more than his annuity for his ſupport. From all his places he acquired no poſſeſſions. The legacy of ten thouſand pounds, left him by the Duchefs of MARLBOROUGH, already mentioned in Chapter V, had amply ſupplied his pecuniary wants; releaſed him from all dependence on his family and friends, and while it emancipated him from the terrors of obligation, it inſpired him with that ſpirit of independence, which may be ſaid to have firſt kindled that blaze, which adorned the remainder of his life. During his ſtay in office he had no levees—he dedicated his whole time to the duties of his ſtation. When he reſigned, many of the principal cities and corporations in the kingdom, preſented him with addreſſes

CHAP. XXI.
1761.

of thanks for his great and important services; and at the same time lamented the cause of his departure from Government.

His successor was the Earl of EGREMONT, who was recommended to Lord BUTE by the Earl of BATH. Upon the accession of GEORGE III. Lord BATH made a tender of his services, which although not accepted publicly, his advice was received *privately*, by Lord BUTE.

Princesses of Brunswick.

But Lord BUTE's principal adviser, and manager of the House of Commons, was Mr. Fox. The circumstance which caused the first advances to an union between them, was the arrival of the two Princesses of *Brunswick*, already mentioned in Chapters XIII. and XIX. That affair had been originally suggested by the Duchess, their mother, sister to the then King of *Prussia*, whom she had solicited to recommend it to GEORGE the SECOND, when at Hanover in the month of July 1755.—The project had certainly the approbation of Mr. PITT at that time, but he warmly disapproved of the *resolution* to accomplish it against the pressing entreaties of the Princess of WALES *; who

secretly

* Lord MELCOMBE in his Diary, mentions this affair in these words:

" She [*meaning the Princess of Wales*] told me that the King had sent to invite the two Princesses of Brunswick; they came, but their mother, the King of Prussia's sister, who was not invited came with them ; We talked of the match—Surely he would not marry her son without acquainting her with it, so much as by letter I said certainly not, as he had always behaved very politely to her. It may be so, she replied, but how can this be reconciled ? In this manner said I: nothing will be settled at Hanover; but when the King comes back, he may say in conversation, and commending the Prince's figure, that he wishes to see him settled before he dies ; and that he has seen such and such Princesses ; and though he would settle nothing, without her participation, yet he could wish to see the Prince settled before his death, and therefore, if she had no objection, he should think one of those Princesses a very suitable party.

" She

secretly wished for an alliance with one of her own family. Mr. PITT's opposition to the resolution of force, was one principal cause of the design being relinquished. Lord BUTE supported the Princess in all points; and Mr. Fox was ready to put his negative on *all* continental alliances—against the Princesses of BRUNSWICK, therefore, they were perfectly united. The resignation of the Duke of CUMBERLAND, which happened in a little more than a year afterwards, the ascendency of Mr. PITT in the closet, and other circumstances, drew Mr. Fox every year into a closer connexion with Lord BUTE. He doubtless saw, that his future rise in the State, must be obtained by his interest

" She paused, and said, No; he was not that sort of man :—but if he should settle the match without acquainting her with it, she should let him know how ill she took it; and if he did it in the manner I mentioned, she should not fail to tell him fairly and plainly, that it was full early...... She was determined to behave so whenever the King spoke to her about it. She thought the match premature: the Prince ought to mix with the world—the marriage would prevent it—he was shy and backward—the marriage would shut him up for ever, with two or three friends of his and as many of hers. That he was much averse to it himself, and that she disliked the alliance extremely: that the young woman was said to be handsome, and had all good qualities and abundance of wit, &c. but if she took after her mother, she would never do here—the Duke of BRUNSWICK indeed, her father, is a very worthy man.—Pray Madam, said I, what is her mother? as I know nothing at all about her.—Why, said she, her mother is the most intriguing, meddling, and also the most satyrical sarcastical person in the world, and will always make mischief wherever she comes. Such a character would not do with GEORGE; it would not only hurt him in his public, but make him uneasy in his private situation; that he was not a wild, dissipated boy, but good-natured and cheerful, with a serious cast upon the whole—that those about him knew him no more than if they had never seen him. That he was not quick; but, with those he was acquainted, applicable and intelligent. His education had given her much pain; his book-learning she was no judge of, though she supposed it small or useless."—*Edit.* 1784, *p.* 354, *&c.*

CHAP. XXI. in the Prince's Court. Upon the accession of GEORGE III. we ac-
1761. cordingly find, that Lord BUTE, who was totally inexperienced in
the wide field of politics, takes Mr. Fox for his principal adviser,
not upon the principles of Government, for upon them they often
differed, but in the gratifications of resentment, and in the arrangements of men. Lord BUTE's other chief adviser was
Lord BATH, whose enmity was principally directed to the Duke
of NEWCASTLE, and his friends, as Mr. Fox's was to Mr.
PITT, and his friends. By these advisers, Lord BUTE was instructed to break all great connections, and to annihilate all
popular influence. The Court adopted these measures, with a
view to increase the power of the crown; and give to the King
an uncontrouled exercise of his influence, under the direction of
his private favour.

Mr. Grenville
wishes to be
made Speaker.
When it was known, that Mr. LEGGE was to be turned out,
Mr. GRENVILLE expressed to his brothers, his desire to succeed
Mr. LEGGE; but Mr. PITT took no notice of his wishes; upon
which a coolness commenced between them. This disappointment occasioned Mr. GRENVILLE to direct his attention to another situation, and probably to another interest. Mr. ONSLOW
having resigned the chair of the House of Commons, Mr. GREN-
VILLE solicited to succeed to that vacancy. He was at this time
Treasurer of the Navy, and had been in that post about seven
years, and in other places. He waited upon the Duke of NEW-
CASTLE; who being still First Lord of the Treasury, was nominally Minister. The Duke asked him if he had mentioned
the matter to Lord BUTE. Mr. GRENVILLE owned he had:
and added, that he had not only the King's approbation, with
his Majesty's gracious assurance of the Cabinet, but the approbation

bation likewife of all his own family. The laft part was undoubtedly a miftake; for the Duke of NEWCASTLE was the firft perfon who informed Lord TEMPLE of Mr. GRENVILLE's overtures. Lord TEMPLE and Mr. PITT were exceedingly offended with their brother, for having made an application to Lord BUTE, without communicating his intention to either of them. From this moment Mr. GRENVILLE feparated himfelf from all his family; and there fubfifted the moft bitter animofity between them, until the month of May, 1765. During that period, Mr. GRENVILLE attached himfelf firft to Lord BUTE, and afterwards to the Duke of BEDFORD.

On the 6th of November, 1761, the new Parliament met. Mr. Fox had, at this time, obtained the fituation he was fo defirous of poffeffing in the late reign, viz. the management of the Houfe of Commons. No man was better qualified for this important truft. He was liberal in his promifes, and honourable in the performance of them. We may judge of his means, by the facts refpecting the Civil Lift only. When Mr. PITT refigned (October, 1761), the King's revenue not only ftood clear of all incumbrances, but there was a balance in the Exchequer, due to the Crown, of between one hundred and thirty and one hundred and forty thoufand pounds. When Lord BUTE and Mr. Fox refigned*, which was in April, 1763, the balance in the Exchequer was not only expended, but the outgoings upon the eftablifhment of the Civil Lift, exceeded the income, to the amount of upwards of ninety thoufand pounds *per annum*.

* Mr. Fox did not refign the Pay Office, but only the management of the Houfe of Commons. Mr. Grenville fucceeded him in that department.

CHAP. XXI.
1761.
Motion for the Spanish papers.

On the 11th of December, 1761, a motion was made in the House of Commons, "That an humble address be presented to his Majesty, that he will be graciously pleased to give directions that there be laid before the House copies of all the memorials delivered by Count FUENTES, to his Majesty's Ministers, relating to the demand of liberty to the Spanish nation to fish on the banks of Newfoundland; and also copies of all memorials delivered by the said Ambassador of Spain, to his Majesty's Ministers, relating to the destruction and evacuation of any establishments made by British subjects on the coasts of Honduras, and relating to the right of cutting logwood there; and also copies of all memorials delivered by the said Ambassador to his Majesty's Ministers, demanding restitution of the prizes taken during this war on the subjects of Spain; together with copies of the answers given by the Court of Great Britain to the Court of Spain on the three above demands."

Mr. Pitt.

Mr. PITT supported this motion. He did not wish, he said, that any part of his conduct should be covered or concealed from the public. On the contrary, he declared it to be his ardent desire to see laid open and revealed, both the motives and actions of every part of his administration. He, therefore, pressed with zeal, the laying before the House every paper relative to the six years negociation with Spain, that the justice and candour of the Crown of England on the one hand, and the chicanery, insolence and perfidy of Spain, on the other, might be apparent to the whole House. [This appeal to so much written evidence, spoke the strongest language of conscious integrity.] Much stress, he added, had been laid without doors, on his refusing the memorial offered by M. BUSSY, relative to the concerns of Spain. In refusing that memorial, he said he had followed the *precedent* of the Court of Spain, which had returned, as inadmissible, a memorial of the King of Great Britain. He thought it was of consequence to the House to know both the *matter* and the *expression* of that memorial, as it related to one of the three points in negociation.

But upon calling for the question, a negative was put upon the motion.

The debate being over, Mr. Fox stood up and said, That if any

particular

particular paper neceffary to the vindication of certain perfons, was specifically moved for, it would be given.

Mr. PITT treated this as a captious offer: he faw through its fallacy, and refufed to accept it. What he earneftly wifhed for, was all the papers relative to the fix years negotiation, which having been refufed, he faid the gentleman who made the offer, very well knew, that he (Mr. PITT) could not mark out, nor call in a parliamentary way, for a fpecific paper, with the contents of which he had been entrufted before, by the King, under the feal of fecrecy.

Mr. PITT took no further part in the debates of this feffion, until the month of May, 1762; when the King fent a meffage to the Houfe of Commons, informing them of the defign of Spain to attack Portugal, foliciting their fupport of his moft faithful Majefty. On the 13th the Houfe in a Committee of Supply, voted one million for that fervice.

Mr. PITT, though not in the King's fervice, fupported the refolution of the committee of fupply. He began with pointing out the neceffity of continuing the war in Germany, and of fupporting the King of Portugal. He obferved, that in times of war, connexions with the continent had always been found political, except in the four unhappy reigns of the Stuarts. Then, turning about to feveral perfons, he very jocularly faid, 'You who are for continental mea‑
'fures, I am with you; and you who are for affifting the King of Por‑
'tugal, I am with you; and you who are for putting an end to the
'war, I am with you alfo; in fhort, I am the only man to be found that
'am with you all.' He then enumerated the fucceffes that attended the Britifh arms in all parts of the world, and the immenfe advantages gained in our trade, which would more than compenfate the great expence we had been at; and which he obferved was a confideration that had been overlooked by thofe who were complaining of the heavy burthen of the war; and in regard to contracting the expences, he entirely agreed with thofe who were for it, and urged, that whoever would effect this falutary work, would deferve the higheft encomiums; but he hoped a diftinction would be made between contracting the expence, and contracting the operations of the war, and defired any one prefent to fhew how the latter could have been, or might ftill be done with fafety: he then remarked, that he did not find any lefs expence attended

CHAP. XXI.
1762.

attended the nation now, than when he unworthily held the seals, or that more was done; and turning to the Marquis of GRANBY, he observed, that he knew his zeal for the service of his country was such, that if he had received his orders, he was sure he would not then be where he was. And as to what the noble Lord * had said, no one doubted his capacity, if his heart was but as good; that as for his own part, he could not tell the reason of the continental expences being greater now than in Queen ANNE's time, unless it was because provender and every thing else in Germany was dearer now than then, and wished the noble Lord had explained that part of his speech, for he did not properly know what to make of it; it carried a something! a suspicion he did not understand! but if he meant that there had not been fair play with the money, he knew nothing of it; and then stretching out his hand, and moving his fingers, said they were clean, there was none of it stuck to them! and that he would second any person, who should move for an enquiry into the money matters; he was anxious to know how it was appopriated, that the whole truth might come out. He observed, that the noble Lord had said, he bled for his country, and he did not wonder at it; that it was his opinion, he ought to throw his body at his Majesty's feet, and there bleed at every pore. He then represented, that in consequence of our withdrawing our troops from Germany, Portugal and the Low Countries, would become a prey to the French and Spaniards; that in point of policy we ought not to suffer it; but that he did not mean to bear Portugal on our shoulders, but only to set him on his legs, and put a sword in his hand. He affirmed, that France was almost a ruined nation, having expended in the last year upwards of eight millions, and had been still losing: that he knew the finances of France, as well as any man in England; and that we, by our successes, were repaid for our expence; that it was wrong and unjust to represent Great Britain in so deplorable a state, as unable to carry on the war, (for there were always strangers in the gallery, who wrote to their friends in Holland, an account of what passed in that place, and the Dutch forwarded it to the French) that it was well known England never was better able

* Lord George Sackville.

to support a war than at present; that the money for this year was raised, and he would answer for it, if we wanted fifteen or twenty millions for next year, we might have it; he therefore strongly recommended the million as desired; that he knew the cry which had been propagated for these three years; You won't be able to raise money to continue the war another year; and yet we all saw the contrary.— He affirmed, that one campaign might have finished the war; (alluding to his own proposal of demanding a categorical answer from Spain). And in answer to the Gentleman * who had said, that the complaints of the Portuguese merchants had not been attended to, he insisted, that so far from it, he had spent many nights in considering them; and referred that Gentleman to what had passed between him and the Ambassador of the Court of Portugal; but they had been abandoned since. He then recommended union and harmony to the Ministry, and declared against altercation, which, he said was no way to carry on the public business, and urged the necessity of prosecuting the war with vigour, as the only way to obtain an honourable, solid, and lasting peace; and proved from the readiness with which supplies had been granted, there would be little danger of a stop on that account, so long as the money was properly applied, and attended with success. He said, he wished to save Portugal, not by an ill-timed and penurious, but by a most efficacious and adequate assistance.

The session closed on the second of June 1762.

The defence of Portugal was undertaken, without making any stipulations in behalf of our merchants, which the opportunity so amply afforded, and who had presented severally memorials to the Courts of London and Lisbon complaining the injustice of the last. So far from taking the least notice of these complaints, Lord TYRAWLEY was sent to Lisbon, in the character of Ambassador. He was, perhaps, the only gentle-

* Mr. Glover.

CHAP. XXI. man in the Britifh dominions, to whom that Court, at another
1762. time, would have made an exception. At this moment, the
Court of Lifbon was under the neceffity of being filent. Upon
a former occafion, Lord TYRAWLEY had rendered himfelf particularly offenfive at Lifbon; and he feems to have been felected
on this occafion, certainly not from motives of friendfhip to
that Court, although it was the moft favourable period for efta-
blifhing every neceffary commercial ftipulation, with clearnefs
and precifion.

CHAP.

[213]

CHAP. XXII.

Resolution of the British Cabinet to make peace— Subsidy to Prussia refused—Negotiation with the Court of Petersburgh, and with the Court of Vienna—Both made known to the King of Prussia— Negotiation with the Court of Turin—Anecdote of the peace of Aix la Chapelle—Pension granted to the Sardinian Minister— Privy Purse and Secret Service—Alterations in the British Ministry—Lord Bute Minister—His Brother at Court—Interesting particulars of the negotiation between Great Britain and France—Lord Bute's wealth—Examination of Dr. Musgrave —Union of the Duke of Bedford and Mr. Grenville—Dismission of the Duke of Devonshire.—Anecdote of the Duke of Newcastle and Lord Granville.

NOTWITHSTANDING the British arms continued successful in every quarter of the world, yet it was the firm and unalterable resolution of the British Cabinet, to make peace, with the utmost expedition. By the partial use which had been made of the press, already mentioned in Chap. XIX. the people of England became divided in opinion, on the subject of continuing the war. The Scottish nation were nearly unanimous in support of Lord BUTE. The British Cabinet were influenced by the same principles, and probably by the same means, which governed the Tory Cabinet of Queen ANNE, at the time of making the peace of Utrecht.

The first consideration of the noble Lord, who now guided the King's Councils, was to reduce the King of Prussia to the necessity of concurring in his pacific disposition. For this purpose,

CHAP. XXII.
1762.
Subsidy to Prussia refused.

purpose, the subsidy, which, according to treaty, had been annually paid to Prussia, was this year refused, contrary to the most solemn engagements, and in direct breach of the national faith—not, indeed, by an open and manly negative in the first instance; but after an infinite number of promises of the money, and evasive answers, to the Prussian resident in London, from the month of January to the month of May, 1762. The cruelty of this sport in the British Minister, was embittered by the perilous situation of the King, surrounded by hosts of enemies, and disappointed of the only assistance he had a right to estimate, in his preparations for the succeeding campaign. However, his good fortune did not abandon him; for in the same moment that Great Britain became his enemy, Russia became his friend. The Empress ELIZABETH died, and the Emperor, PETER III. immediately withdrew from the alliance against him: So that the design of the British Cabinet, in the refusal of the subsidy, was not accomplished. But though not accomplished, it was not abandoned: As soon as it was known in London, that the Emperor, PETER III. was preparing to withdraw himself from the alliance against the King of Prussia, the British Cabinet immediately opened a negociation with the Court of Petersburgh, to prevent, if possible, a separate peace being made, between the new Emperor and the King of Prussia. In this negociation, it was insinuated to the Court of Petersburgh, in very strong terms, that the British Court would behold with great concern, his Imperial Majesty withdrawing from his alliance with the Empress-Queen, and recalling his armies from their co-operation with the troops of the House of Austria—that it was not the wish of the British Court to

Negociatn. with the Court of Petersburgh.

see

see the House of Brandenburgh aggrandized at the expence of the House of Austria.

CHAP. XXII.
1762.

And from an apprehension, that this negociation might not be sufficient to answer the purpose, the plan of another negociation was formed: and the execution attempted, by the most humiliating introduction. This was with the Court of Vienna. To that haughty Court, offers, in the utmost degree degrading, on the part of Great Britain, were made. A renewal of the connexion between that Court and Great Britain, was solicited in terms of supplication. The most earnest assurances were made, that the British Cabinet never desired to see the power of Prussia encreased, by a diminution of the House of Austria— that on the contrary, the British Cabinet would rather see the power of Prussia revert to its primitive electoral state. And to prevent any suspicion of dissimulation, this proposed alliance between Great Britain and Austria, was further offered to be purchased, by some *concessions* to be made in Italy, or *elsewhere*. The British Court, at this time, had no authority to stipulate for any concessions to be made in Italy, in behalf of the House of Austria—consequently the word *elsewhere*, a word of unlimited latitude, must have been meant to include any country, or territory, to which the British influence either did, or could extend. And if we reflect but an instant, on the disposition of the British Cabinet at this time, towards the King of Prussia, there can be no doubt, that this word was intended to apply to some part of the dominions of that Prince.

And with the Court of Vienna.

These acts of proferred treachery, were treated with contempt. The Court of Vienna communicated them to the

Court

CHAP. XXII.
1762.

Both made known to the K. of Pruſſia.

of Peterſburgh; and by the laſt Court, all the documents of both negociations, were communicated to the King of Pruſſia: which explains the cauſe of that coolneſs, which ſubſiſted between that Monarch and the Court of Great Britain, until within a ſhort time of his death.

Negociation with the Court of Turin.

A Third negociation, which was opened with the Court of Turin, was more ſucceſsful; ſoliciting the intereſt of that Court with the Houſe of Bourbon, to repoſe the moſt firm confidence in the pacific diſpoſition of the Britiſh Cabinet; at the ſame time imploring his Sardinian Majeſty, to become the mediator and umpire in all points of diſpute. This was the *ſecond* time, that the Houſe of Savoy had been authorized to diſpoſe of the intereſts of Great Britain to the Houſe of Bourbon. The firſt time was at the peace of Aix la Chapelle; which, not being mentioned by the writers of the time, the reader will find it ſtated in the note*. And of the preſent negociation,

Lord

---

* At the battle of Laffelt, Lord LIGONIER being made priſoner, was introduced to the French King as ſoon as the action was over. The King ſaid to him—*Hé bien, Monſieur de Ligonier, quand eſt ce que le Roy votre maitre nous donnera la paix?* And at the ſame time commanded Marſhal SAXE, and the Duke de NOAILLES, to confer with him next day upon the ſubject; which they did, and aſſured him, that his Majeſty's orders were, that he ſhould be ſent back to the Duke of CUMBERLAND, upon his parole, with the following propoſal of peace.——That the King was ready to make peace upon theſe terms: that France would acknowledge the Emperor, and reſtore all Flanders, except Furnes, in caſe England inſiſted on the demolition of Dunkirk; but if England permitted Dunkirk to continue in its preſent ſtate, France would reſtore Furnes alſo: That England ſhould reſtore the fort and iſland of Louiſbourg; and the Empreſs Queen and King of Sardinia ſhould make an eſtabliſhment for Don PHILLIP; which his Majeſty did not require to be very ſplendid. The propoſal was debated in the Britiſh Cabinet ſeveral times, and the Cabinet

Lord CHATHAM said in the House of Lords, on the second of March, 1770, "That the Court of Turin sold this country to "France in the last peace." If we admit this assertion to have been well founded, and there is no reason to doubt it, the Court of Turin received favours from *both* sides. The British Court were very liberal in the rewards they gave: amongst others, the Sardinian Ambassador, in particular, was gratified with a pension of one thousand pounds per annum upon Ire-

net were divided upon it. Dr. MATY gives some hints of this matter, in section V. of his memoirs of Lord CHESTERFIELD; but he does not seem to have been fully informed. At length the Sardinian Minister in London, prevailed upon the Duke of NEWCASTLE and Mr. PELHAM to reject the proposal, under a pretence that it was incompatible with the treaty of Worms. Whoever will be at the trouble of comparing these terms with the treaty of Aix la Chapelle, will instantly perceive, that they were infinitely more advantageous to Great Britain, than the articles of that treaty.

But there was another circumstance, which marked this influence of the Court of Turin more strongly:—This was the negotiation for peace that was attempted to be opened on the part of the Court of Madrid, by M. WALL, who came through the *Pays Bas* to London, with Marshal SAXE's passport, for that purpose. He had several conferences with the British Ministry on the subject; but when he began to enter upon that part which related to an establishment for Don PHILIP, he was told, that it was expected that Spain should consent to the King of Sardinia's keeping Final, Vigevanasco, part of Pavia and Anghiera, with the free navigation of the Thesin. To this proposal M. WALL refused to give his promise; upon which the negotiation broke off, and M. WALL returned to Madrid. And though these very terms were obtained for the King of Sardinia, by the treaty of Aix la Chapelle, yet as the the conditions of that treaty were not so favourable to Great Britain, as the terms which had been offered to Lord LIGONIER, there can be little doubt of the British interests having been sacrificed, to secure these points for his Sardinian Majesty; who had moreover a subsidy from England, of 200,000l. per annum, by the treaty of Worms.

CHAP. XXII.
1763.

land for thirty one years, commencing the 25th of March, 1763, in the name of *George Charles*, Esq.*

The reduced condition of France, required no entreaty on the part of Turin, to induce her to accept the pacific assurances of

---

* This fact was first mentioned in the House of Commons of Ireland, by Mr. EDMUND SEXTON PERY, now Lord PERY, on the 24th of November, 1763, in these words:

" I shall communicate a fact to this House, from which it will appear that the grant of pensions to aliens, is supposed to be contrary to the sense of the nation, even by the advisers of such grant, and therefore not avowed, though made.—There is a pension, Sir, granted nominally, to one *George Charles*, but really to Count *Viri*, the Sardinian Minister, for negotiating the peace that has just been concluded with the Minister of France. I must confess, Sir, that in my opinion, this service deserved no such recompence, at least on our part; so that, in this case our money is not only granted to an alien, but to an alien, who has no merit to plead. If it is thought a defensible measure, I should be glad to know why it was not avowed; and why, if it is proper we should pay a thousand pounds a year to Count *Viri*, we should be made to believe, that we pay it to *George Charles*?"

The reader will draw his own conclusion from the following account of monies issued for the King's Privy Purse and Secret Service, during the two last years of the reign of the late King, and the three first years of his present Majesty; taken from the 32d vol. of the Journals of the House of Commons, page 514, &c.

Late Reign.

From October, 1758, to October 1759.   To Edward Finch, Esq. for his Majesty's privy purse, 36,000l.
For Secret Service, during the same period, 67,000l.

From October 1759, to October 1760.   To Edward Finch, Esq. for his Majesty's privy purse, 36,000l.
For Secret Service, during the same period, 66,000l.

Present

of the new British Minister. But before this negociation was publicly opened, Lord BUTE had avowedly assumed the character of Prime Minister. He had dismissed the Duke of NEWCASTLE, and all his friends; and had established his omnipotence through every department of the State. He took the Treasury himself, and appointed Mr. GRENVILLE his successor in the Secretary of State's office. Lord ANSON dying at this time, he offered the Admiralty to Lord HALIFAX, who at first refused it, because he wanted to be Secretary of State; upon which Lord BUTE told him, he did not know what he refused; that in patronage, it was next to the Treasury. Lord HALIFAX then took it. He had recalled his brother from Turin, and had appointed Lord RIVERS to that station. When his brother appeared at the levee, his Majesty honoured him with this compliment—"*I have now a* Second *Friend here.*" From the moment that he became Minister, it was the public language at the Court of Versailles, that he *must* make peace, if he wished

Margin notes: CHAP. XXII. 1763. Lord Bute Minister. His brother at Court.

Present Reign.

From October 1760, to October 1761.	To John Earl of Bute, for his Majesty's privy purse, 40,000l.
	For Secret Service, during the same period, 66,000l.
[*Here Mr. Pitt's Administration ends.*]	
From October 1761 to October 1762.	To John Earl of Bute, for his Majesty's privy purse, 48,000l.
	For Secret Service, during the same period, 95,000l.
From October 1762, to October 1763.	To John Earl of Bute for his Majesty's privy purse, 48,000l.
	For Secret Service, during the same period, 72,000l.

CHAP. XXII. to preserve his power; and therefore the assurances of his paci-
1763. fic disposition, and the offers to commence a negotiation, that
Court was prepared to expect.

The correspondence of this negotiation, not having been laid before Parliament, it may not be improper, in this place, to state a few particulars of the negotiation, with some extraordinary circumstances relative to it; which, although they are known to several persons, who have been in certain situations, yet they are not known to the public in general.

Interesting particulars of the negotiation between Great B. and France.
The Duke of BEDFORD set out for Paris on the fifth of September 1762, with full powers to treat; and on the 12th of the same month, the Duc de NIVERNOIS arrived in England. A few hours after the Duke of BEDFORD arrived at Calais, he received dispatches from London, by a messenger who was sent after him, containing some limitations in his full powers. He immediately sent the messenger back with a letter, insisting upon his former instructions being restored, and in case of a refusal, declaring his resolution to return to England. The Cabinet acceded to his Grace's demand. But the most essential articles of the treaty, were agreed upon between M. de CHOISEUL and the Sardinian Minister at Paris, and Lord BUTE and the Sardinian Minister at London, without any other trouble to the Duke of BEDFORD than giving his formal assent. The manœuvre in making the King of Sardinia *umpire*, gave to his Ambassadors the power of decision; consequently the Duke of BEDFORD had very little room for the exercise of his powers; until a circumstance happened, which occasioned a division in the British Cabinet. This was the Capture of the Havannah.

vannah. The news of this event arrived in England on the 29th of September. The negotiation was nearly concluded. In a few days the preliminaries would have been signed.

CHAP. XXII.
1762.

Lord BUTE expressed his fears, that this acquisition would embarrass and postpone the accomplishment of peace, if the negotiation, which was on the point of being finished, should on that account be opened again; and therefore he declared his wish to be, to conclude the peace in the same manner, and on the same terms, which had been agreed upon before the news of this event arrived; without any other mention of it, than the name of it among the places to be restored.

Mr. GRENVILLE opposed this idea. He declared his opinion to be, that if the Havannah was restored, there ought to be an equivalent given for it. And in their deliberations upon this subject, it is certain, that he insisted upon this alternative—either the entire property of Jucatan and Florida, or the islands of St. Lucia and Porto Rico.

Lord BUTE adhered to his first opinion. Upon which Mr. GRENVILLE resigned his place of Secretary of State on the 12th day of October. Lord HALIFAX immediately succeeded to his office; and Mr. GRENVILLE went to the Admiralty, by which he was removed from the Cabinet.

Lord EGREMONT, however, represented to Lord BUTE, in very strong terms, the necessity of an equivalent for the Havannah. Either his Lordship's arguments, or Lord BUTE's fears, so far prevailed, as to occasion an instruction to be sent to the Duke of BEDFORD, to ask for Florida. The Duke had

been

Chap. XXII.
1762.

been informed of the whole dispute in the British Cabinet, by Mr. GRENVILLE, and being entirely of Mr. GRENVILLE's opinion, he added, Porto Rico to his demand. But Lord BUTE and the Sardinian Minister in London, settled it for Florida *only*. At Paris some difficulties arose. The cession of Florida was made without the least hesitation; the French Minister instantly agreed to it; which shews the superior influence of the French Cabinet in this negotiation. But with respect to Porto Rico, the French Minister resorted to chicane and delay. It was at length agreed, to send a messenger to Madrid, with this demand. Fourteen days were allowed for the messenger to go and return. During this period, the Duke of BEDFORD received positive orders to sign the preliminaries. Two days after the preliminaries were signed, the messenger returned; and *it was said*, that Spain purchased the retension of the island. Whether the Sardinian Minister at London, or at Paris, or both, were entrusted on this occasion; or whether any other persons were admitted to the same confidence, are questions for the investigation of posterity. Discoveries of this kind are seldom made, either at, or near the time of the transaction. The offers of LOUIS the Fourteenth to the Duke of MARLBOROUGH, were not known until the publication of DE TORCY's memoirs*. Whatever were the confidential measures, it

---

* " I am willing you should offer the Duke of MARLBOROUGH *four millions*, should he enable me to keep Naples and Sicily for my Grandson, and to preserve Dunkirk with its fortifications and harbour, and Strasburg and Landau, in the manner above explained, or even the same sum, were Sicily to be exempted out of this last article."—*Mem. de Torcy.* T. II. p. 237

" It is not necessary to have recourse to foreign examples. We have a Sejanus of our own. Have we not seen him for a time displaying his exorbitant

it is certain, the Duke of BEDFORD was not entrusted with them. However, as his Grace kept a diary of all public transactions, CHAP XXII. 1761.

"tant treasures, in every kind of princely profusion? Has he not purchased estates, built and adorned villas, erected palaces, and furnished them with sumptuous magnificence? I am sure I speak within compass, when I assert, that within these last three years, [*This was written in the Autumn*, 1765] he has expended between *two and three hundred thousand pounds*. An enormous sum, equal almost to the whole revenues of the kingdom, from which he draws his original! I could wish to be informed by some of those, who are in the secret, how he has acquired such prodigious wealth. I will not suppose he *embezzled the public money*, when he officiously thrust himself into office; because there were so many checks upon him in that department, that he could not easily have done it without associates, or possessing more courage or cunning than I take him to be master of. But how then, has he acquired such amazing riches?— Tell me, ye flatterers of his, was it by *State-jobbing*, or *Stock-jobbing*, that he is become from a needy northern Thane, a potent British noble?— What sinister method has he taken to plunder the nation and escape the iron hand of Justice?—I am aware of the answer, that he has been able to make a purchase, to the amount of ninety-seven thousand pounds, to lay out a large park, and adorn and build two magnificent houses, out of the estate which was left him by a relation three years ago. But such a reply is so false and foolish, that it scarce deserves a moment's consideration; for I will venture to maintain, that the whole sum of his *visible* income, for the last *ten years* put together, will not amount to above 50,000l. As to the estate, it is not his; he is entitled only to part of the annual produce; for two thousand pounds a year were left to his injured brother, on whom he *affectionately turned his back*, as soon as he had possessed himself of his natural inheritance. When this 2000l. per annum is deducted, there will not remain clear to the Favourite above 5000l. a year: And whether this is sufficient to account for all those immense sums, which, to our amazement and indignation, he has lately expended, I leave every impartial person to judge.—*Anti Sejanus*."

It is, no doubt, yet in the public recollection, that a series of political essays, distinguished by the signature of *Anti Sejanus*, appeared in the public prints, in the Autumn of the year 1765. They were supposed to be written by Mr. SCOTT, of Trinity College, Cambridge, under the patronage of Lord SANDWICH. The above extract is made from the paper of the third of August.

CHAP. XXII. actions, in which he had any share; and as Mr. GRENVILLE
1762. kept copies of all his letters on public business, if ever these are laid before the public, and it is hoped they will, many suspicions, which can now only be hinted, will be confirmed, or exploded.

The examination of Dr. MUSGRAVE at the bar of the House of Commons, although it was voted *frivolous*, perhaps will not appear so in the eye of Impartial posterity. As this examination is not in every body's hands, the reader will find an extract from it the note.*

The

* Dr. MUSGRAVE read the following paper at the bar, being the information he laid before Lord HALIFAX for the purpose of instituting an Enquiry.

Narrative of intelligence received at Paris.

1. The first hint I had of the Ministry having been bribed to make the peace, was at the latter end of the year 1763, from Monsieur .... in a private conversation I had with that gentleman. The peace happening to be talked of, he made use of this expression, *On croit à Paris, que milord Bute a eu de l'argent pour cela*. Though the words *on croit* were pretty strong, and though Monsieur ....'s connections gave great weight to them, I considered the thing as an idle rumour, and neither pushed the conversation further at that time, nor made any enquiry about it afterwards.

2. It was not till the latter end of November, 1764, that I began to think the story more worthy attention. Being at that time in company with three gentlemen, an Irishman, a Scotchman, and a Frenchman, a dispute arose about the peace. The Irishman and myself condemning it, the Frenchman remaining silent, the Scotchman alone approving it. The dispute did not last long before the Irishman and the Scotchman had occasion to go away, so that there remained only the Frenchman and myself together. Our conversation falling upon the same topic, he told me that he remembered to have heard, a little before the Duke of BEDFORD's negociation, that a sum of money, amounting to about eight millions of livres, had been sent into England to buy a peace; that the remittance had been made by Monsieur de la BORDE, and another banker,
whose

The coincidence of opinion, which arose between the Duke of BEDFORD and Mr. GRENVILLE, during the preceding negotiation,

CHAP. XXII.
1762.
Union of the D. of Bedford and Mr. Grenville.

whose name he did not know; and that the way this came to be known, was by the clerks talking of it among themselves after dinner. He added, that being himself in company with several gentlemen, who were giving their conjectures, whether peace would hold or no, one of the company decided the question, by saying, *Nous aurons la paix certainement, car nous l'avons achetè.* This was all I heard the first interview.

3. I communicated this account the next morning, to a Mr. Stuart, my patient, who lived in the Rue de l'Echelle, with a Mr. Maclean. Mr. Maclean was then gone out; but upon his coming in, I repeated it to him. It occurred to me, during my conversation with Mr. Stuart, as it did afterwards to Mr. Maclean, that the fact of money being sent over might be true, but that the destination of it might be a mistake: that in short, it might be intended for no other purpose than to buy up English stocks, for the sake of selling them soon after at an advanced price. This account appeared so natural, that I went home in (almost) a full persuasion of its being really the case.

4. The same day, or the day after, I saw the same Frenchman, my informant, again. I put this objection to him. He answered readily no, that was not the case. He knew very well, continued he, that Monst. de la Borde sent over a very large order for stocks, by the Sardinian Ambassador's courier: but the money I speak of was before that time, and at least a month or two before the Duke of Bedford's arrived. Besides, I can tell you the people to whom it was distributed. It was divided among three persons: Lord Bute—here he hesitated for a minute or two. I mentioned to him the name of Lord Holland. He answered no; it was not Lord Holland, that was not the name; it was ...... Mr. Fox. The third, added he, was a Lady, whose name I do not recollect.

This I am pretty sure, was all that passed upon the subject at our second interview.

5. The third interview was, I believe, on Monday, the 3d of December.— I then asked him, whether the third person, whose name he could not recollect, was not ———? He answered no, it was not. That he had heard the name; that it being a name no way familiar to him, he could not at such a distance of time, recollect it of himself; but if it was mentioned, he believed he should know it. At present, added he, I only remember, that it was a Lady, and the mistress of a man of great quality.

6. I had

Chap. XXII.
1762.

gociation, laid the foundation of that union, which subsisted between them, until the death of Mr. GRENVILLE. They perfectly

6. I had hitherto made no enquiries about his authorities. But reflecting, that a person who could know all these particulars, must have been very near the source, I thought proper to ask him, the next time I saw him, from whom he had his information. He answered, from an officer, who, at that time furnished plans to the Duke de Choiseul's office, was of course, greatly connected with it, and moreover dined every day with the principal people of the office: and there, added he, at table, did these gentlemen talk over the affair, not without some satisfaction at its being concluded. Further, says he, this officer, who is now at Cayenne, reasoned thus with me about it: Is it not better to buy a peace at the expence of ten millions, than spend three hundred millions (if we could raise them) to fit our army for the field, which army, so fitted out, could not possibly do us any material service.

7. I had curiosity, continued he, to hear what the Sardinian Ambassador's secretary, who was a great acquaintance of mine, would say to this. Happening to meet him soon after, I told him it was reported, the English had given a great sum to Madame Pompadour, to buy a peace, and asked him if it was true. The answer he made me was in these words; *ah, que vous etes bête! les Anglois donne de l'argent ? et pourquoi faire ? oui, oui, on a donné de l'argent.*

8. He further said, that upon Monsieur Bussy's return from England, one of his secretaries having dropped some hints in company, *à un soupér*, of what was going on in England, was taken up and put into the Bastile, that he might not, by any further indiscretion, discover the whole affair.

9. Upon my mentioning an intention of going to England with the news, he added, that the whole detail of the transaction might be known, either from Monsieur D'Eon if he chuses to discover it, or from a Monsieur L'Escallier, a wine merchant in London, whom the Duke de Nivernois made use of as a secretary.

10. I pressed him about the authenticity of his account; his answer was, as to myself, *Je le crois autant que je crois ma propre existence.* He assured me likewise, that the affair was shamefully notorious in some houses at Paris: *C'est affaire faisoit même beaucoup de scandale dans certaines maisons à Paris.*

11. I think it necessary to take notice of one variation, and the only one that I observed in his account. In the first interview here mentioned, the sum of eight

fectly agreed, *That better terms of peace might have been had— that all was not obtained, which might have been obtained.* But although

eight millions of livres*. In a subsequent one (I forgot which) he said, between five and eight millions: possibly this might be owing to his having heard the sum named in English money, and never having given himself the trouble of reducing it to French; beause the last time I talked with him upon the subject, which I desired to know, as near as possible, the exact sum, he took a little time to recollect himself, and then said, between eight and ten millions of livres; that is, continued he, in English, four hundred thousand guineas.

Extract from the Examination.

What was Lord Halifax's answer to this information?

I would first mention some previous steps. Lord Hertford having asked me, if I thought it matter of further enquiry, I went to Lord Mansfield; he said he chose not to hear it. I then went to Dr. Blackstone, who read my paper of information, and told me, that I should carry it to the Secretary of State; that no Englishman would be averse to enquire into it. I went to Lord Halifax on the 10th of May; he desired me to come again that evening; I then saw him: he took the paper and read it, looked up and stopped; then said, I was recollecting, that that person bought stock at that time, but it might be with his own money. He read my letter to Lord Hertford, said it was a proper one— He said, if I had been in Lord Hertford's place, I would have sent it to ——— and heard what he had to say. On reading the second letter, he said, this might be very deep; I would readily enquire, but it is an affair of such magnitude; and then put a case of a man's being robbed on Hounslow-heath, and going to Justice Fielding, and saying he was robbed by a tall, thin man, and apprehend it was the Duke of Ancaster: there is no difference, only in the size of the purse. He said, if you had any proof, I would make no difficulty of telling it to my royal master. In my letter to Lord Hertford, I mentioned the defectiveness of my information as a proof of the truth of it. Lord Halifax said, I think with you, it is more likely to be true, from his knowing only a few circumstances. The second meeting was a few days afterwards. He did not stick to one objection. I set down a few arguments to use to him, which I left with him; I have in my pocket the same arguments, which I set down a short time after, from my recollection. This is not a copy [read a paper, in substance as follows.]

* Compare this with the first paragraph.

CHAP. XXII. although they were convinced, and the fact lay within their
1762. own knowledge, that the interests of the nation had been sacrificed.

Narrative of intelligence is sufficient for enquiry, though not for accusation, confirmed by Dr. Blackstone. The first of all crimes is hearsay; rare, at first, to stumble upon certainty. All offenders would escape if there was no enquiry. The high quality of offenders is no reason for stopping the enquiry; it must be done speedily; if the common people hear it, and believe it, they might do justice after their own manner. I recommend it to Lord Halifax, as one of the French ministers is here, whether he can be excused for not examining into it, &c.

What said Lord Halifax?

Lord Halifax made no answer to the paper; nor did he controvert one of the arguments.

The next morning I saw Mr. Fitzherbert, Sir George Yonge was there. Mr. Fitzherbert expressed his astonishment at my boldness in going to Lord Halifax. He said he would not have any thing of his writing appear. Mr. Fitzherbert said he had intelligence the French were offering money to get D'Eon's papers back. I went the same day to Lord Halifax, or the next day. Lord Halifax said, I will have nothing to do with the matter. I disbelieve the charge: if I did believe it, as strongly as I now disbelieve it, I should not think this sufficient ground to go upon. I told him it was his duty; he seemed surprized. He said his duty was to take care of the state. I told him that Mr. Fitzherbert had said the French were in treaty for D'Eon's papers. I made my apology for troubling him, and that closed my conversation with Lord Halifax.

(Mr. Fitzherbert) Did you collect from my conversation, that I had the smallest knowledge of D'Eon?

I don't know I did; but Mr. Fitzherbert admitted the reality of the overtures. After the names of the two Lords were mentioned, Mr. Fitzherbert said, did you hear nothing of the Princess of Wales. I said no. Mr. Fitzherbert answered, D'Eon says, the Princess of Wales had some of the money.

From whom had you the information of D'Eon's overtures?

The first was from General Conway. He first gave me a hint of it.

What was that hint?

When I told the story, Mr. Conway asked me if I had seen D'Eon; he said I hear he has dropped hints. I told him I never would see him. I said, I will avoid all possibility of concert with any one. After this, I went to Mr. Hartly,

ficed by the leader of the Cabinet, to his exceffive rage for peace; yet when the preliminary articles of the treaty were fubmitted to

Hartly, and defired him to enquire. He defired firft to confult Sir George Savile. Sir George Savile came to us, I could not tell him the particulars, but only that there was fuch a charge. Sir George Savile thought it was right to confult the Duke of Newcaftle. He went to him. I was not prefent; but I heard, that the Duke of Newcaftle faid, Fox was rogue enough to do any thing, but thought he was not fool enough to do this. The Duke faid he could not advife them to meddle in it; for D'Eon will be bribed, and then you will be left in the lurch. I heard this converfation from Sir George Savile, or Mr. Hartly; from one of them, in the prefence of the other. They both went to the Duke of Newcaftle.

(Mr. Conway). What was the nature of his firft application to me?

The nature of my firft application to Mr. Conway was, I wanted to know how to convey a letter to Lord Hertford, not to be opened, to enquire whether the informant was apprehended. I had defigned prefenting a paper to the Houfe of Commons, fetting forth the information. He afked me the particulars, and faid he would not encourage fuch application to the Houfe of Commons without a fhadow of probability; and then afked if I had heard, that D'Eon had dropped hints, and whether I would go to him. I faid no, I would not. Mr. Conway added, at the fame time, I think it the duty of every man, to come at truth in every ftation.

Had you any intimacy with your informant at Paris?

It would be improper to anfwer that queftion—but they were men of credability.

Had you any other information of D'Eon's overtures, but from General Conway?

The firft intimation was from General Conway; then I applied to Mr. Hartly. Mr. Hartly told me, that D'Eon's letter was fent to Mr. Fitzherbert. Afterwards he informed me more fully, and named the two Privy Counfellors and the lady. He faid, the lady is the Princefs of Wales. I faid, it can't be, becaufe my informant would not have forgot the name; and named another lady, the miftrefs of a man of quality.

Do you underftand this overture of D'Eon's was contained in a letter to Mr. Fitzherbert?

Mr.

CHAP. XXII. to the confideration of Parliament, Mr. GRENVILLE gave them
1762. his approbation by his vote, and the Duke of BEDFORD by his
proxy;

Mr. Hartly told me fo. I met him in a chair, and he faid, all I have heard is, that D'Eon's letter was fent to Fitzherbert; that Mr. Pitt had been confulted, and had written a letter, diffuading them from proceeding. Mr. Hartly never told it me from his own knowledge.

(Dr. Blackftone.) Are you fure I directed you to go to Lord Halifax?

Not directly to Lord Halifax. Doctor Blackftone faid, you muft by all means go to the Miniftry. It is an affair of an alarming nature. He fent three days after to know if I had been; for he faid, if you had not, I fhould think myfelf obliged, as a fervant of the Crown, to go and give it myfelf.

I took a minute of what paffed between us; which I will mention to Dr. M. I took it immediately, and communicated it the fame day to an intimate friend, and it has never fince been out of my cuftody.

Produces a minute taken immediately after Dr. Mufgrave had been with him, the 10th of May, 1765, at half paft eleven o'clock in the morning.

" Dr. Mufgrave came and fhewed me a written converfation between him and Mr. Le Beau, in the latter end of 1763; where he declared, that it was believed at Paris that Lord Bute had received money for the peace; and many other converfations with another French Ambaffador. The fum of the account was this, That eight or ten millions of livres had been remitted by a French banker, juft before the D. of Bedford went to France. That this was divided between Lord B. Mr. F. and a Lady, name not mentioned; and, that Mr. D'Eon or Mr. Defcalier, could inform him of particulars. He alfo fhewed me Lord Holland's letters and anfwers. He told me he had communicated it to General Conway, and that he had learnt from Mr. Fitzherbert that D'Eon tells the fame ftory, except that he mentions the Princefs of Wales, which Dr. M. obferved might be no inconfiftency, if a Maid of Honour's name only was made ufe of, and the money paid over by the Princefs Dowager of Wales. Dr. Mufgrave feemed to be attached to D'Eon's caufe, and believed the ftory of his affaffination being attempted by Count de Guerchy, and his coffers being fearched. He afked me if this was fufficient to juftify bringing it before the Secretary of State. As our acquaintance was fmall, I was furprifed. I told him that the affair was delicate, both as to the things and perfons; and that he fhould well confider the confequences if his friends fhould deny it. He faid his friend was a man of honour, and knew he left Paris for that purpofe. I

begged

[231]

proxy; nor was it until the open breach with Lord Bute in 1765, that the fact concerning the Havannah, was known beyond

CHAP. XXII.
1762.

begged to be excused advising him, but he would do right to confider, that it would depend on conviction of his own mind, and his friends's veracity. It was equally a duty to difclofe fuch a tranfaction on good foundation, and to ftifle it in the birth, if founded on malice or ignorance. We parted, and he feemed inclined to proceed. I don't recollect the converfation he mentions three days after. It might be. I thought him fuch an enthufiaft as might have difordered his imagination."

(Mr. Speaker.) The Honourable Gentleman delivered to me a copy of the paper he has now read; which has been in my cuftody ever fince.

(Dr. Mufgrave.) As to the fecond converfation, Dr. Blackftone will recollect it if I fhew him his note, defiring me to come to him. I have not that note about me, but I am fure it is ftill in my poffeffion. I don't know what he thinks of my enthufiafm, but I remember he trembled, feemed much affected, and let the paper drop, as in great agitation.

(Sir Geo. Yonge.) After I had expreffed my furprize at his coming to me, he told me he had laid the matter before Lord Halifax, who was willing to receive information from any gentleman whatever. He preffed it fo ftrongly that I thought he came with a meffage, but he did not fay that. I faid, if Lord Halifax will fend for me I will wait on him, but I know nothing of the matter, with regard to the fecond meeting at Mr. Fitzherbert's, nor did I know he had told the ftory to Mr. Fitzherbert till I faw it in the papers.

(Mr. Fitzherbert.) I never remember being in the fame room with Sir G. Yonge and Dr. Mufgrave. Dr. Mufgrave came and talked in the fame ftile, and told me the ftory he fays I told him. I don't remember I faid any thing at that time, the Dr. came and told me this ftory. I will do myfelf the juftice to tell all I knew at that time, though I don't recollect I told it him. We were then a good many in a fociety in Albermarle-ftreet. I had an office in that fociety. When he had told me all he had to fay, I wifhed to change the fubject; he would not; fo I told all I knew of it. Captain Cole, a gentleman of general admiffion, had come to me, and faid D'Eon defires me to tell you he is apprehenfive of being taken away by force, on account of a quarrel with Count Guerchy, in which Miniftry would affift him. He defired me to communicate it to the fociety, which I did. He recommended D'Eon as an agreeable man. I communicated it to Sir George Yonge, and defired him to go with me becaufe he could fpeak French, which I could not eafily. No day was appointed. We

never

CHAP XXII.
1762.

yond the small circle of their indispensible confidents. This circumstance indisputably shews, that the Public Interest was not the first consideration with his Majesty's servants at this time. And it is believed, although it is a matter, that perhaps will not be ascertained until some future period, that Lord BUTE's resignation in the month of April 1763, was occasioned by the junction of Mr. GRENVILLE and the Duke of BEDFORD, and the menaces they held out against him, respecting the negotiation for peace——That he compounded for his impunity, by an abandonment of office to the Duke and his Friends. It was, however, the popular opinion, that the political paper, called the *North Briton*, written principally by Mr. WILKES, had raised such a spirit of animosity in the nation against Lord BUTE, that he resigned from an apprehension of popular indignation; and it answered the purpose of more parties than one, at that time, to say so. But Mr. WILKES had no more influence in the resignation of Lord BUTE, than he had in that of Sir ROBERT WALPOLE, or any other Minister. However, until Lord BUTE absconded from his public situation of Minister, no Favourite exercised the power of the Crown, with

---

never did meet. I never knew Mr. D'Eon: I never received a letter from him. As to going on with the conversation, and naming the Princess of Wales, I have nothing to say to that, I have no trace of it in my memory; it must depend on our veracity: nor had I any direct message, but from Captain Cole, as to his apprehensions of being taken away.

(Mr. Speaker.) Dr. Musgrave, would you ask these gentlemen, or either of them, any questions?

(Dr. Musgrave.) I was not prepared for these answers; and I have no questions to ask them.

Motion by Sir George Osborne—That the accusations brought by Dr. Musgrave, are in the highest degree frivolous. Agreed to, January 29, 1770.

more

more pride and infolence. This charge might be proved in in- numerable inftances. But it is not the defign of this work, to relate any occurrence, not immediately connected with Mr. PITT, unlefs the fame has been either omitted, or materially miftated, in the public accounts of the times. Of this latter kind, is the difmiffion of the Duke of DEVONSHIRE.

<small>CHAP. XXII
1762.</small>

During the preceding negotiation of peace, his Grace held the office of Lord Chamberlain, and although in the difcharge of his official duties, he was very frequently attending on the King, yet differing from his Majefty's other fervants on political fubjects, he did not attend any Council held after the commencement of the negotiation. Early in the month of October 1762, he obtained his Majefty's permiffion to go to Bath. While he was at Bath, he received a fummons to attend Council, and the fummons, as ufual, mentioned the bufinefs; which was, the *final* confideration on the preliminary articles of peace. The Duke wrote an anfwer, That as he had not attended any of the *former* Councils on the fubject of the negotiation, he apprehended, that his prefence at the *laft* Council would be improper. At the end of the month his Grace returned to London; and the day after his arrival, being levee day, he went to Court. The King was in the clofet. He fent in his name. The King took no notice. In this particular the Duke was wrong---he was too delicate——he fhould have demanded an audience. He next defired to know, to whom fhould he deliver his key? The King returned an anfwer, That he fhould fend next morning; which he did, and with his own hand, ftruck his Grace's name out of the lift of his Privy Council.

<small>Difmiffion of the Duke of Devonfhire.</small>

CHAP. XXII. The reader will make his own obfervations on this extrordi-
1762. nary conduct. No one need be told, that the CAVENDISHES were amongſt the moſt warm, and moſt determined fupporters of the Revolution in 1688, and of the Houfe of Brunfwick; nor have their virtue and zeal diminifhed, in an oppofition to the moſt fubtle attempts to accomplifh the moſt defpotic defigns.

Diſmiſſion of the Duke of Newcaſtle. Nor has the immediate caufe of the Duke of NEWCASTLE's refignation been lefs miftated. When his Grace found, that the annual convention with Pruffia was not to be renewed, as ufual, he fuggefted another mode, to fave the national honour; and which would, at the fame time, fupport the national dignity, and effentially contribute towards commanding the terms of peace. This was, when the application was made to Parliament, in the month of May 1762, for a vote of credit of one million, his Grace wifhed to extend the fum to two millions. A vote of credit of one million, had been ufual every year of the war. His Grace's intention was to have fupplied the King of Pruffia, with the amount of his annual fubfidy out of the fecond million. But this defign being made known to Lord BUTE, by one of the Secretaries of the Treafury*, almoſt asfoon as it was fuggefted, that Lord oppofed it with the greateft warmth. The Duke finding this oppofition from Lord BUTE, and expecting no better fuccefs in the clofet, he faw his influence at an end—and immediately refigned.

Lord Granville. Mr. WOOD, who had been Mr. PITT's Secretary during the war, fays in the preface to his Effay on Homer, that having

* The political paper, called the North Briton, accufed Mr. S. MARTIN of having *betrayed* the Duke of NEWCASTLE to Lord BUTE. MARTIN was alfo Treafurer to the Princefs of WALES.

waited

waited upon Lord GRANVILLE, Prefident of the Council, when he was dying, with the preliminary articles of the treaty, and read them to him, his Lordfhip declared, "it was the moft honourable peace he ever faw." This anecdote only proves Lord GRANVILLE's attachment to Lord BATH to the laft moment of his life. Dr. FRANKLIN frequently entertained his friends with another anecdote of this Nobleman, which deferves to be remembered. Upon the Embargo being laid on all American veffels laden with corn, flour, &c. in the year 1757, the American agents petitioned againft it, and were heard before the Privy Council. Lord GRANVILLE, who was Lord Prefident, told them, That America muft not do any thing to interfere with Great Britain in the European markets; that if America grew corn, fo did England; that if America fhipped corn, fo did England. Upon which, Dr. FRANKLIN told his Lordfhip, that America could not do any thing that would not interfere with Great Britain in fome refpect or other.---If they planted, reaped, and muft not fhip, the beft thing he could advife his Lordfhip to do, would be, to apply to Parliament for tranfports fufficient to bring them all back again.

Has it not been the misfortune of England, that moft of her great men have frequently fhewn, that they were influenced by very narrow ideas, when exercifing their political talents on national fubjects? If the policy of that part of the Treaty was juft, which extended the Britifh Colonies in America, what benefit could be derived from thofe Colonies, if thefe ideas of reftraint were maintained?

CHAP. XXIII.

Extraordinary preparations for the meeting of Parliament—Preliminary articles of Peace laid before Parliament—Mr. Pitt's Speech against them.

CHAPTER XXIII.
1762.
Extraordinary preparations.

PARLIAMENT met on the 25th of November 1762 †. The most extraordinary provision was made for this event. The Royal Houshold had been encreased beyond all former example. The Lords and Grooms of the Bedchamber were doubled. Pensions were thrown about indiscriminately. Five and twenty thousand pounds were issued in one day, in bank notes of one hundred pounds each. The only stipulation was, *Give us your vote.* A corruption of such notoriety and extent, had never been seen before. There is no example, in any age or country, that in any degree approaches to it. The dole was lavish beyond the probability of account, or possibility of credit. Mr. Fox had the management of the House of Commons, with unlimited powers.

† In the evening of the day preceding the meeting of Parliament, the Members of the House of Commons met, as usual, at the Cockpit. Mr. Fox took the chair, and produced to the company a paper, which he only called *a Speech*, and which he said he would, as usual, read to them. He afterwards produced an *Address*, which he read; and then said, that Lord CARYSFORT and Lord CHARLES SPENCER had been so kind to undertake to move and second *that* address. The same ceremony is observed with respect to the House of Lords. The speech is read by some Peer, who is supposed to conduct the business of that House. The Manager of the House of Commons takes the chair at the Cockpit.

On

On the 29th of November, the preliminary articles of peace with France and Spain, were laid before both Houses.

Chapter XXIII. 1762.

On the ninth of December they were taken into consideration; and a motion was made, to return his Majesty thanks, for his gracious condescension in ordering the preliminary articles of peace concluded between his Majesty and their most Christian and Catholic Majesties, to be laid before them. To assure his Majesty, his faithful Commons were impatient to express to his Majesty, their approbation of the advantageous terms, upon which his Majesty hath concluded preliminary articles of peace. And to lay before his Majesty, the hearty applause of a faithful, affectionate and thankful people, &c. &c. &c.

Preliminaries laid before Parliament.

On this memorable day, Mr. PITT attended in Parliament, notwithstanding he was at that moment afflicted with a severe fit of the gout. He spoke in reply to Mr. Fox, who made the motion.

He began with lamenting his ill state of health, which had confined him to his chamber; but although he was at this instant suffering under the most excruciating torture, yet he determined, at the hazard of his life, to attend this day, to raise up his voice, his hand, and his arm, against the preliminary articles of a treaty, that obscured all the glories of the war, surrendered the dearest interests of the nation, and sacrificed the public faith by an abandonment of our allies. He owned, that the terms upon which he had consented to conclude a peace, had not been satisfactory to all persons; it was impossible to reconcile every interest; but he had not, he said, for the mere attainment of peace, made a sacrifice of any conquest; he had neither broken the national faith, nor betrayed the allies of the Crown. That he was ready to enter into a discussion of the merits of the peace he had offered, comparatively with the present preliminaries. He called for the most able casuist amongst the

Mr. Pitt's speech against the preliminaries. M.S.

CHAPTER XXIII.
1762.

the Minister's friends, who, he saw, were all mustered and marshalled for duty, to oppose him; they made a most gallant appearance, and there was no doubt of the victory on the main question.——If the Rt. Hon. Gentleman, (Mr. Fox) who took the lead in this debate, would risk the argument of comparison, he would join issue with him, even under all the disadvantages of his present situation. His motive was to stop that torrent of misrepretation, which was poisoning the virtue of the country.
(No answer being made, he proceeded.)*

He

* The following paper will, in some degree supply this chasm:

Mr. PITT's negotiation.	Lord BUTE's peace.
Mr. PITT, and *all* the King's servants insisted, " That the French shall abstain from that particular fishery, on all the coasts appertaining to Great Britain, whether on the continent, or on the islands situated in the said Gulph of St. Lawrence; which fishery the proprietors only of the said coasts have constantly enjoyed, and always exercised, saving always the privilege granted by the 13th article of the treaty of Utrecht."	Gives the French " The liberty to fish in the Gulph of St. Lawrence, on condition, that the subjects of France do not exercise the said fishery, but at the distance of three leagues from all the coasts belonging to Great Britain, and fifteen leagues from the coast of the island of Cape Breton, together with the liberty of fishing and drying on a part of the coasts of the island of Newfoundland,."—If the French are as attentive to their interests as we have ever found them to be, they will doubtless call this a grant of the WHOLE FISHERY.
Mr. PITT absolutely refused to cede the island of Miquelon to the French; and the French Minister told Mr. STANLEY, " He would not insist on it." To the cession of the island of St. Peter ONLY, *four indispensible* conditions were annexed*. The cession of the island of St. Peter, as well as some others, was not agreeable to Mr. PITT's own inclination; for it is a fact, that	The islands of St. Peter and Miquelon are both ceded to the French, in full right, without any one of the *four indispensible* conditions. No English commissary is allowed to reside there; our security is on the *present* French King's royal word; but not a syllable is mentioned of any engagement for his successors.

that   Lord

* See in the Appendix, the answer of Mr. PITT to the Ultimatum of France, delivered to M. BUSSY, on the sixteenth of August 1761.

He perceived, that the Right Honourable Gentleman, and his friends, were prepared for only the prefent queſtion. He would, therefore, take a view of the articles, as they appeared upon the paper, on the table.

[*Mr. Pitt was ſo exceſſively ill, and his pain ſo exceedingly acute, that the Houſe unanimouſly deſired, he might be indulged to deliver his ſentiments ſitting—a circumſtance that was unprecedented. Hitherto he had been ſupported by two of his friends.*]

The firſt important article was the fiſhery. The terms in which this article was written, appeared to him, to give to France a grant of the whole fiſhery. There was an abſolute, unconditional ſurrender of the iſlands of St. Pierre and Miquelon, which if France continued to be as attentive to her own intereſt, as we have hitherto found her, would enable her to recover her marine. He conſidered this to be a moſt dangerous article, to the maritime ſtrength and future power of Great Britain. In the negotiation he had with M. Bussy, he had acquieſced in the ceſſion of St. Pierre *only*; after having, he ſaid, ſeveral times, in vain,

that both he and Lord Temple, earneſtly conteſted for the whole exclusive fishery, which they ſaid, ought to be inſiſted upon. But in this, as many other things, they were over-ruled.

Mr. Pitt inſiſted on keeping both Senegal and Goree, on the coaſt of Africa, "For that Senegal could not be ſecurely maintained without Goree;" and M. Bussy "was authorized to conſent to the ceſſion."

Mr. Pitt poſitively refuſed to cede the iſland of St. Lucia to France. His negotiation declares "the ceſſion by no means admiſſible."

Mr. Pitt treated the King of Pruſſia with efficacy and good faith. The anſwer to the French ultimatum, ſays, "As to what regards the *reſtitution* and evacuation of the conqueſts made

Lord Bute gave away the iſland of Goree, which was of the greateſt importance to France, as it ſerves her as a ſecurity in the ſupply of negroes for the French Weſt Indies.

Lord Bute ceded St. Lucia in full right to France.

Lord Bute both deceived and betrayed the King of Pruſſia. He firſt broke the faith of the nation, by refuſing the ſubſidy to that monarch. Then in the preliminary articles of peace, he ſtipulated

Chapter XXIII.
1762.

CHAPTER XVIII.
1762.

vain, contended for the whole exclusive fishery; but he was over-ruled; he repeated he was over-ruled, not by the foreign enemy, but by another enemy. After many struggles, he obtained four limitations to the island of St. Pierre—they were indispensible conditions; but they were omitted in the present treaty. If they were necessary in the surrender of one island, they were doubly necessary in the surrender of two. In the volumes of abuse which had been so plentifully bestowed upon him, by

made by France on the King's allies in Germany, and particularly of Wesel, and other territories of the King of Prussia, his Majesty persists in his demand relative to that subject, in the *ultimatum* of England, viz. that they be *restored* and evacuated." The French having proposed the keeping possession of the countries belonging to the King of Prussia, Mr. PITT returned this answer in writing, which was applauded by *all* the King's Ministers: " I likewise return you as totally inadmissible, the memorial relative to the King of Prussia, as implying an attempt on the honour of Great Britain, and the fidelity with which his Majesty will always fulfil his engagements with his allies."

lated evacuation and *restoration*, with regard to the conquests made on our allies, except the King of Prussia, for whom he stipulated EVACUATION *only*. All the conquests which the French were in possession of, belonging to Hanover, Hesse, Brunswick, &c. amounted to only a few villages, not exceeding one hundred acres of land in the whole. But the places belonging to the King of Prussia, of which the French were in possession, were Cleves, Gueldres, Wesel, &c. Thus Lord BUTE, instead of behaving to the King of Prussia with good faith becoming an ally, acted like an open enemy to him; and left the French at full liberty to evacuate those places, and all others which they held belonging to that monarch, *to whom they pleased*. And lastly, he

said, the dominions of the King of Prussia " *were to be scrambled for.*" That was his phrase in the House of Lords. And it was very near being the case; for as soon as the treaty was signed, the Court of Vienna ordered a large body of troops to begin their march for the Netherlands, with a view to enter those places, the moment the French should evacuate them. The King of Prussia did the same. The Netherlands were thus threatened with becoming the theatre of war; and the French Minister foreseeing, that France must take part in it, he proposed to the King of Prussia, to deliver up all those places to him, provided his Majesty would sign a neutrality for the Netherlands. The King agreed to the proposal, and purchased his territories on that condition.

the

the writers, who were paid, and patronized by thofe, who held great employments in the State, this ceffion of Pierre only, had been condemned, in terms of acrimony. He had been reminded, that the Earl of OXFORD was impeached, for allowing the French liberty to fifh and dry fifh on Newfoundland. He admitted the fact. But that impeachment was a fcandalous meafure, was difapproved by every impartial perfon. In one article, (the feventeenth) the Minifter is accufed of having advifed the *deftructive* expedition againft Canada——Why was that expedition called *deftructive*?—becaufe it was not fuccefsful. Thus have events been confidered by Parliament as ftandards of political judgment. Had the expedition to Canada, under General Wolfe, been unfuccefsful, there is no doubt it would alfo have been called *deftructive*; and fome of the Gentlemen, now in office, would this day have been calling for vengeance upon the Minifter's head.

CHAPTER XXII.
1762.

Of Dunkirk he faid but little. The French were more favoured in this article of the prefent preliminaries, than they had been by any former treaty. He had made the treaty of Aix la Chapelle his guide on this point; but in the prefent treaty, even that requifition was difregarded. *

Of the dereliction of North America by the French, he entirely approved. But the negotiators had no trouble in obtaining this acquifition. It had been the *uti pofsidetis* in his own negotiation, to which the French had readily confented. But Florida, he faid, was no compenfation for the Havannah: the Havannah was an important conqueft. He had defigned to make it, and would have done it fome months earlier, had he been permitted to execute his own plans. From the moment the Havannah was taken, all the Spanifh treafures and riches in America, lay at our mercy. Spain had purchafed the fecurity of all thefe, and the reftoration of Cuba alfo, with the ceffion of Florida only. It was no equivalent. There had been a bargain, but the terms were inadequate. They were inadequate in every point, where the principle of reciprocity was affected to be introduced.

* The neceffary ftipulations concerning Dunkirk have been greatly miftaken. If the reader will take the trouble to turn to the events of 1765, during the Adminiftration of the Marquis of ROCKINGHAM, he will find this matter explained more clearly, than it has hitherto been.

CHAPTER XXIII.
1762.

He had been blamed for confenting to give up Guadaloupe. That ceffion had been a queftion in another place. He wifhed to have kept the ifland——he had been over-ruled in that point alfo—he could not help it——he had been over-ruled many times—on many occafions—He had acquiefced—he had fubmitted——But at length he faw that all his meafures—all his fentiments—were inimical to the new Syftem—to thofe perfons,—to whom his Majefty had given his confidence. But to Guadaloupe thefe perfons had added the ceffion of Martinique. Why did they permit the forces to conquer Martinique, if they were refolved to reftore it? Was it becaufe the preparations for that conqueft were fo far advanced, they were afraid to countermand them? And to the ceffion of the ifland of Cuba, Guadaloupe, and Martiniqne, there is added the ifland of St. Lucia; the only valuable one of the neutral iflands.—It is impoffible, faid he, to form any judgment of the motives, which can have influenced his Majefty's Servants to make thefe important facrifices. They feem to have loft fight of the great fundamental principle, That France is chiefly, if not folely, to be dreaded by us in the light of a maritime and commercial power. And therefore, by reftoring to her all the valuable Weft India iflands, and by our conceffions in the Newfoundland fifhery, we had given to her the means of recovering her prodigious loffes, and of becoming once more formidable to us at fea. That the fifhery trained up an innumerable multitude of young feamen; and that the Weft India trade employed them when they were trained. After the peace of Aix la Chapelle gained France a decided fuperioty over us in this lucrative branch of commerce, and fupplied almoft all Europe with the rich commodities, which are produced only in that part of the world. By this commerce, fhe enriched her merhants, and augmented her finances. The ftate of the exifting trade in the conquefts in North America, is extremely low; the fpeculations of their future are precarious, and the profpect at the very beft, very remote. We ftand in need of fupplies, which will have an effect, certain, fpeedy, and confiderable. The retaining both, or even one of the confiderable French Iflands, Martinico or Guadaloupe, will, and nothing elfe can effectually anfwer this triple purpofe. The advantage is immediate. It is a matter not of conjecture, but of account. The trade with thefe conquefts, is of the utmoft lucra-

tive

tive nature, and of the moſt conſiderable extent; the number of ſhips employed by it are a great reſource to our maritime power. And what is of equal weight, all that we gain on this ſyſtem, is made fourfold to us by the loſs which enſues to France. But our conqueſts in North America are of very little detriment to the commerce of France. On the Weſt Indian ſcheme of acquiſition, our gain and her loſs go hand in hand. He inſiſted upon the obvious connection of this trade, with that of the colonies in North America, and with our commerce to the coaſt of Africa. The African trade would be augmented, which, with that of North America, would all center in Great Britain. But if the iſlands are all reſtored, a great part of the benefit of the colony trade muſt redound, to thoſe who were lately our enemies, and will always be our rivals. Though we had retained either Martinico or Guadaloupe, or even both theſe iſlands, our conqueſts were ſuch, that there was ſtill abundant matter left to diſplay our moderation.

Goree, he ſaid, is alſo ſurrendered, without the leaſt apparent neceſſity; notwithſtanding it had been agreed in the negociation with M. Bussy, that it ſhould remain with the Britiſh Crown, becauſe it was eſſential to the ſecurity of Senegal.

In the Eaſt Indies there was an engagement for mutual reſtitution of conqueſts. He aſked, what were the conqueſts which France had to reſtore? He declared that ſhe had none. All the conqueſts which France had made, had been retaken, and were in our own poſſeſſion; as were likewiſe, all the French ſettlements and factories. Therefore the reſtitution was all from one ſide. We retained nothing although we had conquered every thing.

The reſtitution of Minorca he approved. And that, he ſaid, was the only conqueſt France which had to reſtore; and for this iſland we had given the Eaſt Indies, the Weſt Indies, and Africa. The purchaſe was made at a price that was fifty times more than it was worth. Belleiſle alone, he affirmed, was a ſufficient equivalent for Minorca.

As to Germany, he ſaid, it was a wide field; a tedious and lengthened conſideration, including the intereſts of many hoſtile powers: ſome of them immediately, and others eventually, connected with Great Britain. There might, ſometimes, be policy in the conſtruction

CHAPTER XXIII.
1762.

our measures, to consult our insular situation only. But while we had France for our enemy, it was a scene to employ, and to baffle her arms. Had the armies of France not been employed in Germany, they would have been transported to America; where we should have found it more difficult to have conquered them. And if we had succeeded, the expence would have been greater. Let any one, he said, make a fair estimate of the expence of transports and provisions to that distant climate, and he will find, that in the article of expence, the war in Germany to be infinitely less than in the wilds of America. Upon this principle, he affirmed, that the conquests made in America, had been owing to the employment of the French army in Germany. He said, with an emphasis, that America had been conquered in Germany.

He owned, that several objections had been made to the German war. He thought them frivolous and puerile, factious and malicious. It had been said, that during twelve months after the Marathon of Minden, not a squadron of ships had been sent to make any British conquests: If this be true, will any man say, that France would, the day before the battle of Minden, have made those humiliating concessions she afterwards did make? To what, but her ill success in the German war, was it owing, that she submitted to the most mortifying terms, in the late negotiation with M. Bussy? These facts speak for themselves; and from them it appears, that the cessions offered by France, during the late negotiation, which will always be remembered with glory to Great Britain, were owing to our perseverance in the German war, and to our observing good faith towards our protestant allies on the continent.

Other objections had been made, and while he was upon the subject he would take notice of them. It had been said, that the French subsidies do not amount to half what we pay. The subsidies which the French actually pay, may not; but what they promise amount to double. They subsidize Sweden, Russia, and the Swisses, several Italian States—and if we are to believe their own writers, even the Danes; those subsidies, are most, or all of them, for negative services. They have got nothing by the Swedes; they have got nothing by the

Empress

Emprefs of Ruffia, though fhe has got a great deal for herfelf; they have got far lefs by the Emprefs Queen if we except the honour of having buried above 150,000 of their beft troops in Germany. The Wirtemberghers, it is well known have refufed to ferve them, the Swifs and Italian ftates cannot ferve them, and the Danes give them—a neutrality.

    The fubfidy to Heffe had been arraigned, and falfhood had been added to malignity. But it ought to be remembered, that the treaty with Heffe was made before he came into office; an imputation of crime to him, for not breaking that alliance, came with a very ill grace from them, who made it: they blamed him for confenting to pay the Prince of HESSE a fum of money, for the damage done by the French in his dominions. He was aftonifhed that any fet of men, who rrogated to themfelves the diftinction of friends to his prefent Majefty, fhould reprefent this circumftance, as a crime. Can a people, he afked, who impeached the Tory Miniftry of Queen ANNE, for not fupporting the Catalans at an expence that would have coft fome millions, againft their King, merely becaufe they were our allies. Can a people, who unanimoufly gave 100,000l. as a relief to the Portuguefe, when under the afflicting hand of heaven, merely becaufe they were our allies.—Can a people who indemnify their American fubjects, whom at the fame time they protect in their poffeffions; and even give damages to their own publicans when they fuffer, though in purfuance of our own acts of Parliament.—Can fuch a people, cry aloud againft the moderate relief to a Prince, the ally and fon-in-law of Great Britain, who is embarked in the fame caufe with Great Britain, who is fuffering for her, who, for her fake is driven from his dominions, where he is unable to raife one fhilling of his revenue, and with his wife, the daughter of our late venerable monarch, is reduced to a ftate of exile and indigence? Surely they cannot. Let our munificence, therefore, to fuch a Prince, be never again repeated.

    It had been exultingly faid, that the prefent German war, had overturned that balance of power, which We had fought for, in the reigns of King WILLIAM and Queen ANNE. This affertion was fo far from having the fmalleft foundation in truth, that he believed the moft fuperficial obfervers of public affairs, fcarcely ftood in need of being told, that that balance was overturned long before this war had
exiftence,

CHAPTER
XXIII.
1762.

CHAPTER XXIII.
1762.

existence. It was overturned by the Dutch before the end of the late war. When the French saw, that they had nothing to apprehend from the Dutch, they blew up that barrier, for which our NASSAU's and MARLBOROUGH's had fought. The Louvestein faction again got the ascendancy in Holland; the French monarchy again took the Dutch republic under its wings, and the brood it has hatched has—but let us forbear serpentine expressions. Since the time that the grand confederacy against France took place, the military power of the Dutch by sea and land, has been in a manner extinguished, while another power, then scarcely thought of in Europe, has started up—that of Russia, and moves in its own orbit extrincically of all other systems; but gravitating to each, according to the mass of attracting interest it contains. Another power, against all human expectation, was raised in Europe in the House of Brandenburgh, and the rapid successes of his Prussian Majesty, prove him to be born to be the natural asserter of Germanic liberties against the House of Austria. We have been accustomed to look up with reverence to that House, and the phenomenon of another great power in Germany was so very new to us, that for some time he was obliged to attach himself to France. France and Austria united, and Great Britain and Prussia coalesced. Such are the great events by which the balance of power in Europe has been entirely altered since the time of the grand alliance against France. His late Majesty so passionately endeavoured to maintain or revive the antient balance, that he encountered at home, on that account, opposition to his government, and abroad, danger to his person; but he could not re-animate the Dutch with the love of liberty, nor inspire the Empress Queen with sentiments of moderation; they talk at random, therefore, who impute the present situation of Germany, to the conduct of Great Britain. Great Britain was out of the question; nor could she have interposed in it, without taking a much greater share than she did. To represent France as an object of terror, not only to Great Britain, but Europe, and that we had mistaken our interest in not reviving the grand alliance against her, was mere declamation. Her ruined armies now returning from Germany, without being able, through the opposition of a handful of British troops, to

effect

effect any material object, is the strongest proof of the expediency of the German war.

The German war prevented the French from succouring their colonies and islands in America, in Asia and in Africa. Our successes were uniform, because our measures were vigorous.

He had been blamed for continuing the expence of a great marine, after the defeat of M. CONFLANS. This was a charge that did not surprise him, after the many others, which had been made; and which were equally unfounded and malignant. It was said, that the French marine, after that defeat was in so ruinous a conditions, there was not the least occasion for our keeping so formidable a force to watch its motions. It was true, he said, that the French marine was ruined---No man doubted it---they had not ten ships of the line fit for service: but could we imagine, that Spain, who in a very short time gave him but too much reason to be convinced, that his suspicions were well founded, was not in a common interest with France; and that the Swedes, the Genoese, and even the Dutch, would not have lent their ships for hire?

He begged pardon of the House for detaining them so long; he would detain them but a few minutes longer.

The desertion of the King of Prussia, whom he stiled the most magnanimous ally this country ever had, in the preliminary articles on the table, he reprobated in the strongest terms. He called it insidious, tricking, base, and treacherous. After amusing that great and wonderful Prince, during four months, with promises of the subsidy, he had been deceived and disappointed. But to mark the inveteracy, and treachery of the Cabinet still stronger, he is selected from our other allies, by a malicious and scandalous distinction in the present articles. In behalf of the other allies of Great Britain, we had stipulated, that all the places belonging to them, which had been conquered, should be evacuated and *restored*: but with respect to the places, which the French had conquered, belonging to the King of Prussia, there was stipulated *evacuation* only. Thus the French might keep those places, until

the

CHAPTER XXIII.

1762.

the Auſtrian troops were ready to take poſſeſſion of them. All the places which the French poſſeſſed belonging to the Elector of Hanover, the Duke of BRUNSWICK, the Landegrave of HESSE, &c. did not amount to more than ten villages, or about an hundred acres of land; but the places belonging to the King of PRUSSIA, they were in poſſeſſion of, were Cleves, Weſſel, Gueldres, &c.

Upon the whole, the terms of the propoſed treaty, met with his moſt hearty diſapprobation. He ſaw in them the ſeeds of a future war. The peace was inſecure, becauſe it reſtored the enemy to her former greatneſs. The peace was inadequate, becauſe the places gained were no equivalent for the places ſurrendered.

He was ſo ill and faint, towards the end of his ſpeech, he could ſcarcely be heard. He intended to have ſpoken to ſome points relative to Spain, but he was unable.

He ſpoke near three hours; and when he left the Houſe, which was before the diviſion, he was in the greateſt agony of pain.

The motion was agreed to by a very large majority.

CHAP.

CHAP. XXIV.

Addresses on the Peace---Mr. Pitt against the Excise on Cyder---Lord Bute tampers with the City of London---Denies it in the House of Lords---Proved at Guildhall---A Portrait---Lord Bute resigns.

THE Addresses to the King, which followed the Parliamentary approbation of the preliminary articles of peace, were obtained by means equally corrupt and dishonourable. There was one instance where the seal of a corporation was forged, and more than one where it was feloniously obtained. The City of London refused to address, although the sum of fourteen thousand pounds was offered to complete the bridge. No means were left untried every where to obtain addresses. The Lord Lieutenants had begging letters sent them, to use their influence; and five hundred pounds, secret service, were added to each letter. The sum of five hundred pounds was the notorious price of an address. Some addresses cost a much larger sum. The sum was regulated according to the importance and magnitude of the place, from which the address was obtained. The corruption without doors, was as lavish as it had been within. Of Bath, in particular, being the city Mr. PITT represented, the reader will see the correspondence in the Appendix. This conduct of Administration exhibited to the world two disgraceful things; one, that the people

people were capable of being corrupted; the other, that the King was easily deceived. The former, until this period, might have seemed improbable; the latter might be possible.

Mr. Pitt against the Excise on Cyder. M.S.

Mr. PITT took no other part in the proceedings of this session, until a bill was brought in, laying a duty upon Cyder and Perry, and subjecting the makers of those liquors to the laws of Excise. He opposed this bill very strongly; upon the dangerous precedent of admitting the officers of excise into private houses. Every man's house was his castle he said. If this tax is endured, he said, it will necessarily lead to introducing the laws of excise into the domestic concerns of every private family, and to every species of the produce of land. The laws of excise are odious and grievous to the dealer, but intolerable to the private person. The precedent, he contended, was particularly dangerous, when men by their birth, education, and profession, very distinct from the trader, become subjected to those laws.*

Mr. PITT's *bon mot* in this debate, is remembered for the mirth it occasioned.

Mr. GRENVILLE spoke in answer to Mr. PITT; and although he admitted, that the excise was odious, yet he contended that the tax was unavoidable; Government did not know where they could lay another tax of equal efficiency. The Right Honourable Gentleman, says he, complains of the hardship of this tax---why does he not tell us where we can lay another tax instead of it. And he repeated, with a strong emphasis, two or three times, *Tell me where you can lay another tax!*

Mr. PITT replied, in a musical tone, *Gentle shepherd, tell me where.*

The whole House burst out in a fit of laughter, which continued for some minutes.

Lord Bute tampers with the City of London.

While the bill was pending, the City being alarmed by the extension of the Excise Laws to private houses, presented a pe-

* The principal arguments against this bill, may be seen in two Protests of the Lords,—one on the 29th, the other on the 30th of March, 1763.

tition

tition against the bill; at the same time Sir RICHARD GLYNN* told Sir John Phillips †, that the City had resolved to petition every branch of the Legislature against the bill. Lord Bute was alarmed at the threat to present a petition to the King: and Sir John Phillips, in Lord Bute's name assured the gentlemen of the City Committee, while they were waiting in the lobby of the House of Commons, when the petition was presented to that House, That if they would with-hold their petition to the King, Lord Bute would promise and engage, upon his honour, that the act should be repealed next year. One of the Committee answered ‡, " Who can undertake for " Lord Bute being Minister next year? or for his influence " over Parliament?"

This application not proving successful, a card from Mr. Jenkinson, Lord Bute's *confidential* Secretary, and now Lord Hawkesbury, was brought in the evening to Sir *James Hodges*, Town Clerk of the City; desiring to see him next morning at Lord Bute's, in South Audley-street, upon particular business. Sir James went, and was introduced to Lord Bute, by the Secretary. The Minister requested the Town Clerk, in the most anxious and pressing manner, to acquaint the gentlemen of the City Committee, that if they would not present their intended petition to the King, he would engage, and did then engage, to obtain a repeal of the act next session. Sir James returned into the City, and collected the Committee at his office in Guildhall, and laid before them, a state of the conference he had had with the Minister. The Committee treated the pro-

---

* One of the Members for the City of London. † One of Lord Bute's confidents.   ‡ Mr. Samuel Freeman.

mise with contempt, saying it was no more than a repetition of the same assurance, which had been made to them the preceding day by Sir JOHN PHILLIPS. The petition to the Lords, and the petition to the King, were presented; but without effect.

<small>CHAPTER XXIV.
1763.</small>

Lord TEMPLE presented the City's petition to the House of Lords, (March 28) on the second reading of the bill, and in the course of his speech upon that occasion, mentioned the circumstance of Lord BUTE's tampering with the City Committee.

Upon which, Lord BUTE got up, and assured the House, "*that the whole was a* FACTIOUS LIE."

<small>Denies it in the House of Lords</small>

This assertion was not only too coarse, but too strong, to pass unnoticed.

The Corporation of the City of London immediately assembled, to enquire into the conduct of the Town Clerk. At this enquiry Sir JAMES HODGES acquitted himself to the satisfaction of the whole Court, by a candid and fair narration of all the preceding facts; and at the conclusion, he voluntarily offered to verify the same upon oath. From this enquiry, it was indisputably clear *who was the liar.**

<small>Proved at Guildhall.</small>

Lord

* A PORTRAIT.

"TO draw a character so much beneath the honours of portraiture, would need apology, if the caprice of fortune, in a fit of ill-humour against this nation, had not by giving to the original a situation for which Nature had never designed him, raised him into notice, and made him in the consequences, an object of the public concern. It is only then for the most candid motive of a public utility, to atone for the ignobleness of the personage whose portrait is here exhibited; faithfully taken, feature by feature, without any the least caricature, and too fatally fulfilling the idea of a favourite without merit.

" Constitutionally

[253]

Lord BUTE finding his Cabinet divided upon almost every question that came before them; and fearing, the Duke of BEDFORD's indignation, who was on the point of returning from

"Constitutionally false, without system, and in the most capital points, greatly, to his own disadvantage, so; being, in fact, neither true to others nor to himself: Involved by the necessity of his nature, in that vicious circle of being false because weak, and weak because false.

"Reserved, inward, and darksome; sequestered in some measure from society, taking covert in the shades of embowered life, as the refuge of vanity from the wounds of contempt. Clandestine without concealment--sad without sorrow--domestic without familiarity--haughty without elevation; nothing great, nothing noble having ever marked his character, or illustrated his conduct, public or private: Reducing every thing to his own ideas, that standard of littleness, that mint of falsity. Stubborn without firmness, and ambitious without spirit. A frigid friend, a mean enemy. Nauseously bloated with a stupid, rank, quality pride, without the air, the ease, the manners, the dignity of a gentleman. Ungenerous without any very extraordinary note of avarice; but rather so, through that poverty of head and heart, from which so many people of fortune hug themselves on what they imagine *saved* by the omission of some *little* circumstance that honour, justice, or taste required of them; though by that *little* so saved, they not only lose the *much* they will have sacrificed to their various objects of vanity, but where they bespoke admiration, find no returns for their expence but just censure and derision. And surely in this point of vulgar error, among the low understandings in high life, this poor man was not born to break herd.

"Bookish without learning; in his library of parade, as insensible and unconversable on the great objects of literature, as one deaf and dumb questioned on a concert of music; as little of a judge as a blind man in a gallery of pictures. A dabbler in the fine arts, without grace, without taste. A traveller through countries without seeing them, and totally unacquainted with his own.

"In a dull ungenial solitude, muddling away what leisure he may have from false politics, and ruinous counsels, in stuffing his port-folios with penny prints and pretty pictures of coloured simples, those gazing-traps of simpletons, and garnishing his knicknackatory with mechanical toys, baubles, and gimcracks, or varying his nonsense with little tricks of chemistry; while all these futile puerilities have been rendered still more futile by the gloom of a solemn visage, ridi-

these,

CHAPTER XXIV.
1763.

from Paris, he settled an arrangement in favour of the Duke's friends, and retired from his public station on the eighth day of April 1763. He made Mr. GRENVILLE his successor†, hoping he

culously exhibiting the preternatural character of a grave child. Bagatelles these, which it would doubtless be impertinent, illiberal, and even uncharitable to mention, were it not for the apprehension of his having inspired this most unroyal taste for trifles where it could not exist, but at the expence of a time and attention, of which the nation could not be robbed without capital detriment to it: A circumstance this, that must draw down a ridicule upon his master, not to be easily shaken off, and as much more hurtful to a Prince than a calumny of a graver nature, as contempt is ever more fatal to Government, than even fear or hatred.

"Too unhappily, alas! for this nation, chance had thrown this egregious trifler into a family whom his domestic streights had favourably disposed towards him. How he maintained and improved his footing into a pernicious ascendant, is surely beneath curiosity. So much, however, it would be unfair to suppress, that the attack on the fame of his political maker, was not only treated by him with such an apathy as had nothing in it of a just and noble contempt; but to consummate the ingratitude, one of notoriously the first instigators of the scandal was inrolled among his intimate confidents and supporters, without even this being the only appearance afforded by him of his not being infinitely displeased at the currency of the calumny.

"As to the Royal Pupil, who, by a much misplaced confidence, fell under his management at the tender age of susceptibility of all impressions, it was not well possible for him to prevent a deep-rooted partiality for a choice manifestly not made by him, but for him. In raw, unexperienced, unguarded youth, practiced upon by an insidious study of his inclinations not to rectify, but to govern him by them: captivated by an unremitting attention to humour and perpetuate the natural bent of that age to the lighter objects of amusement; instituted to

† When Mr. GRENVILLE was appointed Secretary of State, he was under the necessity of soliciting his brother, Lord TEMPLE, to permit him to be re-elected for the town of Buckingham; and upon his promotion to the Treasury, he repeated the same act of supplication. His generous brother said, it would have been a disgrace to Government, to have seen the King's first Minister, a mendicant for a seat in Parliament.

he should, by that promotion, appease the Duke's choler.——
It was immediately signified to all the foreign Ministers, that his

an implicit faith in the man who littered his head with trifles, and unable to corrupt his heart, only hardened it like his own against the remonstrances of true greatness, while warping his understanding with the falsest notions of men and things, and especially of maxims of state, of which himself never had so much as an elementary idea; thus delivered up to such a tutor, how could the Disciple possibly escape such a combination?—What of essentially wise or magnanimous could he learn from such a pedlar in politics and manners? No one can impart what himself never had. Honour, gratitude, dignity of sentiment, energy of sincerity, comprehensiveness of views, were not in *him* to inculcate. Obstinacy under the stale disguise of firmness; the royalty of repairing a wrong by persisting in it, the plausible decencies of private life, the petty moralities, the minutenesses of public arrangements, the preference of dark juggle, mystery, and low artifice to the frank, open spirit of government; the abundant sufficiency of the absence of great vices, to atone for the want of great virtues, a contempt of reputation, and especially that execrable absurdity in the sovereign of a free people, the neglect of popularity, were all that the hapless pupil could possibly learn from such a preceptor. Moulded by such an eternal tutorage, imperceptibly formed not to govern, but to be governed; and from being the lawful possessor of a great empire, converted into the being himself the property of a little silly subject; stolen thus away from himself, what remains for us but ardently to pray that, before it is too late, he may be restored to himself; that he may at length, enter into the genuine spirit of Royalty, assume the part he was born to, and have a character of his own?—May he quit a borrowed darkness for native light, never more to exhibit, in any the least degree, the copy of an original, whom not to resemble would surely be the honour! Let him give us the Sovereign himself, not the Favourite at second hand; or still worse yet, the Favourite's *Commis** at second hand! And in this deprecation of detriment and dishonour to himself, there can questionless be nothing disloyal, or disrespectful.

This testimony of a genuine sentiment, takes birth too naturally from the subject with which it is connected to appear a digression; though in such a cause, and in such a crisis of the times, I should have judged even the digressiveness meritorious, and certainly alone the best apology for a portrait, the exhi-

* Lord Hawksbury.

bition

CHAPTER XXIV.
1763.

Majesty had placed his Government in the hands of Mr. GRENVILLE, Lord HALIFAX, and Lord EGREMONT; and as soon as the other arrangements were made, (the particulars of which, the reader will see in the List of Administrations at the end of the work), the session was closed on the nineteenth of April.

bition of which from any motive of pique or personality, would be infinitely beneath the meanest of daubers.

"Here it would be perfectly infignificant to fearch out the diftinction, without a difference to the public, whether, or not, the favourite after that fcandalous defertion, when he as abjectly fneaked out of an oftenfible office in the State, as he had arrogantly ftrutted into it, retains individually by himfelf, or by his appointment of others, the power of continuing that infernal chaos, into which he from the firft plunged affairs, at the time that through his cloudy imbecility it fo foon thickened in the clear of the faireft horizon that ever tantalifed a country with the promife of meridian fplendor. It is enough to obferve, that fince his having delivered up to his own parafites that mafter whom he thus made the centre of their paltry cabals, and the prey of their fordid rapacioufnefs, it appears, at leaft, from the identity of fpiritleffnefs, of infenfibility to honour, of want of plan, and of the total diforder in which we fee things for ever languifhing, that the fame deftructive impulfion ftill fubfifts; while none could collaterally be admitted into any participation of truft, but fuch as would wink hard, and, at leaft, pretend not to fee through that grofs illufion, with which a natural defire of not appearing to be governed, might blind a Prince, without impofing on any but himfelf. The joke of holding committees with refpective minifters of departments, paffes on no one. In vain would the mafter take blame upon himfelf, and father errors not his own. The wires of motion to the will have been too clumfily worked, not to be feen, however they may not have been felt. Add, that the primary caufe may, by the faireft eveftigation, be brought home to that unhappy man, whom chance had thrown into a channel of power to do much good, or much mifchief. The laft he has mechanically done, without, perhaps, much meaning it, coming upon the fcene, with abfolutely every thing in his favour, except himfelf. All prejudice then a-part, mark in him, to his Prince, a tutor without knowledge, a minifter without ability, a favourite without gratitude! The very anti-genius of politics. The curfe of Scotland. The difgrace of his mafter. The defpair of the nation; and the difdain of hiftory."—*Public Advertifer*, *Auguft* 30, 1776.

It

It was upon the speech delivered at the close of this session, that the *North Briton* made those observations, which drew upon the supposed author, an illegal and vindictive exertion of all the power and malice of Government. The particulars of this interesting affair, have been amply stated in several books. In *Junius*'s address to the King, originally published on the 19th of December 1769, are these words, " The destruction of *one* " man, has been for many years, the sole object of your Go- " vernment."

CHAPTER XXIV.

1763.

CHAP. XXV.

Interview between Mr. Pitt and Lord Bute—Conferences between the King and Mr. Pitt—Treaty of Connivance---Mr. Pitt at Court---His remark---Lord Hardwicke's conduct.

EARLY in the month of August 1763, a circumstance happened, which threw the Ministry into some disorder and perplexity. This was the sudden death of the Earl of EGREMONT. The Ministers had rendered themselves odious to the nation by supporting the measures of the late Administration, and the measures of the Court, in the persecution of Mr. WILKES. Notwithstanding Lord BUTE had recommended them to their situations, as the bargain of his own escape; yet he grew impatient under the proscription he had imposed on himself; and apprehending that their removal would be received with satisfaction by the public, he seized this opportunity, which the death of the Secretary of State afforded, and the vacancy of the President's chair, which had not been filled since the death of Lord GRANVILLE, to form a new Administration; not so much with a view of manifesting his influence, as of effecting his own emancipation. He fixed his attention upon Mr. PITT. His wish was to form an Administration under the auspices of that gentleman. For this purpose he sent Sir HARRY ERSKINE to Mr. Alderman BECKFORD, soliciting the Alderman's interest with Mr. PITT, to procure an interview for Lord BUTE. The proposal was accepted, and Lord BUTE

BUTE waited on Mr. PITT, at his houfe in Jermyn-ftreet, on Thurfday the 25th of Auguft, 1763. Lord HARDWICKE in a letter which he wrote to his fon, Lord ROYSTON, gives the following account of this interview, and of Mr. PITT's two conferences with the King; which took place in confequence of it.

CHAPTER XXV.
1763.

"*Wimpole, Sept. 4*, 1763.

"I HAVE heard the whole from the Duke of NEWCASTLE, and on Friday morning *de fource* from Mr. PITT. It is as ftrange as it is long, for I believe it is the moft extraordinary tranfaction that ever happened in any Court in Europe, even in times as extraordinary as the prefent.

"It began as to the fubftance, by a meffage from my Lord B——E to Mr. PITT at Hayes, through my Lord Mayor, to give him the meeting *privately* at fome third place. This his Lordfhip (Lord B.) afterwards altered by a note from himfelf, faying, that as he loved to do things openly, he would come to Mr. PITT's houfe in Jermyn-ftreet in broad day-light. They met accordingly, and Lord B-E, after the firft compliments, frankly acknowledged, that his Miniftry could not go on, and that the **** was convinced of it, and therefore he (Lord B.) defired that Mr. PITT would open himfelf frankly and at large, and tell him his ideas of things and perfons with the utmoft freedom. After much excufe and hanging back, Mr. PITT did fo with the utmoft freedom indeed, though with civility. Lord B——E heard with great attention and patience; entered into no defence; but at laft faid, " If thefe are your opinions, why fhould you not tell them to the " **** himfelf, who will not be unwilling to hear you?"—*How can I, my Lord, prefume to go to the ****, who am not of his Council, nor in his fervice, and have no pretence to afk an audience? The prefumption would be too great.* " But fuppofe his M——y fhould order you to attend " him, I prefume, Sir, you would not refufe it."—*The ****'s command would make it my duty, and I fhould certainly obey it.*

* Sunday

CHAPTER XXV.
1763.
Conferences with the King.

"This was on laſt Thurſday ſe'nnight*. On the next day (Friday) Mr. PITT received from the **** *an open note unſealed*, requiring him to attend his M———y on Saturday noon, at the Q———'s Palace in the Park. In obedience hereto, Mr. PITT went on Saturday at noon-day through the Mall in his gouty chair, the boot of which (as he ſaid himſelf) makes it as much known as if his name was writ upon it, to the Q———'s Palace. He was immediately carried into the cloſet, received very graciouſly, and his M———y began in like manner as his *quondam* Favourite had done, by ordering him to tell him his opinion of things and perſons at large, and with the utmoſt freedom; and I think, did in ſubſtance make the like confeſſion, that he thought his preſent Miniſters could not go on. The audience laſted three hours, and Mr. PITT went through the whole upon both heads more fully than he had done to Lord B——E, but with great complaiſance and douceur to the ****: and his M———y gave him a very gracious accueil, and heard with great patience and attention. And Mr. PITT affirms, that in general, and upon the moſt material points, he appeared by his manner, and many of his expreſſions, to be convinced. Mr. PITT went through the infirmities of the peace; the things neceſſary and hitherto neglected to improve and preſerve it; the preſent ſtate of the nation, both foreign and domeſtic; the great Whig families and perſons which had been driven from his Majeſty's Council and ſervice, which it would be for his intereſt to reſtore. In doing this he repeated many names, upon which his M———y told him there was pen, ink, and paper, and he wiſhed he would write them down. Mr. PITT humbly excuſed himſelf, ſaying, *that* would be too much for him to take upon him, and he might upon his memory omit ſome material perſons, which might be ſubject to imputation. The **** ſtill ſaid, he liked to hear him, and bid him go on, but ſaid now and then, that his honour muſt be conſulted; to which Mr. PITT anſwered in a very courtly manner. His M———y ordered him to come again on Monday, which he did, to the ſame place, and in the ſame public manner.

* Auguſt 25.

"Here

"Here comes in a parenthesis, that on Sunday Mr. PITT went to Claremont, and acquainted the D. of NEWCASTLE with the whole, fully perfuaded, from the ****'s manner and behaviour, that the thing would do; and that on Monday the outlines of the new arrangement would be fettled. This produced the meffages to thofe Lords, who were fent for. Mr. PITT undertook to write to the Duke of DE-VONSHIRE and the Marquis of ROCKINGHAM, and the Duke of NEWCASTLE to myfelf.

"But behold the cataftrophe of Monday†. The **** received him equally gracioufly; and that audience lafted near two hours. The **** began, that he had confidered of what had been faid, and talked ftill more ftrongly of his honour. His M——y then mentioned Lord NORTHUMBERLAND‡ for the Treafury, ftill proceeding upon the fuppofition of a change. To this Mr. PITT hefitated an objection—that certainly Lord NORTHUMBERLAND might be confidered, but that he fhould not have thought of him for the Treafury. His M—— then mentioned Lord HALIFAX for the Treafury. Mr. PITT faid, Suppofe your M. fhould think fit to give his Lordfhip the Paymafter's place. The **** replied,---" But, Mr. PITT, I had de-
" figned that for poor G. GRENVILLE. He is your near relation,
" and you once loved him." To this the only anfwer made was a low bow. And now here comes the bait. "Why," fays his M——,
" fhould not Lord TEMPLE have the Treafury? You could go on then
" very well."---*Sir, the perfon, whom you fhall think fit to honour with the chief conduct of your affairs, cannot poffibly go on without a Treafury connected with him. But that alone will do nothing. It cannot be carried on without the great families who have fupported the Revolution Government, and other great perfons, of whofe abilities and integrity the public has had experience, and who have weight and credit in the nation. I fhould only de-*

† Auguft 29.

‡ This was an idea at that time fo ftrange, that it could not be explained until about fix or feven months afterwards, when an alliance took place between Lord NORTHUMBERLAND's eldeft fon and Lord BUTE's daughter, which in effect made Lord NORTHUMBERLAND a part of Lord BUTE's family, and which feems to have been at this time in contemplation.

ceive

CHAPTER XXV.
1763.

ceive your M------, *if I should leave you in an opinion that I could go on, and your M------ make a solid Administration on any other foot.* "Well, Mr. " PITT, I fee (or I fear) this won't do. My honour is concerned, and " I muſt ſupport it."---*Et ſic finita eſt fabula. Vos valete,* but I cannot with a ſafe conſcience add, *plaudite.* I have made my ſkeleton larger than I intended at firſt, and I hope you will underſtand it. Mr. PITT profeſſes himſelf firmly perſuaded, that my Lord B--- was ſincere at firſt, and that the .... was in earneſt the firſt day; but that on the intermediate day, Sunday, ſome ſtrong effort was made, which produced the alteration.

" Mr. PITT likewiſe affirms, that if he was examined upon oath, he could not tell upon what this negociation broke off, whether upon any particular point, or upon the general complexion of the whole.

" It will certainly be given out, that the reaſon was the unreaſonable extent of Mr. PITT's plan---a general rout; and the Minority, after having complained ſo much of proſcriptions, have endeavoured to proſcribe the Majority. I aſked Mr. PITT the direct queſtion, and he aſſured me, that although he thought himſelf obliged to name a great many perſons for his own exculpation, yet he did not name above five or ſix for particular places. I muſt tell you that one of theſe was your humble ſervant for the Preſident's place. This was entirely without my authority or privity. But the ....'s anſwer was, " Why, " Mr. PITT, it is vacant and ready for him, and he knows he may " have it to-morrow, if he thinks fit."

" I conjectured that this was ſaid with regard to what had paſſed with poor Lord EGREMONT, which made me think it neceſſary to tell Mr. PITT in general what had paſſed with that Lord (not owning that his Lordſhip had offered § it directly in the ....'s name) and what I had anſwered, which he, in his way, much commended.

§ Mr. C. TOWNSHEND's explanation of this refuſal was in theſe words, " Lord HARDWICKE refuſed Lord EGREMONT's offer, becauſe he thought the " beſt of the lay was on the other ſide."

" This

"This obliges me to desire, that you will send by the bearer my letter to you, which you were to communicate to my Lord LYTTELTON, that I may see how I have stated it there, for I have no copy.

"I shall now make you laugh, though some parts of what goes before make me melancholy, to see the .... so committed, and his M. submitting to it, &c. But what I mean will make you laugh is, that the Ministers are so stung with this admission, that they cannot go on (and what has passed on this occasion will certainly make them less able to go on), and with my Lord B-- 's having thus carried them to market in his pocket, that they say Lord B--- has attempted to sacrifice them to his own fears and timidity; that they do not depend upon him, and will have nothing more to do with him. And I have been very credibly informed, that both Lord HALIFAX and GEORGE GRENVILLE have declared, that he is to go beyond the sea, and reside for a twelvemonth or more. You know a certain *Cardinal* was twice exiled out of France, and governed France as absolutely whilst he was absent as when he was present."

To the preceding statement of Lord HARDWICKE, it is proper to make some additions. The five or six other persons, whom his Lordship says Mr. PITT named for places, were the following:—

Lord TEMPLE for First Lord of the Treasury, with power to name his own Board.

Mr. JAMES GRENVILLE for Chancellor of the Exchequer.*

Himself Secretary of State.

Mr. C. TOWNSHEND, Secretary of State, with the management of the House of Commons.

* He was second brother to Lord TEMPLE. He was a man of excellent erudition and fine understanding. When Lord TEMPLE and Lord CHATHAM differed in 1766, he adhered to Lord CHATHAM, and continued in that attachment to the death of his Lordship, whom he did not long survive.

CHAPTER XXV.
1763.

Lord ALBEMARLE at the head of the Army.
Sir EDW. HAWKE at the head of the Admiralty.

Treaty of connivance.

On the Sunday, between the two conferences, certain advice was given, which broke off the negotiation. Lord BUTE had the merit of bringing it on, and to him is to be afcribed the caufe of its failure. It was fignified to Lord BUTE, that if he turned out the Miniftry, his own *impeachment* fhould be the confequence. He took fright; and *again* compounded for his fafety. But the Minifters infifted upon his quitting London, and he agreed to pafs the winter at his new eftate in Bedfordfhire. When this profcription was fettled, the Duke of BEDFORD took the Prefident's chair, Lord SANDWICH was made Secretary of State, and Lord EGMONT had the Admiralty. His Grace taking an official fituation, the Adminiftration acquired the appellation of the *Duke of Bedford's Miniftry*. Lord MELCOMBE'S words are the moft proper commentary on this "treaty of connivance" (as Mr. PITT called it)---" *It is all for quarter day.*"

Mr. Pitt at Court

On the Wednefday (Auguft 31), fubfequent to the laft conference with which his Majefty honoured Mr. PITT, Lord TEMPLE and Mr. PITT went to St. James's to pay their duty to his Majefty, they were both received in the moft gracious manner; and his Majefty in the moft obliging terms faid to Mr. PITT " I hope, Sir, you have not fuffered by ftanding fo " long on Monday." Upon this occafion Mr. PITT faid to his

His remark.

friends, " His Majefty is the greateft Courtier in his Court."

Lord Hardwicke's conduct

Although Lord HARDWICKE and the Duke of NEWCASTLE affected to be well fatisfied with Mr. PITT's conduct in this negotiation, yet Lord HARDWICKE was very defirous of a

place

place at Court, and would certainly have accepted of Lord Egremont's offer, if he could have prevailed upon Lord Bute to have received the Duke of Newcastle and two or three of his Grace's friends at the same time. But Lord Egremont would not undertake a negotiation with Lord Bute for that purpose, and Lord Hardwicke could not open one himself, having no direct communication with Lord Bute, nor any oftensible pretence. Even in the present design of making some alterations in the Ministry, the application was not made to him, but to Mr. Pitt. From motives of policy, he concealed his disapprobation of this preference given to Mr. Pitt. Upon the discharge of Mr. Wilkes by the Chief Justice of the Common Pleas, he attended the levee and drawing-room, accompanied by the Duke of Newcastle, and a few of their friends. Finding this bait not to succeed, he afterwards courted favour, by avowing in all companies, his opinion to be totally different from the judicial judgment of the Chief Justice: and he actually formed a league, with the Duke of Newcastle, and others, to determine in Parliament, that the Chief Justice had done wrong, in releasing a member of Parliament from confinement, for a libel, upon a plea of privilege, by an implied censure, in a vote, declaring, That privilege of Parliament did not extend to a libel. And this accounts for the protest upon that question, not being signed by the Duke of Newcastle, Lord Hardwicke, Lord Rockingham, Lord Sondes, &c. At the meeting of the Lords in the Minority at Devonshire-house, to settle the words of the protest, the Duke of Newcastle excused himself from signing ti, by relating this agreement with his friend Lord Hardwicke; who at that time was confined by sickness, and who died about three months afterwards.

CHAP. XXVI.

Meeting of Parliament—Servility of the Commons; of the Speaker—Verfatility—Vote away their own privilege—Royal Apothegm—The North Briton—Mr. Pitt's fpeech againft the facrifice of Privilege.

ON the fifteenth of November 1763 Parliament met. The moment the Commons were returned to their own Houfe from the Lords, Mr. GRENVILLE and Mr. WILKES rofe together. Each was eager to addrefs the Houfe. Mr. GRENVILLE to deliver the commands of the King—Mr. WILKES to complain of a breach of privilege. By the fettled forms of the Houfe, the breach of privilege ought to have been heard firft. But the Speaker, as previoufly directed, pointed to Mr. GRENVILLE.

The reader muft have perceived in the courfe of thefe fheets, that the corruption of Parliament, or, as it is fafhionably called, the management of Parliament, is become an indifpenfible part of the mechanifm of Government. The particular fervility of the Speaker has been noticed feveral times—by Mr. PITT himfelf, in his fpeech for the repeal of the American ftamp act.

This Parliament, which had been elected while the Whigs were in office—which had fupported them and deferted them---which had fupported Lord BUTE, and deferted him alfo---was now the inftrument of the Duke of BEDFORD and Mr. GRENVILLE:

ville: such measures as they found necessary for the establishment of their situations, this Parliament readily supported. This Parliament voted away its own privilege, in the case of a libel, at the requisition of the Minister, to gratify the King, in accelerating the punishment of Mr. Wilkes*; thereby sacrificing not their own privileges only, but those of their constituents, and posterity. The Lords, adopting a vote of this sort, could affect only themselves. But the privileges of the Commons, are connected with the rights of the people. One cannot be sacrificed, without injuring the other. As the matter now stands, any obnoxious Member or Members, may be easily got rid of. The King, or his Minister, has only to charge him, or them, with being the author or publisher of a libel; or if neither King, nor Minister chuses to be seen in it, they can order the Attorney General to do it, by his information *ex officio.*— When *Charles the First* wanted to seize the five Members, he was too precipitate. Had he taken the modern mode, he would have succeeded. It is related, as one of the Royal apothegms, that his Majesty, speaking of *Charles the First,* said, *He was a good King; but did not know how to govern by a Parliament.*

---

* Mr. Wilkes was discharged from close imprisonment in the Tower, on account of his privilege. The warrant of commitment was not held to be illegal. A Member of Parliament may therefore be committed for a libel before trial. And whether a paper be a libel or not, is a matter of discretion in the judgment of the King, his Minister, or his Attorney General. And as to witnesses, they are always to be had. Algernon Sidney's words, upon the last point, are—" *False witnesses* are sent out to circumvent the most eminent men.
" The tribunals are filled with *Court parasites,* of profligate consciences, for-
" tunes, and reputation, that no man may escape who is brought before them.
" If crimes are wanting the diligence of well chosen officers, and prosecutors,
" with the favour of the Judges, supply all defects. The *law* is made a
" *snare.*"—*Quarto edit. p.* 214.

CHAPTER XXVI.
1763.

Mr. GRENVILLE having delivered the King's meſſage, ſtating that his Majeſty had cauſed Mr. WILKES to be apprehended, and ſecured for writing a libel, and that he had been releaſed on his privilege, &c. the Houſe took this matter *inſtantly* into conſideration; and voted an addreſs of thanks for his Majeſty's gracious communication. The uſual addreſs, in reply to the ſpeech on opening the ſeſſion, was not mentioned this day: And Mr. WILKES's complaint of a breach of privilege, by the impriſonment of his perſon, plundering his houſe, and ſeizing his papers, was put off to the twenty-third.

North Briton a Libel.

The Houſe immediately voted the *North Briton* a libel, although it was one of their own eſſential privileges always to treat the King's ſpeech as the ſpeech of the Miniſter.

The right of either, or both Houſes of Parliament, to declare any paper a libel, which is to be tried by another juriſdiction, may, in ſome future day, become a queſtion. Such a declaration is, undoubtedly, a pre-judgment of the paper; and cannot fail obtaining an influence on the minds of the jury, who are to try the cauſe.

Mr. Pitt on Privilege and the North Briton. M.S.

On the twenty-third of November, Mr. WILKES's complaint of a breach of privilege was taken into conſideration; when it was reſolved, that Privilege of Parliament did not extend to the caſe of writing or publiſhing a libel. On this day Mr. PITT attended, although ſo ſeverely afflicted with the gout, he was obliged to be ſupported to his ſeat. He ſpoke ſtrongly againſt this ſurrender of the privileges of Parliament, as highly dangerous to the freedom of Parliament, and an infringement on the rights of the People. No man he ſaid, could condemn the paper, or libel, more than he did: But he would come at the author fairly, not by an open breach of the

Conſtitution,

Conſtitution, and a contempt of all reſtraint. This propoſed ſacrifice of privilege, was putting every Member of Parliament, who did not vote with the Miniſter, under a perpetual terror of impriſonment. To talk of an abuſe of privilege, was to talk againſt the Conſtitution, againſt the very being and life of Parliament. It was an arraignment of the juſtice and honour of Parliament, to ſuppoſe, that they would protect any criminal whatever. Whenever a complaint was made againſt any Member, the Houſe could give him up. This privilege had never been abuſed; it had been repoſed in Parliament for ages. But take away this privilege, and the whole Parliament is laid at the the mercy of the Crown. This privilege having never been abuſed, why then is it to be voted away? Parliament, he ſaid, had no right to vote away its privileges. They were the inherent right of the ſucceeding Members of that Houſe, as well as of the preſent. And he doubted, whether the ſacrifice by that Houſe was valid, and concluſive againſt the claim of a future Parliament. With reſpect to the paper itſelf, or the libel, which had given pretence for this requeſt to ſurrender the privileges of Parliament, the Houſe had already voted it a libel---he joined in that vote. He condemned the whole ſeries of North Britons; he called them illiberal, unmanly, and deteſtable. He abhorred all national reflections. The King's ſubjects were one people. Whoever divided them, was guilty of ſedition. His Majeſty's complaint was well founded, it was juſt, it was neceſſary. The author did not deſerve to be ranked among the human ſpecies—he was the blaſphemer of his God, and the libeller of his King. He had no connection with him. He had no connexion with any ſuch writer. He neither aſſociated nor communicated with any ſuch. It was true, that he had friendſhips, and warm ones; he had obligations, and great ones; but no friendſhips, no obligations, could induce him to approve, what he firmly condemned. It might be ſuppoſed, that he alluded to his noble relation (Lord TEMPLE). He was proud to call him his relation; he was his friend, his boſom friend; whoſe fidelity was as unſhaken as his virtue. They went into office together, and they came out together—they had lived together, and would die together. He knew nothing of any connection with the writer of the libel. If there ſub-

ſiſted

CHAPTER XXVI.
1763.

fifted any, he was totally unacquainted with it. The dignity, the honour of Parliament, had been called upon to fupport and protect the purity of his Majefty's character; and this they had done, by a ftrong and decifive condemnation of the libel; which his Majefty had fubmitted to the confideration of the Houfe. But having done this, it was neither confiftent with the honour and fafety of Parliament, nor with the rights and interefts of the people, to go one ftep farther. The reft belonged to the Courts below.

When he had finifhed fpeaking, he left the Houfe, not being able to ftay for the divifion.

CHAP. XXVII.

Prince of Brunswick visits Mr. Pitt at Hayes—Question concerning General Warrants—Mr. Pitt's Speech against them.

IN the month of January 1764, the Prince of BRUNSWICK came to England, to espouse the Princess AUGUSTA, the King's sister. When the ceremonies were ended, he paid a visit to Mr. PITT; who was confined to his chamber by a severe fit of the gout, at his seat at Hayes in Kent. This visit was very far from being agreeable at St. James's. The Prince was just come from Berlin; and whether the conjecture was well founded, or not, that he carried a complimentary message from the King of PRUSSIA to Mr. PITT, the visit at least shewed, the high estimation in which Mr. PITT was held by the Prince, the King of PRUSSIA and his allies, who at this time were Russia and Poland: while we were without any ally, and the great Minister of this country, who had conducted the war with so much honour to himself and advantage to the nation, was proscribed at Court and deserted in Parliament. He was retired to Hayes---to his ability, glory and integrity---where this young Prince distinguished him, by the most gracious marks of esteem and affection, filled with sentiments, which were known to be similar to those of the King of PRUSSIA, and the Empress of the North. After this circumstance, his Serene Highness did not experience the most cordial reception at the British Court,

and

<small>CHAPTER XXVII.
1764.
General Warrants.</small>

and he was permitted to embark for the Continent, in a very dangerous and tempeftuous feafon.*

On the fourteenth of February 1764, Sir W. MEREDITH moved, " That a *General* Warrant for apprehending and feizing " the authors, printers and publifhers of a feditious libel, to- " gether with their papers, is not warranted by law." Seconded by Sir G. SAVILE. Although the Conftitution, the law of the land, common fenfe, and the ftrict principles of juftice, all united in condemning a *General* Warrant; yet all the officers of Government, all the fubalterns of Minifters, all the people who call themfelves *King's Friends*, and all whom thefe could command or influence, pertinacioufly defended, not indeed the *legality*, for that was impoffible, but the neceffity of poffeffing a power to iffue thefe warrants, whenever, the Secretary of State in his difcretion fhould think fit. The debate having continued all night, was adjourned to the feventeenth.

<small>Mr. Pitt's fpeech againft them. M.S.</small>

On the adjourned debate, Mr. PITT being able to attend, fpoke in favour of the motion. He began with obferving, that all which the Crown had defired, all which Minifters had wifhed, was accomplifhed in the conviction and expulfion of Mr. WILKES: it was now the duty of the Houfe, to do juftice to the nation, to the Conftitution, and to the Law. Minifters had refufed to lay the warrant before the Houfe be-

* In the pamphlet entitled *Faction Unmafk'd*, there is an anecdote of this Prince, which feems to infinuate, that the effects of this vifit were not confined to an embarkation in ftormy weather. The words are thefe, " When " General SPOERKEN died, the Duke of BRUNSWICK wifhed to fucceed him in " the command at Hanover; and from his having fought our battles, and married " our King's fifter, every body in Germany and England thought his claim fo " juft, he would undoubtedly be appointed; but the Queen's brother, a youth " at that time, was preferred to him." *Edit.* 1790, *p.* 103.

caufe

cause they were conscious of its illegality. And yet these Ministers, who affect so much regard for liberty and the Constitution, are ardently desirous of retaining for themselves, and for their successors, a power to do an illegal act. Neither the law officers of the Crown, nor the Minister himself, had attempted to defend the legality of this warrant. Whenever goaded upon the point, they had evaded it. He therefore did not hesitate to say, that there was not a man to be found, of sufficient profligacy, to defend this warrant, upon the principle of legality. It was no justification, he said that General Warrants had been issued. Amongst the warrants which were laid before the House, to shew the practice of office, there were two which had been issued by himself; but they were not against libels. One was, for the seizure of a number of persons on board a ship going to France; the other for apprehending the Count de St. Germain, a suspected foreigner; and both in a time of war with France. Upon issuing the latter warrant, he consulted his friend, the Attorney General, (who was afterwards Lord Camden) who told him the warrant would be illegal, and if he issued it he must take the consequences; nevertheless preferring the general safety in time of war and public danger, to every personal consideration, he run the risk, as he would of his head, had that been the forfeit, upon the like motive, and did an extraordinary act, against a suspicious foreigner, just come from France; and who was concealed at different times, in different houses. The real exigency of the time, and the apparent necessity of the thing, would, in his opinion, always justify a Secretary of State, in every extraordinary act of power. In the present case, there was no necessity for a General Warrant. Ministers knew all the parties. The plea of necessity could not be urged; there was no pretence for it. The nation was in perfect tranquility. The safety of the State was in no danger. The charge was, the writing and publishing a libel. What was there in this crime, so heinous and terrible, as to require this formidable instrument; which, like an inundation of water, bore down all the barriers and fences of happiness and security? Parliament had voted away its own privilege, and laid the personal freedom of every representative of the nation, at the mercy of his Majesty's Attorney General. Did Parliament see the extent of this

CHAPTER XXVII.
1764.

surrender, which they had made? That they had decided upon the unalienable rights of the people, by subjecting their representatives to a restraint of their persons, whenever the Ministers, or the Attorney General thought proper. The extraordinary and wanton exercise, of an illegal power, in this cafe, admits of no justification, nor even palliation. It was an indulgence of a personal resentment against a particular person: And the condemnation of it is evaded by a pretence that is *false*, is a mockery of justice, and an imposition on the House. We are told, that this warrant is *pendente lite*; that it will come under judicial decision, in the determinations of the Court on the bills of exception; and, therefore, that Parliament ought not to declare any judgment upon the subject. In answer to this, he said, that whenever the bills of exceptions came to be argued, it would be found, that they turned upon *other points*. Upon *other points* he repeated. He was confident in his assertion. He concluded with saying, that if the House negatived the motion, they would be the disgrace of the present age, and the reproach of posterity; who, after sacrificing their own privileges, had abandoned the liberty of the subject; upon a pretence, that was wilfully founded in error, and manifestly urged for the purpose of delusion.

Upon a motion being made for adjourning the debate for four months, the numbers were 234 for the question, and 220 against it.

The Right Hon. CHARLES TOWNSHEND, who at this time was in opposition to the Ministry, said to Mr. PITT as they entered the House, that they should be in the Majority that night. It was certainly his opinion, for he said afterwards to several of his friends, that he was confident they went *into* the House a majority; but that LLOYD*, who had the Minister's *private pocket book*†, made converts before the division.

* Mr. CHARLES LLOYD, who was Mr. GRENVILLE's *private* Secretary.
† The term given to the Minister's List of Members.

CHAP.

CHAP. XXVIII.

Sir William Pynsent leaves his fortune to Mr. Pitt—Similar intention of Mr. Hollis—Present and Note from Wareham—Pitt's Diamond—The Regency—American Stamp Act—Lord Bute resolves to dismiss the Ministers—Gets an audience of the Duke of Cumberland---The Duke sends for Lord Temple---Conference between them---The Duke goes to Mr. Pitt---Applies to Lord Lyttelton---Lord Temple and Mr. Grenville reconciled---Observation—Mr. Stuart Mackenzie dismissed---The King sends for Mr. Pitt --Lord Temple sent for---They refuse the King's offers ---Observation---King's Friends---Conduct of the Duke of Bedford and Mr. Jenkinson---The Duke forms a new Ministry.

THE fame of Mr. PITT's character, of his public virtue and talents, excited no less the admiration of all independent persons at home, than of princes and potentates abroad. Although proscribed the Court of his Sovereign, he maintained a place in the hearts of the people. Although his Majesty's Council had repudiated his advice, and the representatives of the nation had engaged with a more profitable master, yet there were many persons, who saw no disloyalty to the King, nor disrespect to Parliament, (themes which are constantly dwelt upon, whenever a proscribed person is popular) in continuing their esteem and veneration for a great character, of exemplary virtue and unrivalled abilities. Amongst these, was Sir WILLIAM PYNSENT, of Burton-Pynsent, in Somersetshire, a Baronet

CHAPTER XXVIII.
1765.

a Baronet of ancient family, and large fortune; who having no iffue, bequeathed his eftate (of near three thoufand pounds per annum) to Mr. PITT, and his heirs. He died on the 12th of January 1765. There was a contention for the property; and it was countenanced from a quarter, where, it might have been fuppofed the perverfion of juftice never reached. However it was of no avail: the will of the teftator was confirmed.*

Prefent from Wareham.

In the month of Auguft, Mr. PITT went into Somerfetfhire. While he was there an inhabitant of Wareham fent him a falmon, with this note: " I am an Englifhman, and therefore love liberty and you; Sir, be pleafed to accept of this fifh, as a mark of my efteem; were every fcale a diamond §, it fhould have been at your fervice."

During the greateft part of the feffion of the year 1765, Mr. PITT was confined by the gout.

Early in the month of April, his Majefty was afflicted by an alarming diforder. At the firft audience he honoured his Mini-

* It has been confidently afferted, that THOMAS HOLLIS, Efq. who died at at Corfcombe in Dorfetfhire, in the month of December 1773, intended to have bequeathed his eftate to Mr. PITT, but died before he was able to make the arrangement he had in contemplation.

RALPH ALLEN, of Prior Park, Efq. died, in 1764, and left Mr. PITT one thoufand pounds.

§ Alluding to the celebrated diamond, which Mr. PITT's anceftor, THOMAS PITT, Efq. who, in Queen ANNE's reign, was Governor of Fort St. George, in the Eaft Indies, brought from thence, weighing one hundred and twenty-feven carats; and which, being refufed by the Britifh Sovereign, was purchafed by the Regent of France, for one hundred and thirty-five thoufand pounds fterling. It is placed in the Crown of France; and it is to this day called *Pitt's diamond*. For a defcription and reprefentation of this diamond, fee the Mufeum Britannicum, page 69, and tab. 28.

fter

fter after his recovery, he took a paper out of his pocket, containing a speech to both Houses of Parliament, requesting a power to nominate a Regent, with a Council, in case of his death, before his successor was eighteen years of age. His Majesty gave the paper to his Minister, and fixed the day for going to the House. As this was the first notice the Ministers had of the design, they were greatly surprised by it. The speech was written, and the measure was formed, without their participation, or even knowledge. They had submitted to several invasions of their departments, by appointments being made, Ecclesiastical, Civil, and Military; some without their knowledge, and others contrary to their recommendations: But this was a stronger act, and a more indisputable proof, of a secret unresponsible influence, subsisting somewhere, than any other they had met with. They were not very ardent, therefore, in support of the measure. The bill was brought into the House of Lords, agreeable to the portrait given in the speech. " To " vest in me the power of appointing, by instruments in writing, " under my sign manual, either the Queen, or *any other person of* " *my Royal Family*, usually residing in Great Britain, to be," &c. But a doubt arising, on the question, " Who were the Royal Fa- " mily?" It was explained, the Descendants of GEORGE the SECOND. And this explanation was declared by the Secretary of State, Lord HALIFAX, to be perfectly agreeable to the Royal construction. The Princess of WALES (who was descended from another family) being thus excluded, the Ministers conceived they had gained a complete victory over Lord BUTE. But their enjoyment of this opinion, was of very short duration; for when the bill came into the House of Commons, her Royal Highness's name was added,

CHAPTER XXVIII.
1765.
The Regency.

CHAPTER XXVIII.
⌣
1765.

added, on a motion made for that purpose by Mr. MORTON, one of Lord BUTE's friends, immediately after the Queen: Whether Lord HALIFAX did not rightly understand his Majesty, when he reported the question; or whether his Majesty did not rightly understand Lord HALIFAX, is a distinction not worth ascertaining. The original error, was in the writer of the speech, who ought to have been more explicit. Perhaps he designedly, as well as cautiously avoided it; with a view to prevent, what by the family might have been called, invidious observation and personality. But the remedy was made, in a manner more palpably indicative of that secret influence, which dictated and controuled every important measure of Government.*

Lord Bute resolves to dismiss the Ministers.

Whether during the King's late illness, or at whatever moment earlier, or for whatever cause, the Earl of BUTE took a a resolution of removing the Ministers; are points, which can be explained by only those persons, who were at that time in his confidence. The sincere opinion of other persons was, that some representations had been made by the subsisting Ministers, upon the appointment of Sir H. ERSKINE, upon filling the See of Armagh, and other promotions; some of which had taken place contrary to their advice, and others without their

* It was in this session of Mr. GRENVILLE's Administration, that the American Stamp Act was passed; which Mr. GRENVILLE afterwards defended with the warmest zeal and resolution; yet if we may believe Mr. JENKINSON, now Lord HAWKESBURY, who, in such a case, may safely be taken for the best authority, this measure was not Mr. GRENVILLE's. See Mr. JENKINSON's speech in the House of Commons, on the fifteenth of May 1777. Mr. JENKINSON has not yet informed the nation, to whom this measure ought to have been ascribed; though he has explicitly acquitted Mr. GRENVILLE of it.

knowledge;

knowledge; the King was offended; and applied to his favourite, to emancipate him from these importunities. Whether this opinion was well founded, or not, it is certain, that ten days, at least, before any intimation was given to the Ministers of the Regency Bill, the Earl of BUTE obtained, through the interest of the Earl of ALBEMARLE, a private audience of the Duke of CUMBERLAND§. His wish was to bring Mr. PITT into office. His project had failed in the year 1763, through his own cowardice. This year he resolved not to appear in the measure; perhaps he was still influenced by his fears, and therefore, the better to conceal himself, and to give greater weight to his design, his first care was to put the negotiation into the hands of the Duke of CUMBERLAND, with some limitations. After his first audience of the Duke, he and his brother appeared publicly at his Royal Highness's levee, more than once during the time the Regency Bill was in Parliament. These circumstances were not unknown to the Ministers, nor did they scruple to declare to their friends, That the King's confidence was not placed where it ought to be. Yet they did not refuse a necessary measure. But they were particularly blameable for admitting one part of it, which whoever advised, gave bad advice: It was a proposition, for an unexampled encroachment on the inherent fundamental and essential rights of Parliament, and a dangerous precedent, for an addition to the pretensions of the Crown; by entrusting to the *sole and secret* nomination of the Prince upon the throne, the appointment of the person to exercise the regal authority, during a minority.

§ On Sunday evening, April 14. His Royal Highness came to town on purpose.

CHAPTER XXVIII.
1765.

Mr. PITT having declared in Parliament, that he would live and die with his brother (Lord TEMPLE) the confidential contriver of this second project, to bring in Mr. PITT, resolved to make the first application to Lord TEMPLE, with the hope of obtaining his favourable opinion, which was considered the most essential step towards gaining Mr. PITT. Accordingly on the fifteenth of May, the Duke of CUMBERLAND sent for Lord TEMPLE from Stowe†. As soon as possible his Lordship waited on the Duke, who began by informing him, that the King had resolved to change his servants, and to engage his Lordship, Mr. PITT, and their friends, in his service; but first he (the Duke) wished to know *their conditions*. Lord TEMPLE respectfully assured his Royal Highness, that their conditions were not many. The making certain foreign alliances, the restoration of officers (Civil as well as Military) cruelly and unjustly dismissed, a repeal of the Excise on Cyder, a total and full condemnation of General Warrants, and the seizure of papers. His Royal Highness perfectly approved of these conditions, and said they must be agreed to. And then added, that he had a proposition to make—this was, That it was the King's desire Lord NORTHUMBERLAND should be placed at the Head of the Treasury. Lord TEMPLE replied, " He would never come into " office under Lord BUTE's Lieutenant‡." Here the conference broke off. This proposition having been made in the negotiation of the year 1763, when Lord BUTE appeared openly in the measure, left no room to doubt of his Lordship being still the secret adviser of the King, and the secret mover of the present negotiation.

The Duke sends for Lord Temple.

Conference between them.

† His Royal Highness also sent for Mr. JAMES GRENVILLE from Pinner.
‡ Lord NORTHUMBERLAND was at this time Lord Lieutenant of Ireland.

On

On the nineteenth of the same month, which was Sunday, the Duke sent a message to Lord TEMPLE, requesting his Lordship to meet him at Mr. PITT's house, at Hayes in Kent. The Duke was with Mr. PITT, when his Lordship came in, and had made the same proposition respecting Lord NORTHUMBERLAND, which Mr. PITT had refused, as totally inadmissible; upon the same principle, that the refusal had been made by Lord TEMPLE; of which, Mr. PITT had not, until that moment, received the smallest intimation. He assured his Royal Highness, that he was ready to go to St. James's, *if he could carry the Constitution along with him*;—that was his expression.

Next day the Duke sent Lord FREDERICK CAVENDISH to Mr. PITT, with an assurance, that the proposition respecting Lord NORTHUMBERLAND being at the head of the Treasury, was relinquished; provided his Lordship was considered in some other way. Mr. PITT returned the same answer he had given to his Royal Highness. Upon the return of Lord FREDERICK, the Duke offered the Treasury to Lord LYTTELTON, who desired to consult Lord TEMPLE and Mr. PITT. The Duke was displeased with this answer, and immediately went to the King; and having informed his Majesty of the several answers he had received, concluded with advising the King, to continue his present servants.

At the same time, Lord TEMPLE and his brother, Mr. GRENVILLE became reconciled through the mediation of the friends of both parties; who declared, that this reconciliation was no more than domestic friendship, as brothers; and on public principles, only as to measures in future.

CHAPTER XXVIII.
1765.
Obfervation.

It is in their influence on meafures *in future*, that fuch circumftances become interefting to the nation. The reconciliation being effected, Mr. GRENVILLE unbofoming himfelf to his brother, related all the arts and clandeftine fteps of the Favourite; which, if poffible, encreafed his brother's ardour in oppofition to Lord BUTE. Both the brothers now entertaining the fame opinion, there could be little probability of another feparation happening between them. Confequently, *in future*, it muft be fuppofed they engaged to act, and to concert their meafures together.

During the negotiation with the Duke, Parliament had been kept fitting, under an expectation of iffuing writs: But that negotiation having failed, the fubfifting Minifters refolved to vindicate the independence of their fituations, by afferting the due influence, which of right belonged to the refponfibility of their offices, and to create a neceffity of iffuing writs, very different from thofe, which had been in expectation.

Mr. Stuart Mackenzie difmiffed.

The decifive ftroke of this conteft, was the turning out Mr. MACKENZIE, Lord BUTE's brother; which, they declared, they offered to the public as a mark, that the Councils and employments of the State, were not feparated, notwithstanding the late negotiation. And this circumftance gave them a merit in their death, that moft of them would never have acquired in any other way.

There was no ftep they could have taken more perfonally offenfive than this. And to it they added, the difmiffions of Lord NORTHUMBERLAND and Mr. FOX, who had been created Lord HOLLAND. As foon as thefe changes were made, Parliament was prorogued.

The

The King confidered thefe three difmiffions, but moft particularly the firft, as infults to his perfon and dignity. Whether the opinion was fpontaneoufly his own, or whether it was fuggefted to him, is not deferving of an attempt to difcover. The language of the Favourite upon this occafion was—*What do you mean to deftroy the Monarchy?—to annihilate the firft of the three Eftates?*

In confequence of thefe open and avowed acts of hoftility to the Favourite, a refolution was taken to open another negotiation with Mr. PITT. Lord BUTE and the Duke having both failed, the King himfelf undertook this negotiation. His Majefty fent for Mr. PITT. He waited upon the King at the Queen's Houfe, on the twentieth day of June, 1765. The confequence of this audience was, the fending for Lord TEMPLE. And on the 25th they waited on his Majefty together, at the Queen's Houfe; when the following conditions were propofed to them.

1. Mr. STUART MACKENZIE to be reftored.
2. Lord NORTHUMBERLAND to be Lord Chamberlain.
3. The King's Friends to continue in their prefent fituations*.

To the two firft conditions Mr. PITT was not very averfe. Refpecting the laft, he wifhed for fome explanation. But Lord

---

* There were about thirty perfons, who arrogantly affumed this appellation. They affected to belong to no Minifter—to maintain no connection—to court no intereft---to embrace no principle---to hold no opinion. They might more properly have been called the Houfehold Troops, or Janizaries of the Court; becaufe they fupported, or oppofed, the Official Minifters, according to the orders they received from the Favourite.

TEMPLE

CHAPTER XXVIII.
1765.

TEMPLE declared againſt the whole. Upon which the conference ended.——Here it is proper to obſerve, that upon more mature confideration Mr. PITT's changed his ſentiments on the two firſt conditions, and perfectly agreed with his brother.

Obſervation.

The reader's judgment will anticipate any obſervations which can be made on theſe extraordinary occurrences; reſpecting either the humiliation of the King, who defcended from his ſtation to execute the project of his favourite; or the ſuperiority of Mr. PITT, who refifted the entreaties of his Sovereign, when incompatible with the ſervice of the public. Theſe prominent features, are ſo obvious from the plain ſtatement of the facts, that no reader can feel the want of illuſtration. The future hiſtorian may indulge in obſervations and inferences, which the preſent writer dare not. And Truth may find an advocate in a future age, which the venality of the preſent refuſes to endure.

The Duke forms a new Miniſtry.

The King's negotiation having failed, the Duke of CUMBERLAND was again applied to. His Majeſty having reſolved to part with his preſent ſervants at any rate*, his Royal Highneſs had

* It has been ſtated, that this refolution was taken in confequence of ſome expreſſions, which had fallen from the Duke of BEDFORD in his Majeſty's cloſet. One writer ſays, "The Duke of BEDFORD continuing in ſuch a behaviour as no private man could have ſuffered in any one of his inferiors, produced an inftantaneous determination to get rid of ſuch provocations at any rate." *Principles of the Changes in* 1765, *page* 45.

Another, and more popular writer, ſays, "The Miniſtry having endeavoured to exclude the Dowager out of the Regency Bill, the Earl of BUTE determined to difmiſs them. Upon this, the Duke of BEDFORD demanded an audience of the ———, reproached him in plain terms with duplicity, baſeneſs, falſehood, treachery and hypocriſy,-----repeatedly gave him the lye, and left him

had full power to form an administration. The Duke of NEW-CASTLE, the Marquis of ROCKINGHAM, and their friends, thought it their duty to accept of his Royal Highness's invitation. General CONWAY was made Secretary of State, and to him was committed the management of the House of Commons.

CHAPTER XXVIII.

1765.

him in convulsions." *Junius's Letters, the author's own edition, printed by Woodfall,* volume 1, page 171. the note.

And with respect to the particular dismission of Mr. GRENVILLE, another writer has given the following anecdote.---" He had been so completely duped, that for some days after his dismission, he had the vanity to believe the Court retained a partiality for him;---but when he saw, that Mr. CHARLES JENKINSON, whom he knew was the confidant of Lord BUTE, and whom he had carried to the Duke of NEWCASTLE, and for whom he had obtained a pension, for writing a pamphlet on the seizure of the Dutch vessels in 1757, and who for that, and other obligations, he thought would have followed him out of Court——when he discovered that Mr. JENKINSON stayed behind, and that his credit was not diminished at either Carlton House or Buckingham House, he then *saw*, what all the world knew before, that he had been the *dupe of Lord* BUTE's *agent*——that the very man, who owed his original recommendation to him, was the very man who had betrayed him. Perhaps no gentleman ever felt the poignant sting of ingratitude so keenly as Mr. GRENVILLE did upon 'hat occasion." *Faction Unmask'd, p.* 19.

CHAP.

CHAP. XXIX.

New Ministry blamed for accepting—Lord Bute's influence not diminished—Their Apology—Mr. Pitt's Speech against the American Stamp Act—He compliments Mr. Burke.

<small>CHAPTER XXIX.
1765.
New Ministry blamed for accepting.</small>

MR. PITT did not entirely approve of the new Ministry's acceptance. And Lord TEMPLE condemned them in terms of acrimony: he said, if they had followed the example of Mr. PITT and himself, in refusing the allurements of office, the Favourite must have submitted to such conditions, as it might have been thought necessary to impose upon him; which certainly would have been, an absolute and total exclusion of him and his friends, from every situation and channel of secret communication with the Sovereign: there must have been an end of all those unhappy suggestions, which had already distracted the kingdom, and menaced the pervasion of further misfortunes. This might be called violent language, but it was founded in truth and experience; and although the new Ministry were not under the influence of the Favourite, yet his influence was not diminished; it might, perhaps, be said to suffer a temporary abatement, or rather it was his own policy to suspend the exercise of it, until a more suitable opportunity occurred for making another display of his power and versatility.

<small>Lord Bute's influence not diminished.</small>

<small>Their apology.</small>

The new Ministry had this apology fairly to offer.—Out of office they were inadequate to the performance of any service to their country; but in office they might accomplish something, though

though perhaps not so much as they wished; and undoubtedly they should prevent any encrease, or aggravation of the public discontents.—These motives were laudable.—*Gradatim* was Mr. PITT's own word, in a former day.—They might reason justly, that in the present unhappy partiality of the King, the Constitutional exercise of the powers of Government were to be obtained by degrees, not by hazarding a violent convulsion of the State; to which point some of them feared Lord TEMPLE's inflexibility might possibly extend.

When the new Ministers entered their offices, they found that many of their former subalterns, were either dead, sequestered in retirement, or allied to the enemy: even the first Lord of the Treasury was at a loss for a private Secretary of competent talents. An accomplished *Commis* is an inestimable character. Mr. FITZHERBERT, of Tissington in Derbyshire, a gentleman of unexampled philanthropy, and most gentle manners, whose ambition was benevolence, and whose happiness consisted in the administration of kindness, recommended to his Lordship Mr. EDMUND BURKE. The British dominions did not furnish a more able and fit person, for that confidential important situation. He is " the only man, since the age of Cicero, who has united the talents of speaking and writing, with irresistible force and elegance." At the same time, his cousin, Mr. WM. BURKE, of equal diligence, penetration and integrity, was made Secretary to General CONWAY. There was no private interest courted or gratified by these appointments. The merit of the persons was their principal recommendation.

Parliament

CHAPTER XXIX.
1765.
1766.

Parliament met on the seventeenth of December, in order to issue writs for the vacancies, which had been made by the change of the Ministry, and then adjourned to the fourteenth of January 1766, for the dispatch of business. On this day the session was opened with a speech from the throne. On the usual motion for an address, the friends of the new Ministry spoke very tenderly of the disturbances raised in America, in opposition to the Stamp Act, terming them only *occurrences*; which gave great offence to the friends of the late Ministy, by whom that act had been passed.

Mr. Pitt's speech against the American Stamp Act.

Mr. PITT was impatient to speak on this subject: therefore he rose in the early part of the debate. He began with saying, I came to town but to-day; I was a stranger to the tenor of his Majesty's speech, and the proposed address, till I heard them read in this House. Unconnected and unconsulted, I have not the means of information; I am fearful of offending through mistake, and therefore beg to be indulged with a second reading of the proposed address. The address being read, Mr. PITT went on: He commended the King's speech, approved of the address in answer, as it decided nothing, every gentleman being left at perfect liberty to take such a part concerning America, as he might afterwards see fit. One word only he could not approve of, an *early*, is a word that does not belong to the notice the Ministry have given to Parliament of the troubles in America. In a matter of such importance, the communication ought to have been immediate: I speak not with respect to parties; I stand up in this place single and unconnected. As to the late Ministry, (turning himself to Mr. GRENVILLE, who sat within one of him) every capital measure they have taken, has been entirely wrong!

As to the present gentlemen, to those at least whom I have in my eye (looking at the bench, where Mr. CONWAY sat, with the Lords of the Treasury), I have no objection; I have never been made a sacrifice by any of them. Their characters are fair; and I am always glad when

men

men of fair character engage in his Majesty's service. Some of them have done me the honour to afk my opinion, before they would engage. Thefe will do me the juftice to own, I advifed them to engage; but notwithftanding—I love to be explicit—I cannot give them my confidence; pardon me, gentlemen, (bowing to the Miniftry) confidence is a plant of flow growth in an aged bofom: youth is the feafon of credulity; by comparing events with each other, reafoning from effects to caufes, methinks, I plainly difcover the traces of an over-ruling influence.

There is a claufe in the act of fettlement, to oblige every Minifter to fign his name to the advice which he gives his Sovereign. Would it were obferved!—I have had the honour to ferve the Crown, and if I could have fubmitted to influence, I might have ftill continued to ferve; but I would not be refponfible for others.——I have no local attachments; it is indifferent to me, whether a man was rocked in his cradle on this fide or that fide of the Tweed. I fought for merit wherever it was to be found. It is my boaft, that I was the firft Minifter who looked for it, and I found it in the mountains of the North. I called it forth, and drew it into your fervice, an hardy and intrepid race of men! men, who, when left by your jealoufy, became a prey to the artifices of your enemies, and had gone nigh to have overturned the State in the war before the laft. Thefe men, in the laft war, were brought to combat on your fide: they ferved with fidelity, as they fought with valour, and conquered for you in every part of the world: detefted be the national reflections againft them!——they are unjuft, groundlefs, illiberal, unmanly. When I ceafed to ferve his Majefty as a Minifter, it was not the *country* of the man by which I was moved—but *the man* of that country wanted *wifdom*, and held principles incompatible with *freedom*.

It is a long time, Mr. Speaker, fince I have attended in Parliament. When the refolution was taken in the Houfe to tax America, I was ill in bed. If I could have endured to have been carried in my bed, fo great was the agitation of my mind for the confequences! I would have folicited fome kind hand to have laid me down on this floor, to have borne my teftimony againft it. It is now

CHAPTER XXX.
1766.

an act that had passed—I would speak with decency of every act of this House, but I must beg the indulgence of the House to speak of it with freedom.

I hope a day may be soon appointed to consider the state of the nation with respect to America.—I hope, gentlemen will come to this debate with all the temper and impartiality that his Majesty recommends, and the importance of the subject requires. A subject of greater importance than ever engaged the attention of this House! that subject only excepted, when, near a century ago, it was the question, whether you yourselves were to be bound or free. In the mean time, as I cannot depend upon health for any future day, such is the nature of my infirmities, I will beg to say a few words at present, leaving the justice, the equity, the policy, the expediency of the act, to another time. I will only speak to one point, a point which seems not to have been generally understood—I mean to the right. Some gentlemen (alluding to Mr. NUGENT) seem to have considered it as a point of *honour*. If gentlemen consider it in that light, they leave all measures of right and wrong, to follow a delusion that may lead to destruction. It is my opinion that this kingdom has no right to lay a tax upon the colonies. At the same time, I assert the authority of this kingdom over the colonies, to be sovereign and supreme, in every circumstance of government and legislation whatsoever.—— They are the subjects of this kingdom, equally entitled with yourselves to all the natural rights of mankind and the peculiar privileges of Englishmen. Equally bound by its laws, and equally participating of the constitution of this free country. The Americans are the sons, not the bastards of England. Taxation is no part of the governing or legislative power.—The taxes are a voluntary gift and grant of the Commons alone. In legislation the three estates of the realm are alike concerned, but the concurrence of the Peers and the Crown to a tax, is only necessary to close with the form of a law. The gift and grant is of the Commons alone. In ancient days, the Crown, the Barons, and the Clergy possessed the lands. In those days, the Barons and the Clergy gave and granted to the Crown. They gave and granted what was their own. At present, since the discovery of America,

America, and other circumstances permitting, the Commons are become the proprietors of the land. The Crown has divested itself of its great estates. The Church (God bless it) has but a pittance. The property of the Lords, compared with that of the Commons, is as a drop of water in the ocean: and this House represents those Commons, the proprietors of the lands; and those proprietors virtually represent the rest of the inhabitants. When, therefore, in this House we give and grant, we give and grant what is our own. But in an American tax, what do we do? We, your Majesty's Commons of Great Britain give and grant to your Majesty, what? Our own property?—No. We give and grant to your Majesty, the property of your Majesty's Commons of America.—It is an absurdity in terms.

The distinction between legislation and taxation is essentially necessary to liberty. The Crown, the Peers, are equally legislative powers with the Commons. If taxation be a part of simple legislation, the Crown, the Peers have rights in taxation as well as yourselves: rights which they claim, which they will exercise, whenever the principle can be supported by *power*.

There is an idea in some, that the colonies are virtually represented in this House. I would fain know by whom an American is represented here? Is he represented by any Knight of the shire, in any county in this kingdom? *Would to God that respectable representation was augmented to a greater number!* Or will you tell him that he is represented by any representative of a borough—a borough, which perhaps no man ever saw—This is what is called, *the rotten part of the Constitution*. ——It cannot continue a century—If it does not drop, it must be amputated.—The idea of a virtual representation of America in this House, is the most contemptible idea that ever entered into the head of a man—It does not deserve a serious refutation.

The Commons of America, represented in their several assemblies, have ever been in possession of the exercise of this, their constitutional right, of giving and granting their own money. They would have been slaves if the had not enjoyed it. At the same time, this kingdom, as the supreme governing and legislative power, has always bound the colonies by her laws, by her regulations, and restrictions in trade,

trade, in navigation, in manufactures—in every thing, except that of taking their money out of their pockets without their confent. Here I would draw the line,

' *Quam ultra citraque nequit confiftere rectum.*'

He concluded with a familiar voice and tone, but fo low that it was not eafy to diftinguifh what he faid. A confiderable paufe enfued after Mr. PITT had done fpeaking.

Mr. Conway. Mr. CONWAY at length got up. He faid, he had been waiting to fee whether any anfwer would be given to what had been advanced by the Right Honourable Gentleman, referving himfelf for the reply: but as none had been given, he had only to declare, that his own fentiments were entirely conformable to thofe of the Right Honourable Gentleman—That they are fo conformable, he faid, is a circumftance that affects me with the moft fenfible pleafure, and does me the greateft honour. But two things fell from that Gentleman, which give me pain, as, whatever falls from that Gentleman, falls from fo great a height as to make a deep impreffion.—I muft endeavour to remove it.—It was objected, that the notice given to Parliament of the troubles in America was not early. I can affure the Houfe, the firft accounts were too vague and imperfect to be worth the notice of Parliament. It is only of late that they have been precife and full. An over-ruling influence has alfo been hinted at. I fee nothing of it—I feel nothing of it—I difclaim it for myfelf, and (as far as my difcernment can reach) for all the reft of his Majefty's Minifters.

Mr. Pitt. Mr. PITT faid in anfwer to Mr. CONWAY, The excufe is a valid one, if it is a juft one. That muft appear from the papers now before the Houfe.

Mr. Grenville. Mr. GRENVILLE next ftood up. He began with cenfuring the Miniftry very feverely, for delaying to give earlier notice to Parliament of the difturbances in America. He faid, They began in July, and now we are in the middle of January; lately they were only occurrences, they are now grown to difturbances, to tumults and riots. I doubt they border on open rebellion; and if the doctrine I have heard this day be confirmed, I fear they will lofe that name to take that of revolution. The government over them being diffolved, a revolution,

revolution will take place in America. I cannot understand the difference between external and internal taxes. They are the same in effect, and only differ in name. That this kingdom has the sovereign, the supreme legislative power over America, is granted. It cannot be denied; and taxation is a part of that sovereign power. It is one branch of the legislation. It is, it has been exercised, over those who are not, who were never represented. It is exercised over the India Company, the merchants of London, the proprietors of the Stocks, and over many great manufacturing towns. It was exercised over the palatinate of Chester, and the Bishoprick of Durham, before they sent any representatives to Parliament. I appeal for proof to the preambles of the Acts which gave them representatives: the one in the reign of HENRY VIII. the other in that of CHARLES II. Mr. GRENVILLE then quoted the Acts, and desired that they might be read; which being done, he said: When I proposed to tax America, I asked the House, if any Gentleman would object to the right; I repeatedly asked it, and no man would attempt to deny it. Protection and obedience are reciprocal. Great Britain protects America; America is bound to yield obedience. If not, tell me where the Americans were emancipated? When they want the protection of this kingdom, they are always very ready to ask it. That protection has always been afforded them in the most full and ample manner. The nation has run itself into an immense debt to give them their protection; and now they called upon to contribute a small share towards the public expence, an expence arising from themselves, they renounce your authority, insult your officers, and break out, I might almost say, into open rebellion. The seditious spirit of the colonies owes its birth to the factions in this House. Gentlemen are careless of the consequences of what they say, provided it answers the purposes of opposition. We were told we trod on tender ground: we were bid to expect disobedience. What was this, but telling the Americans to stand out against the law, to encourage their obstinacy with the expectation of support from hence? Let us only hold out a little, they would say, our friends will soon be in power. Ungrateful people of America! Bounties have been extended to them. When I had the honour of serving the Crown, while you yourselves were loaded with an enormous debt, you have

given.

CHAPTER XXIX.

1766.

CHAPTER XXIX.
1766.

given bounties on their lumber, on their iron, their hemp, and many other articles. You have relaxed, in their favour, the act of navigation, that palladium of the British commerce; and yet I have been abused in all the public papers as an enemy to the trade of America. I have been particularly charged with giving orders and instructions to prevent the Spanish trade, and thereby stopping the channel, by which alone North America used to be supplied with cash for remittances to this country. I defy any man to produce any such orders or instructions. I discouraged no trade but what was illicit, what was prohibited by an act of Parliament. I desire a West India merchant, well known in the city (Mr. LONG) a gentleman of character, may be examined. He will tell you, that I offered to do every thing in my power to advance the trade of America. I was above giving an answer to anonymous calumnies; but in this place, it becomes one to wipe off the aspersion.

Here Mr. GRENVILLE ceased. Several Members got up to speak, but Mr. PITT seeming to rise, the House was so clamorous for Mr. PITT, Mr. PITT, that the Speaker was obliged to call to order.

Mr. Pitt.

After obtaining a little quiet, he said, Mr. PITT was up; who began with informing the House, That he did not mean to have gone any further upon the subject that day; that he had only designed to have thrown out a few hints, which, Gentlemen, who were so confident of the right of this kingdom to send taxes to America, might consider; might, perhaps, reflect, in a cooler moment, that the right was at least equivocal. But since the Gentlemen, who spoke last, had not stopped on that ground, but had gone into the whole; into the justice, the equity, the policy, the expediency of the Stamp Act, as well as into the right, he would follow him through the whole field, and combat his arguments on every point.

Lord Strange.

He was going on, when Lord STRANGE got up, and called both Gentlemen, Mr. PITT and Mr. GRENVILLE, to order. He said, they had both departed from the matter before the House, which was the King's speech; and that Mr. PITT was going to speak twice on the same debate, although the House was not in a Committee.

Mr. Onslow.

Mr. GEORGE ONSLOW answered, That they were both in order, as nothing had been said, but what was fairly deducible from the King's speech;

speech; and appealed to the Speaker. The Speaker decided in Mr. Onslow's favour.

Mr. PITT said, I do not apprehend I am speaking twice : I did expressly reserve a part of my subject, in order to save the time of this House, but I am compelled to proceed in it. I do not speak twice; I only finished what I designedly left imperfect. But if the House is of a different opinion, far be it from me to indulge a wish of transgression, against order. I am content, if it be your pleasure, to be silent.—Here he paused—The House resounding with Go on, go on: he proceeded:

Gentlemen, Sir, (to the Speaker) I have been charged with giving birth to sedition in America. They have spoken their sentiments with freedom, against this unhappy act, and that freedom has become their crime. Sorry I am to hear the liberty of speech in this House, imputed as a crime. But the imputation shall not discourage me. It is a liberty I mean to exercise. No gentleman ought to be afraid to exercise it. It is a liberty by which the gentleman who calumniates it might have profited. He ought to have desisted from his project. The Gentleman tells us, America is obstinate; America is almost in open rebellion. I rejoice, that America has resisted. Three millions of people, so dead to all the feelings of liberty, as voluntarily to submit to be slaves, would have been fit instruments to make slaves of the rest. I come not here armed at all points, with law cases and acts of Parliament, with the statute book doubled down in dog's-ears, to defend the cause of liberty : if I had, I myself would have cited the two cases of Chester and Durham. I would have cited them, to have shewn, that, even under any arbitrary reigns, Parliaments were ashamed of taxing a people without their consent, and allowed them representatives. Why did the Gentleman confine himself to Chester and Durham ? He might have taken a higher example in Wales; Wales that never was taxed by Parliament, till it was incorporated. I would not debate a particular point of law with the Gentleman: I know his abilities. I have been obliged to his diligent researches. But, for the defence of liberty upon a general principle, upon a constitutional principle, it is a ground on which I stand firm; on which I dare meet any man. The Gentleman tells us of many who are taxed,

and

and are not reprefented—The India Company, merchants, ftock-holders, manufacturers. Surely many of thefe are reprefented on other capacities, as owners of land, or as freemen of boroughs. It is a misfortune that more are not actually reprefented. But they are all inhabitants, and as fuch, are not virtually reprefented. Many have it in their option to be actually reprefented. They have connexions with thofe that elect, and they have influence over them. The Gentleman mentioned the ftock-holders: I hope he does not reckon the debts of the nation as a part of the national eftate. Since the acceffion of King WILLIAM, many Minifters, fome of great, others of more moderate abilities, have taken the lead of Government.

He then went through the lift of them, bringing it down till he came to himfelf, giving a fhort fketch of the characters of each of them. None of thefe, he faid, thought, or ever dreamed, of robbing the colonies of their conftitutional rights. That was referved to mark the æra of the late Adminiftration: not that there were wanting fome, when I had the honour to ferve his Majefty, to propofe to me to burn my fingers with an American Stamp Act. With the enemy at their back, with our bayonets at their breafts, in the day of their diftrefs, perhaps, the Americans would have fubmitted to the impofition; but it would have been taking an ungenerous, and unjuft advantage. The Gentleman boafts of his bounties to America! Are not thofe bounties intended finally for the benefit of this kingdom? If they are not, he has mifapplied the national treafures. I am no courtier of America,—I ftand up for this kingdom. I maintain, that the Parliament has a right to bind, to reftrain America. Our legiflative power over the colonies, is fovereign and fupreme. When it ceafes to be fovereign and fupreme, I would-advife every Gentleman to fell his lands, if he can, and embark for that country. When two countries are connected together, like England and her colonies, without being incorporated, the one muft neceffarily govern; the greater muft rule the lefs; but fo rule it, as not to contradict the fundamental principles that are common to both.

If the Gentleman does not underftand the difference between internal and external taxes, I cannot help it; but there is a plain diftinction distinction between taxes levied for the purposes of raising a revenue, and duties imposed for the regulation of trade, for the accommodation of the subject; although, in the consequences, some revenue might incidentally arise from the latter.

CHAPTER XXIX.
1766.

The Gentleman asks, when were the colonies emancipated? But I desire to know, when they were made slaves? But I dwell not upon words. When I had the honour of serving his Majesty, I availed myself of the means of information, which I derived from my office: I speak, therefore from knowledge. My materials were good. I was at pains to collect, to digest, to consider them; and I will be bold to affirm, that the profits to Great Britain from the trade of the colonies, through all its branches, is two millions a year. This is the fund that carried you triumphantly through the last war. The estates that were rented at two thousand pounds a year, threescore years ago, are at three thousand pounds at present. Those estates sold then from fifteen to eighteen years purchase; the same may now sold be for thirty. You owe this to America. This is the price America pays you for her protection. And shall a miserable financier come with a boast, that he can fetch a pepper-corn into the Exchequer, to the loss of millions to the nation! I dare not say, how much higher these profits may be augmented. Omitting the immense increase of people by natural population, in the northern colonies, and the migration from every part of Europe, I am convinced the commercial system of America may be altered to advantage. You have prohibited, where you ought to have encouraged; and you have encouraged where you ought to have prohibited. Improper restraints have been laid on the continent, in favour of the islands. You have but two nations to trade with in America. Would you had twenty! Let acts of Parliament in consequence of treaties remain, but let not an English Minister become a Custom-house officer for Spain, or for any foreign power. Much is wrong, much may be amended for the general good of the whole.

Does the Gentleman complain he has been misrepresented in the public prints? It is a common misfortune. In the Spanish affair of the last war, I was abused in all the news-papers, for having advised his Majesty to violate the law of nations with regard to Spain. The abuse was industriously circulated even in hand-bills. If administra-

Vol. I.   Q q   tion

CHAPTER XXIX.
1766.

tion did not propagate the abuse, *administration never contradicted it.* I will not say what advice I did give to the King. My advice is in writing, signed by myself, in the possession of the Crown. But I will say, what advice I did not give to the King: I did not advise him to violate any of the laws of nations.

As to the report of the Gentleman's preventing in some way the trade for bullion with the Spaniards, it was spoken of so confidently, that I own I am one of those who did believe it to be true.

The Gentleman must not wonder he was not contradicted, when, as the Minister, he asserted the right of Parliament to tax America. I know not how it is, but there is a modesty in this House, which does not chuse to contradict a Minister. I wish Gentlemen would get the better of this modesty. Even that Chair, Sir, sometimes looks towards St. James's. If they do not, perhaps, the collective body may begin to abate of its respect for the representative. Lord BACON had told me, that a great question would not fail of being agitated at one time or another. I was willing to agitate that at the proper season, the German war: my German war, they called it. Every sessions I called out, has any body any objections to the German war? No body would object to it, one Gentleman only excepted, since removed to the upper House, by succession to an ancient barony, (meaning Lord LE DESPENCER, formerly Sir FRANCIS DASHWOOD;) he told me, "he did not like a German war." I honoured the man for it, and was sorry when he was turned out of his post.

A great deal has been said without doors, of the power, of the strength of America. It is a topic that ought to be cautiously meddled with. In a good cause, on a sound bottom, the force of this country can crush America to atoms. I know the valour of your troops. I know the skill of your officers. There is not a company of foot that has served in America, out of which you may not pick a man of sufficient knowledge and experience, to make a Governor of a colony there. But on this ground, on the Stamp Act, when so many here will think it a crying injustice, I am one who will lift up my hands against it.

In such a cause, your success would be hazardous. America, if she fell, would fall like the strong man. She would embrace the pillars of the State, and pull down the Constitution along with her. Is this

your

your boasted peace? Not to sheath the sword in its scabbard, but to sheath it in the bowels of your countrymen? Will you quarrel with yourselves, now the whole House of Bourbon is united against you? While France disturbs your fisheries in Newfoundland, embarrasses your slave trade to Africa, and with-holds from your subjects in Canada, their property stipulated by treaty; while the ransom for Manillas is denied by Spain, and its gallant conqueror basely traduced into a mean plunderer, a gentleman, (Colonel DRAPER) whose noble and generous spirit would do honour to the proudest grandee of the country. The Americans have not acted in all things with prudence and temper. The Americans have been wronged. They have been driven to madness by injustice. Will you punish them for the madness you have occasioned? Rather let prudence and temper come first from this side. I will undertake for America, that she will follow the example. There are two lines in a ballad of PRIOR's, of a man's behaviour to his wife, so applicable to you and your colonies, that I cannot help repeating them:

<blockquote>
Be to her faults a little blind:
Be to her virtues very kind.
</blockquote>

Upon the whole, I will beg leave to tell the House what is really my opinion. It is, that the Stamp Act be *repealed absolutely, totally*, and *immediately*. That the reason for the repeal be assigned, because it was founded on an erroneous principle. At the same time, let the sovereign authority of this country over the colonies, be asserted in as strong terms as can be devised, and be made to extend to every point of legislation whatsoever. That we may bind their *trade*, confine their *manufactures*, and exercise every *power* whatsoever, except that of taking their money out of their pockets without their consent!

In the course of this debate, Mr. BURKE made his first speech in Parliament. Mr. PITT complimented him upon it, in terms peculiarly flattering to a young man.

CHAPTER XXIX. 1766.

He compliments Mr. Burke.

CHAP.

CHAP. XXX.

Lord Bute refolves to change the Miniſtry again—Difregards the Duke of Bedford—Tries to gain Lord Temple—Meeting at Lord Eglintoun's—Amufes Lord Temple—Lord Strange's aſſertion—Lord Rockingham's requeſt—Affair of Dunkirk—Negotiation with Mr. Wilkes—Propoſition for the Government of Canada---Difapproved by the Chancellor, who adviſes the King to ſend for Mr. Pitt.

CHAPTER XXX.
1766.
Lord Bute refolves to change the Miniſtry again.
Difregards the D. of Bedford.

BEFORE the meeting of Parliament, the new Miniſtry having ſhewn an inclination to reverſe the ſyſtem purſued by their predeceſſors, Lord BUTE, who had been the author of that ſyſtem, took a refolution to remove them. He was no longer terrified by the threats of impeachment. The Duke of BEDFORD had connived ſo long, his Grace could not now bring forward his menaced accuſation, upon any ground or pretence of public principle. He had moreover been recently ſtigmatized by violent marks of popular odium*. His Grace was not at this time, in the judgment of the Favourite, an object of either dread or reſpect.

Tries to gain Lord Temple.

Lord BUTE's attention at this period, was directed to another Nobleman. Since the reconciliation between Lord TEMPLE and his brother Mr. GRENVILLE, there had commenced a coolneſs between his Lordſhip and Mr. PITT, and between his

* By the Spitalfield weavers, who had aſſembled in great multitudes before his houſe. Several partizans of Lord BUTE were ſeen amongſt them.

Lordſhip

Lordſhip and Mr. JAMES GRENVILLE. They imagined from several circumſtances, that their brother had ſupplanted them in his Lordſhip's favour and confidence. To diſſolve all great connexions had been Lord BUTE's favourite maxim, from the moment of his acceſſion to power. Nothing, therefore, could be more favourable to his project than this family diviſion. He reſolved to ſeize the opportunity which this circumſtance ſeemed to offer. Accordingly, a few days after the meeting of Parliament, when Mr. PITT had given the deciſion for the repeal of the Stamp Act (by the preceding ſpeech) which Mr. GRENVILLE had oppoſed, he ſolicited an interview with Lord TEMPLE and Mr. GRENVILLE, for the purpoſe of forming a new Adminiſtration. His firſt application was to Lord EGLINTOUN, between whom and Lord TEMPLE, there ſubſiſted a very warm friendſhip. Lord EGLINTOUN opened his commiſſion to Lord TEMPLE at Lord COVENTRY's, where they dined on the firſt Sunday after the meeting of Parliament. The converſation began upon the affairs of America, in which the three Lords agreed in opinion, that a repeal of the Stamp Act would be a ſurrender of the authority of the Britiſh legiſlature over the Colonies. Lord EGLINTOUN finding that Lord TEMPLE was of their opinion, ſaid to his Lordſhip, " Let us talk no more upon that ſubject here, but let us go to your brother—Has your Lordſhip received no meſſage from him ?" Lord TEMPLE ſaid he had not: and in a few minutes after they went to Mr. GRENVILLE's. This matter had been more explicitly opened to Mr. GRENVILLE, by Mr. CADOGAN, now *Lord Cadogan*, and Mr. GRENVILLE had requeſted Lord SUFFOLK to acquaint the Duke of BEDFORD with it. Upon ſeeing his brother, he inſtantly told him, without being aſked a queſtion, that

Meeting at Lord Eglintoun's.

CHAPTER XXX.
1766.

an opening had been made to him of an accommodation with Lord BUTE, and that he wanted to confult his Lordfhip upon making the Duke of BEDFORD a party to the affair." Lord TEMPLE replied, " that he might do as he pleafed; but, that he, himfelf, would have no concern in the matter."

Another channel to Lord TEMPLE was then purfued. This was by Mr. W. G. HAMILTON, who was in the moft confidential intimacy with his Lordfhip, and who from the time of the feparation of Mr. JAMES GRENVILLE, was intended to be his Chancellor of the Exchequer, if ever he accepted of the Treafury. But Mr. HAMILTON knowing his Lordfhip's temper and refolution, with refpect to Lord BUTE, did not warmly recommend the propofition.

Next day (Monday) Lord EGLINTOUN went to Mr. GRENVILLE'S, to defire him to meet Lord BUTE at his houfe; but Mr. GRENVILLE was gone to the Houfe of Commons; upon which Lord EGLINTOUN went there to him; but meeting with Mr. STUART MACKENZIE, he incautioufly told him of the intended meeting, and that Gentleman immediately informed Lord HOLLAND, who feeing Lord BUTE a few moments after, told his Lordfhip, " That he was going to do a very foolifh thing; but as he had gone fo far he muft not ftop; but give them the meeting, hear what they had to propofe, and then leave them."

Lord TEMPLE called upon his brother, juft as he had returned from the Houfe of Commons. In a minute or two afterwards, Lord EGLINTOUN came in; and being rejoiced to fee his Lordfhip, begged he would ftay there ten minutes, while he he went home. Lord TEMPLE said he could not stop so long; that he was going to the House of Lords upon particular business, and it was growing late. Lord EGLINTOUN then desired he would stay only five minutes. This was refused: Lastly, he requested only three minutes; and this was refused also. But in the expostulation it came out, that it was to meet Lord BUTE, whom Lord EGLINTOUN supposed was, by this time, waiting at his own house, and he wished to fetch him. At length, pressing the matter very earnestly, Lord TEMPLE answered, *By G-d I will not*—that was his expression, and immediately stepped into his carriage.

CHAPTER XXX.
1766.

The Duke of BEDFORD and Mr. GRENVILLE met Lord BUTE at Lord EGLINTOUN's. The conference was very short. Lord BUTE followed Lord HOLLAND's advice—he heard them---and then left them. He afterwards said to Lord EGLINTOUN, that he did not meet the person he wanted to meet (Lord TEMPLE), but the person he did not want to meet (the Duke of BEDFORD). Some time afterwards, Mr. PITT mentioned this meeting in the House of Commons. Mr. GRENVILLE did not deny it; but said, " That the single proposition made, or point spoken of, was relative to the best means of preventing the intended repeal of the Stamp Act. No other subject was mentioned."

Notwithstanding the ill success of this project, Lord BUTE found means through one of the Princess's confidantes, to amuse Lord TEMPLE with assurances, that a *Carte-blanche* would, in a very little time, be offered to him: and this manœuvre was managed so well, he was completely duped by it. He believed the assurances for some time. The design was to engage him

Amuses Lord Bute.

warmly

CHAPTER XXX.
1766.

warmly in the oppofition to the repeal of the Stamp Act; and he fell into the fnare. Having implicitly adopted the American politics of his brother, the American politics of the Court became an eafy, and almoft a natural gradation.

During the progrefs, of the bill for the repeal of the Stamp Act, it was ftrongly infinuated in Parliament, that the bill was very far from being agreeable to the King; upon which Lord ROCKINHAM afferted, that his Majefty's approbation of the the meafure was clear and unequivocal. Next day, Lord STRANGE maintained the contrary—that his Majefty highly difapproved of the bill. Lord ROCKINGHAM was greatly furprifed by this explicit declaration from Lord STRANGE; and at his next audience of the King, he requefted the honour of his Majefty's opinion in writing; which the King refufed to give. This circumftance was an indifputable proof, that notwithftanding the late negotiation had not fucceeded, yet his Majefty ftill withheld his confidence from his prefent fervants. Another change of Minifters was doubtlefs in contemplation; although no frefh applications for that purpofe were yet made.

Lord Strange's affertion.

Lord Rockingham's requeft.

However unfortunate thefe Minifters might be in the clofet, yet they rendered great and important fervices to the country. Their proceedings and conduct are well known; they are to be found in the public accounts of the time: but there is one meafure of that Adminiftration, which has been very imperfectly ftated. It is concerning Dunkirk.

Dunkirk.

This point of frequent and anxious difcuffion, feems to have been miftaken by the Britifh Minifters, prior and fubfequent to Lord ROCKINGHAM. From the peace of Utrecht, in the year 1713

1713, to the month of September 1765, all our demands concerning the demolition of Dunkirk, have originated in a wrong principle. We have infifted upon levelling the ramparts, upon filling up the cunette, &c. Thefe were immaterial points, to which the French Court confented, after fome affected hefitation. The fortifications on the land fide are of no confequence to England. It was the harbour alone, that ought to have engaged our attention. Lord ROCKINGHAM faw this miftake; in his Adminiftration only, was the demolition of the harbour ferioufly attempted: and had he remained a little longer in office, it muft have been accomplifhed. His demands were directed to the jettees, which protect the channel to the harbour, and without which, the harbour becomes totally unferviceable. Thefe jettees are two piers, which project about three quarters of a mile from the harbour, into the fea; and are about twelve feet high, from low-water mark: between them is the channel into the harbour. His Lordfhip ordered a breach to be made in the Eaftern jettee, near the middle, fufficient to admit the fea. All Dunkirk was inftantly filled with alarm. They faw the ruin of the harbour was inevitable. A few tides made the fact clear. The fand was driven through the breach with fuch aftonifhing velocity, it was fully manifeft, the channel muft be entirely choaked in a few days more. Had this breach been made larger, which was intended; and another made lower down, towards the fea, which was alfo intended; the harbour muft have been fo effectually rendered ufelefs, that nothing larger than a row-boat, or a pilot, could have got into it. The French immediately faw the effect of this fmall breach, and inftantly put a ftop to the progrefs of the workmen. The reader is to obferve,

CHAPTER XXX.

1766.

observe, that in all the stipulations our Court has made with France, respecting Dunkirk, a kind of childish delusion has constantly been admitted---this was---the French were to employ their own people to execute our demands, and we were to send our surveyors to examine and report the state of their operation. Our surveyors had no controul over the the workmen: and if the French Governor at any time, chose to put a stop to their labour, we could not oblige them to resume their work. The surveyors might return to England, and upon their report, the British Ambassador at Paris was usually instructed to remonstrate; which commonly produced an evasive answer. The surveyors have been sent back, and the same farce has been played over again. In this manner have the negotiations concerning Dunkirk, been continued, dropped, and revived, from the year 1713. As a proof, that Lord ROCKINGHAM was right in this matter, we need only observe, the conduct of the French, in this particular, since the treaty of 1782, by which we surrendered all claim and concern whatever respecting Dunkirk. Instead of repairing the fortifications, on the demolition of which, we formerly so strenuously insisted, or opening the cunette, or paying any regard whatever to the land side, their whole attention has been directed to *widening, deepening, and enlarging the harbour*. They have made it CAPACIOUS, SAFE, and CONVENIENT. Those who think Dunkirk a place of no danger to the commerce of London, may find their mistake in a future day.

During this Administration, Mr. WILKES returned from France to London; and there was some communication between the Ministers and him. The following is Mr. HUMPHRY COTES's account of this affair; transcribed *verbatim* from his own manuscript.

" Monday

"Monday the 12th of May 1766, Mr. WILKES arrived in town from France, with Mr. MACLEANE (formerly in partnership with Mr. STEWART, in a druggist's store at Philadelphia). He was very intimate with Mr. BURKE, through whose interest he was made Governor of the island of St. Martin. Mr. WILKES had a lodging at Mr. STEWART's, in Holles-street, Cavendish-square. Mr. COTES did not know of his coming, till he saw the account of his arrival in the Evening Post of Tuesday, at his house at Byfleet. He immediately came to town, when he found a note from Mr. WILKES, desiring to see him. He went immediately; when Mr. WILKES acquainted him, that he was come to demand a performance of the repeated promises of the Ministers; which he had in writing, viz. to give him a general pardon, five thousand pounds in cash, in lieu of what he might receive from a fine from Lord HALIFAX, and fifteen hundred pounds *per annum*, for thirty years, upon Ireland. He said he had seen several people from the Ministers, and had great reason to hope for success. He said, the people he had conversed with from the Ministers, expressed great wrath against Lord TEMPLE, for his strong opposition to their measures; that he had told them, he had very many and singular obligations to Lord TEMPLE; and if that was not the case, he had so great a regard for Lord TEMPLE's public and private virtues, that nothing under Heaven, should induce him to do any thing, that would give that noble Lord a moment's uneasiness. He desired me to communicate this to Lord TEMPLE, and to assure him of his best respects; and that he would have paid his respects in person, but as he was in an interesting negotiation with the present Ministers, he hoped his Lordship would excuse him. I went immediately to Lord TEMPLE's bed side, and related

CHAPTER XXX.
1765.

the above to him. He seemed extremely well satisfied with Mr. WILKES's conduct, and wished most heartily, that the Ministers might be as good as their promises. He desired me to convey his kind compliments to Mr. WILKES, and to assure him of his friendship, and approbation of his conduct upon the present occasion: at the same time he told me, that he was very certain that Lord ROCKINGHAM had not the least intention of serving Mr. WILKES, and feared they would deceive him.

" I saw Mr. WILKES next morning, and found Mr. S. LUTTRELL* with him. I thought that a good omen for Mr. WILKES, as I knew LUTTRELL to be a friend of Lord BUTE; and I knew, without that dictator's consent or approbation, nothing would be done for my poor friend. However, I found afterwards, that LUTTRELL only came upon private business. Mr. WILKES was extremely well satisfied with Lord TEMPLE's answer to him, but seemed to think he should succeed with the Ministers. He continued in the same sentiments all that week; though I often told him, from the best and most authentic information, that I heard they never had spoke to the King about him, nor dared they do it. I went out of town, as usual on Saturday, and returned on Monday; when I found my friend much lowered in his expectations; but said he should see Mr. FITZHERBERT next day, and hoped things would go better. The next day he told me, he had got into a *damn'd scrape*, and believed he had been deceived, and that my information was true, viz. that the Ministers did not intend doing any thing for him: he said Mr. FITZHERBERT had asked him, in the name of Lord ROCKINGHAM, for a *carte blanche*, to leave it to his Lordship to do as he thought proper. To which Mr. WILKES

* Afterwards Lord CARHAMPTON.

answered,

answered, that he knew Mr. FITZHERBERT to be a man of honour, and if the business was to pass between them, he should have no sort of objection; but wished Mr. FITZHERBERT to recollect, that he himself had told him the day before, that Lord ROCKINGHAM had broke his word with him ten times, and then wished Mr. FITZHERBERT to declare, whether he would trust him?

"The next day (Wednesday), he seemed to have some more pleasing hopes, having seen Mr. ROSE FULLER*, Mr. G. ONSLOW, the late Speaker's son, and Sir W. BAKER. He then told me, that they had said the King was possessed with a notion, that the Ministers had sent for him, on purpose to embarrass his affairs and that it would take time to disabuse the royal ear. I immediately made enquiry after the truth of this assertion, and found it totally void of truth, and that the name of WILKES had never reached the royal ear, by any of his Ministers. Of this I informed him.

"I found this day (Friday) that they had pressed him much to go back to France, but that he had absolutely refused them; and desired, I would get him a private lodging in Surrey, near the Thames, to facilitate his escape in case of necessity. I went next day to Mr. JOHNATHAN TYERS, who very genteely offered his house at Dorking, but that was thought to be too far off. I went to Byfleet on Saturday, and left him to go on Sunday and see a house Mr. TYERS had provided for him. I offered him

---

* It is an interesting anecdote of this Gentleman, that he was violent in Opposition to several Ministers; particularly on all questions concerning British liberty, and American policy; and that when he died, in the year 1777, it was discovered, he had received a pension from the Court for many years. His warmth, and apparent zeal, induced every Opposition to admit him into their confidence.

Byfleet,

CHAPTER XXX
1766.

Byfleet, but he objected that it would be too public, and that it would be declaring againſt the preſent Miniſters, as they knew my enmity to them.

"On my return on Tueſday, I found he had given over all hopes of ſuccefs from the Miniſters, and defired I would ſee *Philips* (his Solicitor), and Meſſrs. GLYNN and DUNNING, to conſult what was proper to be done, previous to his ſurrender on the Friday following, (the firſt day of Term) as he was firmly reſolved to ſtand all chances; and ſaid he had told Meſſ. BURKE and FITZHERBERT, that he had taken that reſolution, and that if they wanted to ſee a ſteadier man than him, they muſt go to Corſica to find one.

"I appointed *Philips* to meet at Mr. WILKES's next day in the evening, and we went to Serjeant GLYNN's houſe in Bloomſbury-ſquare, who was ſo obliging to accompany us to Mr. WILKES, and ſtayed there the whole evening. Our diſ-courſe ran upon the means to be taken, either to appear per-ſonally, or by Attorney, to reverſe the outlawry; but as the Serjeant had not conſidered of the matter, the conſultation was deferred until next morning, when Mr. DUNNING was to meet.

"I found Sir W. BAKER and Mr. FITZHERBERT at Mr. WILKES's door next morning, going into Sir WILLIAM's cha-riot; who ſaid to me, "That he was going upon an embaſſy for my friend within doors." I found Meſſrs. GLYNN and DUN-NING in the dining room with Mr. WILKES and *Philips*, and a good deal of diſcourſe upon the proceedings, upon writs of error, &c. paſſed; but Mr. WILKES was deſirous to ſuſpend any reſolution being taken, until the return of Sir W. BAKER and Mr.

Mr. FITZHERBERT, which happened in about two hours; when after a long converſation with them, and Lord ROCKINGHAM'S Secretary, Mr. BURKE, who came with them, Mr. WILKES came up ſtairs and told us, that as he could not reverſe his outlawry, either, by error, or appearance, until November Term, and as he did not chuſe to ſurrender and lie in priſon all that time, he had determined to go abroad again. He told me, that they had not given him any money, nor would Lord ROCKINGHAM make him any promiſe, and that he had been forced to borrow one hundred pounds of Mr. FITZHERBERT, as a private friend. He had received one hundred and thirty pounds before, from the ſubſcription of one thouſand pounds *per annum*, promiſed by the Miniſtry, of Mr. FITZHERBERT: which made the whole received of this boaſted affair, fix hundred and thirty pounds for the year 1765. Mr. WILKES ſaid he would certainly come in November, and take his chance.

"Sir W. BAKER aſked Lord ROCKINGHAM what he intended doing for Mr. WILKES? Lord ROCKINGHAM anſwered, Mr. WILKES muſt truſt to his honour. Sir W. BAKER ſaid he would certainly have no objection to do that, but thought that ſomething ſhould be mentioned of his intentions; that if his Lordſhip would give his honour to intercede with the King for his pardon, or do any thing elſe in his power for his ſervice, he would acquaint Mr. WILKES, who would be ſatisfied with reſpect to time, &c. But as to truſting to his Lordſhip's honour at large, he ſhould conſtrue that as a neglect of Mr. WILKES; and ſhould acquaint him, that he had nothing to expect from his Lordſhip; and that he ſhould look upon this, as a ſlight of himſelf. And deſired that Mr. BURKE might go with him to Mr. WILKES, to whom he delivered the above meſſage."

When

CHAPTER XXX.
1766.

Propofition for the Government of Canada.

Difapproved by the Chancellor.

Who advifes the King to fend for Mr. Pitt.

When the peace of the American Colonies had been fettled, the Miniftry took into confideration the State of Canada; for which great province the late Minifters had provided no Conftitution. This defect they conceived it neceffary to fupply. And for this purpofe, they drew the outlines of a plan of Government, preparatory to a bill. This plan, or principal features of one, was fubmitted to the Chancellor (Lord NORTHINGTON), who fo far from approving of it, or offering to correct it, condemned the whole meafure, in the moft violent terms of indignation and intemperance. It is to be obferved, that the Chancellor had never been cordially their friend; and he feemed eagerly to feize this opportunity of expreffing his diflike. His manners were not of the moft gentle kind, nor was his language very polifhed, whenever he indulged in his natural difpofition of reproach; harfh and bitter, vulgar and brutal, were epithets frequently applied to him. And, perhaps, upon no event in his life, they were more juftly merited than the prefent. He went to the King, and complained to his Majefty of the unfitnefs of his fervants: he told the King, in terms of the utmoft plainnefs, that the prefent Minifters could not go on, and that his Majefty muft fend for Mr. PITT.

It is eafy to conceive, that this advice was agreeably received. In confequence of it, his Majefty commiffioned the Chancellor to confer with Mr. PITT, on the fubject of a new arrangement.

CHAP.

CHAP. XXXI.

Lord Northington opens his Negotiation with Mr. Pitt—Duke of Grafton refigns—Several Perfons refufe Places—An eighteen days Journal—Mr. Pitt fees the King—Lord Temple fent for, and goes to the King—Conference between Mr. Pitt and Lord Temple at Hampftead—They differ and feparate—Lord Temple has an audience of the King—Returns to Stowe—Mr. Pitt created Earl of Chatham—His extraordinary Grants—Mr. Townfhend Manager of the Houfe of Commons—Several Perfons refufe Places---Lord Rockingham refufes to fee Lord Chatham---Mr. Stuart Mackenzie reftored---Lord Chatham not united with Lord Bute.

LORD NORTHINGTON opened his negotiation with Mr. PITT, through the channels of the Duke of GRAFTON and Mr. CALCRAFT. Mr. PITT was at that time at his new eftate in Somerfetfhire; from which place he was fent for. He arrived in London on the eleventh of July; and the fame evening he had a conference with Lord NORTHINGTON.

The Duke of GRAFTON had lately refigned his office of Secretary of State, and attached himfelf to Mr. PITT: this attachment he had publicly avowed in the Houfe of Lords*.

---

* His Grace faid in the Houfe of Lords, "That he had no objection to the perfons, or to the meafures of the Minifters he had recently left; but that he thought they wanted ftrength and efficiency to carry on proper meafures with fuccefs; and that he knew but one man who could give them that ftrength and folidity *(meaning Mr. Pitt)*; that under him, he fhould be willing to ferve in any capacity, not only as a General Officer, but as a Pioneer, and would take up a Spade and a Mattock."

[314]

CHAPTER XXXI.
1766.

When it was indisputably clear, that Lord ROCKINGHAM's Administration was not honoured by the countenance and support of Mr. PITT, not only the Duke of GRAFTON, but several other persons* refused to contribute their assistance; from an apprehension, that a new Administration would in a short time be appointed; of which, each man flattered himself with becoming a part, under the idea of forming a more comprehensive system. Nobody doubted the honour and integrity of Lord ROCKINGHAM: it was even admitted, that his Administration had been regulated, and conducted on the purest principles of Patriotism; yet there was not virtue enough in the country to support him.

Several persons refuse.

Those who assert, that Lord BUTE was not consulted, nor gave any advice upon this occasion, must forget all the preceding facts, since the death of GEORGE the SECOND; and must deny his nocturnal visits, at this time to the King's mother at Carlton House†. Lord NORTHINGTON did not indeed, begin his

Eighteen days Journal.

---

* Lord SHELBURNE refused the Board of Trade, and Col. BARRÉ Vice Treasurer of Ireland.
  His Lordship refused also the Embassy to Paris.
  Lord NORTH refused the Exchequer, also Vice Treasurer of Ireland.
  Lord TOWNSHEND refused to go to Paris or Madrid.
  Lord EGMONT refused the Seals resigned by the Duke of GRAFTON.
  Lord HARDWICKE refused them likewise.
  Lord LYTTELTON refused a Cabinet situation.

† *An eighteen Days faithful Journal, ending a few Days previous to the Ministry's kissing hands in* 1766.

Tuesday, June 24, 1766. From Audley-street, the Favourite set out about one o'clock, in a post-coach and four, for Lord LICHFIELD's at Hampton Court, and came home again at ten at night; went out directly after in a chair to

Miss

his negotiation with Mr. PITT, under the immediate and per- CHAPTER XXXI. fonal directions of Lord BUTE, but Lord BUTE's influence pervaded through a higher channel.

1766.

Lord

Miſs VANSITTART's, maid of honour to the P. D. of W. in Sackville-ſtreet; ſtaid there but a very little while, and then went to Carlton Houſe, and returned home about twelve o'clock.

Wedneſday 25. From Audley-ſtreet, the Favourite ſet out in a chair, at half paſt ſix in the evening, went into Sackville-ſtreet, as before, ſtaid there till paſt ten, then went to Carlton Houſe, and returned home about twelve.

Thurſday 26. From ditto, the Favourite ſet out at half paſt ſix in the evening in a chair, went into Sackville-ſtreet as before, ſtaid there till ten, then went to Carlton Houſe, and came home at twelve.

Friday 27. At ſeven this morning the Favourite ſet out from Audley-ſtreet, for his ſeat in Bedfordſhire.

Sunday 29. The Earl returned from Bedfordſhire this day to dinner; ſet out as before at a quarter paſt ſix for Sackville-ſtreet, ſtaid there till about ten, then went to Carlton Houſe, and came home at twelve.

Monday 30. From Audley-ſtreet, the Favourite ſet out in a chair a quarter paſt ſix, went into Sackville-ſtreet, ſtaid there till about ten, then went to Carlton Houſe, and came home as uſual at twelve.

Tueſday, July 1. From ditto, at half paſt ſix in a chair to Sackville-ſtreet, ſtaid there till ten, then to Carlton Houſe, and thence home at twelve.

Wedneſday 2. From ditto, ditto, ditto, and ditto.

Thurſday 3. At ſix this morning the Favourite ſet out from Audley-ſtreet for his ſeat in Bedfordſhire.

Saturday 5. The Favourite returned to Audley-ſtreet from ditto this day to dinner; at half paſt ſix went to Sackville-ſtreet, ſtaid there as uſual till about ten, then to Carlton-houſe, and afterwards came home about twelve.

Sunday 6. At half paſt ſix to Sackville-ſtreet as uſual, about ten to Carlton Houſe, and home at twelve as before.

Monday 7. At three quarters paſt ſix to Sackville-ſtreet as uſual, about ten to Carlton Houſe, and home at twelve.

Tueſday 8. At half paſt ſix to Sackville-ſtreet, about ten to Carlton Houſe, and home at twelve.

Wedneſday 9. At half paſt ſix to Sackville-ſtreet, about ten to Carlton Houſe, and home at twelve.

Thurſday

CHAPTER XXXI.
1766.

Mr. Pitt fees the King.

Lord NORTHINGTON offered Mr. PITT a *Carte Blanche*. Although Mr. PITT did not dispute his Lordship's authority or veracity, in making this offer, yet he wished to have it confirmed by the King. Mr. PITT was introduced to the King at Richmond. The conference was very short. His Majesty confirmed the offer made by his Chancellor; and added, that he had no terms to propose—He put himself into his *(Mr. Pitt's)* hands. This was on Saturday the 12th of July*, In the evening Mr. PITT had another conference with the Chancellor, and afterwards with General CONWAY, with whom he settled the principal arrangements. Next day (Sunday) the Chancellor, by his Majesty's command, sent for Lord TEMPLE, who was at Stowe, in Buckinghamshire. His Lordship came to town on the fourteenth. Next day he waited on the King at Richmond, before he saw Mr. PITT. The King acquainted his Lordship with the offer that had been made to Mr. PITT; and added, that he expected his Lordship would assist Mr. PITT in forming the arrangements. Next day, which was the 16th,

Lord Temple sent for.

Thursday 10. This morning at seven the Favourite and his lady set out from Audley-street for Bedfordshire.

Saturday 12. Returned this day from Bedfordshire to dinner; and, being Lord MOUNT STUART's birth-day, he went out at *eight* this evening to Sackville-street, staid there till past ten, then went to Carlton House, and returned home about twelve.

Sunday 13. At half past six to Sackville-street, staid there till past ten, then to Carlton House, and home at twelve.

Monday 14. At half past six to Sackville-street, staid there till ten, then to Carlton House, staid there till past twelve, and then home.

N. B. The curtains of the chair, from Audley to Sackville-street, were constantly drawn, and the chair taken into the house.

* *Vide* the dates, of the last three days, of the preceding eighteen days journal.

" his

"✝ his Lordship received a very affectionate letter from Mr. Pitt, then at North End, Hampstead, desiring to see his Lordship there, as his health would not permit him to come to town. His Lordship went; and Mr. Pitt acquainted him, that his Majesty had been graciously pleased to send for him, to form an Administration; and as he thought his Lordship "*indispensable*," he desired his Majesty to send for him, and put him at the head of the Treasury; and that he himself would take the post of Privy Seal. The Commoner then produced a list of several persons, which he said *he* had fixed upon to go in with his Lordship; and which, he added, was not to be altered. Lord TEMPLE said, that he had had the honour of a conference with his Majesty at Richmond the evening before, and that he did not understand, from what passed between them, that Mr. PITT was to be *absolute Master*, and to form *every part* of the Administration; if he had, he would not have given himself the trouble of coming to Mr. PITT upon that subject, being determined to come in upon an *equality* with Mr. PITT, in case he was to occupy the most responsible place under Government. And as Mr. PITT had chosen only a *side-place*, without any responsibility annexed to it, he should insist upon some of his friends being in the Cabinet offices with him, and in whom he could confide; which he

CHAPTER XXXI.

1766.

Conference between Mr. Pitt and Lord Temple at Hampstead.

✝ This account of the Conference between Mr. PITT and Lord TEMPLE at Hampstead, and the subsequent audience of the King, are taken from a pamphlet called *An Enquiry*, &c. Lord CHESTERFIELD, in his letters to his son says, this pamphlet was written by Lord TEMPLE. But his Lordship was mistaken. The pamphlet was written by Mr. HUMPHRY COTES, assisted by another person. It is, however true, that the particular facts, stated in this account of the conference and of the audience, were communicated by Lord TEMPLE, in conversation, to Mr. COTES; who, without Lord TEMPLE's participation, caused them to be published.

thought

thought Mr. PITT could have no objection to, as he muſt be ſenſible he could not come in with honour, unleſs he had ſuch nomination; nor did he deſire, but that Mr. PITT ſhould have his ſhare of the nomination of *his* friends. And his Lordſhip added, that he made a *ſacrifice* of his brother Mr. G. GRENVILLE, who notwithſtanding his being entirely out of place, and excluded from all connection with the intended ſyſtem, would nevertheleſs, give *him* (Lord TEMPLE) all the aſſiſtance and ſupport in his power: that it was his idea to conciliate all parties, which was the ground that had made Mr. PITT's former Adminiſtration ſo reſpectable and glorious, and to form upon the ſolid baſis of *Union,* an able and reſponſible Adminiſtration; to brace the relaxed ſinews of Government, retrieve the honour of the Crown, and purſue the permanent intereſt of the public: but that if Mr. PITT inſiſted upon a ſuperior dictation, and did not chuſe to join in a plan deſigned for the reſtoration of that *Union,* which at no time was ever ſo neceſſary, he deſired the conference might be broke off, and that Mr. PITT would give himſelf no further trouble about him, for that he would not ſubmit to the propoſed conditions.

" Mr. PITT, however, inſiſted upon continuing the conference; and aſked, who thoſe perſons were whom his Lordſhip intended for ſome of the Cabinet employments? His Lordſhip anſwered, that one in particular, was a noble Lord of approved character, and known abilities, who had laſt year refuſed the very office now offered to him (Lord TEMPLE) though preſſed to it in the ſtrongeſt manner, by the Duke of CUMBERLAND, and the Duke of NEWCASTLE; and who being their common friend, he did not doubt Mr. PITT himſelf had in contemplation.

tion. This worthy and respectable person was Lord LYTTEL-
TON. At the conclusion of this sentence,'Mr. PITT said, Good
God! how can you compare him to the Duke of GRAFTON,
Lord SHELBURNE, and Mr. CONWAY? Besides, continued he,
I have taken the Privy Seal, and he cannot have that. Lord
TEMPLE then mentioned the post of Lord President: upon
which Mr. PITT said, that could not be, for he had engaged the
Presidency: but, says he, Lord LYTTELTON *may have a pension.*
To which Lord TEMPLE immediately answered, that would
never do; nor would he stain the bud of his Administration
with an accumulation of pensions. It is true, Mr. PITT
vouchsafed to permit the noble Lord to nominate his own Board;
but at the same time insisted, that if two persons of that Board,
(T. TOWNSHEND, and G. ONSLOW, Esqrs.) were turned out,
they should have a compensation, i. e. *Pensions.*

" Mr. PITT next asked, what person his Lordship had in his
thoughts for Secretary of State? His Lordship answered, Lord
GOWER, a man of great abilities, and whom he knew to be
equal to any Mr. PITT had named, and of much greater alliance; and in whom he meant and hoped to unite and conciliate a great and powerful party, in order to widen and strengthen
the bottom of his Administration, and to vacate even the idea
of Opposition; thereby to restore unanimity in Parliament, and
confine every good man's attention to the real objects of his
country's welfare. And his Lordship added, that he had never
imparted his design to Lord GOWER, nor did he know whether
that noble Lord would accept of it*, but mentioned it now,

* Lord TEMPLE afterwards wrote to Lord GOWER, to excuse the mention
he had made of his name.

only as a comprehenſive meaſure, to attain the great end he wiſhed, of reſtoring unanimity by a reconciliation of parties, that the buſineſs of the nation might go on without interruption, and become the only buſineſs of Parliament. But Mr. PITT rejected this propoſal, evidently *healing* as it appeared, by ſaying, that he had determined Mr. CONWAY ſhould ſtay in his preſent office, and that he had Lord SHELBURNE to propoſe for the other office, then held by the Duke of RICHMOND; ſo that there remained no room for Lord GOWER. This Lord TEMPLE ſaid, was coming to his firſt propoſition of being ſole and abſolute dictator, to which no conſideration ſhould ever induce him to ſubmit. And therefore he inſiſted upon ending the conference; which he did with ſaying, That if he had been firſt called upon by the King, he ſhould have conſulted Mr. PITT's honour, with regard to the arrangements of Miniſters, and have given him an equal ſhare in the nomination; and that he thought himſelf ill-treated by Mr. PITT, in his not obſerving the like conduct."

Here the conference ended.

Next day Lord TEMPLE had an audience of the King in the cloſet; when his Lordſhip told his Majeſty, in ſubſtance, " That Mr. PITT's terms were of ſuch a nature, he could not poſſibly accept of them conſiſtently with his honour: that he had made a ſacrifice of his brother to Mr. PITT's reſentment, in order to accommodate with him; but that Gentleman inſiſted upon bringing in a ſet of men, ſome of whom were perſonal enemies to his Lordſhip, and with whom he had differed upon the moſt eſſential points of Government; and would not permit him to name one friend for the Cabinet, in whom he had

had an entire confidence: and had assumed a power to himself, to which his Lordship never could submit; for if he did, the world would say, with great justice, that he went in like a child, to go out like a fool. That his wish was, to retrieve the honour of the Nation by an Administration formed upon a broad bottom, and composed of men of the best abilities, without respect to party, which his first and principal view was to extinguish and annihilate, as much as possible, in order that the whole attention of Parliament might be confined to the great objects of national concern. That he had never been a suitor to his Majesty, either for himself or his friends, for any place of honour or emolument; he did not even seek the present offer; yet he was extremely willing to sacrifice his own peace and leisure, to the service of his Majesty and the country, provided he could do it with honour; but that, he added, was in his own disposal, and he would not make a compliment of it to any man.

CHAPTER XXXI.
1766.

"In the evening (of the same day) the noble Lord told Lord NORTHINGTON, that the farce was at an end, and the masque was off: His Lordship need not have sent for him from the country, for there was no real wish or intention to have him in the Administration."

Lord TEMPLE returned to Stowe. The natural disposition of this noble Lord, was the most amiable that can be conceived, to his friends. But when offended, his disapprobation was warm and conspicuous—his language flowed spontaneously from his feelings; his heart and his voice always corresponded. With such a temper, it was not probable that the cause of his separation

And returns to Stowe.

CHAPTER XXXI.
1766.

ration from Mr. PITT, would either be concealed, or indifferently expressed.

Mr. Pitt created Earl of Chatham.

Mr. PITT having made choice of the office of Privy Seal for himself, was necessarily created a Peer. This was announced to the Public, in the London Gazette in the following words——
"*St. James's, July* 30. The King has been pleased to grant unto the Right Honourable WILLIAM PITT, and his heirs male, the dignity of a Viscount and Earl of Great Britain, by the name, style and title of Viscount PITT, of Burton-Pynsent, in the county of Somerset, and Earl of Chatham, in Kent."—A List of the persons, to whom his Lordship distributed the offices of State, may be seen at the end of the work*. Although he continued Mr. CONWAY in his post of Secretary of State, yet he

Mr. Townshend has the House of Commons.

gave the management of the House of Commons to Mr. TOWNSHEND ; and Lord GRANBY was put at the head of the

* But the following extraordinay grants are proper to be mentioned here.—Having made Lord NORTHINGTON, President of the Council, it was stipulated, that whenever his Lordship should resign that post, he should receive during his life a pension of 4000l.

Also the reversion of the Hanaper was secured to him for two lives, after the demise of the Duke of CHANDOS ; salary supposed to be per annum 1350l.

The reversion of a Teller of the Exchequer for Lord CAMDEN's son. Salary about per annum 3500l.

A pension to Lord CAMDEN on the Irish Establishment, in case he should lose his post of Lord Chancellor before there is a vacancy in the Exchequer for his son ; per annum 1500l.

A pension to Col. LIGONIER for life, on England ; per annum 1500l.

A surrender of the borough of Orford to Lord HERTFORD ——

Mr. STANLEY appointed Ambassador to Russia, but never went ——

Lord BRISTOL appointed Lord Lieutenant of Ireland, but never went ——

An additional pension to Prince FERDINAND, on the Irish Establishment, per annum 2000l.

Army.

Army. Before Lord CHATHAM had finally settled his arrangements, he made several offers to different persons of great weight and consideration, with a view of strengthening his Ministry, and of detaching them from their friends. But that superiority of mind, which had denied him the usual habits of intercourse with the world, gave an air of austerity to his manners, and precluded the policy of a convenient condescension to the minutiæ of politeness, and fascinating powers of address. He made an offer of Secretary of State to Lord GOWER, whom he had refused, when proposed for that office by his brother. He made offers to the Duke of PORTLAND, Mr. DOWDESWELL, and several others. But in such terms of hauteur, as seemed to provoke, though unintentionally, the necessity of refusal*. They were all rejected. He then waited upon Lord ROCKINGHAM, at his house in Grosvenor-square; but Lord ROCKINGHAM, who was at home, refused to see him.—These circumstances chagrined him considerably. He now found, for the first time in his life, that splendid talents alone, were not sufficient to support the highest situations; that the Government of a Party and the Government of a Nation, were as distinct in their features as in their principles. He now felt the loss of his brother, Lord TEMPLE, whose gracious affability procured him the esteem of all ranks of people, while the splendor of his own talents commanded their admiration. These two great men united, made a host against the world; but when separated, they became the instruments of two factions;

CHAPTER XXXI.
1766.

Several persons refuse places.

Lord Rockingham refuses to see L. Chatham.

* To one, of the most amiable and gentle manners, an abrupt message was sent, "That he might have an office if he would." To another, "That such an office was still vacant." To a third, "That he must take such an office, or none."

CHAPTER XXXI.
1766.

both of them without intending it, and for some time without perceiving it: Lord CHATHAM of the Court, and Lord TEMPLE of the Opposition.

One of the first acts of Lord CHATHAM's Administration, was the restoration of Mr. STUART MACKENZIE.—He did this in the handsomest manner possible.—When Mr. MACKENZIE was first appointed to the *sinecure* of Privy Seal for Scotland, he was honoured with the royal assurance, that he should enjoy the place for his life. But the Duke of BEDFORD had obliged his Majesty to break his promise in the year 1765, in order to convince the nation, that he [the Duke] was not under the influence of Lord BUTE. Lord CHATHAM thought this removal such a flagrant violation of the royal promise that he made this reparation of the King's private honour one of the first acts of his Ministry, without regarding the unpopularity of the measure. This circumstance indisputably proves, that Lord CHATHAM was not unfavourably disposed to the King's friendships, nor even to his partialities. And if we reflect a moment, upon the great political talents of his Lordship, and the wonderful effects of his return to office in the year 1757, we may safely say, that every public interest, and every private attachment might have been at this period, as harmoniously arranged, and would probably have been honoured with equal success, and supported by similar unanimity, *had he found the same fidelity in the closet*.

Mr. Stuart Mackenzie restored.

The restoration of Mr. S. MACKENZIE, the fact of his own Peerage, and his sudden difference with Lord TEMPLE, gave cause and credit to a suspicion, which all the minions of the Court assiduously encouraged and circulated, that in a very short time

time prevailed throughout the kingdom, of his having *joined* the Earl of BUTE. However strong the appearances were, it is certainly true, that the suspicion was unfounded. What was said of Lord ROCKINGHAM, on a similar pretence of suspicion, might with equal veracity be said of him also----—" That with the Earl of BUTE he had no personal connection, nor correspondence of Council: he neither courted him, nor persecuted him."*

CHAPTER XXXI.
1766.
Lord Chatham is not united with Lord Bute.

* By Mr. BURKE.

CHAP.

CHAP. XXXII.

Embargo on the Exportation of Corn—State of Parties—Conference between Lord Chatham and the Duke of Bedford at Bath—Conference between Lord Chatham and Lord Edgcumbe—Its consequences—The Admiralty offered to Lord Gower—Conduct of the Court—Second Conference with the Duke of Bedford—Breaks off.

<small>CHAPTER XXXII.
1766.
Embargo on the exportation of corn.</small>

THERE never was known in England so wet a summer as that of this year. From the month of March to the month of August, there were not successively two fair days. This uncommon season injured the corn harvest prodigiously. Towards the end of the summer, when the extent of the injury was manifest, Ministers held several Councils upon the subject. At length they issued a proclamation, commanding an embargo to be laid on the exportation of corn. Lord CHATHAM did not attend any of these Councils. To the second Council he sent his opinion in writing, which was in favour of the embargo. When Parliament met, Ministers defended their conduct upon this particular point, by the same arguments, and avowed the same doctrines which had been used in defence of similar arbitrary measures by the STUART's. The Constitution was very ably supported by Lord MANSFIELD, Lord TEMPLE and Lord LYTTELTON. And their arguments were afterwards published in a pamphlet, entitled *A Speech against the suspending and dispensing Prerogative*. Many people ascribed this speech to Lord MANSFIELD.

Mansfield. But they were mistaken. The pamphlet was written under the eye of Lord Temple, by a gentleman at the bar, who was present at the debate, and who was also assisted in the composition by Lord Lyttelton.

CHAPTER XXXII.
1766.

A few days after the proclamations were issued respecting the embargo*, Lord Chatham retired to Bath, for the benefit of his health. During his stay at Bath, the Duke of Bedford came there for the same reason. Lord Chatham solicited an interview with his Grace. His Lordship's view was, to detach the Duke from Mr. Grenville. His own penetration suggested to him the necessity of this attempt; and however inconsistent he might seem, in his offers to accomplish his design; the fact shews, that men of the greatest talents are not always influenced by the strict rules of consistency. Lord Chatham was not unacquainted, that a powerful and violent opposition was forming against him. It was menaced, that this opposition would consist of the late Ministry, whom for distinction's sake, and because the Duke of Newcastle was yet alive, was sometimes called the *Pelham*'s; of the relations of his own family, and their friends, who, though a junior and a minor party, were yet a growing one; and of the *Bedford* interest, which at that time was respectable, firm and compact. The two last interests were united. His design was to separate them; and to strengthen his Administration by an acquisition of the Duke of Bedford. He therefore opened his conference with his Grace, by making the strongest assurances, that he should be particularly happy to see the King's Administration

State of Parties.

Conference between Lord Chatham and the Duke of Bedford.

* They were dated Sept. 26, 1766.

countenanced.

CHAPTER XXXII.
1766.

countenanced and fupported by his Grace's approbation and intereft. The Duke making no reply to this exordium, Lord CHATHAM proceeded by faying, that he would frankly lay before his Grace, the principal meafures he intended to purfue.

Firft. He intended to keep the peace inviolate, and to keep a watchful eye over the Princes on the Continent, that they did the fame.

Secondly. He would enter into no continental connections, nor make any fubfidiary treaty with any European power.

Thirdly. He would obferve fuch a ftrict and rigid œconomy, as fhould command the approbation of the moft frugal Member of Parliament.

The Duke replied, that thefe were the very meafures for which he had always declared and contended. They were *his* meafures, and he would certainly fupport them, whether his friends were in, or out of office.

Not a word was fpoken of America, nor of any arrangements.

They parted in fimilar conceptions, that this interview was only a prelude to another. And this accounts for a great part of the *Bedford intereft* being neuter at the meeting of Parliament.

Lord CHATHAM's next ftep was, an attempt to divide the *Newcaftle intereft*. He began with Mr. SHELLEY, the Duke's near relation. To him, he promifed the Staff of the Treafurer of the Houfhold; which at this time was in the hands of Lord EDGCUMBE. In his expectations of accomplifhing this defign,

he

he was too sanguine. It is true, he procured the dismission of Lord Edgcumbe, and the appointment of Mr. Shelley; but the dismission of Lord Edgcumbe was attended with consequences, which rather weakened, than strengthened his Administration; and so far from dividing, or dismaying his opponents, rather cemented their union, and provoked their resentment.

Chapter XXXII.
1766.

The particulars of this dismission were as follows:

* " About the 20th of November 1766, the minister sent a note to Lord E. acquainting his Lordship, "That a great Per‑ sonage had determined upon making some alterations in his " servants; and that he [the Minister] should be glad to see " Lord E. in Bond-street, or he would wait upon his Lordship " in Upper Grosvenor-street." Lord E. directly waited upon the Minister in Bond-street. The Minister began with highly commending his Lordship's abilities, his virtues, his integrity, and recited the contents of his letter. Then, after many pauses, and inarticulate sounds, he said, " He was very sorry for it, was " extremely concerned it should happen so——but—a—it was " necessary---a---." Here Lord E. stopped him short, and bluntly demanded " if his post was destined for another." The Mini‑ ster, after a little pause, and uttering a few broken sentences, acknowledged that it was, and that it had been so for some time. Lord E. then proceeded to remind him of the measures of the late Opposition; " that he had, four years, steadily and " and uniformly supported those measures; measures which he " [the Minister] had approved and adopted; and which were " now happily effected: that he had never deserted any of the

Conference be‑ tween Lord Chatham and Lord Edgcumbe

* From the Political Register, vol. I. page 275.

Vol. I   U u   " great

CHAPTER XXXII.
1766.

"great queſtions upon the ſubjects of the liberties and intereſts
"of his country; and expreſſed his aſtoniſhment that this treat-
"ment ſhould be the reward of a conduct that had manifeſtly
"the approbation of, and was agreeable to the ſpirit and princi-
"ples of the Miniſter, while in Oppoſition." The force of
theſe truths, and this concluſion, obviouſly made an impreſſion
upon the Miniſter; and he ſaid, "that however unwilling a
"Great Perſonage was to encreaſe the number of his Lords of
"the Bedchamber, yet he [the Miniſter] would nevertheleſs
"venture to place his Lordſhip upon that liſt." Lord E. directly made anſwer, "That however willing he really was to
"hold ſome place, in order that he might continue in office
"with his friends, and ſupport the meaſures of Government, yet,
"after this uſage, he would not take any place, nor reſign that
"which he held, to any but the Great Perſonage himſelf." And
added, "that it was extremely impolitic thus to turn out perſons
"of rank; perſons of great Parliamentary intereſt." The Miniſter burſt out—"Oh!" ſaid he, "if that be the caſe, *let me
"feel myſelf!* I deſpiſe your Parliamentary intereſt! I do not
"want your aſſiſtance!" And added, "that he truſted to the
"uprightneſs of his meaſures, for the ſupport and confidence
"of the K——, and the favour and attachment of the people;
"and acting upon theſe principles," ſaid he, "*I dare look in the
"face the proudeſt connections of this country!*" They parted.

"Two days after, Lord E. received a note ſignifying a Great
Perſon's deſire of his ſtaff. On Monday the 24th of November, 1766, he waited on the Great Perſon, who ſaid, "that he
"was very ſorry to part with his Lordſhip, of whoſe ſervices he
"had

"had a very high opinion, as well as of his Lordship's abilities, and attachment to his person, and especially because his Lordship had no mixture of factious principles in his disposition; But," says he, "My Ministers tell me it must be so;" and added, "that the idea of the bed-chamber was purely his own." Lord E. returned the Great Person his sincere and most humble thanks for the good opinion he was pleased to entertain of him; and expressed the great obligation he was under for it, and the more so," added he, "for not pressing the bed-chamber upon me; all which, more than pay me for the ill usage of your Ministers." The staff was given up, and Mr. SHELLEY appointed Treasurer of the Houshold.

CHAPTER XXXII.
1766.

"Next day the Earl of BESSBOROUGH, who was one of the joint Post-masters, offered to make room for Lord E. by proposing to resign that post in favour of his Lordship, and taking the bed-chamber, which had been offered to that Lord. But this obliging offer was rejected. Upon which the Duke of *Portland*, the Earls of *Besborough* and *Scarborough*; and Lord *Monson*, resigned the next day, which was Wednesday, November the 26th, 1766. And these resignations were immediately followed by those of Sir *Charles Saunders*, Sir *William Meredith*, Admiral *Keppel*, &c."

Its consequences.

In consequence of these resignations, Lord *Chatham* resolved to renew his overtures to the *Bedford interest*. The office of first lord of the Admiralty, which Sir *Charles Saunders* had resigned, he immediately tendered to Lord *Gower*. But that Lord did think proper to accept it (though he did not refuse it) without first consulting the Duke of *Bedford*, who at this time was at Wooburn.

Admiralty offered to Lord Gower.

CHAPTER XXXII.
1766.

Wooburn. And having given this anfwer to Lord *Chatham*, he went on the 28th to Wooburn to confult his Grace. Next day Lord *Chatham* had a long conference in the clofet. He laid open the plan of his intended alliance with the *Bedford intereft*, to fill the vacancies occafioned by the late refignations. But the conduct of the great leader of this intereft, when laft in office, had created fo violent a prejudice againft him, Lord *Chatham* found the execution of his plan to be impracticable in the whole extent that he defigned it; for he intended to have included the Duke himfelf in his new arrangement. But he was entreated to abandon all thoughts of that Nobleman. He was promifed the warmeft, the fulleft, moft fincere, and moft effectual fupport. He yielded to thefe affurances, or, as he faid afterwards, he could not refift them: and feveral vacant offices were filled before Lord *Gower* returned from Wooburn. The names of the perfons appointed, will fufficiently diftinguifhed the intereft which prevailed. Lord *Le Defpencer*, who had been Lord *Bute*'s Chancellor of the Exchequer, was made Poftmafter; Mr. *Jenkinfon*, who had been Lord *Bute*'s *private* Secretary, was made a Lord of the Admiralty. The reft the reader will find in the Lift of Changes at the end of the Work. By this arrangement, Lord *Chatham* feemed to be entirely united to the Court. He certainly trufted to the promifes which had been made, for his fupport; and he gave them full credit, becaufe he believed them to be fincere.

Second conference with the Duke of Bedford.

On the firft of December Lord *Gower* returned from Wooburn, with the Duke of *Bedford*. A few hours after their arrival in London, the Duke waited on Lord *Chatham* in Bond-ftreet. The conference between thefe two noble Peers was very fhort. Lord *Chatham*'s purpofe was to conceal the engagement

he

had made with the Court. The Duke's idea was, that the negotiation begun at Bath, and continued with Lord *Gower*, was still open. His Grace therefore requefted fome of the vacant offices for his friends, and an Englifh Peerage for the Marquis of *Lorne*, now Duke of *Argyll*. He afked nothing for himfelf; but added, that the meafures which had been avowed at Bath, he expected were ftill to be purfued. Lord *Chatham* began with putting a pofitive and unqualified negative on the Peerage of Lord *Lorne*. Then, as to the offices, he faid, there were very few vacant. He had beftowed the Admiralty upon Sir *Edward Hawke*, and given to Mr. *Jenkinfon* and Sir *Piercy Brett* the two vacant feats at that Board, and Lord *Le Defpencer* was deftined for the Poft-office. And as to meafures, he obferved, he had never altered his opinion of the peace, it was the fame that he had declared in Parliament: And with refpect to Pruffia, he was refolved to fupport and maintain the alliance with that monarch. From thefe anfwers the Duke was convinced, that all thoughts of negotiation were at an end, and next morning his Grace returned to Wooburn.

CHAP. XXXIII.

Further Arrangements—Lord Chatham regrets the loss of Lord Temple—Siezed with the Gout at Bath, and at Marlborough—Comes to Hampstead—Another Change meditated—General Conway wishes to resign—Lord Northington wishes to resign—King's Message to Lord Chatham—Duke of Newcastle is very anxious to preserve the Union of the Opposition—Application to Lord Rockingham—Declaration of the Duke of Bedford—Declaration of the Duke of Newcastle---Conference at Newcastle House---Breaks off---Importance of the Minister of the House of Commons---America the true cause---Second Conference at Newcastle House---Anecdotes of Mr. Lownds's Tickets, and of the Judges' Tickets---Lord Rockingham waits on the King---Lord Holland advises the King.

CHAPTER XXXIII.
1766.
Further arrangements.

WITH a view to detach some of the Duke of *Bedford*'s Friends from his Grace's interest, Lord *Chatham*, in ten days after the preceding negotiation was closed, gave the same Peerage to the Marquis of *Lorne*, which he had refused to the request of the Duke: And at the same time Mr. *Nugent*, who was placed at the head of the Board of Trade, was created Lord *Clare*. But the American business, usually managed and transacted at that Board, was transferred to the office of the Southern Secretary of State; and the Board itself was reduced to the state of a board of reference only. As soon as Lord *Chatham* had made this alteration, and a few other lesser arrangements he went into Somersetshire.

Although

Although the vacant offices were filled, yet he was far from being satisfied with the choice he had been obliged to make of several of the individuals, or with the union he had been obliged to accept. And he regretted, more than any other circumstance, the loss of his brother, Lord *Temple*---because he felt that loss more and more every day.---He now felt the loss of a repository of his confidence---the solace of his hours of affliction. Grief, vexation, and disappointment, preyed upon his nerves; which, though in early life, naturally strong, were now become weak by age and infirmity. His Peerage had diminished his popularity. A considerable part of his Ministry, consisted of men, who had been appointed through necessity, not through choice; and this circumstance being notorious to those, whom he had selected in the first instance, inspired them with a spirit of envy and ambition, to become the rivals of his situation and power. He was agitated by contending passions---a mind sometimes vigorous, and often depressed---his body tortured by pain, and imprisoned by infirmity---he fell into a paroxysm of the gout at Bath, which seemed to threaten his extinction. In the month of February 1767, he attempted to return to London, but was unable to proceed further than Marlborough; where he lay until March, and then finished his journey. He retired to a house he had hired at Hampstead; but was in so feeble a state, he could not attend to any public business. He remained at Hampstead some time, having sold his estate at Hayes, in Kent. The air of Hampstead was too sharp for his disorder— that of Hayes he thought suited him better; therefore he wished to re-possess his former habitation; which being made known to Mr. *Walpole*, the purchaser, he very politely gratified his Lordship

CHAPTER XXXIII.
1766.

Lord Chatham regrets the loss of Lord Temple.

Seized with the gout at Bath.
1767.
And at Marlborough.
Comes to Hampstead.

CHAPTER XXXIII.
1767.

Lordship, notwithstanding he had bought the place for his own residence.

During his absence, Mr. *Townshend* in some degree assumed the reins of Government. He supposed Lord *Chatham*'s state of health to be such as would totally, and for ever, preclude his return to public business. He therefore meditated the accomplishment of some alliances, with a view of forming another Administration for the establishment of his own power. In this project he was joined by General *Conway*. They cultivated a favourable understanding with Lord *Rockingham*. Their first object was the removal of the Duke of *Grafton*; but Lord *Chatham* arriving in the vicinity of London, the design was abandoned, and the Duke and Mr. *Townshend* became reconciled.*

Another change meditated.

During Lord *Chatham*'s stay at Hampstead, the King sent frequent messages to him, desiring him not to be concerned at his confinement, or absence from public business; for that he [the King] was resolved to support him.

Gen. Conway wishes to resign.

† "Early in the month of June, General *Conway* declared to several of his friends, that he had resolved to resign his office of Secretary of State; because his situation was of late become very disagreeable to him, not only from having been frequently over-ruled in his opinions respecting measures; but from his being sensible, that he was acting in opposition to his friends, and particularly to those friends, with whom he anxiously

* They had differed upon the affairs of India.

† From the Political Register, (with several corrections and additions) vol. 1, page 201.

wished

wished to be re-united. And he made the same declaration, or something not very unlike it, to the King; but at the same time said he would stay till a succeſſor was appointed. In conſequence of this declaration, he ceaſed to tranſact any buſineſs in his office, and circular letters were ſent to the Ambaſſadors for four weeks together, ſignifying that he was out of employment.

CHAPTER XXXIII.
1767.

Towards the end of June, Lord *Northington* declared to the King his reſolution to reſign, on account of his ill ſtate of health, and real inability to attend the public buſineſs; and adviſed the King to ſend for the Duke of *Bedford*, Lord *Temple*, and Mr. *Grenville*, whom he had before publicly declared *were equal to their offices*.

Lord Northington wiſhes to reſign.

This, though an expected event, bore no relation to the preceding declaration of Mr. *Conway*, nor were the two perſons in the ſmalleſt degree connected.

A few days after the riſing of Parliament, which was on the ſecond day of July, the King wrote a letter with his own hand to Lord *Chatham*, who lay ſick at Hampſtead, acquainting him of his reſolution to make ſome alterations in his ſervants, and deſiring his aſſiſtance or advice. Lord *Chatham* returned a verbal anſwer to this effect, "That ſuch was his ill ſtate of health, that his Majeſty muſt not expect from him any further advice, or aſſiſtance, in any arrangement whatever."

King's meſſage to Lord Chatham.

It being now certain, that application muſt be made to ſome part of the Oppoſition, the Duke *Newcaſtle* who dreaded nothing ſo much as a diviſion of them, and therefore had for ſome time ſtrongly recommended a firm union among them, againſt the ſecret

D. of Newcaſtle anxious to preſerve the union of the Oppoſition.

CHAPTER XXXIII.
1767.

secret defigns of the Favourite; whom, he fufpected would repeat his old trick of dividing them. His Grace converfed with the friends of all the leaders in the Oppofition; and preffed with particular affiduity and extraordinary ardor, the great and indifpenfible neceffity of a faithful and fteady adherence to each other. He fhewed the advantages which muft refult from fuch an union, and exhibited the wretched and ruined fituation into which any part of them muft inevitably fall, if they fuffered themfelves to be feduced from their friends. His Grace took infinite pains to unite the houfes of *Ruffel* and *Wentworth*; left, by the fecret machinations of the Favourite, (againft whofe pernicious influence no Adminiftration had hitherto been able to ftand, the moment he chofe to become their enemy) either of them fhould be over-reached, or drawn in by a principle of miftaken duty; when, in reality, it was a much more effential duty, and a matter of ftrict juftice, to enquire after the author of the public grievances, than to connive at the protection afforded him. With a view to the final accomplifhment of this union, fo extremely interefting to the welfare of the country, the Lords *Gower*, *Weymouth* and Mr. *Rigby*, dined with his Grace at Claremont; and a few days afterwards (July 5, 1767) the Marquis of *Rockingham* and feveral of his friends, dined likewife with his Grace at the fame place.

At this period we will leave the Oppofition, and turn to the proceedings of the Court.

In confequence of the *verbal* anfwer received from Hampftead, the Favourite applied to his former affociate, Lord *Holland*, who had fo materially affifted him in procuring an appro-

bation

bation of the late peace, and other measures. That person sent him his advice on Sunday morning, July the fifth; soon after the receipt of which, the Favourite set out for Richmond; and it was remarkable, and much taken notice of at the time, that the King did not come to town that day. Whatever was the plan then adopted for a new arrangement of Ministers is not exactly known; and if it were, might be more decently guessed than related. Certain it is, that that part of the Opposition supposed to be the least hostile to the Favourite, was immediately applied to. The Duke of *Grafton* wrote a letter, by order of the Court, to the Marquis of *Rockingham*, "requesting his Lordship's return to Court, to assist in the present critical situation of affairs." This naturally brought on an interview between the Duke and the Marquis; when, among other things, his Grace said, " That he was tired of his office, and wished his Lordship might be his successor." Lord *Rockingham* asked, " Whether his Grace said this from his own, or the authority of an higher power." The Duke said, " he could not answer that question." The conference broke off; but two days after was renewed; when Lord *Rockingham* asked, the Duke, " whether he was treating with the King's Minister, or with the Duke of *Grafton*." The Duke answered, " with the King's Minister." Lord *Rockingham* then said, " he would not conclude upon any thing without the advice and participation of his friends."

Accordingly, on Saturday July 11, he set out for Wooburn; where he found Lord *Albemarle*, who had stopped there in his way to Buxton; when the above particulars were laid before his Grace, he said, " that as the Great Personage had made choice

choice of the Marquis of *Rockingham* for his Minister, he should readily acquiesce in that nomination, for the sake of putting an end to parties, and of restoring unanimity, so peculiarly wanting at this time in the management of the public business; but though he renounced all pretensions to any place or emolument for himself, yet he did not mean that his friends should, for that reason, be excluded: on the contrary, he stipulated, that they should be considered in the new arrangement; and upon that condition he chearfully offered his support to the Administration. And added, that if the King had made choice of himself to treat with, he should have expected the same kind of renunciation from his Lordship, regarding himself personally, and his friends should, in like manner, have been taken care of. However, his Grace said, that all this was conditionally only, for that he and Lord *Temple* and Mr. *Grenville* were one, and that he would not proceed without consulting them.—The information given concerning the plan was, that as to measures, particularly American measures, Lord *Rockingham* hoped they might be settled to the joint satisfaction of the Duke of *Bedford*, Lord *Temple*, and Mr. *Grenville*, and as to men, Lord *Rockingham* declared for a wide and comprehensive system.—The answer returned to this communication by Lord *Temple* and Mr. *Grenville* was, that they concurred in the idea of a comprehensive Administration, as the likeliest to be permanent, and that they were ready to support such an Administration, though out of office, (Mr. *Grenville* having before insisted, that his name should not be mentioned for any office, having determined long ago not to be obtruded on the King) provided they adopted such measures as could satisfy them, and particularly the capital measure of asserting and establishing the sovereignty of Great Britain.

over

over America; lastly, that if this were the case, though they did not mean to take places themselves, they would use their best offices with their friends to accept of honourable and becoming situations in Government.

CHAPTER XXXIII.
1767.

It must not be forgot, that the Duke of *Newcastle* said precisely the same. Thus, these four great and respectable persons, of acknowledged ability and great experience, agreed to sacrifice themselves in order to restore tranquility to the public, unanimity to the King's Councils, and to establish an able and permanent Administration, composed of men of talents, judiciously selected from all parties. Lord *Rockingham* impressed with this idea, and following, as he had done, in his conferences with the Duke of *Bedford*, the advice and direction of his friend, Lord *Albemarle*, returned to London, with full powers to treat upon the formation of a new Administration, upon a *broad and comprehensive system*. The Duke of *Grafton* was made acquainted with this, and desired to report it to the King, which he did on the 15th of July. His Majesty took two days to consider of it. On Friday the 17th, an answer was said to be returned to the Duke of *Grafton* to this effect, " That the King adopted and approved of the idea of a *comprehensive system*, and hoped it was not meant to exclude his friends, and those about his person; for the rest, he entirely agreed."

Declation of the Duke of Newcastle.

This answer being given to Lord *Rockingham*, his Lordship sent for the Duke of *Bedford*, who came to London on Sunday evening, the 19th of July.

On Monday, July the 20th, it was agreed that there should be a meeting of the several persons in town, at Newcastle-house

Conference at Newcastle-house.

that

CHAPTER XXXIII.
1767.

that day, and accordingly there came the Dukes of *Bedford, Newcastle, Richmond* and *Portland*; the Marquis of *Rockingham*; the Earl of *Sandwich*; Viscount *Weymouth*; Mr. *Dowdeswell*, Mr. *Rigby*, and Admiral *Keppel*.

Mr. *Rigby* read a letter from Mr. *Grenville*, wherein that gentleman promised his support to the new Administration, out of office, provided the dependance and obedience of the colonies were asserted and maintained. Much altercation instantly arose upon reading this letter. The Marquis of *Rockingham* was warm: the Duke of *Bedford*, remarkably cool and temperate. At length, Lord *Sandwich* said, "that it was needless to debate about that letter, for he was certain they all meant the same thing; that their conduct respecting the colonies, must be regulated by the future behaviour of the colonies, and not by any regard or retrospect to former transactions. If the colonies, added his Lordship, are dutiful and loyal, there will be no occasion to exercise any extraordinary power over them; and if they should be otherwise, he did not doubt but all present, as well as their friends, would join in every proper and necessary measure to enforce obedience. This reasoning being approved of, and all uniting in the same sentiment, Mr. *Dowdeswell* took up the letter, and struck out the two words *asserted* and *maintained*, and put in *supported* and *established*. Here all altercation upon this subject entirely ended, Mr. *Rigby* folded up the letter, and put it into his pocket, and there was not another word uttered concerning it.

They then came to the arrangement of men to the great offices; the subject upon which they had met. The Marquis of *Rockingham* proposed himself for the first Lord of the Treasury;

fury; with the powers ufually annexed to that poſt, and Mr. *Dowdeſwell* for his Chancellor of the Exchequer; to all which the Duke of *Bedford* agreed. The Marquis next propoſed Mr. *Conway* for Secretary of State, and *Miniſter of the Houſe of Commons.* To which the Duke of *Bedford* ſaid, "that he had for two ſeſſions ſeen ſufficient proofs of Mr. *Conway*'s inability in a Civil capacity, ever to agree to that propoſal; that he thought the Military was Mr. *Conway*'s proper line; that he had always entertained a very high opinion of him as a military officer; that he had not the leaſt objection to Mr. *Conway*'s being amply provided for on the military eſtabliſhment; nay, to his being gratified to the utmoſt of his wiſhes."

The Marquis of *Rockingham* ſaid, "that it was a propoſal from which he could not recede;" and other words to the ſame effect. Upon which Mr. *Rigby* ſaid, "that they ſtopt at the threſhold, and that it was needleſs to go any further into the matter."

Here the conference ended.—No other particulars or conditions were even mentioned.

In a corrupt ſyſtem of Government, the *Miniſter of the Houſe of Commons, or Manager*, as he is ſometimes called, is the firſt *efficient** Miniſter in the State. His conſequence cannot be more clearly ſhewn than by the abrupt concluſion of the preceding conference.—After ſo many oppoſite intereſts had been reconciled, and ſo many great ſacrifices had been made, to remove individual jealouſies, and to eſtabliſh public harmony—all theſe were

---

* A diſtinction firſt made uſe of by Lord MANSFIELD—between efficient and official—between confidential and oſtenſible.

but

CHAPTER XXXIII.
1767.

but as a phantom—they all vanished in a moment—when the appointment of this *new Minister* came under discussion. Each party wished to nominate him. They differed, and separated upon that point only—not in a contention for places, but in a contention for *power*. Whoever is the Minister of the House of Commons, has the power of directing the measures of Government. Lord *Rockingham* wanted Mr. *Conway*, because he intended to persevere in his own system, with respect to America. The Duke of *Bedford* intended to have nominated Mr. *Rigby*, because he intended to pursue the Court system, which Mr. *Grenville* had adopted, of taxing America. Ame-

America the true cause.

rica was therefore the true cause of this conference breaking off. Subsequent events have proved, whose policy was right. Had Lord *Rockingham* been Minister, America would still in all probability have belonged to the Crown of Great Britain. Or had this system of appointing a Minister of the House of Commons, been abandoned, that, and other important benefits, would, no doubt, have continued; because the Members would have been left to the free exercise of their own judgment.

It is impossible to dismiss this point without a short apostrophe, on the alarming state of British depravity. If the administration of annual bribes to the Members of the Legislature, independent of the influence of places, public and private, is become so necessary, and the practice so mechanical, as to comprise the *most essential department* of Government—is it not a matter of indelible disgrace on the Nation, and on the Constitution? There is no species of corruption to be found in the antient Governments, that equals it. It is a perfect parricide. The British Empire has been dismembered by it—so fatally true

is

is that maxim of Lord *Burleigh,* " *that England can never be undone but by her Parliament* *.

Notwithstanding the conference ended, in the manner that has been already related, the Earl of *Sandwich* having occasion to make a visit to the Duke of *Newcastle,* his Lordship went next morning (Tuesday, July 21), when the Duke took an opportunity of resuming the subject of the preceding conference: " He earnestly conjured his Lordship to exert his abilities, and employ all his good offices in endeavouring to reconcile the parties who had differed; he urged again, and again, the necessity of their agreeing upon this important occasion: he trembled for the mischiefs and dangers which must arise from a division of their strength and interest; and concluded with repeatedly supplicating, in the strongest terms, that they might be

---

* Of the many FACTS which might be stated, the following may serve for a specimen:

Towards the end of the session, the Secretary of the Treasury, Mr. BRADSHAW, one day accosts Mr. LOWNDES (Member for Bucks) with, *Sir, you have voted with us all the winter; some return is usually expected upon these occasions; and as we are much obliged to you for your constant support, if you chuse to accept of two hundred Lottery Tickets at Ten Pounds each, they are at your service.* Mr. LOWNDES bowed, expressed his great friendship for the Secretary, and accepted of the offer; adding only, That as the session was just upon the close, he should, as soon as it was finished, go into the country upon his private affairs; and begged the tickets might be sent to such a one, his banker; which the Secretary having promised to comply with, they parted. Mr. LOWNDES went to Winslow. The tickets were delivered: none, however, were sent to Mr. LOWNDES's, banker. The reason of which was, they had been distributed among that part of the Common Council, who voted against the Livery having the use of Guildhall. Mr. LOWNDES, hearing nothing of the tickets, wrote to his banker, who returned for answer, that he had not received, nor heard

CHAPTER XXXIII.
1766.
Second conference at Newcastle-house.

be brought together again to his house that evening." Lord *Sandwich*, waited on the Duke of *Bedford*: and the Duke of *Newcastle* went himself to the Marquis of *Rockingham*. Accordingly the following five met at Newcastle-house that evening, viz. the Dukes of *Bedford* and *Newcastle*, the Marquis of *Rockingham*, Mr. *Dowdeswell*, and Mr. *Rigby*. When the Marquis insisting on the proposal he had before made respecting Mr. *Conway*, and declaring that he would not agree to any arrangement in which Mr *Conway* was not included in that capacity, and the Duke of *Bedford* refusing to agree to it, the conference finally broke off.

Lord Rockingham waits on the King.

Next day, Wednesday, the Marquis of *Rockingham* waited on the King at St. James's, and respectfully acquainted his Majesty, that he had met his friends, who had agreed to his proposal

heard of, any tickets. Mr. LOWNDES next wrote to Mr. BRADSHAW, who in his answer " begged a thousand pardons ; that the matter had quite slipped his memory ; that the tickets were all disposed of, except five-and-twenty, which were at his service." Mr. LOWNDES meanly accepted of the twenty-five, and they were sent to his Banker's.—By these tickets he probably cleared about one hundred pounds. Such was his *douceur* for voting one session with the Duke of GRAFTON.

In a late Parliament, the Nabob of ARCOT had nine Members in his interest—Might not any European Prince have twice that number by the same means ?—Do not these facts speak stronger than a thousand arguments, the necessity of a Parliamentary Reform ?

But it is further remarkable, and in the breast of every honest man it must be matter of sincere lamentation, that douceurs have been given to the Judges.—Sir RICHARD ASTON, in particular, was seen selling his tickets in 'Change Alley ; and when the Fact was mentioned to him at the Old Bailey at dinner, he confessed it, and said, he had as good a right to sell his tickets, as Mr. Justice WILLES, or any body else.—Is not this circumstance a full answer to all the encomiums on the independence of the Judges ?

of

of his being firſt Lord of the Treaſury; but that they had differed in providing for Mr. *Conway*, and that in conſequence of that difference, he had no plan of Adminiſtration to lay before him. The King thanked his Lordſhip for the pains he had taken, and the regard he had ſhewn for his ſervice; but added, *that he never knew the Treaſury was intended for his Lordſhip* †.

From the concluſion of this anſwer it is clear, that either the Marquis of *Rohkingham* greatly miſtook the Duke of *Grafton* in the conferences he had with his Grace; or that his Grace was not ſufficiently candid and explicit in his converſations with the Marquis.

The Marquis of *Rockingham* waited on the Duke of *Bedford* (Thurſday July 23), and expreſſed his deſire that no diffe-

† The moment the Marquis of Rockingham came out of the King's cloſet, Lord Holland was immediately introduced to his Majeſty; with whom he continued ſome time.——In Lord Bath's pamphlet *(Seaſonable Hints, edit.* 1761, *p.* 37*)*, of which Mr. Burke ſays, *(Thoughts on Diſcontents, edit.* 1770, *p.* 23*)*, " there firſt appeared the idea of ſeparating the Court from " the Adminiſtration,"—are the following lines:—

" Though the wings of prerogative have been clipt, the influence of the Crown is greater than ever it was in any period of our hiſtory. For when we conſider, in how many boroughs the Goverment has the voters at its command ; when we conſider the extenſive influence of the money corporations, ſubſcription jobbers, and contractors ; the endleſs dependence created by the obligations conferred on the bulk of the gentlemens' families throughout the kingdom, who have relations preferred, in our navy, and numerous ſtanding army : when, I ſay, we conſider how wide, how binding a dependence on the Crown is created by the above particulars ; and the great, the enormous weight and influence which the Crown derives from this extenſive dependence upon its favours and power ; *any lord in waiting, any lord of the bed-chamber, any man, may be appointed Miniſter.*"

A doctrine to this effect, was the advice which Lord Holland gave his Majeſty.

CHAPTER XXXIII.
1766.

rence might arife between them on account of what had paffed, but that they might continue in the fame union and friendfhip as before; which was accepted.

On Friday July 24, Mr. *Conway* attempted to renew the negotiation with the Marquis of *Rockingham*, feparately; but the Marquis refufed to leave his friends.

All negotiation being now at an end, the leading perfons in Adminiftration met to confider on what fhould be their future conduct. They all agreed to remain in their places."

CHAP.

CHAP. XXXIV.

Mr. Townshend resolves to be Minister—Dies—Lord North appointed—Lord Chatham goes into Somersetshire—The Bedford Interest join the Ministry—Duke of Bedford's Apology to Mr. Grenville, and Mr. Grenville's Answer—Lord Chatham returns to Hayes—French purchase Corsica—Difference between the Duke of Bedford and Lord Shelburne—Lord Rochford resigns—Lord Shelburne resigns—Fine Diamond Ring presented to his Majesty —Lord Rochford made Secretary of State, with the reasons— Lord Chatham resigns—Lord Townshend continued in Ireland.

MR. TOWNSHEND observing, that no notice had been taken of him in the preceding negotiation for a change of Ministers, resolved to resent this contempt, with which he had been treated. Administration had been for some time without a leader, and was still considered to be in that subordinate capacity. Lord *Chatham* was thought to be irrecoverable. This situation seemed to afford him an opportunity, for the uncontrouled exercise of his talents. He determined to embrace it. Therefore he instantly joined the Court, with the most full and explicit declaration of sincerity. His alliance was favourably received; and he gave a proof of his power, by creating his lady, an English Peeress, with the remainder to his son. Had he lived, he would have been first Lord of the Treasury before the ensuing session of Parliament: and Mr. *Yorke* was to have been his Chancellor. His death, which happend early in the month.

month of September, put both the Court and the Miniſtry into freſh difficulties. Every effort had been made to form a new Adminiſtration in vain. Every party had been ſolicited, individuals ſeparately, and connections jointly, without ſucceſs. But there was one part of the Royal Family, that had not publicly appeared in any of theſe negotiations: this was the *Princeſs of Wales*.

Mr. *Townſhend*'s place of Chancellor of the Exchequer was offered to ſeveral Gentlemen, who refuſed to accept of it. At length it was thought of giving it to Lord *Barrington*, *pro tempore*. Lord *Mansfield* attempted to open a negotiation with the Duke of *Bedford*. But his Grace refuſed to enter into any ſeparate treaty. Lord *North*, who, during Mr. *Grenville*'s Adminiſtration had been entruſted with all the motions againſt Mr. *Wilkes*, was deſired to ſucceed Mr. *Townſhend*, but he declined it. The *Princeſs of Wales* went to the King. His Lordſhip was again entreated—he took time to conſider of it—he conſulted his father.—After heſitating three weeks; he yielded. The *Princeſs*'s influence prevailed. Mr. *Thomas Townſhend*, now Lord *Sidney*, ſucceeded Lord *North* at the Pay-office, and Mr. *Jenkinſon* ſucceeded Mr. *Townſhend* at the Treaſury.

In making this arrangement, no communication was had with Lord *Chatham*, by either the Court or the Miniſtry. As ſoon as his health permitted, he retired into Somerſetſhire. His departure from the vicinity of the metropolis, though he had not been conſulted in any buſineſs whatever, was conſidered by the Miniſtry as a kind of dereliction. However, he continued to hold the Privy Seal.

Lord

The Duke of *Grafton*, who sometime ago wished to resign, on account of Lord *Chatham*'s infirmity*, now changed his opinion; but Lord *Northington* and General *Conway* still expressing their desire to resign, his Grace resolved to try the friends of the Duke of *Bedford* once more. If they had refused, he must have resigned, and a new Administration must have been formed. But the persons to whom his Grace made his offers, could not withstand the temptation any longer; they separated from their friends and allies; thereby preventing the appointment of an able and powerful Administration, and bargained to support the present, which seemed to consist of the remnants and refuse of several parties. Lord *Gower* was made Lord President, in the room of Lord *Northington*; Lord *Weymouth* Secretary of State, in the room of Mr. *Conway*; Mr. *Rigby* Vice-treasurer of Ireland, in the room of Mr. *Oswald*, who had a large pension and a lucrative reversion. Lord *Hillsborough* was made Secretary of State for America†. Lord *Sandwich* made Postmaster, &c. While the negotiation for these changes was under consideration, the Duke of *Bedford* said to Mr. *Grenville*, "That he "hoped it would not be considered as a breach of good faith, "if his friends thought themselves at liberty to accept of any "offers which might be made to them of public employments."

Mr.

CHAPTER XXXIV.
1767.

Bedford interest join the Ministry.

Duke of Bedford's apology.

---

* Lord BRISTOL gave the same reason for resigning the Lieutenancy of Ireland at the end of July, "That he had no hope of having the advice, direction, and assistance of Lord CHATHAM." Upon which Lord TOWNSHEND was appointed.

† The creation of this new office, and the character of the noble Lord who was appointed to it, were such strong marks of the designs, the plan, and the resolution taken, with respect to the Colonies, that an alarm instantly went forth

CHAPTER XXXIV.

1767.
Mr. Grenville's anfwer.

Mr. *Grenville* replied, "That he left to his Grace's own judgment, whether, (fetting every private compact and agreement afide) the acceffion of his friends to the prefent Miniftry, was not a breach of good faith to themfelves, and to the public?"

Lord Chatham returns to Hayes.

1768.

Before thefe negotiations were concluded, Lord *Chatham* returned from Somerfetfhire to his old feat, at Hayes, in Kent; but fo exceedingly ill and infirm, he was quite unable to tranfact any bufinefs. Early in the month of February, 1768, the Privy Seal being officially neceffary, was put into commiffion for a few weeks, but in the month of March it was re-delivered to him. The Duke of *Grafton*, who had been to him the moft obfequious of men, and was now proceeding at the helm without that pilot, whom he lately deemed indifpenfible, did not venture to turn him out; though Lord *Briftol* and Lord *Egmont* were candidates for his place.

Parliament met on the 24th of November 1767, and was diffolved on the 12th of March, 1768. Lord *Chatham* did not attend during the feffion.

A few weeks before the diffolution of Parliament, Mr. *Wilkes* returned to England, and at the general election, was elected

forth amongft them. Nothing could more clearly fignify, that the Court were preparing to make them the objects of fome extraordinary meafures—fince *another* Secretary of State, with a complete eftablifhment of office, had been appointed feparately and diftinctly, for this department—at a time of great inconvenience to his Majefty—when the Civil Lift was deeply in arrear. His Lordfhip's firft important act of office, was fending Lord BOTTETOURT, Governor of Virginia; and his apology for it was, *That the nomination came from a higher authority*.

Lord CHESTERFIELD fays in his letters, that Lord BUTE was backwards and forwards at this time—from Luton to London.

Member

[353]

Member for the county of Middlesex. All the circumstances of which, have been amply related in several publications.

CHAPTER XXXIV.
1768.

During the last year the French Court purchased of the Genoese, the claim of that republic to the island of Corsica. And this year a French army landed, on the island, to take possession of it. This was an unprecedented kind of purchase. The French might, with the same propriety, have purchased the Spanish claim to the Netherlands, or Jamaica. This addition to the French Monarchy, alarmed the Courts of London and Turin. Mr. *George Pitt*, (afterwards Lord *Rivers*), the British Minister at Turin, having resigned at the General Election, on the promise of a Peerage, the Ministry were divided on the appointment of a successor. Lord *Lansdown*, then Lord *Shelburne*, was for Lord *Tankerville**, and the Duke of *Bedford* for Sir *W. Lynch*. The latter was appointed. But this was not the only instance in which the Secretary of State had been over-ruled, in the affair of Corsica. He considered the accession of Corsica to France, an object of importance to Great Britain; and being deeply impressed with this opinion, he instructed Lord *Rochford*, the the British Minister at the French Court, to remonstrate strongly against this acquisition to France. The French Minister treated the remonstrance with contempt. The fact is, he knew the sentiments of the British Court better than the British Minister. In a short time, Lord *Rochford* found that his instructions were disavowed by his own Court. Upon receiving this information he resigned his diplomatic character, and returned

French purchase Corsica.

Difference between the D. of Bedford and L. Shelburne.

Lord Rochford resigns.

* His Lordship was one of the five Lords, who voted against the American Declaratory Bill in 1766. The other four were the Lords Cornwallis*, Torrington, Shelburne, and Camden.
* For this vote Lord Chatham made Dr. Cornwallis Archbishop of Canterbury.

Vol. I.   Z   to

<small>CHAPTER XXXIV.
1768.
Lord Shelburne resigns.

Lord Rochford made Secretary of State.</small>

to London. The Secretary of State now discovering the dupe he had been made, and the deceptions which had been practised upon him, resigned also‡. When the Court of Turin saw, that the British Cabinet were indifferent to the aggrandizement of France, the King of Sardinia immediately attached himself to the House of Bourbon. Upon the resignation of Lord *Lansdown*, Lord *Rochford* was made Secretary of State, in the month of October 1768. But to relieve the French Minister from the indelicacy of corresponding with a person whose veracity he had disputed, Lord *Weymouth* was removed from the Northern, and placed in the Southern Department, and Lord *Rochford* was made successor to Lord *Weymouth*.

<small>With the reasons.</small>

Lord *Rochford* was made Secretary of State through fear, not through friendship. The chiefs of the interior Cabinet dreaded his laying open the scene of negotiation at Paris. If he had laid this information before Parliament, the whole machinery of the Ministry must have fallen to peices. The system of a Double-Cabinet must have become so apparent to the whole nation, and the hypocrisy of the Court so perfectly unveiled, that it may be presumed, from the ordinary feelings of mankind to repeated insults and indignities, that no man of the smallest spark of

‡ But Sir JOHN MACPHERSON in his memorial, [*printed in the answer to the letter from Mahomed Ali Chan. Appendix, page* xii.] says "the Earl of SHELBURNE was dismissed at the *instigation* of the Duke of GRAFTON."—We learn also from this memorial, That his Majesty was graciously pleased to receive from the Nabob of ARCOT, whose forts are garrisoned by our troops, and whose army is commanded by our officers, *a fine diamond ring*, through the hands of Governor PALK. The world is not ignorant of many other magnificent presents from the East. But as the Governor was once in holy orders, the ceremony of investing the royal finger with this mystic sign of alliance, may be considered as something divine.

honour,

honour, who was not leagued with the Court, as *party* in some criminal transaction, or deeply distressed in the means of subsistence, would continue one moment to uphold, or connive at, a system, that had for its objects, the debasement of the English nobility, the extension of the power of the Crown, and the humiliation of the pride of the nation.——But Lord ****** wanted another place, and upon condition of his silence, he was gratified. Thus the French got Corsica. What they gave for it, the prudence of the parties hath hitherto concealed*.

Lord *Chatham* had for sometime entertained thoughts of resigning. This event decided him. The appointment of Lord *Hillsborough* Secretary of State for the Colonies, was such an outrage of his American system, and the atchievement of Corsica by France, was such an abandonment of his European policy, that they were the principal causes of his resignation. He did not go to Court when he resigned, but sent the Privy Seal by Lord *Camden*.

* On the first of August 1768, (the anniversary of the Hanoverian succession) Lord BUTE set out for Bareges in the South of France. In the succeeding winter a violent dispute arising between Lord TOWNSHEND, Lord Lieutenant of Ireland, and several of the great Lords of that kingdom, the Ministry conceived it necessary to change the Lord Lieutenant; but they could not agree in the choice of a successor. The Duke of BEDFORD was for Lord SANDWICH, and the Duke of GRAFTON for Lord HARCOURT. This disagreement occasioned the return of Lord BUTE in the Autumn of the year 1769. He settled the difference between these Dukes, by not accepting the recommendation of either; but continuing Lord TOWNSHEND, who had been appointed under his own influence. Their Graces submitted to his controul; and then he returned to the Continent. This accounts for Lord TOWNSHEND staying in Ireland four years, being the time of the usual residence of two Lord Lieutenants.

This

CHAPTER
XXXIV.

1768.

This was the laft place he held under the Crown.

His refignation was an event that had been long expected, and therefore it occafioned no furprife to the Public, nor diftrefs to the Miniftry. The Duke of *Grafton* having completed his alliance with the *Bedford Intereft*, eftimated himfelf fully adequate to all the difficulties and burthens of the State. Lord *Camden* attached himfelf to his Grace, and continued in office.

END OF VOLUME I.

www.ingramcontent.com/pod-product-compliance
Lightning Source LLC
Chambersburg PA
CBHW020226240426
43672CB00006B/436